Netscape Navigator™ 6 in 1

by Jennifer Fulton and Nat Gertler

A Division of Macmillan Computer Publishing
201 West 103rd Street, Indianapolis, Indiana 46290 USA

To my late father, Edward Flynn, whom I miss so much. Dad, thanks for all your encouragement and for always believing in me. J.F.

To Simon's Rock College, a unique institution that specializes in taking the younger student. Without the Rock, I could not have gotten where I am when I have. N.G.

International Standard Book Number: 0-7897-0807-8

Library of Congress Catalog Card Number: 96-68586

98 97 96   8 7 6 5 4 3 2 1

Interpretation of the printing code: the rightmost double-digit number is the year of the book's first printing; the rightmost single-digit number is the number of the book's printing. For example, a printing code of 96-1 shows that this copy of the book was printed during the first printing of the book in 1996.

Screen reproductions in this book were created by means of the program Collage Complete from Inner Media, Inc, Hollis, NH.

Printed in the United States of America

Publisher
Roland Elgey

Vice President and Publisher
Marie Butler-Knight

Publishing Manager
Lynn E. Zingraf

Editorial Services Director
Elizabeth Keaffaber

Managing Editor
Michael Cunningham

Acquisitions Editor
Martha O'Sullivan

Product Development Specialist
Lori Cates

Production Editor
Audra Gable

Copy Editor
San Dee Phillips

Book Designer
Kim Scott

Cover Designer
Nathan Clement

Production Team
*Marcia Brizendine, Jerry Cole, Chad Dressler, CJ East, DiMonique Ford, Jessica Ford,
Bryan Flores, Trey Frank, Jason Hand, Damon Jordan, Daryl Kessler, Michelle Lee,
Bobbi Satterfield, Kelly Warner, Paul Wilson, Jody York*

Indexer
Craig A. Small

Special thanks to C. Herbert Feltner for ensuring the technical accuracy of this book.

Acknowledgments

The authors wish to thank these hard-working people at Que for their contributions in the construction of this book: Lori Cates, Herb Feltner, Audra Gable, San Dee Phillips, and the production team.

I would like to thank my husband Scott for his constant support and love.
—Jennifer Fulton

Thanks to Pat Quinn and Steve Gerber, for their assistance in getting illustrations; to Stephen Le Hunt, for his handy HTML reference; and to the fine folks at Netscape, without whom this book would be pretty dang pointless.
—Nat Gertler

Trademark Acknowledgments

Contents

Part 4: Netscape Plug-Ins and Helper Applications

213

Part 5: Using HTML and the Netscape Extensions to Create Web Pages   371

Part 6: Designing and Publishing Web Pages with Netscape Gold   483

Introduction

Congratulations! You've just selected Netscape Navigator, the world's most popular Web browser, to be your guide through the World Wide Web. The only problem now is, you need to figure out how to use it. Of course, you're not looking forward to having to deal with manuals and Help systems that never tell you what you really want to know—at least, not without making you waste a lot of time searching. No, with a schedule as busy as yours, what you really need is a straightforward guide that'll teach you what you need to know in the shortest amount of time.

Welcome to *Netscape Navigator 6 in 1*, a book designed for busy people like you. Nobody has the luxury of sitting down uninterrupted for hours at a time just to learn Netscape. That's why *Netscape Navigator 6 in 1* doesn't attempt to teach you everything at once. Instead, each Netscape feature is presented in a single self-contained lesson, designed to take only a short time to complete. So whenever you have a few minutes to spare in your busy day, you can easily complete a lesson on navigating the Web, using Web search tools, completing forms, or downloading files.

Who This Book Is For

Granted, *Netscape Navigator 6 in 1* might not be the right book for everyone. But if you can slide your way around Windows without too much help, it is the book for you. If you know a little bit about the Internet but you don't know anything at all about Netscape Navigator, the World Wide Web, FTP, Gopher, and all those other funny sounding Internet names, this is *definitely* the book for you.

Netscape Navigator 6 in 1 is perfect for people who have busy schedules, a need to get up and running quickly, and a few ten-minute segments every day in which to learn. If this description fits you, *Netscape Navigator 6 in 1* is your book.

On the other hand, if you're a person who has plenty of time to learn, or if you're an experienced computer user who wants to know all the details about Netscape Navigator, I suggest that you pick up a copy of Que's *Using Netscape Navigator* instead.

How This Book Is Organized

Netscape Navigator 6 in 1 is organized into six parts:

- **Netscape Navigator and Netscape Gold 3.0**   This part teaches you the basics of using Netscape Navigator and Netscape Navigator Gold.
- **Netscape News**   In this part, you'll learn how to use Netscape's news-reader to view and post messages to Internet newsgroups.
- **Netscape Mail**   This part shows you how to send and receive electronic messages (e-mail) with Netscape.
- **Netscape Plug-Ins and Helper Applications**   In this part, you'll learn how to download and install plug-ins and helper applications, special programs that extend the capabilities of Netscape so it can play video and sound files, among other things.
- **Using HTML and the Netscape Extensions to Create Web Pages**   Want to publish your own private Web page? In this part, you'll learn how.
- **Designing and Publishing Web Pages with Netscape Gold**   Designing Web pages using HTML commands can be a daunting task. In this part, you'll learn how to use the HTML editor in Netscape Gold to provide the proper HTML commands.

 Hey, Slow Down! I'm New to This!   If you're new to the Internet and the World Wide Web, be sure to read the sections "What Is the Internet?" and "What, Then, Is the World Wide Web?" later in this introduction.

Each part is divided into several lessons. Because each of the lessons takes only 10 minutes or less to complete, you'll quickly master the skills you need. In addition, the straightforward, easy-to-understand explanations and numbered lists within each lesson guide you quickly and easily to your goal of Netscape mastery.

Conventions Used in This Book

The following icons are included throughout the text to help you quickly identify particular types of information.

Tip icons mark shortcuts and hints for saving time and using Netscape more efficiently.

Term icons point out easy-to-follow definitions that you'll need to know in order to understand Netscape and how it fits into the scheme of the World Wide Web.

Caution icons mark information that's intended to help you avoid making mistakes.

In addition to the special icons, you'll find these conventions used throughout the text:

On-screen text	On-screen text appears in bold type.
What you type	Information you need to type also appears in bold.
Items you select	Items you need to select or keys you need to press also appear in bold type.
`Computer output`	Long sections of computer text appear in a monospace font.

What Is the Internet?

The Internet is simply a collection of interconnected networks. These networks are located within many universities, businesses, libraries, government offices, and research facilities all over the world. The Internet links these various networks so that people all over the world can share their information. When you connect to the Internet, you can access the information on such computers and view it, save it, or print it.

Even just a few years ago, if you connected to the Internet, what you saw wasn't very pretty. Typically, you connected to an Internet provider, typed in a series of very weird UNIX commands (as shown in Figure I.1), and eventually got to something useful.

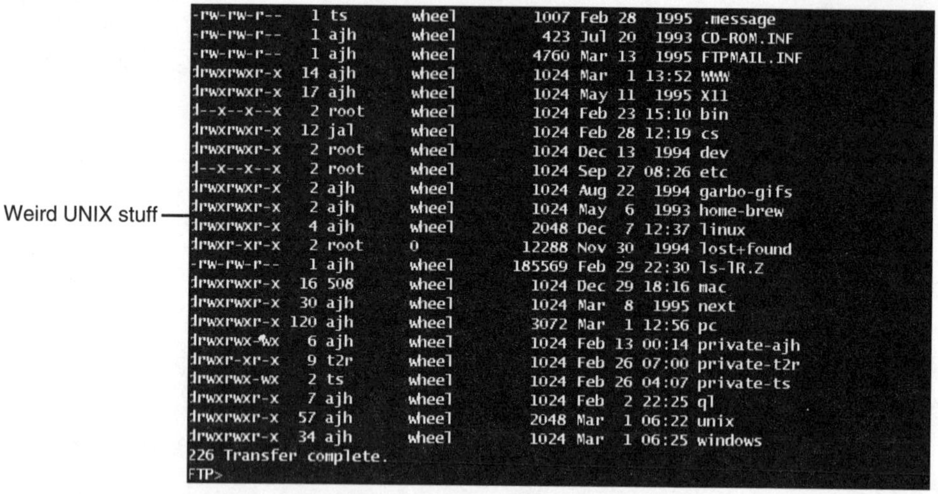

```
-rw-rw-r--    1 ts      wheel      1007 Feb 28  1995 .message
-rw-rw-r--    1 ajh     wheel       423 Jul 20  1993 CD-ROM.INF
-rw-rw-r--    1 ajh     wheel      4760 Mar 13  1995 FTPMAIL.INF
drwxrwxr-x   14 ajh     wheel      1024 Mar  1 13:52 WWW
drwxrwxr-x   17 ajh     wheel      1024 May 11  1995 X11
d--x--x--x    2 root    wheel      1024 Feb 23 15:10 bin
drwxrwxr-x   12 jal     wheel      1024 Feb 28 12:19 cs
drwxrwxr-x    2 root    wheel      1024 Dec 13  1994 dev
d--x--x--x    2 root    wheel      1024 Sep 27 08:26 etc
drwxrwxr-x    2 ajh     wheel      1024 Aug 22  1994 garbo-gifs
drwxrwxr-x    2 ajh     wheel      1024 May  6  1993 home-brew
drwxrwxr-x    4 ajh     wheel      2048 Dec  7 12:37 linux
drwxr-xr-x    2 root    0         12288 Nov 30  1994 lost+found
-rw-rw-r--    1 ajh     wheel    185569 Feb 29 22:30 ls-lR.Z
drwxrwxr-x   16 508     wheel      1024 Dec 29 18:16 mac
drwxrwxr-x   30 ajh     wheel      1024 Mar  8  1995 next
drwxrwxr-x  120 ajh     wheel      3072 Mar  1 12:56 pc
drwxrwx-wx    6 ajh     wheel      1024 Feb 13 00:14 private-ajh
drwxr-xr-x    9 t2r     wheel      1024 Feb 26 07:00 private-t2r
drwxrwx-wx    2 ts      wheel      1024 Feb 26 04:07 private-ts
drwxrwxr-x    7 ajh     wheel      1024 Feb  2 22:25 ql
drwxrwxr-x   57 ajh     wheel      2048 Mar  1 06:22 unix
drwxrwxr-x   34 ajh     wheel      1024 Mar  1 06:25 windows
226 Transfer complete.
FTP>
```

Weird UNIX stuff ——

Figure I.1 Under UNIX, the Internet is a scary place.

UNIX   UNIX is the language of the Internet, just as DOS is the language of most PCs. UNIX, like DOS, is an operating system. To use it, you type commands at a prompt (a reminder from the operating system that it's waiting for a command) to instruct the operating system what to do (to list the files in the current directory, for example).

As you'll see in a moment, the World Wide Web gave the Internet a pretty face—an interface that made the vast resources of the Internet easier to locate, view, print, and save. In order to connect to the Web portion of the Internet, you need a Web browser such as Netscape Navigator or Netscape Gold. I'll tell you more about Web browsers in a moment. But first, read more about the Web.

What, Then, Is the World Wide Web?

The World Wide Web (known as simply WWW) is a subset of the Internet. You can think of the Web as a large book whose pages are located on various parts of the Internet. You start on one page of this vast "book" and instead of turning from one page to another with your fingers, you click on some text or a fancy picture, and you're taken to a different Web page.

Home Page Your starting point when you connect to the Web through your Web browser. With Netscape Navigator, for example, you usually start on the Netscape home page. A home page is filled with links to other Web pages. The Netscape home page contains links to the pages Netscape deems important.

Home Sweet Home You can create your own home page and fill it with links to your favorite Web pages. See Part 5, "Using HTML and the Netscape Extensions to Create Web Pages," and Part 6, "Designing and Publishing Web Pages with Netscape Gold," for more information.

The pages of this "book" are actually a set of interconnected documents containing information on an array of topics. There's no telling what you might find on a Web document (Web page). You'll probably find text and graphics, but you might also find sound and video clips that you can play just by clicking them. You might even find fancy animations, such as a live stock ticker. Figure I.2 shows a Web page that contains many of these elements.

Embedded graphic

Click here to play a sound clip.

Click here to play a video clip.

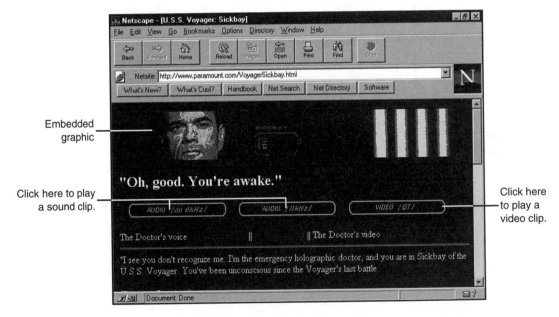

Figure I.2 A Web page often contains many elements.

The pages of the World Wide Web are connected like the threads of a large spider web. This enables you to jump from one Web page to another simply by following its "thread."

The documents or *pages* that make up the Web are connected through *links* that are sometimes called hypertext or hypermedia links. To jump from the current Web page to some other related page on the Web, you simply click a link. A link, by the way, is usually some highlighted text or a colorful graphic (see Figure I.3).

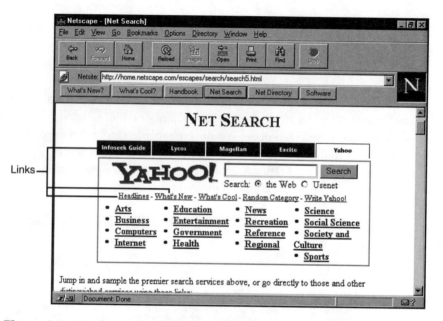

Figure I.3 Links can connect you to a related Web page.

This is how a link works: imagine that you're connected to the Web and you're currently looking at a Web page that contains current news headlines. You click one of the headlines (which is actually a link), and you jump to a Web page detailing a recent plane crash.

TERM   **Link**   Highlighted text or a graphic that, when clicked, takes the user to a related Web page.

Understanding Web Browsers

A Web browser is a program that connects you to the World Wide Web, a subsection of the larger Internet. As you learned earlier, the Web is like a large book whose "pages" you can read in whatever order you choose. With your Web browser, you can jump from page to page on the Web, download files, view graphics, and create bookmarks of your favorite Web pages. Netscape Navigator is one of the more popular Web browsers, but there are others, including NCSA Mosaic and the Internet Explorer.

You might be wondering how Netscape Navigator finds a particular page within the vast Internet forest? You see, each Web page has its own address or *URL* (pronounced "U-R-L"). By entering a URL into the Location/Go to box in Netscape, you tell Netscape to jump directly to the Web page you want to view. You can give Netscape similar instructions by clicking a link, which provides the proper address to your Web browser so that you are transferred to the right Web page.

URL   Short for Uniform Resource Locator, a URL is the address of a Web page. With the proper address, you Web browser can connect you directly to any page on the World Wide Web. A *link* is simply a pointer to a particular Web page; it supplies your Web browser with the proper address for connecting to the linked Web page.

A typical URL (Uniform Resource Locator) looks like this:

http://www.mcp.com/que/new_users/new.html

The first part of a URL tells you which *protocol* was used on that particular Web page. A protocol is a set of rules that define how information should be exchanged between two points. In this example, http:// tells you that the page was sent to you via HyperText Transfer Protocol. HTTP is the most common protocol used on the Web; it defines how information is sent from place to place over the Web.

By the way, the ht in HTTP stands for *hypertext*. Most Web pages are written in a language called HyperText Markup Language, or HTML, which provides Web page creators with the means for formatting text, displaying graphics, and creating links between Web pages.

Hypertext Specially formatted text that provides a link to another document or another part of the same document. You'll find hypertext in most Help systems. When you click a hypertext word such as *save*, you're taken to the part of Help that tells you how to save your work. On the Internet, hypertext (more correctly called *hyperlinks*) provides a link to a particular Web document (Web page).

The second part of the URL (www.mcp.com/que/new_users/new.html in our example) tells you the actual address—sometimes called the server address or host name—of the Web page. The slash marks (/) separate the parts of the address. Here's how the whole address breaks down: www.mcp.com is the address of an Internet server; /que/new_users/ refers to a subdirectory on that particular Internet server; and new.html is the name of the document (Web page) that will be displayed if you type in the complete www.mcp.com/que/new_users/new.html address.

Internet Server A fast, large-capacity PC connected directly to the Internet. You connect to the Internet by connecting through your Internet provider's server. From there, you can jump from Web site to Web site, moving from one Internet server to another.

Large corporations such as Macmillan have their own Internet servers connected to the Internet. When you connect to http://www.mcp.com, you're connecting to the Macmillan server. Once connected, you can view the files stored on that server—provided those files are located in a directory to which you've been given access. (Many Internet servers have private areas that the general public can't reach.) Smaller corporations and individuals who can't afford their own servers rent space on Internet servers.

If you don't know the address of a particular Web page, but you know the information you want to locate, you can use one of several Web search tools such as Lycos, InfoSeek, or Yahoo to look for applicable pages. See Part 1 Lesson 8 for more information. Once you find a page that's useful, you can save its address so that you can visit it later. You can also print a page or save it so you can open it later within Netscape.

Other Cool Things Your Web Browser Can Do

In addition to HTTP, Web browsers support other protocols, such as FTP and Gopher. An FTP site contains files that you can download to your PC. In the old days, you had to use an FTP program such as WS_FTP to connect to an FTP site, but nowadays, it's more convenient to use Netscape's built-in FTP program to download files from an FTP site. You can also use Archie, a tool for searching for files on FTP sites through Netscape, as you'll learn in Part 1, Lesson 12. Figure I.4 shows an FTP site displayed in Netscape.

Figure I.4   You can visit FTP sites with your Web browser.

You can also access a Gopher site with Netscape, instead of using a separate Gopher program such as WS Gopher. A Gopher site organizes its information using a menu system. Gophers are typically found at universities and research facilities, and they usually contain computer-related files and technical documents. You can use the Gopher search tools through Netscape to find what you need on the Gopher servers. You'll learn about using Gopher search tools in Part 1 Lesson 12.

You can do other things with Netscape as well. For example, you can *telnet* to an open system (a computer system that allows other people to sign in as a guest), from which you can run programs, search for files, and copy them to your PC. Basically, with Telnet, you can log onto some other computer and do anything you could do if you were actually sitting in front of that particular computer.

With Netscape's built-in newsreader, Netscape News, you can connect to a newsgroup and exchange messages and information with other people who have similar interests, and with Netscape's built-in e-mail program, Netscape Mail, you can send and receive electronic messages over the Internet. You'll learn more about Netscape News (shown in Figure I.5) and Netscape Mail in Parts 2 and 3.

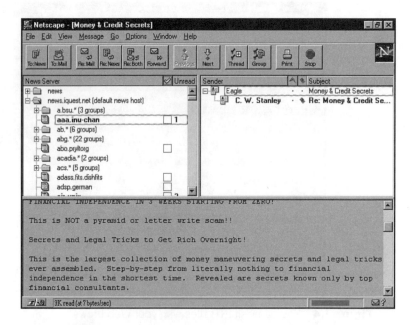

Figure I.5 Netscape News lets you discuss common interests with other people through Internet newsgroups.

Netscape also enables you to use in-line plug-ins and helper applications (programs designed to work with Netscape, which display or run file types that Netscape can't handle). In-line plug-ins and helper applications enable you to do such things as chat (type messages back and forth with other people in a live format), view videos, play sound files, and browse through "virtual worlds." You'll learn more about the in-line plug-ins and helper apps in Part 4.

Each of these protocols (http, ftp, and so on) uses a particular format for its address. Table I.1 shows you the format for the URLs used by each of these protocols.

Table I.1 Internet Addresses by Protocol

Protocol	Address Format and Sample Address
HTTP	http://*server_name/document_path/document_name* **example:** http://www.memphis.edu/egypt/main.html
FTP	ftp://*server_name/file_path/file_name* **example:** ftp://ftp.winsite.com/pub/pc/win95/winzip.exe
Gopher	gopher://*server_name/document_type/selector* **example:** gopher://gopher.senate.gov/1
Telnet	telnet://*user_name:password@server_name* **example:** telnet://jfulton:secret@delphi.com
News	newsrc://*newsgroup:first_article-last_article* **example:** newsrc://news:/misc.writing

Netscape Navigator and Netscape Gold 3.0

Finding and Installing Netscape

In this lesson, you will learn how to download a copy of Netscape Navigator or Netscape Navigator Gold from the Internet.

Comparing Netscape Navigator and Netscape Navigator Gold

Before you download anything, you need to decide which Netscape you want to use: Netscape Navigator or Netscape Navigator Gold (sometimes called Netscape Gold for short). Here's a rundown of what you'll get with Netscape Navigator 3.0:

- All the same features Netscape Navigator 2.0 had, such as built-in e-mail and newsreader programs, support for Java apps and JavaScript, and frames support.
- The LiveAudio feature with which you can play audio files embedded in Web pages.
- The LiveVideo feature with which you can play AVI video files.
- The Live3D feature with which you can play 3-D (VRML) files.
- CoolTalk, a feature that enables Netscape to create a virtual telephone over the Internet, complete with chatting and whiteboard capabilities.
- The *personal certificates* (enhanced security), which allow you to conduct business over the Internet more safely.
- Capability for expansion by means of in-line plug-ins and helper applications.

- Capability to customize the size of the Netscape Mail and Netscape News windows.

Netscape Navigator Gold offers the same features as Netscape Navigator, plus a few more.

- An easy-to-use Web page editor for creating your own Web pages.
- A JavaScript editor for creating your own custom JavaScript programs.
- Templates and design tools for creating cool-looking Web pages, plus a set of predesigned home pages, colorful backgrounds, and Java applets that make your Web pages jump!
- The Netscape Page Wizard, which walks you step by step through the entire process of creating your first Web page.
- The capability to publish changes to your Web pages at the click of a button.
- The Netscape Page Starter Site, a one-stop resource for all of your Web publishing needs.
- The Netscape Gold Rush Tool Chest, a collection of Web page templates.

Basically, if you're not interested in creating your own Web pages, save a few bucks and get Netscape Navigator. On the other hand, if you think you might want to create your own Web page, the additional features built into Netscape Gold are well worth the price.

Downloading Netscape

Netscape Navigator and Netscape Gold are available for purchase at any software store, or you can download them from the Internet. Just because you download your copy of Netscape doesn't mean it's free. You're allowed to download Netscape to try it out, but once you decide to keep it, you will need to register it and pay a small fee for its use. The fee, by the way, is the same whether you buy your copy of Netscape at a software store or download it from the Internet.

Nothing's Free Even if your Internet service provider included a copy of Netscape with its startup files (which you downloaded after logging in the first time), you'll still have to pay to register Netscape and any other *shareware* programs you decide to keep.

To register your copy of Netscape or Netscape Gold once you decide to keep it, you'll install Netscape and then connect to the Netscape home page. You'll enter basic information into an on-screen form, and Netscape will charge your credit card for the purchase. (If you don't register your copy of Netscape, it will expire—cease to operate—after a specified time.)

A Word About Security   The form into which you enter your personal information is secured, which means that a high level of security prevents all but the most clever of Internet users from being able to obtain any of the information it contains. However, no system that allows free access (such as the Internet) can be totally secure. If you feel uncomfortable sending your private information over the Internet, you might prefer to purchase Netscape at a software store instead of downloading it.

If you decide to download Netscape from the Internet, you'll need an FTP program, which was more than likely included with the files you downloaded from your Internet service provider the first time you connected to the Internet. In the following steps, you'll learn how to download Netscape Navigator or Netscape Navigator Gold using the FTP program WS_FTP. If you use a different FTP program, the steps will vary a little.

FTP Phooey   If you shudder at the prospect of using an FTP program to download Netscape, and you just happen to know someone who already has a Web browser, why not talk that person into downloading it for you? (Using a Web browser to download stuff from the Internet is much easier than using an FTP program.) He or she enters the same FTP address used in step 5 of the following steps, but makes a slight change to reflect that he's entering the address in a Web browser and not an FTP program:

ftp://ftp5.netscape.com

Windows 3.1 Users   If you use Windows 3.1, follow the steps below to download Netscape. Then follow the steps in "Downloading Win32s" to download an additional file called Win32s, which Windows 3.1 needs to make Netscape Navigator and Netscape Navigator Gold work.

Downloading Your Copy of Netscape

To download Netscape, follow these steps:

1. Connect to your Internet service provider in the usual manner and start WS_FTP.

2. If necessary, click **Connect**, and the Session Profile dialog box shown in Figure 1.1 appears.

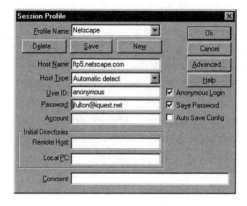

Figure 1.1   Set up a connection to Netscape's FTP site.

3. Click **New**.

4. In the **Profile Name** text box, type **Netscape FTP**.

5. In the **Host Name** text box, type **ftp5.netscape.com**.

I Can't Connect   If you have trouble connecting to Netscape's FTP site, try a different address such as ftp2.netscape.com, ftp3.netscape.com, or ftp4.netscape.com.

CAUTION

6. Select the **Anonymous Login** check box, and type your e-mail address in the **Password** box.

7. Click **Save** and click **OK**.

8. After you connect to the Netscape FTP site, change to the **/3.0/windows** directory. (Just double-click a directory name to change to it; the directories on the Netscape site should be shown on the right side of the WS_FTP window.)

I Want Netscape Gold To download Netscape Gold, change to the **/3.0gold/windows** directory instead.

9. On your Local System (shown on the left side of the WS_FTP window), change to the temporary directory in which you want to store the file, as shown in Figure 1.2.

Change to a temporary directory on your system.

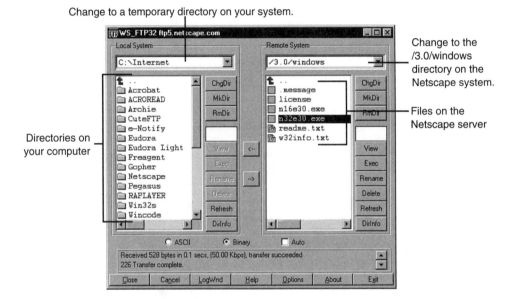

Change to the /3.0/windows directory on the Netscape system.

Files on the Netscape server

Directories on your computer

Figure 1.2 Set up your directories for the download.

10. Double-click the **n32e20.exe** (for Windows 95) or **n16e20.exe** (for Windows 3.1) file to download it to the temporary directory. (For Netscape Gold, double click **g32e20.exe**.)

11. When you're through, click **Cancel** to cancel the connection. Then click **Exit** to exit WS_FTP. Finally, disconnect from the Internet.

If you use Windows 95, you're ready to install Netscape now. Jump to the section "Installing Netscape" to proceed. If you use Windows 3.1, follow the steps in the next section before you try to install Netscape.

Downloading Win32s

If you use Windows 3.1, you'll need to download the Win32s file in order to get Netscape Navigator to work properly. Follow these steps:

1. Connect to your Internet service provider and start WS_FTP.

2. Click **Connect**, and the Session Profile dialog box appears.

3. Select **Microsoft** from the **Profile Name** drop-down list.

"Microsoft" Is Not an Option   If your FTP program doesn't include a setting for Microsoft's FTP site, add one as described in the previous section. Use the address ftp.microsoft.com.

4. After you connect to Microsoft, double-click the **/Softlib /MSLFILES** directory to change to it.

5. On your Local System, change to the temporary directory in which you want to store the file (see Figure 1.3).

Change to a temporary directory on your system.

Change to the /Softlib/ MSLFILES directory on the Microsoft system.

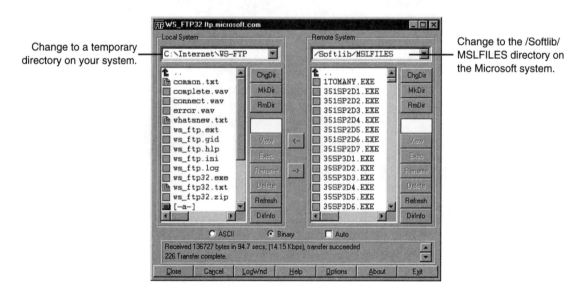

Figure 1.3   Choose your directories.

6. Double-click the **pw1118.exe** file to copy it to your hard drive.

See the section "Installing Win32s" for help installing the win32s.exe program *before* you install Netscape itself.

Installing Netscape

After you download Netscape Navigator or Netscape Gold, you need to install it. This process is not terribly complex, and toward the end of it, you'll connect to the Internet and register your copy of Netscape.

You'll also be given an opportunity at that time to download a variety of in-line plug-ins, such as video, audio, and virtual reality players. Don't feel like you have to make your selections now. You'll probably want to learn more about the basics of Netscape before you start enhancing it with a lot of other applications. Part IV shows you how to return to this screen to download and install various in-line plug-ins and helper apps when you're ready for that.

Installing Win32s

If you use Windows 3.1, you should have downloaded the pw1118.exe file, which you need to install before you install Netscape. (If you use Windows 95, skip this section.) The pw1118.exe file is compressed (zipped), which means that the separate files that make up the program have been compressed into one single file that's smaller and easier to download. To install it, you decompress the file and then begin the installation process.

CAUTION

What If I Use Windows 95?   If you use Windows 95, you should *not* install Win32s. Install Win32s only if you're installing the 16-bit version of Netscape (for Windows 3.1).

Follow these steps to install Win32s:

1. If you haven't already done so, open File Manager and copy the pw1118.exe file to a temporary directory.
2. Double-click the **pw1118.exe** file, and it decompresses its files into the temporary directory.
3. Double-click the **wb2s120.exe** file to decompress its files.
4. Double-click the **setup.exe** file.
5. When you see a message telling you to close your other Windows programs, do so and click **Continue**.
6. The Win32s Setup Target Directory dialog box (shown in Figure 1.4) requests confirmation that it has found your Windows directory. Verify the directory name and click **Continue** to proceed with the installation.

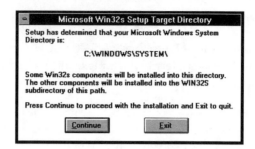

Figure 1.4 Make sure that Win32s found your Windows directory.

7. Click **OK**, and Win32s is installed in the SYSTEM subdirectory of Windows 3.1.

8. In the Freecell Setup dialog box (which appears next), click **Continue** to load Freecell, a game you can use to test Win32s.

9. Verify the Freecell path and click **Continue**. Then click **OK**.

10. Click **Continue** to restart Windows.

11. Double-click the **Freecell** icon (located in the Games program group) to start the game. If it starts, Win32s is set up correctly. Exit Freecell.

Nothing Happens If you can't get FreeCell to work, there is a problem with your Win32s setup. Try installing it again, making sure that it correctly identifies your Windows directory.

CAUTION

Installing Netscape Navigator

During the Netscape Navigator installation, you'll be given a chance to register your copy of Netscape. It's very important that you do this. If you don't register your copy, it will expire (become unusable) after a brief period.

For Windows 3.1 Before you install Netscape Navigator, make sure that you've installed Win32s if you are running Windows 3.1. See the previous section for help.

TIP

Follow these steps to install Netscape Navigator or Netscape Navigator Gold:

1. Open **File Manager** or **Explorer** and double-click the **Netscape** file. It decompresses its files into the temporary directory.

2. You're asked if you want to continue with setup. Click **Yes**.

3. When you see a warning telling you to close your other Windows programs, do so and click **Next**.

4. Netscape displays its destination directory. If the destination directory is okay, click **Next**. If you want to change it, click **Browse**, select the desired directory, click **OK**, and then click **Next**.

What If It Doesn't Exist? If the directory you want to use doesn't exist, you'll see a message asking if you want the setup program to create it. Click **Yes**.

CAUTION

5. You'll see a message asking you if you want to install CoolTalk, a feature that enables you to call people on the phone using the Internet. Click **Yes** to install CoolTalk, or click **No** if you don't want to install it. (Although phoning over the Internet is a bit slow and tedious, it does save you long distance charges.)

6. Next, you're asked if you want to add CoolTalk Watchdog to the Startup group. If you have a permanent Internet connection, click **Yes**. Otherwise, click **No**.

7. You need to connect to Netscape's home site to complete the setup (see Figure 1.5). So connect to the Internet first, and then return to this dialog box and click **Yes**.

After you've connected to the Internet, click here to continue.

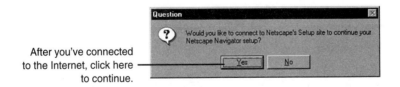

Figure 1.5 Connect to Netscape's home site to complete the installation.

8. Read the license agreement and click **Accept**.

9. You're connected to Netscape's home site, where you will complete the Netscape Navigator setup. Click **Continue**.

10. The screen shown in Figure 1.6 appears, telling you that you need to register your copy of Netscape. To register, click the **User Identification Form** link.

I'm Not Sure! If you really aren't sure that you're going to keep Netscape, you can click **Continue** twice and skip to step 22.

Click here to register your copy.

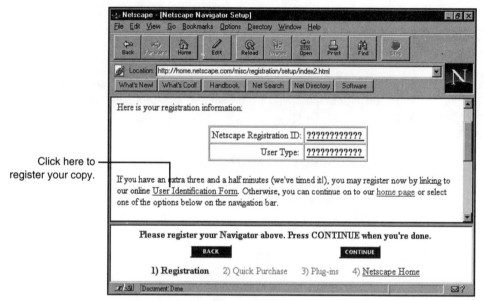

Figure 1.6 You need to register your copy of Netscape.

11. Next, you'll see a screen asking you to select the option that best suits your situation: are you a student, are you evaluating Netscape, or have you already purchased Netscape? If one of these descriptions fits you, click the option to select it. If none of them fits you, proceed with step 12.

12. Click **Continue**.

13. In order to register, you must complete the form on this Web page. Some items are optional; others are not. You must complete all required fields.

14. Scroll down the page and continue to fill in information. When you've completed all the required fields, click **Submit Information**.

15. You'll see a warning; click **Continue**.

16. Next, you're assigned a registration number. Click **Continue**.

17. Select a type of Navigator license from the drop-down list shown in Figure 1.7. Then click **Continue with Purchase**.

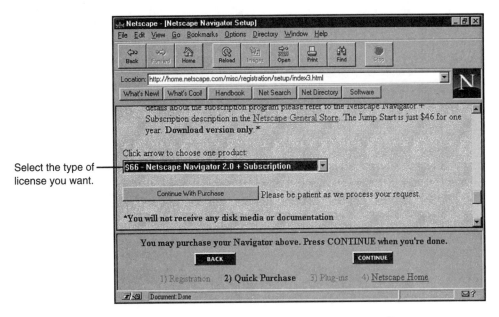

Select the type of license you want.

Figure 1.7 Once you have a registration number, select a license.

I Want Manuals, Too! If you want to purchase the complete Netscape package in the box (complete with manuals and so on), do *not* select a Navigator license in step 15. Instead, scroll up to the top of the screen and click **General Store**, and then follow the steps there. Netscape will ship you the complete Navigator package in a few weeks, after it processes your order.

18. Click **Continue**.

19. Netscape Setup takes you to a secured Web page so you can enter credit card information to pay for your purchase. Click **Continue**.

20. Enter your credit card information and click **Place Order.**

21. Verify your order and click **Continue**.

22. As Figure 1.8 shows, you're now given the opportunity to download a number of in-line plug-ins (special programs designed to enhance Netscape Navigator). You probably have no idea at this time which ones you might want. If that's so, click **Continue** to skip this part.

If you want to download a few plug-ins that you've already been told about, scroll through the list until you find what you want, and then click its link to begin the download process. Select a directory in which to save the program and click **Save**. Click **Continue** when you're through.

13

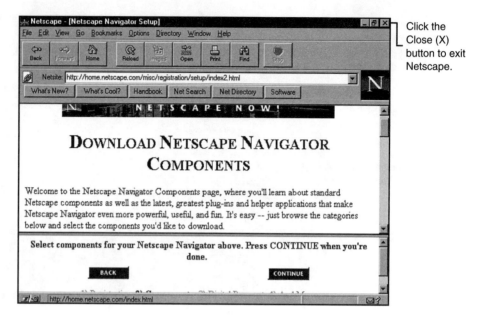

Click the Close (X) button to exit Netscape.

Figure 1.8 You can download plug-ins to enhance Netscape.

23. Next you're taken to a screen where you can apply for a certificate called a digital ID. A certificate allows you to identify yourself to others with whom you might do business over the Internet. If you want to apply for an ID, click **Free Digital ID**. If not, click **Continue** and skip to step 32.

24. You'll see a warning; click **Continue**.

25. Complete the Digital ID form, and then click **Continue**.

26. Verify your information and click **Continue**.

27. Read the Subscriber Agreement and click **Accept**.

28. Click **Submit**.

29. Enter your password as shown in Figure 1.9 and click **OK**.

30. Enter the nickname you want to be known by when you use your certificate, and then click **OK**.

31. Click **Continue**.

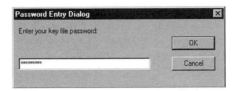

Figure 1.9 Enter your certificate password.

32. You're done! From the Netscape home page (shown in Figure 1.10), you can browse the Internet, create your own Web page , or shop at the Netscape General Store—whatever you want.

33. When you finish browsing the Net, click the **Close** (X) button, or open the **File** menu and select **Exit** to close Netscape.

34. Disconnect from the Internet.

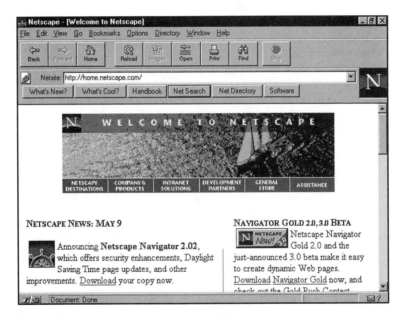

Figure 1.10 The Netscape Navigator home page.

35. When you see a message telling you that Setup is complete, click **OK**.

36. If you want to review the README file, click **Yes**.

In this lesson, you learned how to download a copy of Netscape and install it. In the next lesson, you'll learn how to navigate the Web with Netscape.

Navigating Netscape

In this lesson, you will learn how to move from page to page on the Web.

Starting Netscape

Before you can start Netscape, you need to connect to your Internet service provider. If you use Windows 3.1, follow these steps to connect to the Internet and start Netscape:

1. Double-click the **Trumpet Winsock** icon.
2. Open the **Dialler** menu and select **Login.**
3. If necessary, enter the phone number of your service provider and press **Enter**.
4. Enter your user name and your password. After connecting, you should see the message **Script completed.** Underneath, you'll see **SLIP ENABLED**. Minimize the Trumpet Winsock window if you want.
5. To start Netscape, double-click the **Netscape Navigator** or **Netscape Gold** icon.

If you use Windows 95, you should already have an Internet icon. You created it using the Dial-Up Networking program when you set up your Internet account. Follow these steps to connect to the Internet and start Netscape:

1. Click **Start**, select **Programs**, select **Accessories**, and click **Dial-Up Networking**.
2. Double-click the icon you created for connecting to the Internet, and the Connect To dialog box appears.

3. If you normally enter your logon name and password through a terminal window after connecting to your service provider, don't enter them in the Connect To dialog box. Instead, click **Connect**.

   If you don't use a terminal window to connect to your service provider, enter your logon name and password now and click **Connect**. Then skip to step 7.

4. If a terminal window appears, enter your user name and password. (The password will not appear on-screen.) If you are using a SLIP or CSLIP connection, continue to step 5. If not, click **Continue** and skip to step 7.

5. Use the scroll bars if necessary to see the IP address to which you've been assigned. Write this number down and click **Continue**.

6. Enter the IP address you wrote down and click **OK**.

7. You are connected to the Internet. To start Netscape, click **Start**, select **Programs**, and click **Netscape**. Then double-click the **Netscape Navigator** or **Netscape Gold** icon.

Understanding Netscape's Screen

When you start Netscape, you go directly to the Netscape home page. From the home page, you can go anywhere you want (as you'll see in a moment). Figure 2.1 shows the Netscape home page and points out some of its important elements.

Your home page is your starting point. As you gain more experience with the Internet, you may want to change your home page to some favorite Web page, or you may want to create your own Web page, filled with links to your favorite places on the Web. (A *link*, as you may recall, is a graphic or some highlighted text that you click to go to the associated Web page.) You'll learn how to change your home page in Part 1 Lesson 6; you'll learn how to create Web pages in Parts 5 and 6.

The Navigator screen contains the following elements:

Menu bar   Like other Windows programs, Netscape provides a number of menus from which you can select commands.

Toolbar   Netscape also provides a toolbar for quick access to common commands.

Location box   This box displays the address of the current Web page. You can enter an address (URL) in this box to jump directly to the associated Web page.

Link icon   Click this icon to create shortcuts to your favorite Web pages (see Lesson 3).

17

TERM

Location/Netsite/Go to Box   The name of the Location box changes depending on what you are currently doing in Netscape. When you're viewing and working in a Web page, it is called either "Location" or "Netsite" and shows the address of the current page. If you click in the text box and begin typing a URL, the name changes to "Go to."

Frames   Netscape's home page can be broken into frames so you can navigate Netscape's Web site more easily. Not all Web pages use frames, and very few allow you to turn them on and off. In any case, you click within a frame to activate it. Your browser will display frames only if you turn the feature on (which you'll learn how to do in Lesson 4).

Link   Click a link to jump to an associated Web page. (You'll learn more about links in a moment.)

Status bar   The status bar provides you with information about what Netscape's up to.

Netscape icon   This icon gives you subtle hints about Netscape's activity. When you switch from one Web page to another, comets streak across the big **N**, indicating that Netscape is busy grabbing the image of the new page. Sometimes it takes quite a while to change from one page to another. But if you see the comets, you know for sure that Netscape is still working, and that it hasn't gotten hung up somewhere.

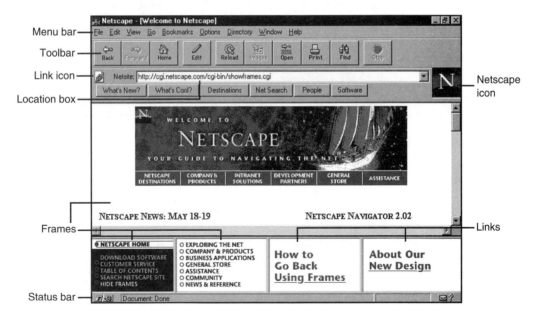

Figure 2.1   When you start Netscape, you immediately see the Netscape home page.

Below the Location box, Netscape Navigator provides a toolbar of buttons that are actually links to popular Web sites. These buttons are available to you at all times, no matter what Web site you're linked to. Here's a rundown of what each button does:

What's New This button jumps you to a page with links to the newest Web pages. If you're looking for someplace new to visit, start here.

What's Cool This button jumps you to a page with links to the coolest, hippest Web pages (according to Netscape). If you're looking for something new and different, start here.

Destinations Need information fast? Then click here for links to great Web pages on news, finances, sports, software, hardware, travel, entertainment, and so on.

Net Search This button jumps you directly to a Web search tool such as Excite!, Yahoo, InfoSeek Magellan, or Lycos. From time to time, Netscape changes the Web search tool to which this is linked, so you can never be quite sure which one you'll get. You'll learn how to search the Web for information in Lessons 8 and 9.

People Looking for a long-lost friend or an old flame? Click here for links to the best people locators. See Lesson 10 for more help.

Software This button takes you to a location on Netscape's home site where you can find updates or upgrades to your Navigator software, as well as add-ins and other useful Internet tools.

Newsgroups If you use Netscape Navigator to access the newsgroups from the Usenet portion of the Internet, you'll see a button here that takes you to Usenet's "root directory."

Using Links to Jump to a Page

A link often appears as a bit of highlighted text or as a graphic. To use a link, simply click it. When you do, Netscape moves you to the Web page whose address the link contains.

Before you click a link, you might want to know where it will take you. To find out, point to the link, and the address of the associated Web page appears in the status bar (see Figure 2.2).

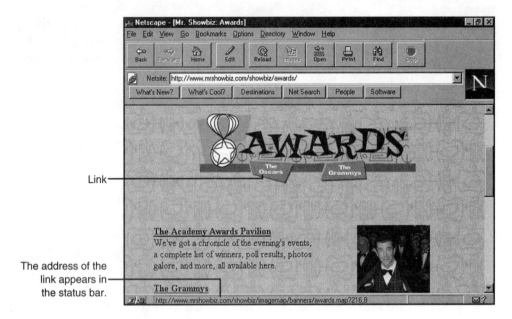

Link ⸻

The address of the
link appears in⸺
the status bar.

Figure 2.2 Click a link to use it.

Most links appear as blue text to begin with. However, once you click a link, it changes to purple. Netscape does this so that if you return to the original page later, you can easily see which links you've followed. (Sometimes, you may run into colors other than blue and purple, but you get the idea.)

What to Do When a Link Fails

If the link you click on points to a Web page that has moved, you'll get an error message saying **File not found.** If that happens, you can try deleting the last part of the address and pressing Enter again to retry it. For example, if you clicked a link that pointed to the address http://www.movies.com/actors/gibson.html, and it didn't work, try erasing gibson.html. If that doesn't work, try deleting actors/ too. If you can connect to www.movies.com, you may be able to pick up the trail to your favorite actor's Web page.

If you get the error message **Document contains no data**, it's usually because the address to which the link refers is incomplete. For example, a normal link will look something like http://www.news.com/current/headlines/ clinton.html. If the link's address is http://www.news.com/current/headlines/, there's no document to which Netscape can connect. Try connecting to just http://www.news.com. From there, you can probably find a link with the complete address of the page you want.

CAUTION

Sometimes a Page Just Won't Load One way to know if Netscape is stuck is to watch the status bar; Netscape displays its progress there. If nothing happens, or if it just plain takes too long, you may want to try reloading the page. To do so, click the **Stop** button, and then click the **Reload** button.

If you click a link to a type of file that Netscape doesn't recognize (such as a unique video or sound format), it probably won't play. Instead, you'll see a message telling you that you don't yet have a viewer configured to handle the file. If that happens, click the **Cancel Transfer** button in the dialog box. In Part 4, you'll learn how to download and install the proper in-line plug-ins and helper apps that enable Netscape to handle unknown file types.

You might click on a link and get the error message **Netscape is unable to locate the server: xxxx. The server does not have a DNS entry**. If so, try clicking the link again. If it still doesn't work, then there may be a typo in the link's address, or the page to which the link refers may no longer exist. This kind of error could also mean that your Internet connection has been broken. Dial into your service provider again and retry the link.

TIP

Busy Signal? If a page is popular, a lot of people might be trying to connect to it at the same time. In such a case, you'll probably get one of two error messages: **Connection refused by Host** or **Too many users, try again later.** Try again at a less busy time, such as early in the day or late at night.

Returning to Previously Viewed Pages

As you move from one Web page to another, Netscape Navigator and Netscape Gold save the history of where you've been so you can easily return to any previously viewed page. However, Netscape tracks the history for the current session only; that history is erased when you exit the program.

TIP

What If I Find a Page I Like? If you find a Web page that you plan to visit often, you can save its address permanently. See Part 1 Lesson 5 for details.

Using the history feature in Netscape Navigator is a lot like reading a book: to return to a previously viewed page, you move backward in the "book." In Netscape, you can move backward as many pages as you like simply by clicking the **Back** button (see Figure 2.3). After you back up, you can return to where you were by moving forward through previously viewed Web pages. Simply click the **Forward** button. If you want to return to your starting point, you can click the **Back** button until you get there, or you can click the **Home** button. Either way, you return to your home page, which by default is the Netscape home page.

Move forward if you back up too far.

Move backward through the pages you've seen.

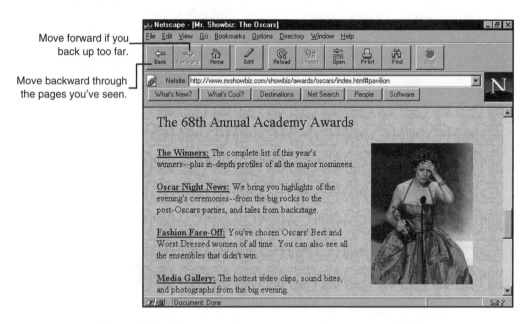

Figure 2.3   You can easily move to a previously viewed Web page.

Nothing Happens When I Click the Button   If the Forward (or Backward) button is gray, you have moved to the end (or the beginning) of the history. You can't select the button again because you've moved as far forward or backward in the history as you can.

CAUTION

Working with Frames   When a Web page uses frames, moving to a previously viewed page is a bit trickier than described here. See Part 1 Lesson 4 for more details.

CAUTION

You can also jump directly to any previously viewed page by selecting it from the history list. Just follow these steps:

1. Open the **Window** menu and select **History**. The History dialog box shown in Figure 2.4 appears.

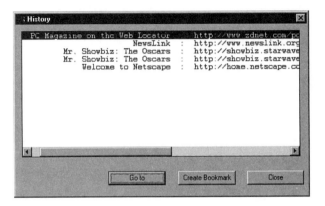

Figure 2.4 The History dialog box.

2. Select the page you want to view and click **Go to**. The page you select appears in the Navigator window.

3. Click the **Close** button to remove the History dialog box from your screen.

Exiting Netscape

When you're ready to exit Netscape, use whichever of the following methods is appropriate for your system:

- **Windows 3.1** Open the **File** menu and select **Exit**, or double-click the **Control-menu** box to exit Netscape. Disconnect from the Internet by returning to Trumpet Winsock, opening the **Dialler** menu, and selecting **Bye**.

- **Windows 95** Open the **File** menu and select **Exit**, or click the **Close** button to exit Netscape. To disconnect from the Internet, return to the Connect To dialog box and click **Disconnect**.

In this lesson, you learned how to start Netscape, how to navigate through the Web using links and Netscape's history feature, and how to exit Netscape. In the next lesson, you'll learn how to enter an address so that you can jump directly to a particular Web page.

Using Addresses (URLs)

In this lesson, you will learn how to use addresses (URLs) to move directly to a Web page.

Understanding Addresses (URLs)

As I've mentioned in the previous lessons, each Web page has its own address, or URL (Uniform Resource Locator). A typical URL looks something like this:

http://www.ticketmaster.com/events/ev_home.html

If you know the address for a particular page you want to see, you can type it in the Location/Go to box in Netscape. When you press Enter, you jump directly to the Web page you want.

Where Do I Get the Address for a Page?   If you don't know the address for a particular page or even which pages you might want to view, you can search for applicable pages using a Web search tool such as InfoSeek, Yahoo, or Lycos. See Part 1 Lesson 8 for more information on those tools. You can also get addresses for hot Web sites from any of several Internet magazines such as *The Net*, *Websight*, *Net Guide*, and *Internet World*. In addition, many companies now include their Web page addresses in their advertising.

A Web address identifies an official Internet resource. Every URL has two parts: the *content identifier* and the *location*. Take another look at our sample address, and then we'll break it down.

http://www.ticketmaster.com/events/ev_home.html

The first part, the http:// part in our sample, is the content identifier (or content-id for short). The content-id tells Netscape which protocol or language was used to create the current page. The http:// identifier tells Netscape that this page was written using HyperText Transfer Protocol (http for short). As you learned in Lesson 2, Netscape supports other protocols as well, such as ftp://, gopher://, telnet://, and news://. This allows you to connect to other resources through the Web. For instance, you can link to a site's FTP directory or to a Usenet newsgroup just as easily as you can link to another Web page—just by clicking the link.

How Can I Tell Which Resource a Link Will Connect Me To?
If you want to see what type of resource you're jumping to before you click its link, point to the link but don't click. The address of the link appears in the status bar. The content-id at the beginning of the address tells you whether the link connects to a Web page (http://) or some other type of resource.

The second part of the sample address, www.ticketmaster.com/events/ ev_home.html, identifies the location of the particular Web page or resource. To understand the location better, you need to divide it into two smaller parts. The first part is the *domain name* or *host name*. Each computer connected to the Internet has a unique name that makes it easy to identify it from the thousands of other computers connected directly to the Web. Your PC doesn't have a domain name, but your service provider's does because it's connected to the Web. (You connect to the Web through your service provider's domain.) So the address www.ticketmaster.com refers to the Web-managing portion (www) of a computer called ticketmaster.com. The .com part, by the way, tells you that this computer is basically used for commercial (business) purposes. Other popular extensions include .gov for government, .edu for education, .pub for public, and .net for Internet service provider.

The second part of the location is the name of a particular Web resource. This name looks very much like a directory path because that's exactly what it is. You see, every Web page is actually just a document file that exists on some computer connected to the Web. These directory paths follow the UNIX format, which means that they use forward slashes (/) in place of the backslashes (\) you're used to seeing in DOS and Windows. So the address in the sample will connect you to a document called ev_home.html, located in the events directory of the ticketmaster computer.

No Document Name? Some addresses don't provide an actual document name. For example, you might be given the address http://www.weather.com, which connects you to the Weather Channel's computer. When you connect, that system automatically displays the Weather Channel's home page (a document file located on that computer). You'll encounter a lot of systems set up this way, so don't worry when you uncover an address that doesn't end in a document name.

Using Addresses to Jump to a Page

Once you have the address of a Web resource you'd like to visit, it's easy to jump to that page. Just follow these steps:

1. Click in the **Location** box. The address of the current page becomes selected so that you can replace it with something else.

2. Type the address you want to go to, as shown in Figure 3.1. (You'll probably notice that the text box's name changes to "Go to" as you type.) Make sure that you use forward slashes (/) to separate the parts of the address, and that you use the proper case.

Case Is Important Note that the address www.Weather.com (for example) is different from www.weather.com. The use of upper- and lowercase letters is *very* important. Make sure that you write down addresses correctly and that you enter them correctly.

3. Press **Enter**, and you're taken to the Web resource at the address you entered.

You can also open the **File** menu and select **Open Location** to enter an address if you want. Simply type the address in the Open Location dialog box and click **Open** to jump to that Web page.

After you enter an address, your Web browser keeps it in a list of most recently typed addresses (see Figure 3.2). To return to a previously entered address (even one from an earlier session), click the **Location** drop-down arrow and select an address from the list.

Running Start If you want to be able to start Netscape with a particular Web page automatically displayed (but you don't want to make it your home page), you can save the page's URL with a shortcut icon. See Lesson 5 for details.

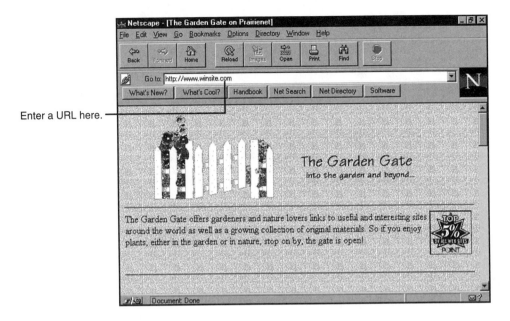

Enter a URL here.

Figure 3.1 Enter a URL in the Location/Go to text box.

Select a previously
entered address.

Figure 3.2 Netscape keeps track of other addresses you've entered.

Using an Address from a Disk

Right now, it's popular for Internet magazines such as *The Net* to include a
CD-ROM or a disk, complete with their list of "hot" Web sites. Basically, the
disk will contain one or two html pages with links pointing to the current
"hottest" Web sites. They also contain a few downloaded Web pages so you can
browse a site before you actually go there. (This saves you time and money
when searching for an appropriate site.) Figure 3.3 shows a page from a disk
included with the magazine *Net Power*.

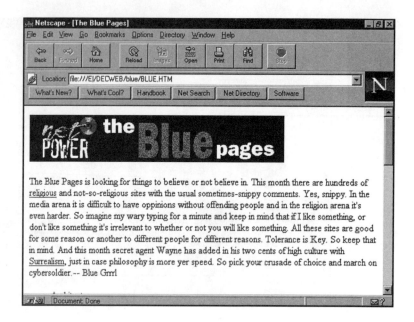

Figure 3.3   Many Internet magazines include disks that can lead you to popular Web sites.

To use one of these disks, pop it into your computer and follow these steps:

1. Start Netscape, but don't connect to the Internet yet.
2. Immediately click the **Stop** button to prevent Netscape from wasting time trying to load its home page.
3. Open the **File** menu and select **Open File**.
4. Switch to the disk drive that contains the magazine's disk, and select an html document.
5. Click **Open**. The html document appears on-screen.
6. Search the document for a Web site in which you're interested. If you find a link you like, connect to the Internet first, and then come back to Netscape and click the link. You're taken to that Web site.

In this lesson, you learned how to enter addresses (URLs) into Netscape to move around the Web. In the next lesson, you'll learn how to work with Web pages that contain frames.

Working with Frames

In this lesson, you will learn how to navigate a Web page that has frames.

What Is a Frame?

A *frame* is a section of the Netscape window. Just as panes divide a real window into smaller sections, frames divide the single Netscape window into smaller sections of information. Frames are typically used to organize a lot of material in a small space so that you can easily jump directly to whatever you're looking for. Figure 4.1 shows the Netscape home page with the frames feature turned on.

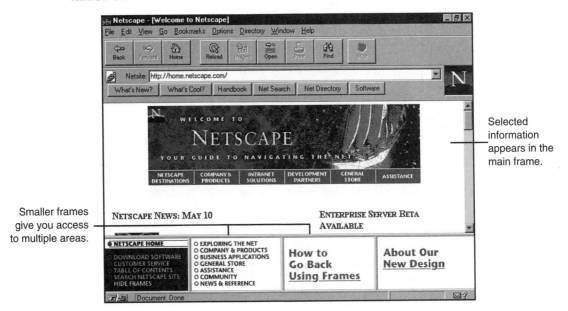

Selected information appears in the main frame.

Smaller frames give you access to multiple areas.

Figure 4.1 Netscape's home page uses frames to organize information.

Not all Web sites use frames. Among those that do use them, the number of frames varies. Some Web sites use only two frames, while others divide the window into several frames. The person who creates the Web page controls the size of the frames, so you won't be able to adjust a frame's size. However, if only part of a frame's information is currently visible, you can scroll in order to view the rest of it.

The contents of each frame is actually a separate Web document (Web page) with its own URL. Therefore, a window with frames can actually display several Web pages at once—each in its own frame. A lot of Web sites are designed so that when you click on a link within a frame, the Web page to which it is linked appears in a corresponding frame (see Figure 4.2). With both pages still visible, you can view new information while referring to information on a previous page.

Make a selection in this frame…

…and your selection appears in this frame.

Figure 4.2 You can keep two Web pages visible in frames and easily switch back and forth.

Don't Be Surprised If you click a link that points to a site that does not use frames, that Web page will fill the entire Netscape window.

CAUTION

In some cases, the contents of a frame may not change. For example, a special message or a map of the Web site may be fixed in a frame within the Netscape window to provide a constant reference point for the user as he moves through the site.

The frame on the left side of the window shown in Figure 4.3 allows the user to quickly jump from section to section in the Web site by clicking on the appropriate link (such as Overview, What's New?, or Concert Reviews). And because the top frame doesn' t change, the user can just as easily jump from any of those locations back to the Clouds in My Coffee page.

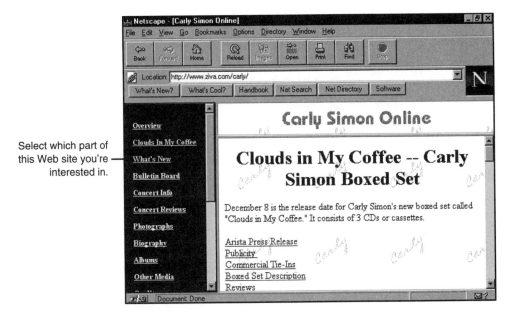

Select which part of this Web site you're interested in.

Figure 4.3   One frame might remain constant as a reference point.

Working on a Framed Web Page

It's easy to navigate your way around a framed Web site. For example, let's weave our way around the winter ski report section of the *Boston Globe* site located at http://www.boston.com/sports/wintact/winguide/winpoframe.html. Figure 4.4 shows the page at that site.

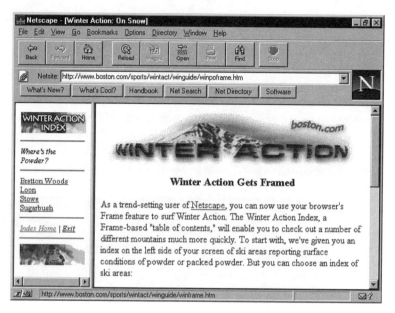

Figure 4.4 How's the powder?

Follow these steps to navigate the site:

1. Connect to the Internet and start Netscape.

2. In the **Location/Go to** text box, type **http://www.boston.com/sports/ wintact/winguide/winpoframe.html** and press **Enter**.

3. You use links on a framed Web page as you would the links on any other page: click a link to go to the corresponding Web page. For example, click **Bretton Woods** in the frame on the left of the page, and the frame on the right changes to display information on ski conditions at Bretton Woods (see Figure 4.5).

4. Notice that the left frame didn't change. A lot of Web sites use this technique in order to give you an *anchor*, or stable reference point. Suppose, now, that you decide you want to see the ski conditions at Stowe instead. Click its link in the left frame.

5. Use the scroll bars, as shown in Figure 4.6, to view information on the part of the page that's not visible.

Click here...

...to view this information.

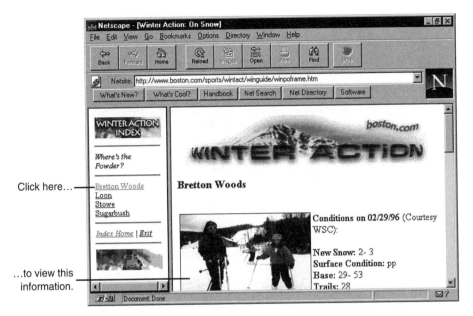

Figure 4.5 What's happening at Bretton Woods.

To view more information, you can scroll within a frame.

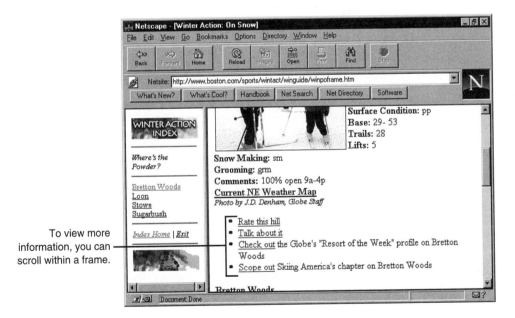

Figure 4.6 Digging deeper.

6. Dig deeper into the *Boston Globe* Web site by clicking the **Rate this hill** link shown in Figure 4.6. The view in the second frame changes again. Figure 4.7 shows the resulting page.

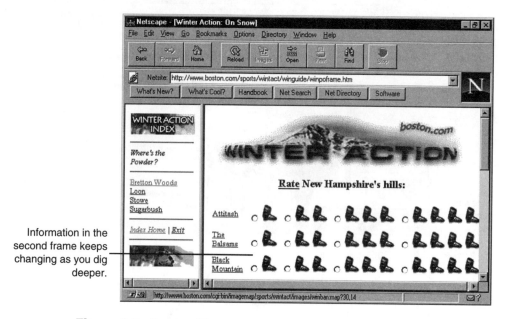

Information in the second frame keeps changing as you dig deeper.

Figure 4.7   Deeper still.

7. To return to the Bretton Woods page in frame two, for example, click the **Back** button. Unlike what you learned in Lesson 2, on a framed Web page, clicking the Back button does not move you back to the previous whole Web page. Instead, clicking the Back button moves you back one *frame* at a time. You can click Back as many times as necessary to back up to the frame you want to see. (If you click the Back button enough times, you will eventually get back to the last previously viewed whole Web page.) After you move back, click the **Forward** button to return to the previously viewed frame.

CAUTION

Is Using the Back Button a Hassle?   The problem with a framed system is that it's difficult to get back to the last whole Web page you visited. To do that, you can keep clicking the Back button until you move past all the frames you've viewed on the current Web site, or you can just use the History window. To do that, open the **Window** menu, select **History**, select the site you want to return to, and then click **Go to**.

8. When you finish practicing with frames, close Netscape and log off the Internet.

Navigating the Netscape Home Page

When you turn on the Show Frames feature, Netscape's home page is divided into five frames. The main frame at the top of the screen displays the entire Web page in a scrollable window. To view more of the main page, use the scroll bars.

On a framed Web page, one or more of the frames usually contain a basic outline of the Web site, which you can use to quickly locate information. This is true of Netscape's home page, as you'll see when you follow these steps to navigate it:

1. Connect to the Internet and start Netscape. Netscape's home page appears.

2. To view frames, scroll to the bottom of the Netscape home page and click the **Show Frames** button (see Figure 4.8). Frame number one (the main frame) displays the information you select from the other frames. The second frame (the first frame at the bottom of the Netscape home page) contains an outline of the Netscape system. If you click one of those options, the associated page appears in the main frame.

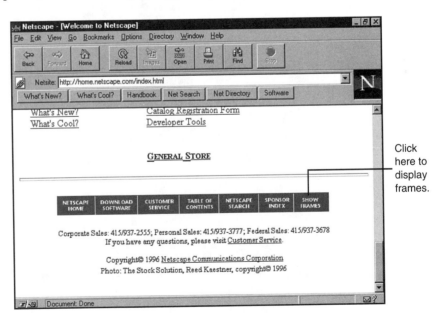

Click here to display frames.

Figure 4.8 You can redisplay frames at any time.

3. Click **Company & Products** in the second frame, and the main frame changes to display your selection. The third frame also changes to display the outline of the Company & Products page (see Figure 4.9).

4. Select **Netscape Products** from the third frame. The Netscape Products page appears in the main frame, and the fourth frame changes to display an outline of the Netscape Products page. This technique enables you to see where you've already been and where you can go from here—all at the same time.

I Want to Go Home   To return to the home page at any time, click **Netscape Home** in the first frame.

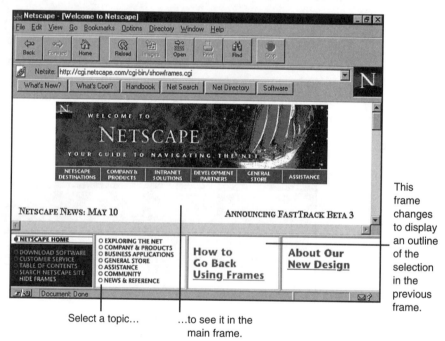

Select a topic...   ...to see it in the main frame.

This frame changes to display an outline of the selection in the previous frame.

Figure 4.9   The frames at the bottom of the page show you where you've been.

5. If you find an especially interesting page on the Netscape site and you want to get rid of the frames so you can see more of it, click the **Hide Frames** option in the first frame at the bottom of the window. Netscape hides the frames and devotes the whole window to the page displayed. To display the frames again, scroll down to the bottom of the page and select **Show Frames** (refer to Figure 4.8).

Go Back! You can also click the **Back** button on the Netscape toolbar to return to the framed version of this page.

6. When you finish navigating the Netscape home page, exit Netscape and disconnect from the Internet.

In this lesson, you learned how to navigate framed Web pages. In the next lesson, you'll learn how to save the locations of your favorite Web pages so that you can return to them quickly.

Creating and Using Bookmarks

In this lesson, you will learn how to insert bookmarks for your favorite Web pages so that you can return to them at any time.

Saving a Bookmark

You'll probably find that browsing the Web is like browsing through the pages of a large book. When you find a particular passage in a book that you want to be able to find again quickly, you insert a bookmark. You can do the same thing with your Web browser: when you find a particular Web page you like and plan to return to often, you add a bookmark.

When you create a bookmark in Netscape, Netscape saves the address for the displayed Web page. Because the addresses are often long and complex, creating bookmarks for your favorite Web pages saves you the time and trouble of trying to remember and enter them correctly.

CAUTION

On the Move   Occasionally, the address of a page changes. Because there's a big market in Web space rental these days, companies tend to move from one provider to another. When that happens, the company's Web page address changes. So a bookmark that took you to your favorite site last week might not be valid this week. You can usually use one of the Internet search tools described in Part 1 Lesson 8 to find the new address. Once you do, jump to the section "Organizing Bookmarks" (later in this lesson) to learn how to use Netscape's bookmark editor to change the old address.

The steps for creating a bookmark in Netscape Navigator and Netscape Gold are the same:

1. Go to the Web page whose address you want to save.

2. Open the **Bookmarks** menu and select **Add Bookmark**. Netscape saves the address of the current Web page.

Marking a Single Frame   If you want to create a bookmark for a frame (a section of a Netscape page), the process is a bit different. See "Saving a Bookmark for a Framed Web Page" for help.

After you create a bookmark for a page, you can return to that Web page at any time using one of following methods:

- To return to a page whose address you've saved, open the **Bookmarks** menu and select the page from the list as shown in Figure 5.1. (Your newest bookmark appears at the bottom of the list.)

- If you have the address stored in a bookmark folder (a group of related bookmarks), select the folder from the **Bookmarks** menu, and a cascading menu appears. Select the page you want to jump to from that menu. (See the upcoming section "Organizing Bookmarks" for information on how to store your bookmarks in a bookmark folder.)

Trade Places   You can trade bookmark files with your coworkers if you want. First, have your friend copy his bookmark file to a disk. (The file is called bookmark.htm, and it's in the Netscape directory.) Insert his disk in your computer, open the **Window** menu and select **Bookmarks**. Then open the **File** menu and select **Import**. Select the file on the disk and click **Open**. Voilà! His bookmarks are added to the bottom of your bookmark list.

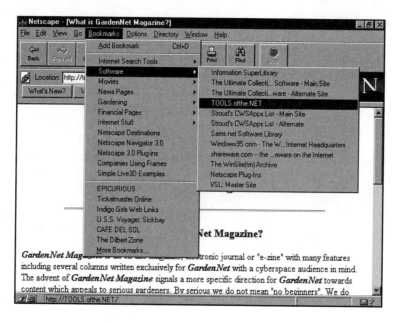

Figure 5.1   To return to a bookmarked page, select it from the Bookmarks menu.

Saving a Bookmark for a Framed Web Page

As you learned in Lesson 4, some Web pages break the normal Netscape window into small sections called frames. The contents of each frame is actually a Web page with its own URL. Therefore, a framed window actually displays several Web pages at once—each in its own frame. However, the fact that multiple Web pages are displayed makes it difficult for Netscape to determine which one you want to create a bookmark for. Follow these steps to save a bookmark for an individual frame:

1. Point to the link for the frame whose address you want to save. (Do not point to the frame itself, but to the link that you clicked to get the frame to appear. If the link is not visible, click the **Back** button, or right-click in the frame and select **Back in Frame** as needed.

2. Right-click the link, and a shortcut menu appears (see Figure 5.2).

3. Select **Add Bookmark**.

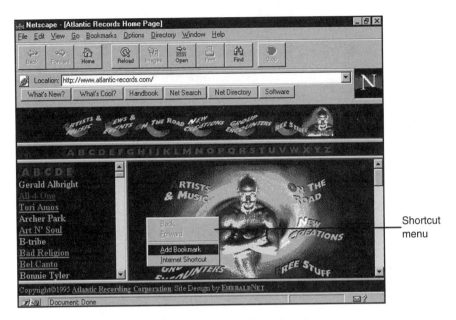

Figure 5.2 Use the shortcut menu to create a bookmark for a frame.

You can return to the page whose address you saved at any time by opening the **Bookmarks** menu and selecting it. You're taken to the page at the saved address, but the page does not appear in its frame. Instead, it takes up the entire Netscape window.

Creating a Shortcut for a Web Page

If you often visit a certain Web page at the beginning of your Netscape session, you might want to set up that page as your home page. You'll learn how to change the home page in Part 1 Lesson 6.

On the other hand, if you don't want to make the page your permanent home page, you can simply create a shortcut for it. When you create a shortcut, an icon for the Web page appears on the desktop. Then all you have to do is double-click the icon, and Netscape starts up and automatically jumps to that Web page. (It's kind of like creating a temporary starting point that you can use whenever you want.)

Windows 95 Only   Sorry, but only Windows 95 users can create a shortcut icon.

CAUTION

To create a shortcut for a Web page, follow these steps:

1. Jump to the page for which you want to create the shortcut.

2. Click the link icon to the left of the Location/Go to text box.

3. Drag the link icon onto the Windows 95 desktop, and the shortcut icon appears.

To start Netscape and jump to that Web page, double-click the shortcut icon. You can also drag the icon off the desktop and drop it into an open Netscape window to change to that page.

Organizing Bookmarks

Netscape enables you to sort your bookmarks, organize them in folders, and add comments. If you save very many bookmarks, you'll soon appreciate that you can organize them into a usable list.

You might create a folder so you can store similar bookmarks together. To create a bookmark folder, follow these steps:

1. Open the **Window** menu and select **Bookmarks**. The Bookmarks window appears.

2. In the bookmarks list, click where you want the folder to appear.

3. Open the **Item** menu and select **Insert Folder.** The Bookmark Properties dialog box appears.

4. Type a name and a description for the folder and click **OK**.

5. To add an existing bookmark item to the folder, drag it to the folder as shown in Figure 5.3.

6. Click the **Close** button to close the Bookmarks window.

CAUTION

Can't I Just Put a Bookmark Where I Want It?   Unfortunately, when you add a bookmark using the Add Bookmark command, it is automatically placed in the main bookmarks directory. After you save your bookmark, you can open the Bookmarks window and drag a bookmark to the folder in which you want to keep it. If you want to place the bookmark in a particular folder to begin with, you must create the bookmark manually using the Insert Bookmark command in the Bookmarks window.

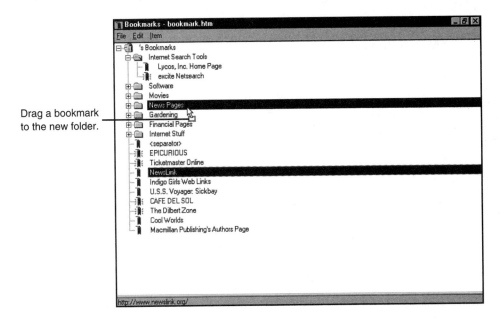

Drag a bookmark
to the new folder.

Figure 5.3 You can organize your bookmarks into folders.

TIP

Let's Separate! One way to group bookmarks together is to use separators. To place a separator between two bookmarks, click the first bookmark, open the **Item** menu, and select **Insert Separator**. The next time you open the Bookmarks window, a separator line appears below the bookmark you selected.

You can delete a bookmark folder by selecting it and pressing **Delete**. Of course, when you delete a folder, you delete all the bookmarks in it. So be careful!

When working in the Bookmarks window, you can hide the items in a folder by clicking the minus sign in front of the folder icon. To display the items in a closed folder, click the plus sign in front of the folder icon.

Creating an Alias

If you use folders to organize your bookmarks, from time to time you might want to place the same bookmark in more than one folder. You can do that by creating an *alias*, or copy, of the original bookmark. An alias is tied to the original in a unique way: if the original is changed somehow (for example, if you add a description), Netscape also changes the alias to keep them in synch.

You can create multiple aliases for the same bookmark if necessary. Follow these steps to create an alias:

1. Open the **Window** menu and select **Bookmarks**.

2. Select the bookmark you want to copy (make an alias of).

3. Open the **Item** menu and select **Make Alias**. The alias appears under the original bookmark.

4. Drag the alias (the copy) to wherever you want it.

Adding Bookmark Descriptions

Sometimes adding a description can help you identify an obscure bookmark later. (Although you can add a description for a bookmark, you see that description only when you open the Properties window.) Follow these steps to add a description to an existing bookmark:

1. Open the **Bookmarks** menu and select **Go to Bookmarks**.

2. To change the description for a particular item, select it, open the **Item** menu, and select **Properties**. The Bookmarks Properties dialog box appears (see Figure 5.4).

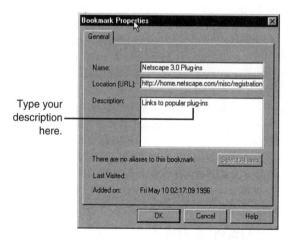

Figure 5.4   Add a description to your bookmark so you can identify it.

3. (Optional) In the **Name** text box, change the name of the item if necessary.

4. In the **Description** area, type a description for the selected bookmark. Then click **OK**.

The Page Moved! If the Web page associated with one of your bookmarks has moved and you know its new location, you can follow these steps to change its address. Type the new address in the Location/Go to text box.

Checking What's New on Bookmarked Pages

The Internet changes constantly, and sometimes it's a struggle to keep up. What's the best way to find out what's new?

One way is to have Netscape check your bookmarked pages and notify you of which ones contain new information. Then you only have to visit the changed pages to get a quick update on your favorite topics. It couldn't be simpler—and you don't waste any time visiting Web pages whose information hasn't changed since your last visit.

Follow these steps to set Netscape to check your bookmarked pages:

1. Open the **Window** menu and select **Bookmarks**.

2. (Optional) If you want to check only a few bookmarks, select them by pressing **Ctrl** and clicking each of the bookmarks you want to check. (If you want Netscape to check all your bookmarks, skip this step.)

3. Open the **File** menu and select **What's New?**.

4. Choose whether you want Netscape to check all bookmarks or only the selected ones.

5. Click Start Checking. Netscape verifies each bookmark by attempting to connect to its associated Web site. As Netscape works, it displays its progress in the dialog box shown in Figure 5.5. (The amount of time it takes to check out your bookmarked pages will vary, depending on the number of Web sites you selected. You can click Cancel to stop Netscape at any time.)

6. When Netscape finishes checking your bookmarks, it displays a message saying so. Click OK.

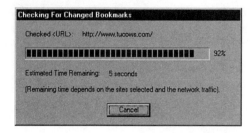

Figure 5.5 Netscape displays its progress as it checks your bookmarks.

If you return to the Bookmarks window, you might see that some bookmark icons have changed. Bookmarks that point to pages whose information has changed are marked with a highlighted icon as shown in Figure 5.6. Bookmarks that could not be checked are marked with a question mark icon.

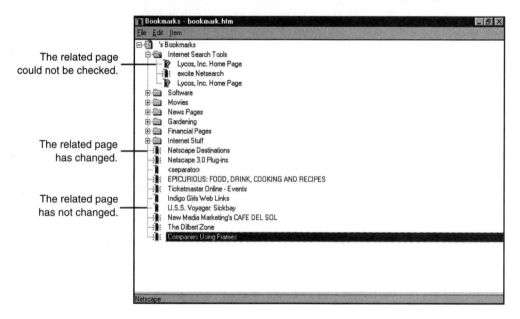

Figure 5.6 Netscape marks your bookmarks as it goes along.

In this lesson, you learned how to create and organize bookmarks. In the next lesson, you'll learn about other Netscape features you might want to try.

Other
Netscape
Features

In this lesson, you will learn about other things you can do with Netscape, such as creating a second window within your browser.

Creating a Second Netscape Window

At some point while cruising the Web, you're going to want to be in two (or more) places at once. In Netscape Navigator and Netscape Gold, you can visit as many Web pages as you want at the same time by placing each page in its own window.

To create a second Netscape window, follow these steps:

1. Open the **File** menu and select **New Web Browser**.

2. A new Netscape window appears, displaying the Netscape home page (or your home page if you've changed it).

3. Type the address of a new Web page in the **Location/Go To** text box and press **Enter**. The associated page appears in that Netscape window. Figure 6.1 shows two Netscape windows.

4. Repeat steps 1 through 3 to open additional Netscape windows.

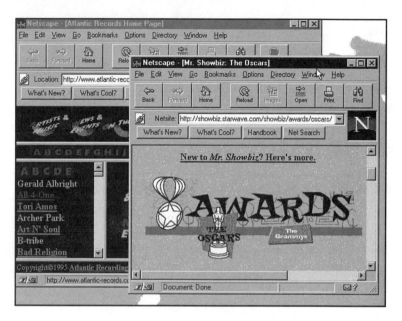

Figure 6.1   You can view more than one Web page at a time.

Because these windows are independent of one another, you can minimize, maximize, or resize any window to fit your needs. In Windows 95, you can arrange your open windows by right-clicking the taskbar and selecting **Cascade**, **Tile Horizontally**, or **Tile Vertically**. To arrange windows in Windows 3.1, open Program Manager's **Window** menu and select either **Cascade** or **Tile.**

To switch from window to window, open the **Window** menu and select the window you want to go to. You can also use the Windows 95 or Windows 3.1 task list to switch from one Netscape window to another. To close a Netscape window, click its **Close** button, or open the **File** menu and select **Close**.

Designating a Different Home Page

Normally, when you start Netscape Navigator or Netscape Gold, you're connected to the Netscape home page. From the home page, you can explore the World Wide Web however you like. But if you often visit the same Web page, why not make it your starting point?

Make Your Own You can also create your own Web page, filled with links to all your favorite spots on the Web, and designate it as your home page. You'll learn how to create Web pages in Part 5 and Part 6.

Once you decide which page you want to use, follow these steps to change your designated home page:

1. Open the **Options** menu and select **General Preferences**. The Preferences dialog box appears.

2. If it isn't already selected, click the **Appearance** tab to see the options shown in Figure 6.2.

The address of
your home page

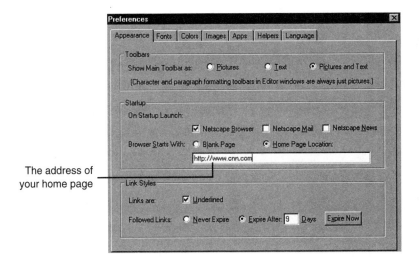

Figure 6.2 Choose any Web page to be your home page.

3. In the **Browser Starts With** text box, enter the address of the Web page you want to use as your home page. If you want to use an HTML file that's on your hard disk, substitute the word "file" for "http" in the address (as in file://C:/Netscape/myhomepage.html).

4. Click **OK**.

49

Saving and Printing Web Pages

You'll often find things on the Web that you want to hang onto. Of course, if you just want to be able to visit the page again, you can create a bookmark for it as described in Lesson 5. However, if you want to save the information on the page, a bookmark might not work because the next time you visit that Web page, it might contain different information. Or, if the page contains a lot of information, you might want to save it so you don't waste online time reading it all. Luckily, both Netscape Navigator and Netscape Gold enable you to print a Web page or to save it so you can view it later.

To save a Web page, follow these steps:

1. Open the **File** menu and select **Save As**. The Save As dialog box appears.

2. Change to the directory in which you want to save the Web page.

3. Enter a name for the document in the **File name** text box and click **Save**.

To view the document later, open the **File** menu and select **Open File**. Then select the document you want to view and click **Open**. The document appears in the Netscape window. You do *not* have to be online to view a saved document.

CAUTION

Where Are the Graphics?   If the Web page you save contains fancy graphics, they won't be in your saved copy. If you really want the graphics, you must save each one separately. To save a graphic, right-click it and select **Save Image as** from the shortcut menu. Then enter a name for the graphic and click **Save**. (For best results, save the graphic in the same directory as your document.) If you save the graphics to the same directory as the Web page, they will appear when you open the document later—at least most of the time. If a graphic doesn't load after you open your saved document, right-click its placeholder and select **Load Image** from the shortcut menu.

If you don't want to save the Web page to your hard disk, you can just as easily save its contents by printing it. To print a Web page, click the **Print** button, or open the **File** menu and select **Print**. In the Print Range area of the Print dialog box, select **All**. Then click **OK**.

Speeding Up Netscape

Most Web pages have a lot of pretty graphics. The trouble is, it can take a long time for Netscape to load and display all those graphics on your system. Meanwhile, you sit—waiting very impatiently, I'm sure.

To speed up Netscape, you can set it so that it doesn't display the graphics. Instead, Netscape displays a small placeholder as shown in Figure 6.3. If you switch to a page whose graphics you want to load and display, you can do it with a single click.

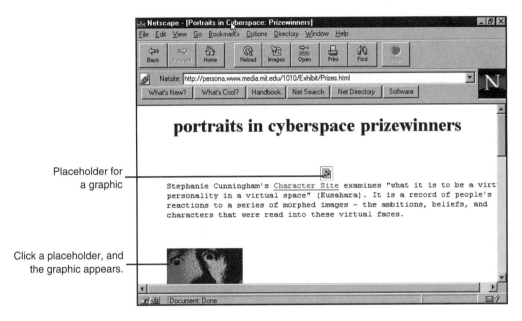

Placeholder for a graphic

Click a placeholder, and the graphic appears.

Figure 6.3   You can speed up Netscape by not displaying graphics.

To set up Netscape so that it doesn't display graphics automatically, open the **Options** menu and deselect **Auto Load Images** (remove the check mark from in front of the option to turn it off). From then on, when you switch to a new Web page, its text appears, and placeholders appear where the graphics normally would. If you decide you want to view a graphic, just click its placeholder. Or, to load all the graphics at one time, click the **Images** button on the Netscape toolbar.

Getting Help

Netscape provides *online* help for its software. Therefore, to get help, you must connect to the Internet first. When your Internet connection is established, open the **Help** menu and choose one of the following commands:

- **About Netscape** Choose this command to find your Netscape version number.
- **About Plug-ins** Select this command to learn more about Netscape *plug-ins*.

Plug-Ins Similar to helper apps, plug-ins are special programs designed to enhance Netscape Navigator and/or Netscape Gold. For example, the RealAudio plug-in enables Netscape to play sound files embedded in a Web page in real-time.

- **Registration Information** Select this to register your copy of Netscape.
- **Software** Want to find out about other products Netscape offers? Select this command to do just that.
- **Handbook** Choose this command if you need help using Netscape.

Create Your Own Help If you use Netscape's Help system a lot, your online time adds up quickly. You might want to save Help pages you need and read them later after you log off. Follow the steps in the section "Saving and Printing Web Pages" to do that.

- **Release Notes** This command provides information about dealing with known "bugs" (glitches in the software).
- **Frequently Asked Questions** Select this command to see a list of often asked questions about Netscape and to find answers to them.
- **On Security** Select this to find out more about how Netscape can help keep your information secure.
- **How to Give Feedback** If you have a suggestion, select this command to learn how you can pass it along.
- **How to Get Support** This command gives you access to more help.
- **How to Create Web Services** If you're thinking about creating your own Web page, Netscape has a lot of help to offer you.

In this lesson, you learned how to open a second Netscape window, change your home page, print and save Web pages, speed up Netscape, and get help about Netscape. In the next lesson, you'll learn how to complete on-screen forms.

Filling Out Forms

In this lesson, you will learn how to complete on-screen forms that you may encounter while surfing the Web.

What Is a Form?

At some Web pages you visit, you may be asked to fill out a *form*. A form is simply a "dialog box" placed on a Web page. You're probably already familiar with dialog boxes; they're part of every program you use, including Netscape, your word processor, your spreadsheet program, and Windows. Dialog boxes enable you, the user, to provide additional information that a program might need in order to complete a task. When you save a file for the first time, for example, you use the options in a dialog box to select a directory in which to save the file and to enter a name for it.

On the Web, you don't use dialog boxes. Instead, you fill out forms to provide the information needed to complete a task. For example, when you use one of the Web search tools such as Yahoo, InfoSeek, or Lycos, you complete an on-screen form to tell the search tool what you want to search for. Similarly, you might complete a form to leave an opinion on someone's Web page, or to provide an e-mail address to which the owner of the Web page may respond. The uses for forms are as vast as the Web itself.

Be Careful Out There! As you'll learn later in this lesson, the Web is not a secure place. Anyone else can obtain the information you give out (if he or she is determined enough). So be careful when you enter information in a form.

CAUTION

As you might expect, an on-screen form looks like a large dialog box, complete with text boxes, list boxes, check boxes, and option buttons. Figure 7.1 shows an example of a form you might fill out on the Web.

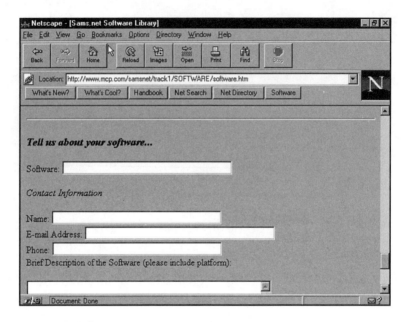

Figure 7.1 A Web form looks like a dialog box.

If you know your way around a basic Windows dialog box, you'll do fine with Web forms. Basically, you make your selections and type in whatever information is needed. Then you click a button such as Send Now, Accept, or Search to tell the system that you've finished completing the form. That's it!

Completing a Form

When you encounter a form on a Web page, treat it as you would a Windows dialog box. (Keep in mind that you should protect private information on the Web; see the next section for a discussion about security issues.)

Follow these guidelines when completing forms:

- To enter text in a Web form, click in the text box and type your information (see Figure 7.2).

- If the form uses option buttons or check boxes, click the option you want to select. (Remember that you can select only one option button in a group.)

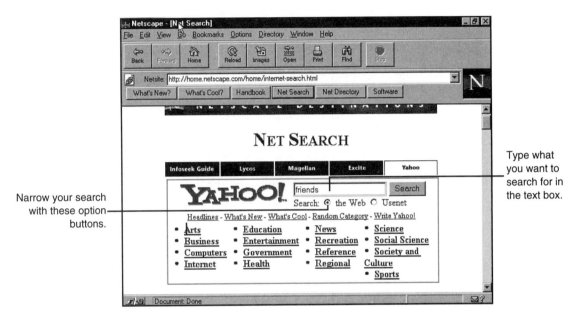

Narrow your search with these option buttons.

Type what you want to search for in the text box.

Figure 7.2 Entering information in a form is like completing a dialog box.

- To use a list box, click the drop-down arrow to open the list (see Figure 7.3). Then click on your selection.

- When you finish filling in the form, click the appropriate command button. (On the form in Figure 7.2, for example, you would click **Search**.)

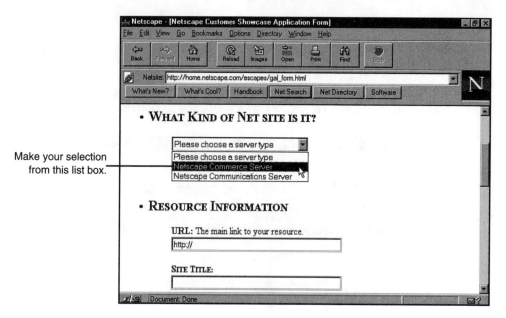

Make your selection from this list box.

Figure 7.3   Some forms use list boxes.

Security Issues

The Internet is an open system. This means that, despite what some people may want you to believe, any information you enter into a Web form is not completely secure. If a person tries hard enough, he or she can access your information eventually.

CAUTION

It Bears Repeating   Be very cautious about completing any Web form that asks for private information such as your social security number, your credit card numbers, and even your phone number. There's always a chance that someone who's unauthorized could get the information you provide.

Although no system is completely secure, some systems are more secure than others. The person who creates a Web site can make the site more secure by using the protocol https instead of the usual http. You can tell whether a Web page uses the https protocol by looking at its address; it will have the https prefix instead of http. In addition, Netscape tells you when you're connected to a secure Web page by displaying a complete key icon at the left end of the status bar. A broken key icon represents a nonsecure page.

What If I Forget to Look? Don't worry if you forget to see whether a page is secure before you complete a form. If the system is not secure, Netscape Navigator or Netscape Navigator Gold will provide a final warning in the form of a large dialog box that's hard to miss.

Another way to improve security is with *certificates*. You might remember that during installation you were asked if you wanted to sign up for a security certificate (digital ID). If you chose to do so, you provided your e-mail address and some other personal information, and in return, you received a certificate file that contained your digital ID. When doing business over the Internet at a secure site, you might be asked for that certificate in order to access the site. The digital ID replaces multiple passwords for accessing the secure site. In other cases, you might be asked for a certificate in order to validate a charge card order. This prevents any potential thief from successfully using your credit card number or your password for a secure site; he won't have the certificate file needed to complete the transaction. See Lesson 19 for more information on certificates and Internet security.

You should check out a page's security level before you complete any forms that ask for personal information such as your social security number or credit card numbers. Also, keep in mind that even if you're connected to a secure Web page, the person to whom you're giving your private information should also be suspect. In other words, just as you might exercise caution when giving your private information over the telephone, you should get to know something about any person or company with whom you're planning to share personal information.

In this lesson, you learned how to complete Web forms. In the next lesson, you'll learn how to search for information on the Web.

Searching for Information on the Web

In this lesson, you will learn how to search the Web for information using the most popular Web search tools.

How Search Tools Work

Up to this point, you've probably found the information you were looking for on the Web by jumping from one link to another or by entering the URLs (addresses) for specific Web pages. Although they work, those are not the most efficient methods.

A better way to locate what you need is to use *Web search tools*. With a search tool, you fill out a form describing what you want to search for and click a Search button, and the search tool looks through its list of Web pages to find a match. As it searches, it makes a note of the number of *hits*, or matches, it finds for each Web page.

TERM

Hit   A match between your search criteria and something found in the description of a Web page. The more hits the tool finds within its description of a particular Web page, the more likely it is that the Web page contains the information you want.

When it finishes searching, the search tool lists the sites it thinks match your search criteria. This list is basically a set of links pointing to various Web pages, arranged so that the pages with the most hits (matches) are at the top. You browse through this list and click the links for the Web sites you want to visit.

Obviously, for the best results, you should start with the pages at the beginning of the list. If you want, you can save your search results so you can browse through them later. To do so, follow the steps for saving a Web page in Lesson 6.

TERM   **Search Tool**   A searchable index of Web pages. Popular Web search tools include Yahoo, Lycos, and Excite!.

Because each search tool maintains its own independent list of Web pages, some search tools are better than others. You'll soon find your favorite. Netscape makes it easy to connect to the most popular search tools, including InfoSeek, Excite!, Yahoo, Lycos, and Magellan.

Search tools typically fall into two categories based on how you specify the information you want to find. With one type of tool, you simply enter a word or two to search for, and click a button to start the search. The popular search tool called Lycos works this way. To use the other type of tool, you select a major category, a subcategory from that, another subcategory, and so on until you find what you need or until you've narrowed the subject matter for the search. The popular search tool Yahoo works in this manner (although it also has a search box in which you can type specific words to search for).

In this lesson, I'll walk you through the specific steps for using Lycos and Yahoo. Many other search tools that you might want to try are available. Table 8.1 contains a list of other tools and their URLs.

Table 8.1   Web Search Tools

Search Tool	Address
Alta Vista	http://altavista.digital.com
Excite!	http://www.excite.com
InfoSeek	http://guide.infoseek.com
Magellan	http://www.mckinley.com
New Riders Official World Wide Web Yellow Pages	http://www.mcp.com/nrp/wwwyp/
Open Text Index	http://www.opentext.com/omw/f-omw.html
Point	http://www.pointcom.com

Quick Seek   You can access one of several popular Web search tools by clicking the Net Search button at the top of the Netscape window. Note, however, that Netscape changes the search tool associated with this button from time to time so you don't really know which search tool you'll get when you click it. It might be Excite!, Magellan, InfoSeek, Lycos, or Yahoo, for example.

Web Only   The search tools you'll learn about in this lesson work only for information on the World Wide Web. Remember that the Web is only one part of the Internet. If a search tool doesn't find any pages that match your criteria, you can still search other parts of the Internet such as FTP or Gopher sites. You'll learn how to search FTP sites in Lesson 11 and Gopher sites in Lesson 12.

Getting Better Results

As you'll see in a moment, most of the Web search tools function in a similar manner. Basically, you type in what you want to search for, click a button, and off it goes. For example, you could search for the word "fishing," and the search tool would make a list of pages that have "fishing" somewhere in the description.

Forget It   The Web search tools ignore certain words, including "a," "an," "the," "it," and common words such as "computer" and "Internet," so don't bother to use those words in your search. One or two well-chosen words are always best ("Windows utilities" or "stock quotes," for example).

Typing a simple search term like "fishing" will probably result in a long list of potential Web sites that you'll have to wade through. To make your search more effective, try to narrow it by using more specific search text. For example, you might type "bass fishing" or "fresh water fishing" instead of just "fishing."

The better search tools allow you to narrow your search further by setting additional criteria. For example, if you enter "vegetable gardening," most search tools will come up with a list of Web sites that mention either the word "vegetable" or the word "gardening." But the better search tools allow you to specify an exact match, which tells the tool that you want a listing of only the Web sites that contain both "vegetable" and "gardening."

Another common mistake is typing a word that can be found in other words that do not relate to what you want. For example, if you type "stock," you might find matches for stocks, stock brokers, stockyards, soup stock, and stock exchange. If the search tool you're using allows you to specify exact matches only, choose that option in order to avoid this problem.

Using Lycos

Lycos is popular because it's one of the best search tools. If you can't find what you're looking for by browsing the Web, chances are you'll find it with Lycos. But if that's not enough, you can also access two other helpful tools through Lycos: Point and A2Z (A to Z). Point provides direct links that *point* you to the more popular pages on the Web. A2Z is an alphabetical listing of popular Web pages.

Like most Web search tools, Lycos provides a simple text box into which you enter the word or words you want to search for. Lycos also offers options with which you can narrow the search and improve the results. To use Lycos, follow these steps:

1. Type **http://www.lycos.com** in the **Location/Go to** text box and press **Enter**. You'll find yourself at the main Lycos screen, shown in Figure 8.1.

Figure 8.1 You can search the Web with Lycos.

A Faster Way You can also access Lycos with Netscape's Net Search button. As you learned earlier, Netscape connects you to one of several search tools when you click this button. Even if the button doesn't take you directly to Lycos, the Web page to which you are connected will provide a link to it.

2. If you do not want to limit your search, type the word or words you want to search for in the **Find** text box. Click **Go Get It**, and you are finished.

   If you want to narrow your search, do not type anything in the Find text box. Instead, proceed with step 3.

3. Click **Enhance your search**. The Lycos Search Form appears (see Figure 8.2).

4. Type the word or words you want to search for in the **Query** text box.

5. Normally, Lycos lists Web pages that contain any of the search words. If you want Lycos to list only pages that contain *all* of the search words, open the first **Search Options** drop-down list and click **match all terms (AND)**.

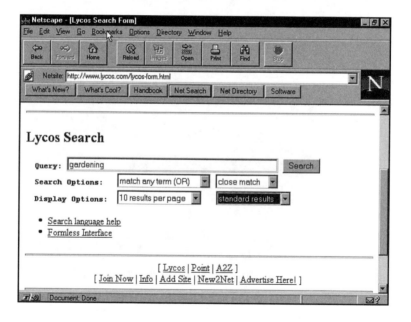

Figure 8.2 Use these options to narrow your search in Lycos.

6. If you want Lycos to list only the Web pages with a lot of hits, open the second **Search Options** drop-down list (on the right) and select an option that specifies how close you want your matches to be.

7. Lycos normally displays 10 matches at a time. To display more matches per page, open the first **Display Options** drop-down list and select a different number.

8. Lycos also displays a brief description for each match. To control the length of this description, open the second **Display Options** drop-down list (on the right) and choose **summary results** (short), **standard results** (medium), or **detailed results** (long).

9. When you're ready to start the search, click the **Search** button.

Lycos performs the search and displays a list of items that match your search criteria. Click any item to jump to the associated Web page. Remember that the pages with the most hits (the ones which come closest to matching your search criteria) appear at the beginning of the list. If the list fills more than one page, scroll down to the bottom of the page and click the link that advances you to the next page of search results. If necessary, you can return to a previous search results page by clicking the **Back** button at the top of the Netscape window.

Save That Search!   You can save your search results on a single page by opening the **File** menu and selecting **Save As**. You can then view the saved Web page later by starting Netscape and opening the file (see Lesson 6). You can also save the results with a bookmark by opening the **Bookmarks** menu and selecting **Add Bookmark**. The only problem (if you want to call it that) is that the bookmark saves the search criteria—not the results. So when you revisit the page, you might find that the results have changed because new Web pages have been added and others have been dropped from the Internet.

Using Yahoo

Yahoo, like Lycos, enables you to search its listing of Web pages by entering a few keywords. However, it also provides you with another way of searching. In Yahoo, you can browse for what you're looking for by selecting a category that interests you from the Yahoo Web page. From there, you can select another category and another, until you've narrowed your search sufficiently. At the bottom of the screen, you'll see a number of sites that fit the category you selected. So by using Yahoo's category method, you can even find a Web page without entering any keywords at all.

In addition, Yahoo lets you combine the two methods. You can select a few categories first and then enter a keyword to search for. This enables you to limit your search to a smaller portion of the Web.

Another Way   You can also access Yahoo with Netscape's Net Search button. As you learned earlier, Netscape connects you to one of several search tools when you click this button. Even if the button doesn't take you directly to Yahoo, the Web page to which you are connected will provide a link to it.

To select a category that interests you in Yahoo, follow these steps:

1. Type **http://www.yahoo.com** in the **Location/Go to** text box and press **Enter**. You'll see the Yahoo opening screen shown in Figure 8.3.

2. Click a category that interests you. For example, click **Arts**.

3. Yahoo presents a list of subcategories. Continue clicking links until you find a category you like.

4. Click a link to jump to that Web page.

Alternatively, you can search for a keyword within a category. Simply enter a keyword or two into the text box, and click the **Search** button. Yahoo searches for the requested topic and displays a list of links that match your entry. Click an entry to change to that Web page.

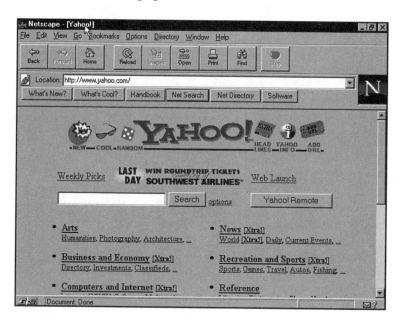

Figure 8.3   With Yahoo, you can search for a Web page by category.

Narrow That Search   You can narrow your Yahoo search as you did with Lycos—by looking for only exact matches, for example. To do so, click the **Options** link next to the Search text box. Make your selections to limit the search, enter keywords to search for, and click **Search**.

After jumping to a particular Web page, you can return to the list of items that Yahoo found by clicking the **Back** button.

Search Twice   If your search results were pretty skimpy, Yahoo allows you to search the Web again using a different Web search tool. At the end of the list of found items, Yahoo provides links to other search tools. Click one, and the other search tool automatically performs a search using the same search criteria.

In this lesson, you learned how to use several different Web search tools. In the next lesson, you'll learn how to perform other types of searches.

Other Searches to Try

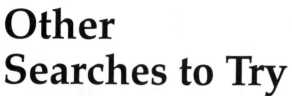

In this lesson, you learn how to search within a Web page's text, as well as how to search for articles with WAIS.

Searching a Web Page

Some Web pages are not well organized; looking for information on such a page is like looking through a junkyard for an overhead cam shaft for a '68 Camaro Z-28. Instead of wasting your time searching through the "junk" that fills most Web pages, you can search for the specific information you need. Follow these steps:

1. Open the **Edit** menu and select **Find**, or click the **Find** button. The Find dialog box appears.

2. Type the text you'd like to search for in the **Find what** text box (see Figure 9.1).

Enter the text to search for.

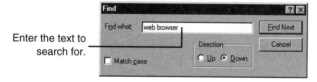

Figure 9.1 You can search for text on a Web page.

3. (Optional) If you want the text to exactly match the use of upper- and lowercase letters you typed, click **Match case**.

4. Click **Find Next**. Netscape finds the first occurrence of your keyword(s). Click **Find Next** as necessary to continue the search.

5. When you're done, click **Cancel**.

End of the Road When Netscape reaches the end of the Web page, you'll see the message **Search string not found.** Click **OK**.

CAUTION

Searching Databases Using WAIS

If you're searching for information for a report or research paper, or if you simply need more information than you can find on most Web pages, you should try WAIS. WAIS (Wide Area Information Server) is a search tool that enables you to search numerous databases on the Internet for helpful articles and research information.

What Makes WAIS Different? WAIS searches the entire text within each article for your keywords. This is unlike a search on a Gopher site, which compares only the title of each article to your keywords.

TIP

In the past, WAIS was very difficult to use (it was really only for people with a penchant for pain). Thankfully, that's not true anymore. To use WAIS, you first connect to a WAIS server. Try one of the following addresses:

> http://www.einet.net
>
> http://sunsite.unc.edu
>
> http://wais.wais.com
>
> http://www.ai.mit.edu/the-net/wais.html
>
> http://www.ecrc.gmu.edu/title.html

To use WAIS, follow these steps:

1. Enter the address of a WAIS server in the **Location/Go to** text box and press **Enter**. (For example, type **http://www.einet.net**.)

2. Select an area of interest by clicking on it (see Figure 9.2). Then narrow this category further by selecting more specific categories until you find what you want. (Alternatively, you can type keywords you want to search for in the text box provided, and click **Search** to begin the search.)

3. Like other search tools, WAIS displays the results of your search as a list of links. Click a link to view any article of interest.

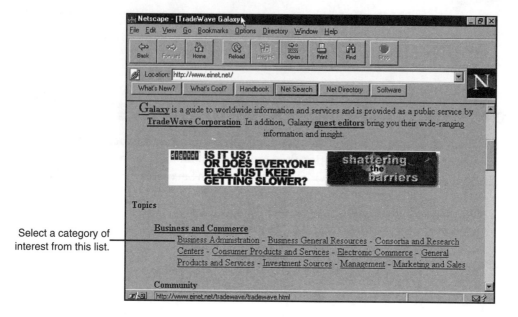

Select a category of interest from this list.

Figure 9.2   Some WAIS servers allow you to select a category of interest.

Uppercase vs. Lowercase   Some WAIS servers use case-sensitive searches, which means it searches for your keywords exactly as you type them. For best results, always use proper case when typing keywords.

CAUTION

Improving Your Results

Unlike other search tools, WAIS lists only articles that contain *all* of the keywords you enter. So if you type "car sales," you'll get articles that contain both the word "car" and the word "sales."

Some WAIS servers allow you to use the following search operators between the keywords you type:

AND   Tells WAIS to get articles that contain all of the keywords you enter. (Some WAIS servers provide a list of articles that contain any of the keywords but not necessarily all of them; in those servers, you might need to use AND.)

OR   Use this to broaden the search criteria to include articles that contain any of the keywords, such as "vegetable" or "gardening," but not necessarily "vegetable gardening."

NOT   Use this to exclude articles that contain a particular keyword. For example, if you want information on archeology, but you're not interested in ancient Egypt, you could type "archeology NOT Egypt."

ADJ   Specifies that the keywords must be adjacent in the article to count as a "hit." For example, if you ran a search for "bass fishing," you'd get articles that contain both the word "bass" and the word "fishing," but not necessarily "bass fishing." However, if you typed "bass ADJ fishing," WAIS would find articles that contain the words "bass fishing" together.

In addition to these search operators, you can use parentheses to group search criteria, as in "golfing (florida OR hawaii)." You can also use an asterisk (*) to search for partial words. For example, if you search for "elect*," you'll get hits such as "elect," "election," and "electorate."

In this lesson, you learned how to search a Web page and how to use WAIS. In the next lesson, you'll learn how to search for people on the Internet.

Searching for People on the Internet

In this lesson, you learn how to search for friends and coworkers on the Web.

"Fingering" a Person

Looking for a person on the Internet is not easy. First of all, there's no master user list that you can search to find your missing friend. In fact, some Internet providers do not allow access to their user lists, which makes your search a lot harder. But to have any chance of finding someone on the Internet, you need to know roughly where to look. That leads us to *finger*.

Finger is a tool that you can use to locate a user for whom you have at least a partial e-mail address. Obviously, if you had an e-mail address for the person, you wouldn't be wasting your time looking all over the Internet for him. But it is handy if the address you have is incomplete—and its usefulness doesn't end there. Finger can also tell you whether an e-mail message reached its intended recipient, it can tell you whether a message has been read, and it can sometimes provide a street address and phone number for your friend.

When you want to try using finger, the first thing you have to do is connect to a finger gateway. Here are some addresses you can use:

> http://www.nova.edu/Inter-Links/cgi-bin/finger.pl
> http://www.cs.indiana.edu/finger/gateway
> http://cei.haag.umkc.edu/people/brett/finger.html
> http://www-bprc.mps.ohio_state.edu/cgi_bin/finger.pl
> http://www.louisville.edu/~jadour01/mothersoft/gf/
> http://www.middlebury.edu/~otisg/cgi/HyperFinger.cgi

http://rdixon.ocx.lsumc.edu/!fingint

http://www.interlink.no/finger

To use finger, follow these steps:

1. Type the address of a finger gateway in the **Location/Go to** text box and press **Enter**.

2. Enter the e-mail address of the person you're looking for in the search text box.

3. Press **Enter** to start the search. Finger lists its results in a screen similar to the one in Figure 10.1.

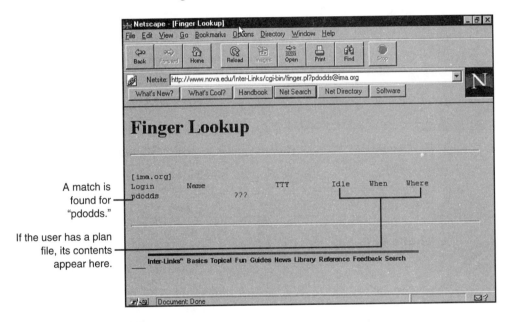

A match is found for "pdodds."

If the user has a plan file, its contents appear here.

Figure 10.1 Finger displays its results.

Sometimes finger displays a *plan* file for the person you are searching for. If it does, you'll find additional information such as a person's address and phone number in that plan file.

TERM

Plan A text file that contains additional information about a person (such as his name, address, and phone number). Since the contents of a plan file is only displayed when someone fingers you (is searching for you) you might want to create this simple text file, fill it with information you want others to know, and place it in your directory on your service provider's computer.

Using Whois to Find Someone

Although the function of Whois is similar to that of finger, Whois might be a bit more useful than finger because it allows you to search for a person using only the person's last name.

To search with Whois, you must first connect to a Whois gateway. Try one of the following gateways:

> gopher://sipb.mit.edu/70
> gopher://gopher.indiana.edu
> gopher://whois.slac.standford.edu
> gopher://gopher.bsu.edu
> gopher://gopher.caltech.edu
> gopher://gopher.fsu.edu:70/11/Phones
> gopher://whois.dfci.harvard.edu

Follow these steps to search for another user with Whois:

1. Type the name of a Whois gateway in the **Location/Go to** text box and press **Enter**.

2. Click **Internet Whois Servers**, **Phone Books**, **Internet Resources**, **Information Resources**, or a similar link.

What's NetFind? Sometimes, instead of connecting to a Whois server, a link will take you to a NetFind server. If that happens to you, skip down to the section "Using NetFind" later in this lesson.

3. You'll see a list of searchable sites. Click the one you think contains the name you're looking for.

4. Type the name of the person you're looking for. (Type either the first name or the last name, but not both.) For example, type **Flynn**. If you're not sure how the name is spelled, type as much of it as you know. (For example, if you're unsure whether to type Flynn or Flinn, just enter **Fl**.)

5. Press **Enter**. Whois runs the search and lists its results. Figure 10.2 shows the results of a Whois search for "Flynn."

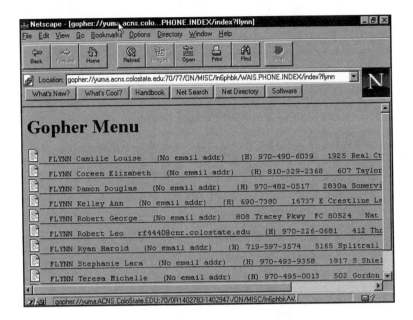

Figure 10.2 You can search for people using Whois.

Sometimes Whois displays the handle (nickname) for the person you are looking for. You might be able to obtain additional information (such as the person's address or phone number) if you search again using the person's handle instead of his name.

Using NetFind

Some of the links you come across when using Whois will be connected to a NetFind server instead of a Whois server. To get to NetFind, you'll need a Telnet program. Follow the steps in Lesson 11 to download one from the Internet. Then use the **Options**, **General Preferences** command to tell Netscape which Telnet program you use. You'll probably need to repeat this step in your Telnet program to tell it which Web browser you use.

Once you're set up and you telnet to a NetFind site, you log in using the name **netfind**. From there, you can select the menu option you want to search.

To search, type the last name of the person you're looking for and type additional *keys*. A key might be the name of the city or state where the person resides, or the department he works in (if you're searching for someone associated with a university). If you type more than just a name, include the search operator AND, like this:

flynn AND indiana

If everything works correctly, you should see a list of results. Good luck!

Other Ways to Search for People

Although finger and Whois are the best ways to locate people on the Internet, there are other search sites you can try. However, most of them charge you something (most searches are under $100). If you're looking for another way to find someone, though, try one of these electronic detectives:

Nationwide Investigations
        http://www.nwin.com
Ritchie's Investigative Service
        http://tmen.ns.net/jack.htm
People Locator Service
        http://www.clickit.com/bizwiz/homepage/plsform.htm
Internet Address Finder
        http://www.iaf.net

Quick Search   You can access links to many of the best Web people locators by clicking the **People** button at the top of the Netscape window.

If you don't want to pay someone to search for the address of an old friend, you can try looking for the person at http://www.Four11.com, a not-for-profit search tool. All they ask is that you add your name to their list.

Finally, if you know that the person you're looking for uses a certain online service, such as CompuServe, you (or someone you know who also uses that service) can search the service's member list for your lost pal. You never know what might work.

In this lesson, you learned how to search for people on the Web. In the next lesson, you'll learn how to copy (download) files from the Internet.

Downloading Files

In this lesson, you will learn how to download files from the Web using a variety of methods.

A Word About FTP

One of the main reasons people connect to the Internet is to download a copy of a *shareware* program such as WinZip (a Windows interface for PKZIP) or Eudora (an Internet e-mail program). The Internet uses *FTP* (File Transfer Protocol) to handle the process of transferring files over the Internet to your computer. Netscape comes with built-in FTP support, so you don't need a separate FTP program to download files from the Internet. However, you can always use one if you want.

Shareware   The programs that you'll find on the Internet are mostly shareware. Shareware programs are not free. You can download a shareware program from the Internet and use it for a short trial period. If you decide to keep the program, you must register it and pay a small fee. Instructions on how to do that are often included in a text file that you receive with the program's other files.

Why Bother with an FTP Program?   Although you can use your Web browser to download files, FTP programs often make the process easier in a number of ways. First, they contain preset links to the most common FTP sites—something a Web browser lacks. Second, you can download multiple files at once with an FTP program, but not with a Web browser. Third, some FTP sites (such as government sites) have restricted access; if you need to access a restricted FTP site, you will need to use an FTP program so that you can enter the required password.

Files available for downloading are stored on FTP sites. Many Web pages provide links to these sites, and because Web pages use HTTP, the process of locating a file and then downloading it to your system is very easy. Of course, if you don't mind weaving your way through endless menus in search of a particular file, you can use Netscape to connect directly to an FTP site. In this lesson, you'll learn how to download files from Web pages and directly from FTP sites.

Locating a File on the Web

There are several good sources for files on the Web. Of those, some sites allow you to search for just about any kind of software, while others specialize in Windows apps, Internet apps, and so on. Search tools such as Lycos, Yahoo, Excite!, and InfoSeek often supply links to the more popular software sources. However, if you don't feel like searching around, try some of the good general sources listed in Table 11.1.

Table 11.1 General Software Sources

Source	URL
Shareware.com	http://www.shareware.com
Windows95.com	http://windows95.com
BC's Win95 Net Apps	http://bcpub.com/w95netapps.html
Thor's WinTools	http://TOOLS.ofthe.NET
Winsite Archive	http://www.winsite.com
Papa Winsock	http://papa.indstate.edu:8888/ftp/main.html

If you're looking for Internet apps in particular, try some of the sites listed in Table 11.2.

Table 11.2 Internet Software Sources

Source	URL
Stroud's main site	http://www.cwsapps.com
Stroud's second main site	http://www.stroud.com
Stroud's main alternate site	http://www.enterprise.net/cwsapps

Source	URL
Stroud's second alternate site	http://cwsapps.wilmington.net
TUCOWS main site	http://www.tucows.com
TUCOWS main alternate site	http://tucow.niia.net

When you connect to one of these pages, you'll typically find a search tool that you can use to find your file. In other cases, files are categorized by type so that all you have to do is select a category that interests you, and then select your file from among those listed. Once you find your file, downloading it from the Web is an easy process, as you'll soon learn.

Searching for Files on an FTP Site with Archie

If you have trouble locating the program you're looking for on the Web, you might want to go directly to the source: an FTP site. To search for a file on an FTP site, you use *Archie*. Archie servers search FTP sites periodically for downloadable files, which they store in a database. To use it, you connect to an Archie site and ask for the file you want, and Archie searches its database for a match. If it finds one, Archie provides the location (the FTP site and directory) of your file. You can then use Netscape or an FTP program to download the file.

CAUTION

First Things First In order to search for files with Archie, you'll need an Archie program; Netscape cannot perform this function for you. I use WS-Archie for Windows 95, which I downloaded from Stroud's (http://www.cwsapps.com). You'll find the Windows 3.1 version there as well. See "Downloading a File from the Web" (later in this lesson) for details on connecting to Stroud's to get such a program.

Your Archie program comes with a built-in list of addresses for popular Archie sites. Keep in mind as you try different Archie sites that some are more up-to-date than others. So if you don't find a particular file at one site, try looking for it on another one.

To locate a file on an FTP site with WS-Archie, follow these steps:

1. Connect to the Internet in the usual manner and start WS-Archie.

2. In the **Archie Server** drop-down list, select the Archie site you want to search. You're connected to the Archie site you selected.

3. Enter the file name you want to search for in the **Search for** text box. For example, to locate an FTP program for yourself, type **ws_ftp32.exe** (see Figure 11.1).

CAUTION

No Name?   Unfortunately, in order to find a file using Archie, you must know the file's name. You can't search on a partial file name. If you don't know the exact name for a file you need, you should use the Web search tools instead, as explained in Lesson 8.

TIP

Limit Your Search   If you want to limit your search to a particular domain, enter its name in the Domain text box. For example, if you know that your file is on a government site somewhere, enter **.gov** in the **Domain** text box. Other domains include .com (for business or commercial use), .edu (for educational use), and .net (for commercial Internet service providers).

4. Click **Search**, and Archie goes to work searching for the file (in this case ws_ftp32.exe).

5. When the Archie program finds your file, it displays the file's location in the area just below the search criteria (see Figure 11.2). Click the plus sign (+) in front of any item listed to see its contents.

6. (Optional) To view more information about the file (such as its size and when it was last modified), click it. The expanded information appears in the area near the bottom of the window.

7. When you're ready, make a note of the file's location, and then click the **Close** button to exit your Archie program.

8. Use Netscape or an FTP program to download the file you found (see "Downloading a File from the Web" or "Downloading a File from an FTP Site").

Type what you
want to search for.

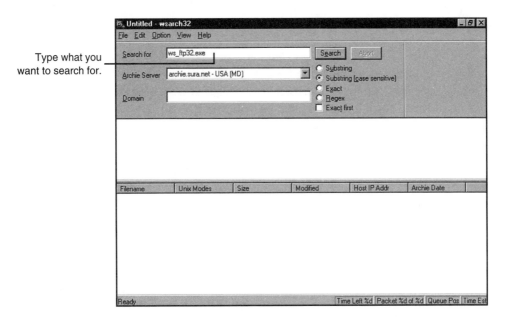

Figure 11.1 Use an Archie program to search FTP sites for files.

The FTP site where
the file is located

The file

Expanded information
about the file

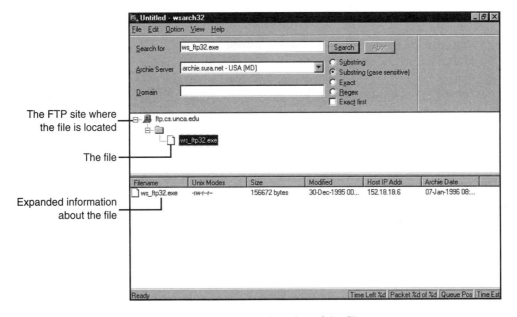

Figure 11.2 Archie displays the location of the file.

Downloading a File from the Web

Once you've located a file you want, you're ready to download it to your PC. Netscape makes downloading files as simple as point-and-click. Basically, you *point* to a link to a file on an FTP site, and then you *click* to begin the downloading process. You can choose whether you want the downloaded file placed in an existing folder or a new folder that you create.

Beware of Viruses! Downloading contaminated files to your PC is the most common way you can get a computer virus. You can protect yourself and your data by double-checking every file you download. Create a folder called Downloads and place all downloaded files in it. Then use your antivirus program to verify that the files you've downloaded are virus-free.

CAUTION

Most files available for download from the Internet have been *compressed*. Compressing a file makes it smaller so that it can be downloaded more quickly. After you download a file from the Internet, you'll probably have to decompress it using a utility called PKUNZIP. You can identify zipped (compressed) files by the file extension .ZIP.

Some compressed files are *self-extracting*, which means that you won't need PKUNZIP (or a similar utility) to decompress them. When you double-click a self-extracting file, it decompresses automatically, placing its newly restored file(s) in the current directory. Self-extracting zip files have the file extension .EXE. (As a side note, keep in mind that not all files that end in .EXE are zipped files.)

The easiest way to unzip files is to use WinZip (which contains a licensed copy of the PKZIP Utilities). So before you start downloading files from the Internet, download a copy of WinZip and install it.

Nothing's Free Remember that WinZip is a shareware program. If you decide to keep WinZip beyond the trial period, you need to register it and pay a small fee for its use.

CAUTION

When you're ready to download files from the Internet, follow the steps below. (See the next section for more on downloading files from an FTP site.)

1. Connect to the Internet and start Netscape.

2. Enter the address of the Web site from which you want to download a file. You might try one of the addresses given earlier for popular software sites such as Stroud's and TUCOWS. Another place where you can find files on the Internet is Shareware.Com. Type **http://www.shareware.com** in the **Location/Go to** text box and press **Enter**.

3. Shareware.com allows you to search various FTP sites for the file you want. To search for a file, click **SEARCH**.

4. Select the category of files to search. For example, select **MS-Windows (all)**.

5. Enter the type of file you want in the **Search word** text box. For example, type **virus** as shown in Figure 11.3. You can enter a second word to search for in the additional search box, if you'd like.

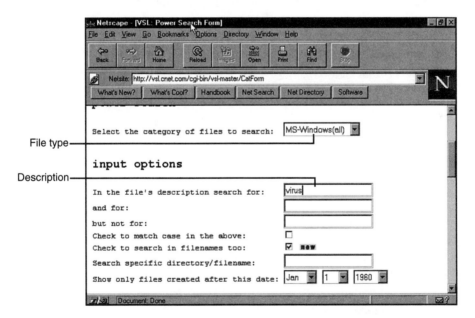

Figure 11.3 Enter a type and description for the file you want.

TIP

How to Get What You Want If you know the *exact* file name of the program you want to search for, you can enter it in the **Search specific directory/filename** text box instead of following step 5.

6. Click **start search**. The results of your search will appear at the bottom of the screen.

CAUTION

I Didn't Get What I Wanted! If you didn't get the results you wanted, click the **Back** button and change the information on the form, making it as specific as possible. For example, if you search for "anti-virus" and get nothing, you might try searching for "virus."

7. To download a file, click its name. A page appears with links to various FTP sites that contain your file.

8. Click a four- or five-star site (see Figure 11.4); they're considered the most reliable.

Click here to
download the file.

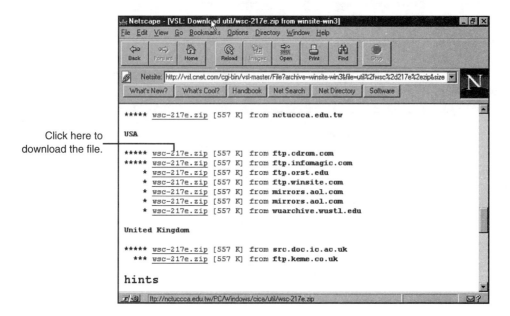

Figure 11.4 Select a site from which to download your file.

Busy Signals Don't choose a site just because it's close to you; sites that are nearby will often be very busy. Instead, pick a site in a time zone where it is the middle of the night. It should be less busy.

9. If the file you're downloading is compressed (zipped), you'll see the Unknown File Type dialog box. Click **Save File**.

What a View You can configure Netscape so that you can view files prior to downloading them. For example, you can link WinZip to Netscape and view compressed files by clicking them. (See Part 4, Lesson 1 for help.) Of course, if you link WinZip to Netscape, you can't just click the file to download it. No, in that case, you press and hold **Shift** and click the file name to override the Netscape viewer.

10. Select a directory in which to save the file and click **Save**. After the file is downloaded, you're returned to the Netscape screen.

Downloading a File from an FTP Site

Many people locate the files they want to download on the Web, and many Web pages feature links to FTP sites. However, those sites are often busy. In such cases, you might find it easier to connect directly to an FTP site with Netscape.

You can connect to one of several FTP sites and rummage around for a file, but it's easier if you have the address of the file's exact location on the FTP system. You might get that address in any number of ways. You might, for example, find the address for a file in a book or a magazine that recommends that particular program, or you might locate the address for a file through an Archie program (see "Searching for Files on an FTP Site with Archie" for more information). Table 11.3 lists some popular FTP sites where you can start.

Table 11.3 Recommended FTP Sites

Site	URL
CICA Windows Archive	ftp.winsite.com
Netscape	ftp1.netscape.com
Mosaic	ftp.NCSA.uuic.edu
Oakland Archives	oak.oakland.edu
Microsoft	ftp.microsoft.com

Table 11.3 Continued

Site	URL
America Online	ftp.aol.com
Mirrors to Popular Sites	mirrors.aol.com
SimTel Archives	ftp.coast.net
ESNET	ftp.esnet.com
GARBO Archives	garbo.uwusa.fi

What's the Password?   A computer such as an FTP server that allows you access to its files is called a *host computer*. You are its guest. To gain entrance, you need the password. In most cases, the password is "anonymous." In other cases, it is something like "guest." Sometimes the server also requires that you enter your e-mail address as the password. If you use Netscape, it takes care of the general login process. However, if you use an FTP program to download a file, you'll need to enter a password.

Once you log onto an FTP site, you'll see its public folders (those files and folders to which you've been given some level of access). You can move about these folders in much the same way that you move from folder to folder within File Manager or the Explorer. When you find the right folder, you select the file you want by clicking it.

To download a file from an FTP site, follow these steps:

1. Type the address of the FTP site you want to visit in the **Location/Go to** text box and press **Enter**. You'll type the address in the format ftp://
ftp.*domainname*, as in ftp://ftp.esnet.com. You're connected to the FTP site, starting in its root directory.

2. To change to another directory, click it. For example, if you know that your file is located in the /pub/mirrors/windows95/miscutil directory, you click the **pub** directory, and then the **mirrors** directory, and eventually the **windows95** and **miscutil** directories (see Figure 11.5).

A Faster Way   If you know the address of your file, you can enter it into the Location/Go to text box. In our example, you could type the address **ftp://
ftp.esnet.com/pub/mirrors/windows95/miscutil** in the **Location/Go to** text box and press **Enter**.

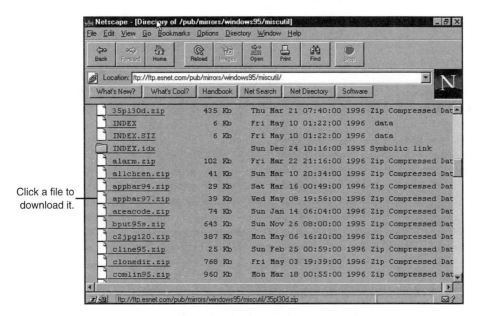

Click a file to
download it.

Figure 11.5   Change to the directory that contains your file.

3. To download a file, click its name.

4. If the file you're downloading is compressed (zipped), you'll see the Unknown File Type dialog box. Click **Save File**.

5. Select a directory in which to save the file and click **Save**. After the file is downloaded, you're returned to the Netscape screen.

In this lesson, you learned how to download files from the Internet. In the next lesson, you'll learn how to navigate a Gopher site with Netscape.

Visiting a Gopher Site

In this lesson, you will learn how to connect to a Gopher site and search for items of interest within Gopherspace.

What Is Gopherspace?

The Gopher system originated at the University of Minnesota, whose Internet engineers promptly named it after the U of M mascot. Gopherspace was designed to create an interconnected index of files and documents located on various Gopher servers throughout the Internet. You navigate Gopherspace using a menu system.

How Do I Get to Gopherspace?   Gopherspace (like the Web) is a subset of the Internet. You can connect to Gopherspace using a Gopher program, but it's easier to use Netscape and connect to Gopherspace through the Web.

When you connect to a Gopher server, you see a menu of subjects. Select a subject off the main menu (directory), and you'll see another menu (subdirectory) with which you narrow your choice. This continues until you get to something useful, such as a text document or a graphic file that you can view, download, or print.

For example, suppose you start by selecting Publications from the main menu. Then you select something like Consumer News from the next menu. Eventually, you find a document you want to look at, such as "How to Get Cheap Airline Tickets." In other words, you browse Gopherspace just as you might browse the Web, but instead of clicking links, you select subjects from Gopher menus. There's even a way to search for information in Gopherspace, as you'll see later in this lesson.

Not everything on a Gopher menu actually resides on that particular Gopher server. But don't worry; as you move from menu to menu, you're automatically connected to whichever server contains the proper information.

Ask Forms   While browsing Gopherspace, you might also encounter *ask forms*, which are like dialog boxes. These forms help you search special Gopher+ sites for information.

Gopher+ Sites   Gopher+ sites are enhanced versions of regular Gopher sites; they are called "enhanced" because they provide ask forms for quick searching, and usually provide more than one version of a file for downloading.

Connecting to a Gopher Site

When you connect to a Gopher server, what you see looks something like Explorer or File Manager: a menu with icons for folders (directories), text files, program files, and so on. To change from one menu (directory) to another or to select a file, you click the appropriate icon. You'll encounter the following icons in Gopher menus:

   Directory   When you click this icon, the directory's contents are displayed as another menu.

   Document   You can read a document by double-clicking this icon.

   Search   This icon represents some type of search tool, such as a Veronica or Jughead.

Veronica   An Internet search tool that you can use to find resources at a Gopher site. Veronica searches all Gopher sites to find the something that matches your criteria.

Jughead   A Gopher search tool that's similar to Veronica. However, unlike Veronica, Jughead searches only the current Gopher site to find the specified resources.

The information you typically find in Gopherspace varies considerably from what you find on the Web. Most Gopher servers are associated with universities, so the information in Gopherspace tends to be fairly academic. If you need to do research, though, you'll probably find more information in Gopherspace than you will on the World Wide Web.

You can travel Gopherspace with a Gopher program or with Netscape. As you may recall from Lesson 3, a Web browser such as Netscape can handle many protocols. A *protocol* is the language in which the information on a particular Web page is written. Even though HTTP is the most common protocol on the Web, Netscape can handle many other protocols as well, including FTP and Gopher.

Basically, this means that you can connect to a Gopher site by typing its address in Netscape's Location box. A Gopher address looks like this:

> gopher://gopher.tc.umn.edu

The first part of the address tells Netscape to use the gopher protocol to read the information on the site. The second part is the actual address of the Gopher site.

When you're ready to try out Gopher, check out the Gopher server named above or one of these others:

> gopher://gopher.uc.wlu.edu
> gopher://gopher.nd.edu
> gopher://gopher.ait.psu.edu
> gopher://gopher.uiuc.edu

To connect to a Gopher site with Netscape, follow these steps:

1. Connect to the Internet as usual and start Netscape.

2. To connect to a Gopher site, type its address in the **Location/Go to** text box and press **Enter**. Netscape displays the opening Gopher menu (see Figure 12.1).

3. Continue to change from menu to menu until you find a file you want to view, print, or download.

Moving Up One Level   To return to the previous menu, click Netscape's **Back** button.

4. To view a file, click it. You can then print it by clicking the **Print** button. To download a file, press and hold **Shift** and click the file name.

CAUTION

Search Forms If you encounter a search form during your travels in Gopherspace, see the next section, "Searching for Items with Veronica and Jughead," for help.

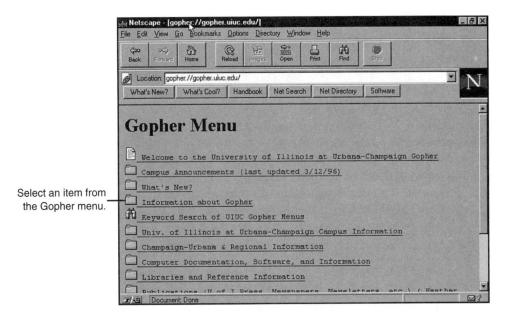

Select an item from the Gopher menu.

Figure 12.1 You surf Gopherspace using menus.

Searching for Items with Veronica and Jughead

Gopher provides two search tools you can use to locate items in Gopherspace: Veronica and Jughead. Veronica searches for your item all over Gopherspace, while Jughead searches only the current Gopher server. You can identify Veronica and Jughead searches on Gopher menus by their distinctive magnifying glass icon.

Faster Searches   Because it takes a long time to search Gopherspace, Veronica allows you to choose between searching all of Gopherspace and searching directory names only.

When you select Veronica or Jughead from a Gopher menu, you're taken to an ask form (similar to a dialog box). Enter the information for which you want to search. Veronica or Jughead locates an item for you, which you can view by clicking it.

Search Tips

In the ask form, if you type a search string such as "English poetry," Veronica or Jughead searches for any item with both the words "English" AND "poetry" in it. Keeping your search very specific like this means that you'll have fewer results to wade through.

You can use NOT in a search string to narrow a search even more if you want. For example, you could type "poetry NOT French" to display all kinds of poetry except French poetry. You can also use the asterisk wild-card character (*) to aid your search. The asterisk represents any character or characters in a search string. For example, if you were to type "drug*," you'd get "drug," "drugs," and "drugstore" among your results. Note, however, that you can't use an asterisk in the middle of a search string (as in dr*g). All you'll get for your cleverness is an error message.

You can also use OR in your search string—but it's not very useful. If you type the string "English OR poetry," Veronica or Jughead will display all files that contain either the word "English" or the word "poetry." This actually expands your search area, when your primary goal is probably to narrow the search. Therefore, you should avoid using OR in your search string if possible.

What's OR For?   Okay, there is one way to use OR to aid in a search. If you are looking for information on English or Irish poetry, you can use the search string "poetry (English OR Irish)," which includes parentheses to group the two related items. This will find items related to either English poetry or Irish poetry.

Normally, Veronica limits its results to the first 200 items it finds that match your search string. You can also narrow a search by limiting the number of items listed, and/or by limiting the type of file Veronica searches. (Jughead doesn't allow you to limit your searches in this manner.)

- To limit the number of files listed in the result, add **-m***number* to the end of your Veronica search string, like this:

     english literature -m10

- To have Veronica list everything it finds, add **-m** but don't type a number, like this:

     english literature -m

- To limit the type of file Veronica searches for, add **-t***type* to the end of your search string, where *type* is a number from Table 12.1. Your search string might look like this:

     utilities -t1

   This example requests a search for only file type #1, which finds directories.

Table 12.1 Valid File Types

Number	Type
0	Text file
1	Directory
2	CSO name server (phone book)
4	Mac HQX file (BINHEX)
5	PC binary file (program file)
6	Uuencoded file
7	Gopher menu
8	Telnet session
9	Binary file
s	Sound
e	Event
I	Image (other than GIF file)
M	MIME e-mail message
T	TN3270 session
c	Calendar
g	GIF image
h	HTML document

Searching Gopherspace

To search Gopherspace with Netscape, follow these steps:

1. To start your search, double-click a magnifying glass or similar icon (such as a Phone icon). You're connected to a Veronica or Jughead search site.

I Can't Find a Veronica or Jughead Site!   Some Gopher sites don't actually list Jughead as an option. Look for a Search option instead, such as "Search Gopher titles at the University of Minnesota." To locate a Veronica site, try typing the address gopher://liberty.uc.wlu.edu:70/11/gophers/veronica or gopher://peg.cwis.uci.edu:70/11/veronica. Both of these list Veronica sites.

2. Enter the keyword(s) you want to search for and click **Search** or press **Enter**. If you enter "Oklahoma weather" as in Figure 12.2, for example, you'll get any item that contains both the word "Oklahoma" and the word "weather."

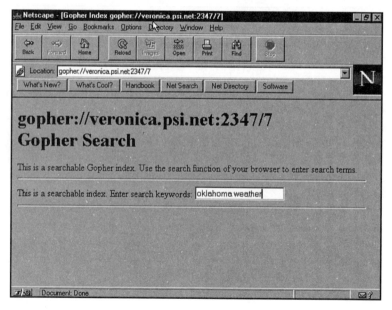

Figure 12.2   You can search Gopherspace with Veronica or Jughead.

3. The results of your search appear on-screen. To view a file, click it. If a folder appears, you can click it to display its contents.

In this lesson, you learned how to search Gopherspace with Netscape. In the next lesson, you'll learn how to view and save graphics.

Viewing and Saving Graphics

In this lesson, you will learn how to view graphic files with Netscape and how to save them to your PC.

A Word About Graphic Viewers

Netscape can display the ordinary graphics, such as jpeg and gif images, that you find on most Web pages. However, to display certain graphic files (bmp, pbm, pgm, and tiff files, for example), Netscape requires some help, which it gets from *in-line plug-ins* and *helper applications*.

Helper apps and in-line plug-ins do just what their names suggest: they help Netscape perform tasks it was not originally designed to do. The difference between in-line plug-ins and helper applications is a small one that has to do with the method in which they enhance Netscape's capabilities. You'll learn more about helper applications and plug-ins in Part 4.

In addition to a helper app or in-line plug-in that enables Netscape to display graphic files, you'll probably need helper apps and in-line plug-ins to play sound in real-time, to view incompatible 3-D worlds, or to print PDF documents. You'll learn how to download and install various in-line plug-ins and helper apps in Part 4; here, you'll learn how to install a graphic viewer.

CAUTION

I Don't Have the Right Viewer If you click a link to a graphic file that your viewer can't display, you'll see a dialog box asking you what to do. You can save the file to your hard disk for later viewing, you can configure a viewer now, or you can cancel the entire operation.

Downloading and Installing a Graphic Viewer

There are several graphic viewers that you might want to use with Netscape, including LView Pro, VuePrint, ACDSee, or ViewDirector. In addition, you might need to install Fractal Viewer if you think you'll encounter any fractal graphic files (which have the .FIF extension) and FIGleaf Inline or InterCAP Inline if you want to display CGM (Computer Graphics Metafiles). If you need to view CAD (computer aided design) drawings, you'll need a good viewer such as DWG/DXF by SoftSource, WHIP!, or SVF by SoftSource.

You can find Netscape-related files such as graphic viewers in a number of places on the Web. If you don't already have your favorite sources, try one of the ones in Table 13.1.

Table 13.1 Sources for Graphic Helper Apps and In-Line Plug-Ins

Site	URL
Stroud's main site	http://www.cwsapps.com
Stroud's second main site	http://www.stroud.com
Stroud's main alternate site	http://www.enterprise.net/cwsapps
Stroud's second alternate site	http://cwsapps.wilmington.net
TUCOWS main site	http://www.tucows.com
TUCOWS main alternate site	http://tucow.niia.com
Shareware.com	http://www.shareware.com
Windows 95.com	http://windows95.com
Thor's WinTools	http://TOOLS.ofthe.NET
Winsite Archive	http://www.winsite.com
Sams.net Software Library	http://www.mcp.com/samsnet/track1/Software/software.htm

Follow these steps to download and install a graphic viewer:

1. Connect to the Internet and start Netscape.

2. Enter the address of a source, such as **http://www.cwsapps.com**, in the **Location/Go to** text box and press **Enter**.

3. Locate the file you want to download. (At Stroud's, for example, you need to first click the Stroud's logo to get to the main menu. Then you click **Graphic Viewers** to get to a list of available graphic viewers.)

4. Select a viewer and click it to download it.

5. If the file is compressed (zipped), you'll see the Unknown File Type dialog box, shown in Figure 13.1. Click **Save File**.

Figure 13.1 The Unknown File Type dialog box.

6. Select a directory into which to save the file, and click **Save**. When the download is complete, you're returned to the Netscape window.

The process to install your new viewer will vary from viewer to viewer, but here are the basic steps:

1. Open File Manager or Explorer and change to the directory/folder into which you downloaded your file.

2. Double-click the zipped file to start WinZip. If the file you downloaded is self-extracting—if it ends in .EXE—WinZip will not start. Instead, the file will decompress (unzip) itself into the current directory, and you can skip to step 5.

WinZip WinZip is a handy utility that makes using PKUNZIP and PKZIP a lot easier. PKUNZIP is the DOS utility that you use to unzip (decompress) the files you get off the Web. If you don't have a copy of WinZip, get back on the Internet and download it (you can find WinZip at http://www.shareware.com). Install WinZip on your system, and then come back here to finish installing your new viewer. (WinZip includes a copy of the PKZIP and PKUNZIP utilities.) Note that WinZip is a shareware program, which means that, after a short trial period, you're required to register it and pay a small fee. *Be sure you do that.*

3. Click the **Extract** button, select a directory into which you want the decompressed files placed (the same directory as the zipped file is okay), and then click **Extract** again.

4. Close WinZip, and then switch to the directory that contains the decompressed files. You'll probably find something called SETUP.EXE or INSTALL.EXE.

5. Double-click the **SETUP.EXE** or **INSTALL.EXE** file to start the installation process.

CAUTION

I Don't See a Setup File   Some smaller programs don't really have an installation routine. If you don't find a setup file, the program is probably already installed. Double-click a **README.TXT** or similar file and read it. This usually clears up any questions you might have about installation. Then double-click the main file (such as lviewp.exe) to start the program to test it.

If the graphic viewer you selected is an in-line plug-in, when you double-click it, it decompresses and starts its setup routine automatically. Follow the on-screen instructions to link the in-line plug-in to Netscape.

If the graphic viewer you selected is a helper application, you need to start Netscape and tell it where the graphic viewer is located. Follow these steps:

1. Start Netscape. (You don't need to connect to the Internet to complete these steps.)

2. Open the **Options** menu and select **General Preferences.**

3. In the Preferences dialog box that appears (see Figure 13.2), click the **Helpers** tab.

4. From the **File type** list, select a file type associated with your viewer. For example, LView Pro supports BMP files, so select that.

5. Add additional extensions for this file type in the **File Extensions** text box. For example, if there were any additional extensions associated with bit-map files (there aren't), you'd type those extensions in the File Extensions box.

6. Click **Launch the Application.**

7. Click **Browse,** and the Select an Appropriate Viewer dialog box appears.

8. Select your application's main program file and click **Open.** (For example, switch to the LView Pro directory and select the lviewp.exe file.)

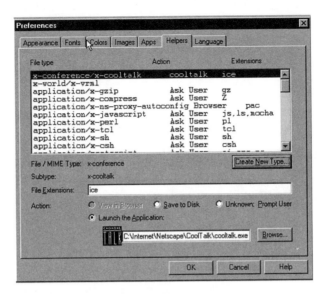

Figure 13.2 Options for installing your graphic viewer.

9. Repeat steps 4 through 8 to associate your graphic viewer with other file types as needed. For example, LView Pro also supports PPM, PGM, PBM, and TIFF files, so you should repeat the steps for each of those file extensions.

10. When you're done, click **OK**.

If you need a graphics file type that is not listed, you can add it. Click the **Create New Type** button and enter **Graphic** under **Mime Type**. Enter the file type (such as jpeg, bmp, or tiff) under **Mime SubType** and click **OK**. Follow the previous steps to associate your graphic viewer with the new file type.

From now on, whenever Netscape encounters a file type that matches one associated with your graphic viewer, it will automatically launch the appropriate program (such as LView Pro) and display the graphic for you.

Saving a Graphic to Your PC's Hard Disk

You can save to your hard disk any graphic you encounter during your Web surfing sessions. If you save a graphic to your hard disk, you can view it later or reuse it for your own purposes (as a desktop background, for example).

Graphic Royalty   If you do reuse a graphic for any commercial reason—such as republishing it on the Web—you should make sure that the graphic is in the public domain (meaning that you do not have to pay a royalty to use it).

CAUTION

To save a graphic to your hard disk, follow these steps:

1. Right-click the graphic.
2. Select **Save Image As**, and the Save As dialog box appears.
3. Select a directory in which to save the graphic, and click **Save**.

Can't See What You're Getting?   Some graphics aren't visible because you need a graphic viewer to view them. Even so, you can right-click the link itself to save the graphic to your hard disk. If you want to preview the graphic first, click the link and let Netscape load the appropriate graphic viewer. You can then save the file to your hard disk by using the viewer's **File, Save As** command.

TIP

In this lesson, you learned how to install a graphic viewer for Netscape and how to save a Web graphic to your hard drive. In the next lesson, you'll learn how to play Java applets.

Finding and Playing Java Applets

In this lesson, you will learn how to find and play Java applets, as well as the basics of putting JavaScript applets into a Web page.

Understanding Java

Java is a hot topic on the Internet right now—but what exactly is it? Java is a programming language you can use to create small miniprograms (called *applets*) that you can embed in Web pages. Java applets can be played on any type of computer—Windows, Mac, or UNIX, which makes them perfect for inclusion on Web pages.

TERM

Applet A small single-purpose application such as a loan calculator or a tic-tac-toe game. Java applets cannot run by themselves; you must use a compatible Web browser (such as Netscape) in order for them to work.

Java applets take many forms, including painting programs, games, and animations. Because Java is still in developmental stages, most of the examples of Java applets you'll find out on the Internet are experimental—designed more to test the limitations of Java than to provide a meaningful function. However, Java is fast becoming a standard, and as such, it will be used more and more as an integral part of a functional Web page.

Examples of Java Applets

You'll often encounter a Java applet without even knowing it. If you run into some part of a Web page that seems to function almost automatically, then you've probably run into a Java applet (see Figure 14.1). For example, some financial Web pages include a "live" stock ticker; that automation is a Java applet.

With Java, parts of a Web page can be updated

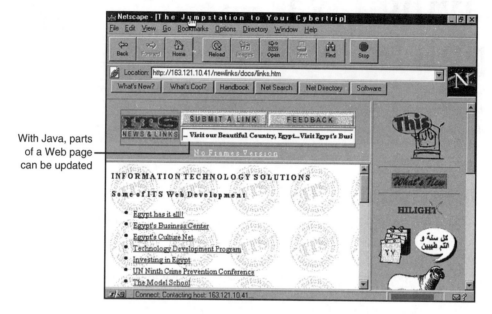

Figure 14.1 A Java applet can automatically update portions of the Web page with current information.

The benefit of including Java applets in a Web page is live interaction with the user. For example, a Java applet might perform a calculation for you—*live*—based on information you just entered into a form. In addition, a graph embedded in the Web page might change to reflect your variable input (see Figure 14.2).

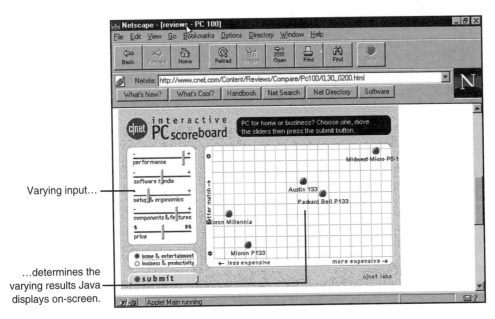

Varying input...

...determines the
varying results Java
displays on-screen.

Figure 14.2 A Java applet can change the display according to varying user input.

Some Java applets draw the reader's attention to particular parts of the Web page, such as blinking or scrolling text. Other Java applets such as a cute animation, a video that is replayed automatically, or a game (see Figure 14.3) are just for fun.

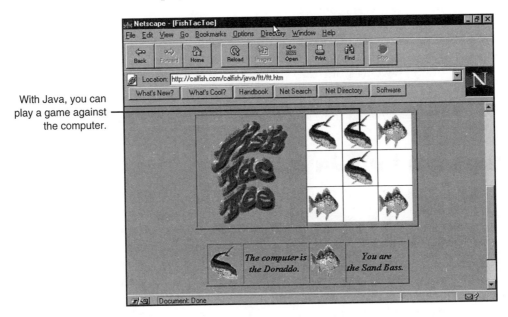

With Java, you can
play a game against
the computer.

Figure 14.3 Some Java applets are just for fun.

You could run into a Java applet just about anywhere on the Web, but because Java is still kind of new, you might want to go to the source (Sun Microsystems) first to see some demonstrations. Their Web site is located at http://java.sun.com. To visit the Sun site and play one of the demos, follow these steps:

1. Connect to the Internet and start Netscape.
2. Type the address **http://www.javasoft.com/applets** into the **Location/Go to** text box and press **Enter**.
3. Click **applets**.
4. Click **Games and Other Diversions**.
5. Select a demo from the list. For example, click **Hangman**. The game you select appears on-screen. To play Hangman, select a letter that you think belongs in the missing phrase. Continue to select letters until you uncover the phrase or you're hung.
6. When you finish playing the demo, you can click the **Back** button to return to the list of applets and select another demo if you want.

The following list names a few of the other sites where you can find Java applets.

http://www.gamelan.com

http://www.pointcom.com/gifs/home/java.html

http://www.jars.com

http://www.java.co.uk

http://www.apletware.com/finders

http://www.vector.co.za/vst/java/vstj-01.htm

http://www.teamjava.com/links

http://www.rssi.com/info/java-info.html

Understanding JavaScript

JavaScript is a set of commands that you place within a Web page to make it more interactive. For example, you can insert a JavaScript command to create an animated control button such as a spinning wheel. With JavaScript, you can ask the user some questions on a form, and then you can respond in varying ways, based on his answers. JavaScript also contains the commands needed to embed a Java applet—a program you create with the Java programming language—into a Web page. But if you don't plan to create your own Web pages, you don't need to worry about JavaScript.

However, if you want to create a Web page with some pizzazz, you can include some simple JavaScript commands within the HTML code for your page. For example, this script by Tomer and Yehuda Shiran (which you can copy, if you like) allows you to add a nice clock to your Web page:

```
<html>
<head>
    <title>The JavaScript Date and Time</title>
    <meta name="GENERATOR" content="Mozilla/2.01Gold (Win32)">
<script>
<!--
/* This script and all others are copyright (c) 1996 by Tomer Shiran
and Yehuda Shiran. They will all be posted in our upcoming book on
JavaScript, along with many others. The book will give you the
ability to write scripts and not just copy them. Feel free to steal
the code. Drop me a line if you choose to do so. Thanks. */
var Temp;
var CurHour; var CurMinute; var CurMonth; var CurDate; var CurYear;
    var DayNight;

getData()
function getData() {
        var location = getPath();
        var ImageOpen = '<IMG SRC="'+location+'dg'
        var ImageClose = '.gif" HEIGHT=21 WIDTH=16>'
        var Copyr='This script and all the others are copyright &#169
        1996 by <BR>
        <BLINK><STRONG>Tomer Shiran</STRONG>'+'</BLINK> and
        <BLINK><STRONG>Yehuda Shiran</STRONG></BLINK>. Please feel
        free to '+'copy <BR>this script and add it to your homepage.'
        Temp = ""
        var now = new Date();
        CurHour = now.getHours();
        CurMinute = now.getMinutes();
        CurMonth = now.getMonth();
        CurDate = now.getDate();
        CurYear = now.getYear();now = null;
        CheckData();
        Temp += "<CENTER><TABLE BORDER=3 CELLPADDING=4><TR><TD>"
        Temp += "The current time is: "
        for (Count = 0; Count < CurHour.length; Count++) {
                Temp += ImageOpen + CurHour.substring (Count,
                Count+1) + ImageClose
        }
        Temp += ImageOpen + "c" + '.gif" HEIGHT=21 WIDTH=9>'
        for (Count = 0; Count < CurMinute.length; Count++) {
                Temp += ImageOpen + CurMinute.substring (Count,
                Count+1) + ImageClose
        }
        Temp += "<p>The current date is: "
        for (Count = 0; Count < CurMonth.length; Count++) {
```

103

```
                            Temp += ImageOpen + CurMonth.substring (Count,
            Count+1) + ImageClose
                }
            Temp += ImageOpen + "p" + '.gif" HEIGHT=21 WIDTH=9>'
            for (Count = 0; Count < CurDate.length; Count++) {
                    Temp += ImageOpen + CurDate.substring (Count,
                    Count+1) + ImageClose
                }
            Temp += ImageOpen + "p" + '.gif" HEIGHT=21 WIDTH=9>'
            for (Count = 0; Count < CurYear.length; Count++) {
                    Temp += ImageOpen + CurYear.substring (Count,
                    Count+1) + ImageClose
                }
            Temp += "</TD><TD>"+Copyr+"</TD></TR></TABLE></CENTER>"
            return(Temp)
        }

    function getPath() {
            PathEnd=location.href.lastIndexOf('/', location.href.length-1);

            FinalPath=location.href.substring(0, PathEnd+1);
            return(FinalPath);
    }

    function CheckData() {
            if (CurMinute < 10) {CurMinute = "0" + CurMinute} else
            {CurMinute = "" + CurMinute}
            CurHour = "" + CurHour;
            CurMonth = ++ CurMonth;
            CurMonth = "" + CurMonth;
            CurDate = "" + CurDate;
            CurYear = "" + CurYear;
    }

    document.write(Temp);

    // -->
    </script>
    </head>
    <body>

    <h1 align=center>The JavaScript Date and Time
    <br>24 Hour Clock</h1>

    <p><b>This is an example of presenting the date and time graphically
    using JavaScript only. This example is from the book we are currently
    writing on JavaScript.</b></p>

    <p> A set of images is available for
    <a href="http://www.geocities.com/Hollywood/4250/digits.zip">
    downloading</a>.
    You may use any set of digit images which match the following names:
```

```
</p>

<ul>
<li>The digit image files (<i>dg0.gif</i> through <i>dg9.gif</i>)
</li>

<li>The colon and point separators (<i>dgc.gif</i> and <i>dgp.gif
</i>)
</li>
</ul>

<p>If you would like to use this clock in middle of the page, just
copy the SCRIPT section to the desired place. The table can be
removed by deleting the specified lines in the source. </p>

<p>Help me make the JavaScript book suitable for your needs. <a
href="http://www.geocities.com/Hollywood/4250/suggest.htm">Send
me comments and suggestions</a> so I know what coverage you would
like to see. </p>

<p><a href="http://www.geocities.com/Hollywood/4250/index.html">
<img src="headsm.gif" border=0 height=38 width=250 align=center></a>
</p>

</body>
</html>
```

The JavaScript commands appear between the <SCRIPT> and </SCRIPT> tags.
The rest of the codes you see here are HTML commands.

Want to Learn More?   If you'd like to learn more about JavaScript so that you can create your own scripts, pick up a copy of *The Complete Idiot's Guide to JavaScript*, also from Que.

Because JavaScript is interactive, you can program many such examples, where your Web page gets information from the user and then acts on it.

In this lesson, you learned about the purpose of Java applets and how to recognize them. You also learned how JavaScript code is incorporated into a Web page. In the next lesson, you'll learn about VRML.

Playing in a VRML Virtual World with Live3D

L E S S O N 15

In this lesson, you will learn about VRML virtual reality files and how to view them using Live3D.

Understanding VRML

In Lesson 14, you learned about a programming language called Java, with which you can make your Web page interactive. VRML, *Virtual Reality Modeling Language*, is similar to Java. With the VRML programming language, you can create animations on your Web pages, run video files, and respond to user input.

CAUTION

Sounds Cool! Let's Go! Before you decide to add VRML animations to your Web page, let me warn you: coding VRML instructions is a lot more difficult than using HTML. However, as with HTML, several editors out there (such as Virtual House Space Builder) make the process of working with the VRML language less of a pain.

The main difference between VRML and Java is that you can use VRML to create a virtual world—a world that seems to have three dimensions, complete with texture, light, and shadow. Why is 3-D so important? A person can navigate a three-dimensional Web site very intuitively by seemingly "walking through" the site (see Figure 15.1). With 3-D, even simple animations can make a Web site come alive. In addition, VRML creates the potential for 3-D Web-based games such as flight simulators, DOOM clones, and the like.

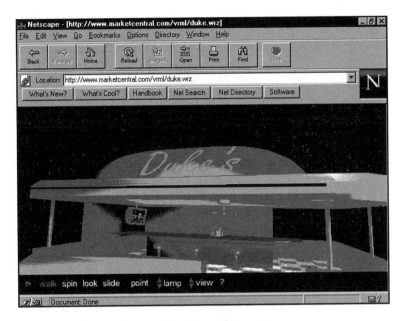

Figure 15.1 A VRML applet can simulate a 3-D world.

What Is Live3D?

Live3D is Netscape's own entry into the VRML plug-in field. To get into that market, Netscape bought out Paper Software, who had created the earlier popular VRML product WebFX (which is no longer available).

A VRML (*Virtual Reality Modeling Language*) browser is used to navigate three-dimensional scenes called *worlds*. These worlds are described in files using the VRML language. Other VRML browsers covered in this book include VRealm Browser, VR Scout, WebSpace, and WorldView. Like some of these other browsers, Live3D uses its own extensions to the existing VRML 1.0 specification, extensions that Netscape has proposed for inclusion in VRML 2.0. The most important of these allow for objects in the world to move; in VRML 1.0, everything in the world stood still.

In addition, Live3D supports streaming audio and video mixed in with the world. It also allows the world to be integrated with Java programs, allowing it to be used for virtual reality games, conferences, and more. These are benefits that give Live3D an edge over other VRML browsers, but it remains to be seen whether people will actually develop worlds that take advantage of this. Because experimenting with these browsers is free, you should try several and see which works best for you.

There are separate versions of Live3D available for 16-bit versions of Windows (such as Windows 3.1) and 32-bit versions (Windows 95 and NT). At the time of this writing, it was only available in a *beta* version (a test version), which could only be used for a fixed period of time.

Finding and Playing VRML Applets

Numerous Web sites on the Internet include VRML applets, one of which you'll visit in a moment. To visit a VRML Web site, you need a compatible VR plug-in or helper app. Netscape comes with a VRML viewer called Live3D built right in. So you've probably already got what you need. But if you somehow encounter a VRML site that doesn't work with Live3D, you can add other VR viewers as needed. Part 4 covers additional VR viewers you might want to try and contains complete instructions on how to install each one.

The Fast Way   Live3D is designed to support files that end with .wrl (a *world* file) or .wrl.gz (a *world* file *geometrically zipped* or compressed). If you're offered the option of viewing the same world as a .wrl or a .wrl.gz file, pick the latter because it will download faster.

Closing Time   VRML is powerful, but it takes a toll on your PC. To keep up, your PC will need a fast CPU and a lot of memory to run most VRML apps. If you notice that your PC is a lot slower when running a VRML applet, close as many other applications as you can.

Follow these steps to visit the Live3D test site:

1. Connect to the Internet and start Netscape.
2. Type the address **http://home.netscape.com/comprod/products/navigator/ live3d/examples/examples/examples.html** in the **Location/Go to** text box and press **Enter**.
3. A tree appears in the left pane, as shown in Figure 15.2. To view the tree from different angles, move the mouse pointer. For example, to "walk" closer, drag the mouse pointer toward the tree.

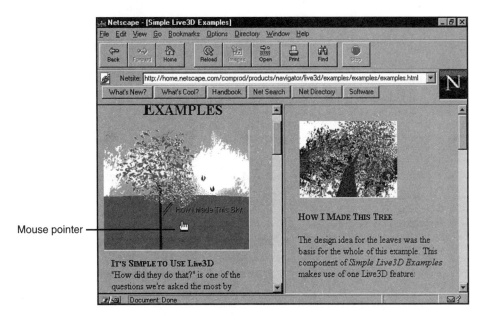

Mouse pointer

Figure 15.2 Change your view by dragging the mouse pointer.

4. If you want to know more about how a particular object (such as the tree, the sky, or the ground) was rendered, click it. Details about the object then appear in the right pane.

5. (Optional) You can use the Navigation Bar to help you explore this virtual world. Right-click inside the VRML window, select **Options**, and then select **Navigation Bar**. The Navigation Bar appears at the bottom of the window. Here's a brief description of each control:

Walk In Walk mode, you move in a lateral plane, as along a surface. To move, drag the mouse in the direction in which you want to "walk." For example, drag the mouse forward to move toward an object; drag backward to move away.

Spin In Spin mode, you move around a point in space as if you were tethered to it. Spinning will seem like flying. To spin, drag toward the point around which you want to rotate.

Look In Look mode, you are stationary, but the view changes as you look left, right, up, or down. To look left, drag the mouse pointer left; to look down, drag the mouse pointer downward; and so on.

Slide   In Slide mode, you move quickly in a single direction without spinning. To slide, drag the mouse pointer in the direction in which you want to go.

Point   In Point mode, you move toward an object by pointing at it. When you click the object in Point mode, you move toward it.

Lamp   This controls your "miner's lamp," making the light brighter or dimmer as you choose. The lamp is not active in all VRML worlds.

View   Takes you back to the starting point or to one of several other viewpoints. Select the viewpoints you want with the up or down arrows, and then click **View** to move there.

6. To leave the VRML world, click the **Back** button.

Check out these other popular sites that contain VRML applets.

http://www.virtus.com/vrmlsite.html

http://www.virtuocity.com

http://www.construct.net/projects/planetitaly/Spazio/VRML/siena.wrl

http://www.tcp.ca/gsb/VRML/

http://cedar.cic.net/~rtilmann/mm/vrmllink.htm#SITES

http://www.sdsc.edu/vrml

http://www.ele.vtt.fi/projects/vrp/html/VRMLLinks.html

http://www.netscape.com/comprod/products/navigator/live3d/
    cool_worlds.html

http://www.marketcentral.com/vrml

http://netmar.com/~bpmc/toystore/install.htm

http://www.graphcomp.com/vrml

http://www.intel.com/procs/ppro/intro/vrml/nav.wrl

http://www.pointcom.com

http://www.photomodeler.com/vrml.html

http://soho.ios.com/~rwcsj29/index2.html

http://www.virtpark.com/theme/worlds/ab2.wrl.gz

http://www.zdnet.com/~zdi/vrml/content/vrmlsite/outside.wrl

http://www.ncsa.uiuc.edu

In this lesson, you learned about virtual reality on the Internet. In the next lesson, you'll learn about listening to sound files.

Listening to
Sound Files
with LiveAudio

In this lesson, you learn how to play sound files embedded in Web pages.

What Is LiveAudio?

LiveAudio is Netscape's built-in sound file player. Whereas in the past you had to install a sound file helper application or in-line plug-in to play a sound file, now Netscape will automatically play any WAV, MIDI, AU, or AIFF sound file you select.

How does LiveAudio work? Whenever you select a sound file on the Web, Netscape displays the LiveAudio player console shown in Figure 16.1. As you'll learn later in this lesson, the player console contains simple controls with which you pause, stop, or replay a sound file. In addition, the console enables you to adjust the volume easily.

CAUTION

What About RealAudio? If you have heard of RealAudio (the in-line plug-in for Netscape), you may be wondering how RealAudio is different from LiveAudio. While LiveAudio does a great job of playing simple audio files, RealAudio allows you to listen to near-to-live audio transmissions over the Internet. Think of it as radio for the Internet. You'll learn more about the RealAudio plug-in in Part 4 Lesson 15.

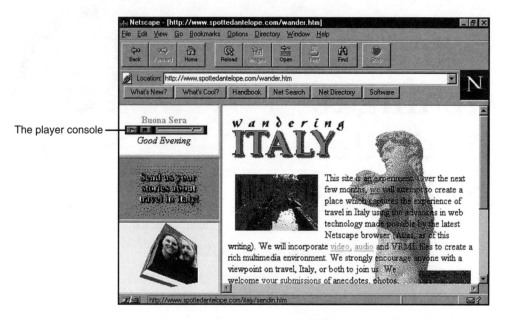

The player console ────

Figure 16.1 Netscape can now play sound files automatically.

Playing a Sound File

On the Web, you might encounter a sound file just about anywhere. When you do, LiveAudio takes over automatically—there's no setup involved.

Sound Card Required Of course, for LiveAudio to work, your PC must be equipped with a sound card.

CAUTION

If you're anxious to test LiveAudio, follow these steps to visit a Web site that uses audio files as background music for a series of three-dimensional worlds.

Big Shock To tour some of the worlds at Headspace, you will need to install a plug-in called Shockwave for Director. See Part 4 Lesson 4 for information on how to do this.

CAUTION

1. Connect to the Internet and start Netscape.

2. In the **Location/Go to** text box, type the address: **http://www.headspace.com/offworld/index.html** and press **Enter**.

3. Scroll down the page until you see the list of worlds you can visit (see Figure 16.2). Click **Desert of The Flat Earth**.

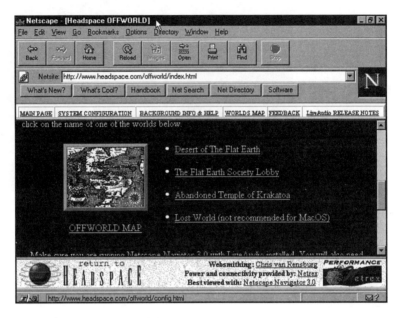

Figure 16.2 Select a world to visit.

4. A new window opens, and the desert world appears. The audio file downloads and begins to play. At the same time, the player console appears. Because the audio files at Headspace OFFWORLD are short, you won't need to tamper with the console. (You'll learn how to use the console in the next section.)

5. To explore this world, click an arrow button, as shown in Figure 16.3. You can also investigate items in the world by clicking them.

6. To leave the world, click the window's **Close** (X) button.

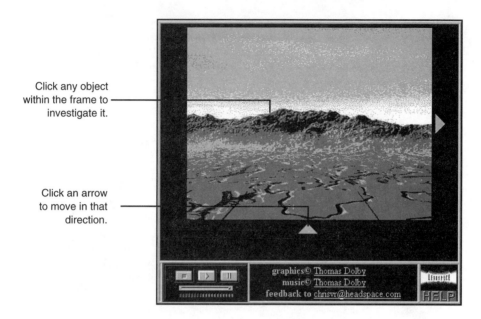

Click any object
within the frame to
investigate it.

Click an arrow
to move in that
direction.

Figure 16.3   Have fun exploring this new world.

Not Fast Enough?   You might notice that it takes a while for Netscape to play the audio file. That's because the entire file must be downloaded before Netscape can begin playing it. If you get impatient with this, you might want to try another audio plug-in (such as TrueSpeech or Crescendo Plus) that uses a faster method called *streaming*. Streaming allows audio files to be played as they are being downloaded. See Part 4 Lesson 7 for information on TrueSpeech or Part 4 Lesson 14 for more on Crescendo Plus.

Using the LiveAudio Console

When an audio file is playing, you might want to adjust its volume. Or perhaps you'll want to pause it for a moment, or to replay the entire audio file. All of these tasks are easy to do with the player console. The following steps take you to a Web site that features a musical audio file. Work through them to learn about using the player console.

1. Connect to the Internet and start Netscape.

2. In the **Location/Go to** text box, type the address **http:// www.thevervepipe.com/music.html** and press **Enter**. The Verve Pipe Web page appears (see Figure 16.4).

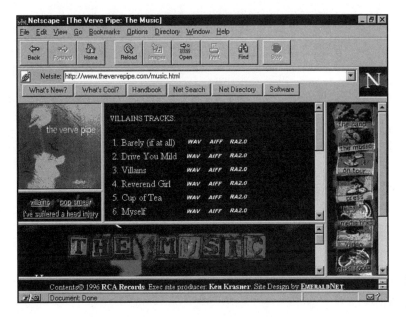

Figure 16.4 Welcome to The Verve Pipe.

3. The main frame displays a list of songs. Click in the WAV column or the AIFF column next to one of the songs to select it. The file is downloaded, and then the player console appears as shown in Figure 16.5.

Figure 16.5 You can control the audio file with the player console.

4. Use the player console's buttons as described here to control the audio file:

Click the **Stop** button to stop the audio file from playing.

Click the **Play** button to replay the audio file.

Click the **Pause** button to pause the recording temporarily. Then click **Pause** again to restart the recording where it left off.

Drag the volume control indicator to the left to decrease the volume, or to the right to increase it.

In this lesson, you learned how to play audio files with LiveAudio. In the next lesson, you'll learn how to play video files.

Playing Video
Files with
LiveVideo

In this lesson, you learn how to play video files embedded in Web pages.

What Is LiveVideo?

LiveVideo is Netscape's built-in video file player. LiveVideo supports the AVI file format. Anytime you click a link to an AVI video file, LiveVideo automatically plays it. Figure 17.1 shows an AVI video file playing with LiveVideo.

The LiveVideo console —

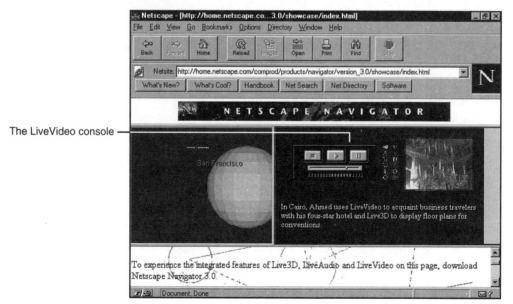

Figure 17.1 With LiveVideo, you can play embedded video files.

LiveVideo's console makes it easy for you to pause, stop, rewind, or replay the video file according to your needs. You can even fast forward the video frame by frame.

CAUTION

One Might Not Be Enough AVI is not the only video format used on the Internet. You might also run into such video formats as QuickTime or MPEG. To play one of them in Netscape, you have to download and install a compatible video player. See Part 4 for details.

Playing a Video File

Because LiveVideo is built into Netscape, you don't have to do much to play an embedded video file. The following steps take you to a Web site that includes a video file you can play to experiment with LiveVideo.

1. Connect to the Internet and start Netscape.

2. In the **Location/Go to** text box, type the address **http://www.spottedantelope.com/wander.htm** and press **Enter**.

3. Because this is a multimedia site, LiveAudio kicks in automatically and plays the greeting, displaying its player console in the upper-left frame. (For more information on LiveAudio, see Lesson 16.) In the lower-left frame, Live3D plays a three-dimensional animation. Click the word **video**, and a short video plays in the middle frame (see Figure 17.2).

4. Scroll to the bottom of the screen and click **story index**.

TIP

3-D Navigation You can also navigate this Web site by clicking the appropriate side of the spinning cube (in the lower-left corner). To change to the story index, click the picture of the leaning Tower of Pisa as it spins into view.

5. Select a story to view. For example, click **The Adventures of Bill and Linda, Part 1: Arrival!**.

6. Scroll down and click the words **train station** to start the video of Bill and Linda's arrival in Italy (see Figure 17.3).

7. (Optional) When the video ends, click the **Back** button and select another video to view.

The video appears
in this frame.

Click here to play
a video.

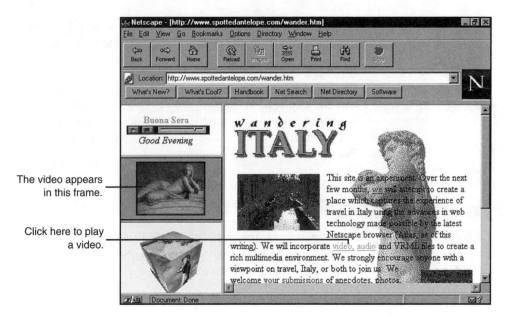

Figure 17.2 Welcome to Italy.

Click here to start
the video.

The video appears
in this frame.

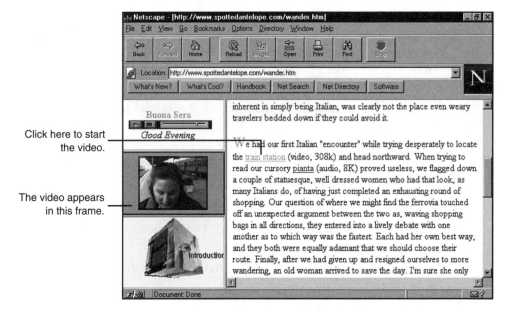

Figure 17.3 Bill and Linda at the train station.

CAUTION

Not So Fast! Although it's good at playing video files, LiveVideo is not terribly fast. The reason is that LiveVideo must download the entire video file *before* it can begin playing the file. If you have a need for speed, you might try to find a *streaming* video player such as VDOLive, StreamWorks, or PreVU. Streaming video players are capable of playing video files as the files are being downloaded. See Part 4 Lessons 5, 8, and 16 (respectively) for information about these plug-ins.

Using the Video Controls

LiveVideo makes it easy for you to replay a video file. You can also pause the video or forward it to the end if you want. And if you're a real videophile, you can advance or reverse the video frame by frame. To use the video controls, follow these steps:

1. After the video is downloaded and begins playing, right-click the video window. A shortcut menu appears, as shown in Figure 17.4.

Figure 17.4 You can control the video with the commands on this shortcut menu.

2. Select the appropriate command:

Play Restarts the video after it's been paused.

Pause Temporarily halts the video.

Rewind Returns the video to the beginning.

Forward Advances the video to the end.

Frame Back Reverses the video one frame at a time.

Frame Forward Advances the video one frame at a time.

In this lesson, you learned how to play AVI video files. In the next lesson, you'll learn how to talk over the Internet with CoolTalk.

Talking Over the Internet with CoolTalk

In this lesson, you learn how to use Netscape and the Internet to make a "telephone" call.

What Is CoolTalk?

CoolTalk is an Internet telephone tool that enables you to take part in real-time audio conferencing and data sharing. You use CoolTalk as you would a telephone: you talk into a microphone attached to your PC's sound card, and CoolTalk sends your voice over the Internet to your colleague. CoolTalk includes speed dialing and call screening features, and it even has a mute button! And by using the Internet as your telephone, you can eliminate long-distance charges for business and personal calls.

There's One Catch... You can use CoolTalk only if the person you want to call also has a copy of CoolTalk (which is included with Netscape 3.0).

CAUTION

CoolTalk also includes a chat tool (with which you "talk" by typing what you want to say) and a white board (through which you can share text and graphical data). There's even a phone book that you can use to store the e-mail addresses of the people you talk to often. And as if all these features weren't enough, CoolTalk provides an "answering machine" that can record messages sent by other CoolTalk users while you're away from your computer (assuming you're connected to the Internet, of course). If you do not have a sound card, you can still use the Chat Tool (which allows you to type messages you want to send) and the White Board (which lets you transfer graphics and annotate them during a virtual meeting).

Setting Up CoolTalk

Unlike Netscape's other features, CoolTalk has its own setup program, which you must run before you can use it.

Check It Twice Before you begin, make sure that your PC's speakers and microphone are connected and turned on.

Follow these steps to set up CoolTalk:

1. Open File Manager or Explorer and change to the \Netscape\CoolTalk directory. In Windows 95, that directory is under the Program Files\ Netscape\Navigator directory.

2. Double-click the file **COOLTALK.EXE**. The CoolTalk Setup Wizard appears.

3. Click **Next>**.

4. If your PC doesn't have a sound card, click the **I don't have a sound card in my computer** option to select it. Click **Next>**. (Without a sound card, you can't make voice calls, but you can type messages and collaborate on projects using the White Board.)

5. Select your modem speed as shown in Figure 18.1, and then click **Next>**.

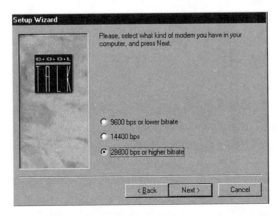

Figure 18.1 Select your modem's speed from this list.

6. You'll see a message telling you to shut down any programs that might be using your PC's audio system. Do so, and then click **Next>**.

7. CoolTalk checks your system to determine the brand of your sound card. Verify that the correct sound card was selected and click **Next>**.

8. You should hear the message "Welcome to CoolTalk." If you do, click **Next>**. If you don't hear the message, make sure that your speakers are properly connected, turned on, and cranked up. Then click **Try playing the audio again**.

9. To have CoolTalk test the 8 KHz *sampling* rate, click **Next>** when you see the dialog box shown in Figure 18.2). If you don't want CoolTalk to perform a test at 8 KHz, check the **Skip this test** check box before you click **Next>**, and then skip to step 13.

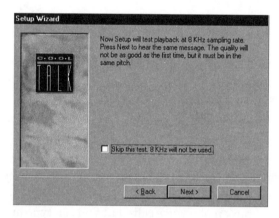

Figure 18.2 CoolTalk tests your sound system.

10. If the test sounded okay, click **Next>**. If not, select the appropriate option and click **Try playing the audio again**.

11. To have CoolTalk test the 5 KHz sampling rate, click **Next>** when you're asked about it. If you don't want CoolTalk to perform a test at 5 KHz, check the appropriate box before you click on **Next>**, and then skip to step 13.

12. If the test sounded okay, click **Next>**. Otherwise, select the appropriate option and click **Try playing the audio again**.

13. Next, CoolTalk tests the *recording* level at 8 KHz. Make sure your microphone is plugged into your sound card and is on. Click **Next>**, say a few words into the microphone, and click **Next>** again. If you don't want CoolTalk to perform the recording test, select the appropriate option before you click on **Next>**, and then skip to step 15.

14. If the test sounded okay, click **Next>**. Otherwise, select the appropriate option and click **Try playing the audio again**.

15. CoolTalk is ready to conduct the performance test. Click **Next>** to begin. (This test can take several seconds.)

16. When you see a message telling you the results of the test and indicating whether your computer is powerful enough to run CoolTalk, click **Next>**.

17. To complete your business card (as shown in Figure 18.3), click **Next>**. The Login field contains the name by which you'll be known online. The Name field contains your real name. These are the only two required fields. Complete the other fields only if you want to.

Photogenic? If you have a photo image file, you can include it with your business card. To do so, click the folder icon and select the file that contains a scanned version of your photograph.

18. You're done with setup! Click **Finish**.

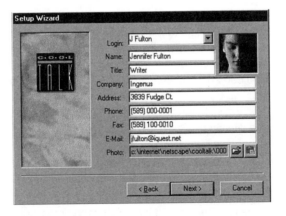

Figure 18.3 Here's your calling card.

This setup procedure is a one-time process. The next time you run CoolTalk, the CoolTalk program window appears immediately so you can start making phone calls. If you want to change settings later, you can run Setup Wizard again by opening the Help menu and selecting Setup Wizard.

Starting a Conference

To start a conference, you send an invitation to the person with whom you want to talk. In order to send the invitation, you'll need that person's e-mail address. If you don't know the person's address, there's a chance that you'll be able to obtain it from Netscape—that is, if the person you're looking for has ever used CoolTalk.

Save That Address For convenience, CoolTalk lets you save the addresses that you use most often in a permanent address book. You'll find detailed instructions later in this lesson.

The person(s) with whom you want to conference must also have Netscape 3.0. In addition, in order to receive your invitation, they must be connected to the Internet and running CoolTalk.

Don't Forget Your CoolTalk If you use the Internet every day, and you're afraid that you might miss an invitation to conference, make sure that you include the CoolTalk Watchdog in your Startup group so that it will be loaded every time you start Windows. You were given this option during installation, but you can also do it manually. The Watchdog is a small program that does nothing but watch for invitations. When you get an invitation, it lets you know, and then it loads CoolTalk. You'll find the Watchdog program (WDOG.EXE) in the \Netscape\CoolTalk directory.

Never Miss a Message If you want to make sure that you don't miss any important voice messages when you're away from your computer, you can have CoolTalk record incoming phone messages for you with the Answering Machine. See the upcoming section "Using the Answering Machine" for more information.

To start a conference, follow these steps:

1. Connect to the Internet and start CoolTalk.

2. Open the **Conference** menu and select **Start**. The Open Conference dialog box appears.

3. Enter the address of the person you want to invite, using one of the following methods:

- If the person you want to invite is listed in your Address Book, double-click his or her name in the Address Book list.

- If the person you want to invite is not listed in the Address Book, click the **IS411 Directory** tab, and select the person's name from the list by double-clicking it.

- If the person you want to invite isn't listed in the Address Book or the IS411 listing, add him or her to the Address Book. Click the **Address Book** tab, enter the person's e-mail address in the upper text box, and click **OK** (see Figure 18.4).

CoolTalk sends an invitation to the person you selected. If that person is currently connected to the Internet and is running CoolTalk, and if he is not involved in a conference, he will receive your invitation.

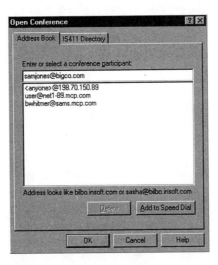

Figure 18.4 Add an address to the Address Book.

No Speed Limit If you call this person often, you can add him to speed dial by clicking the **Add to Speed Dial** button after you've entered his address. Speed buttons appear at the bottom of the CoolTalk window. To use one, you just click it.

4. Repeat step 3 to invite others to join your conference.

5. If the person accepts your invitation, your connection is established. You can talk into your PC's microphone, and you can hear his voice through your speakers.

6. When you want to leave the conference, open the **Conference** menu, select **Leave**, and click **Yes**, or just close the CoolTalk window.

Trouble Connecting?   If CoolTalk appears to have trouble connecting to the person you've called, try using the person's absolute Internet address (such as 198.71.145.89) instead of his or her relative address (bjones@anywhere.com). To find out someones's absolute address, click the big **CoolTalk** button and click the **Host** tab.

CAUTION

Trouble Hearing?   If you're having trouble hearing what's being said, click the **plus** button at the end of the Playback Audio meter. To increase the volume of your speech, click the **plus** button at the end of the Record Audio meter. The status bar shows the recording and playback level (the maximum is 3) as you set it.

CAUTION

Using the White Board

CoolTalk comes with what it calls a "White Board," which you can use to send images to the people you're talking to. You can mark up these images (by drawing an arrow to an important part of the image, for example) as much as you need to. (As you work with the White Board, you might notice a slight drop in the performance of the voice transfers.)

Images loaded to the white board exist on the Image layer. When you make marks on the image using the tools on the Toolbar, those marks exist on the Markup layer. This enables you to erase your markups without reloading the image.

Follow these steps to use the white board:

1. In CoolTalk, click the **White Board** button. The White Board program starts.

2. To load an image, open the **File** menu and select **Open,** or click the **Open File** button. Change the file type if necessary, and then change to the directory in which the file is located. Select the file and click **Open.** Figure 18.5 shows a file open on the White Board.

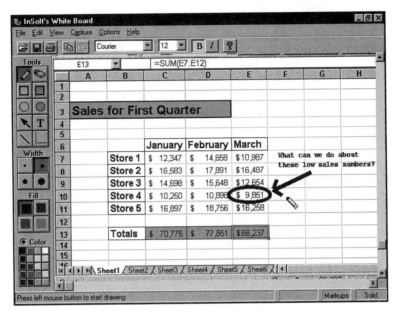

Figure 18.5   The White Board lets you share image files over the Internet.

Screen Capture   If you use Windows 95, you can capture all or part of the screen as an image. To capture the entire desktop, open the **Capture** menu and select **Desktop**. To capture an open window, open the **Capture** menu, select **Window**, and then click that window's title bar. To capture part of the screen, open the **Capture** menu, select **Region**, and then drag over the area you want to capture.

3. After an image is loaded, it is automatically sent to the other attendees. If necessary, you (or the others) can mark up the image with the Toolbar tools described next. (You can change the width of drawn objects with the Width buttons, and you can change the fill color of filled objects.)

Freehand Line   Draw lines, curves, and other shapes freehand.

Eraser   Erase markups or parts of the image (depending on the Options menu setting).

Rectangle   Draw a perfect rectangle.

Filled Rectangle   Draw a rectangle filled with color.

Circle   Draw an ellipse. To draw a perfect circle, press and hold the **Ctrl** key while drawing.

Filled Circle   Draw an ellipse filled with color.

Pointer   Draw an arrow.

Text   Insert text.

Line   Draw a straight line.

Perpendicular Line   Draw a line that is perpendicular to one of the sides of the window.

4. To close the White Board, open the **File** menu and select **Close**.

Start Over   You can completely remove your markups by selecting the **Edit, Clear Markups** command. You can remove both your markups and the image itself by selecting the **Edit, Clear White Board** command.

Too Chatty   Be choosy when using the White Board. Every time you start to draw on it, the White Board becomes the focus for all the other attendees. This means that if someone is trying to type a message in the Chat window, she will be interrupted mid-sentence because her PC will bring the White Board to the front of all open windows. If she tries to return to the Chat window and you continue to draw, you'll continue to interrupt her. So be courteous and use the White Board only when you know that you "have the floor."

Using the Chat Tool

If your PC does not have a microphone, or if your words are not coming through loud and clear, you can simply type what you want to say. To do that, you use CoolTalk's Chat tool. Follow these steps to do that:

1. In CoolTalk, click the **Chat Tool** button. The Chat Tool window opens.

2. Type what you want to say in the lower section of the window, as shown in Figure 18.6.

I Don't Like to Type! You can load a text file instead of typing, if you want. Just click the **Include** button, select the text file you want to load, and then click **Open**.

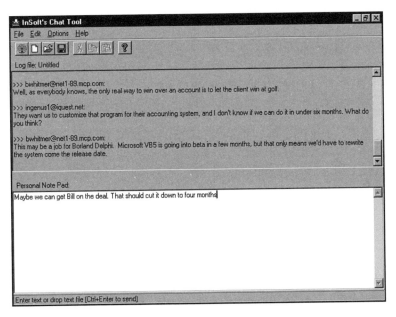

Figure 18.6 With the Chat Tool, you type what you want to say.

3. When you're ready to send your text, press **Ctrl+Enter** or click the **Send** button.

4. Your conversation is recorded in the Log File portion of the window. To save the log, click the **Save** button or open the **File** menu and select **Save**.

5. To close the Chat Tool, open the **File** menu and select **Close**.

Using the Answering Machine

If you're afraid of missing a request to conference while you're away from your desk, you can have anyone who tries to contact you via CoolTalk leave a voice or text message for you on CoolTalk's Answering Machine.

To use the Answering Machine, you must be connected to the Internet, and CoolTalk must be running (but you can't be in a conference). When someone tries to contact you with CoolTalk, a dialog box appears, asking if you want to answer the phone. If you don't pick up, the Answering Machine automatically answers, sending a message and your recorded greeting to the caller. This message gives the person the option of leaving a voice message. If the caller does not have a microphone or sound card, he or she can invoke the Chat Tool and leave a text message. You can play back your messages when you return to your computer.

The Answering Machine works like any desktop model; it answers after a few rings, plays your recorded greeting, and takes a message for you. When you return to your PC, you can replay the messages you've received.

To record your greeting, first leave any conference you might be in. (Remember that the Answering Machine options are not available when you are in an active conference.) Then follow these steps:

1. Open the **Conference** menu and select **Options**. The Options dialog box appears.
2. Click the **Answering Machine** tab.
3. Click the **Record Greeting** button at the bottom of the dialog box.
4. Speak your greeting into your PC's microphone. When you finish recording, click the **Stop Recording** button.
5. Click **OK** to close the dialog box.

Once you've recorded your greeting, you're ready to use the Answering Machine. Follow these steps:

1. Turn on your modem, connect to the Internet, and start CoolTalk.
2. Click the **Answering Machine** option to turn it on. (The button appears to be pushed in when the Answering Machine is on.)

When you return to your desk, if you have messages, the Read Messages button displays a number that indicates how many messages you have. To listen to a message, follow these steps:

1. Click the **Read Messages** button, and the Incoming Message list appears.

2. Select the message you want to play, and then click the **Play** button.

3. You can stop playing the message at any time by clicking the **Stop** button.

4. To return the call, click the **Call Back** button.

5. You can save the message by clicking the **Save WAVE File** button. To delete the message, click the **Delete Message** button.

In this lesson, you learned how to use CoolTalk to carry on a conversation over the Internet. In the next lesson, you'll learn how to keep your private information secure over the Internet.

Securing Your System

In this lesson, you will learn about Internet security issues and how to do your part toward keeping your private information secure.

Understanding Internet Security

When it comes to security of your data, the issue is twofold. First of all, it's important that "unknown parties" don't intercept or otherwise interfere with security of private data transmitted over the Internet. Second, it's important that you secure the data already on your computer against hidden viruses that might be a part of any item you download from the Internet. You'll learn how to deal with basic security concerns in this lesson; in Lesson 20, you'll learn what you should do to prevent a computer virus from destroying your data.

Now, back to those "basic security concerns." Contrary to what you might have been told, the Internet was never intended to be used as a medium for secure communications. The Internet is basically an open system. This means that information you send over the Internet can never be completely secure; individuals who have a certain amount of know-how and a distinct lack of morals can acquire data not intended for their eyes.

When you send data over the Internet, it goes through a countless number of other computers in a technological game of connect-the-dots before it reaches its intended destination. Data is chopped up into several pieces in the sending process, and each of those pieces might take a different route to the final destination. Therefore, it's highly unlikely that anybody along the way would accidentally acquire an entire message intact. However, if somebody were to try hard enough, it is possible to intercept all the necessary pieces of a message and read it. So if you decide to do business over the Net using your credit card number or other personal data, you need to keep in mind that there's always a chance that your private information might be intercepted by the wrong party.

Although you cannot change the design of the Internet, you do have a measure of control over the safety of the data you send over the Internet. In this chapter, you'll learn some ways in which you can make the Internet more secure. You'll also learn the ways in which Netscape lets you know when you're connected to a nonsecure system.

CAUTION

Private Information Because of the open nature of the Internet, you need to be very careful when completing any Internet form that asks for private information such as your Social Security number, credit card numbers, and even your phone number. Netscape Navigator will warn you whenever you're about to enter any type of data from a form into a nonsecure system, so there's no way that you can transmit data in a nonsecure manner without knowing it.

How to Know If a Site Is Secure

Netscape created a protocol called the *Secure Sockets Layer* (SSL) for encrypting information sent over the Internet. The Web server to which you're connected either uses this protocol, or it doesn't—there isn't anything you can do about it. In other words, the security of your data is dependent on the *server* to which you are sending it, and there's nothing *you* can do within Netscape to "turn on" SSL.

When SSL is active, you won't notice any differences in the way you use Netscape Navigator. What is different is the manner in which information is sent between you and the Web server to which you're connected. The information you exchange is encrypted using a scheme to which only your computer and the server are privy. You can tell when SSL is active by looking at the lower-left corner of the Navigator window. If you see a broken key icon, you know you're connected to a standard nonsecure Web site. If you see a key that's intact, you're connected to a secured site on which SSL is active. And, with SSL enabled, it would take a long time for even an expert to decipher your information.

In addition to the key icon, Netscape lets you know when you're connected to a secure site by changing its *colorbar* from gray to blue (see Figure 19.1). And another noticeable surface difference is in the URL of the site with which you're communicating. Secure Web pages use the protocol https instead of the usual http. So in addition to looking for the telltale key icon at the bottom of the screen, you can look for https:// in the address of the page you're on. Figure 19.1 shows the Navigator screen as it displays a secure Web site.

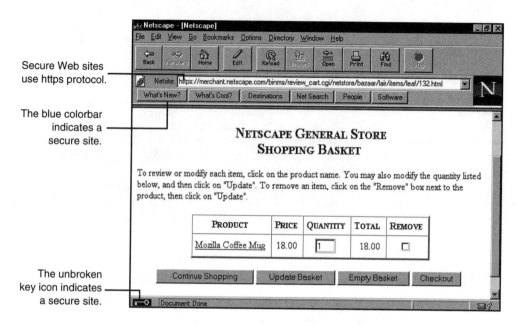

Secure Web sites
use https protocol.

The blue colorbar
indicates a
secure site.

The unbroken
key icon indicates
a secure site.

Figure 19.1   You can tell if you're connected to a secure Web site.

SSL can be used on almost every part of the Internet. Whether you're reading a Gopher menu, browsing an FTP list, or reading a Web page, SSL might be active, so always check the key icon to be sure.

It bears repeating: you can't do hardly anything to secure the data you're sending; the security of data transmission over the Internet is controlled by the Web server to which you're connected. If the server with which you're communicating sends Web pages with https instead of ordinary http, everything you send or receive will be secure. Obviously, if the server uses http protocol, the data you send or receive from that server is not secure.

A similar state of affairs holds true for Usenet news. When you're using Netscape News to read messages from or post messages to Usenet newsgroups, you'll know whether your news server supports SSL by looking at its URL (in the title bar of the Netscape News window). The address will begin with snews:// instead of the usual news://.

If you're communicating with a secure news server, all messages you send to newsgroups—regardless of which group you're sending to—will be secure during the transmission. Once your message is posted on Usenet, however, that message is still public. Every person who subscribes to that newsgroup can still read it, even if he or she is using an ordinary news server.

So why bother with the security protocol? You may want a degree of privacy, even anonymity, when posting Usenet messages. If you subscribe to a role-playing game group, for instance, and you use a pseudonym like "Zoltar the Omnipotent," you don't want an enterprising enemy magic-wielder to intercept one of your move messages, trace it to its source, eliminate it, and post his own message in its place using your pseudonym. SSL security measures do protect the transmission of your Usenet messages, making sure that your readers see only what you want them to see.

What You Can Do About Security Concerns

Before you complete any form that asks for personal information such as your Social Security number or credit card numbers, you should check the page's security. Remember that if the Web page is nonsecure (if the key icon is broken and the URL address starts with http://), the data you send back will also be nonsecure. If the key icon is intact and the address starts with https://, your data will be encrypted because your computer and the server are communicating with one another using a secure protocol.

If you are asked to provide personal information on a nonsecure page, you simply should not answer the solicitation for private information. Even if you know that the company running the server is reputable, if it does not use the https protocol, you need to be careful.

Netscape is also keeping tabs on the security of your Internet transactions. By default, Netscape notifies you when you're about to submit data on a form through a nonsecure channel, by displaying the dialog box in Figure 19.2.

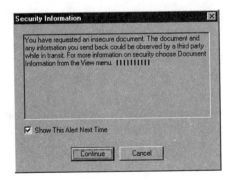

Figure 19.2 Netscape gives you this final warning before you submit nonsecure data.

If you're interested in the degree of security being used on a Web page (for instance, what types of algorithms are currently being employed in its encryption), click the key icon in the lower-left corner of the screen. You'll see the Security Information box, which includes a message telling you that transmissions to and from the secured page are encrypted while en route. To find out more about this, click the **Show Document Info** button in the Security Information box, or open the **View** menu and select **Document Info.** In the bottom frame of the Document info window, the Security entry tells you what measures are in effect to protect the Web page you're currently viewing. Most of the time, this entry will state **Status unknown** (which generally means the page is nonsecure). If you're looking at an ordinary Web page, you'll probably see the **Status unknown** indicator. If the Web page is secure, you'll see the name of the security method being used instead, as shown in Figure 19.3.

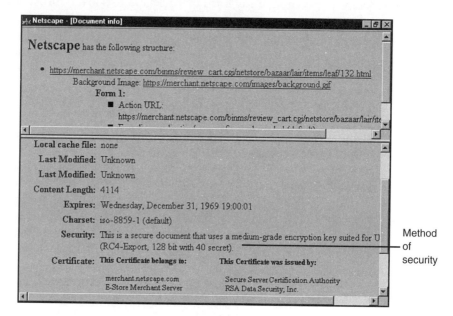

Method of security

Figure 19.3   Netscape tells you what is securing your data.

Things Aren't Always What They Seem   For reasons unknown, sometimes, you'll see the words **Status unknown** on a secure Web page. This probably indicates that some method of security has been used, but that method is unknown to Netscape.

136

A Word About EDI

If you frequently do business over the Internet with only a handful of select clients, you may want to ask your Internet service provider if it supports Electronic Data Interchange (EDI). Using special software in conjunction with your e-mail, EDI sets up a special mailbox on your service provider's computer to be used exclusively for messages sent between you and your designated trading partners. Messages between you and your partners are automatically sent to this mailbox, where the service provider encrypts them. Only the messages' final recipients have the tools necessary to decrypt them. There is some cost involved with EDI, but you might find that using EDI is much safer and much less expensive than using express delivery services to ensure privacy.

Banking and Buying Stuff on the Internet

When it comes to the issue of Internet security, one area of concern is the process of paying for purchases. Most users fear the idea of a hacker getting ahold of their charge card numbers and running up thousands of dollars worth of charges on their accounts. Sure, there are limits to which you're supposed to be liable, but this kind of thing can really mess up your credit rating (or at the very least, it will be a huge inconvenience).

However, suppose you see something on the Net that you can't resist—some great new piece of shareware or a hard-to-find antique, for example. Is it possible to buy something over the Internet without risking your credit rating?

CAUTION

Buyer Beware! Even if you feel safe spending your hard-earned e-cash online, you still should know something about the merchant with whom you are dealing. Once a purchase is made, if the merchant fails to ship your merchandise, or if it arrives broken or damaged, you won't be able to picket the guy's storefront (or take someone to court who does business halfway around the world).

The answer to that question may soon be a resounding, "Yes." Several companies are gearing up to offer various forms of e-cash (electronic cash) for use in transactions over the Net. One company, DigiCash, offers a system that allows a user to set up an account with a bank by mailing it a check and an application. After the account is set up, the bank sends you electronic "cash," in the form of an encrypted e-mail message containing a unique combination of 64-bit numbers. You send your e-cash to whomever you want, and they forward it back to

137

the bank for verification. If the number matches the cash in your account, the e-cash is transferred to the recipient's account. Every number is issued only once, so you can't "copy" your e-cash. The unique numbering system also makes fraud an improbability.

Another company, CyberCash, offers a software-based solution. When you find something you want to buy online, you ask the merchant to send you an electronic invoice. You use CyberCash software to add your encrypted credit card number to the invoice, which you then send back to the merchant. The merchant adds a confirmation number and sends the whole thing to a CyberCash server on the Internet. That server decrypts it and sends it through its banking system as a normal credit card transaction.

A variation on this theme is offered by First Virtual. With First Virtual, you apply for an account, and First Virtual assigns you an ID number. To buy something online, you send the merchant your number. The merchant sends it to First Virtual, who sends an e-mail to you for confirmation. If you confirm the purchase, First Virtual processes the transaction and charges your credit card.

In this lesson, you learned about security on the Internet. You learned how to determine if a Web page is secure, and ways to avoid having your credit card number stolen online. In the next lesson, you learn to avoid viruses on the Web.

Avoiding Viruses

In this lesson, you learn about computer viruses and how to prevent them from infecting your system as you work on the Internet.

What Is a Virus?

A computer virus is a program that hides itself inside another file. If you use the other file, the virus attaches itself to your system, where it often destroys data and can render your system inoperable. Although some viruses are simple pranksters that display annoying messages on your screen, many are extremely dangerous to your data. For example, a virus might prevent you from starting your PC, or it might damage your files so that you can no longer use them. In any case, computer viruses are a serious business.

A virus can only enter your system by way of an outside file. Typically, your system becomes infected when you unknowingly copy a diseased file onto the hard disk from some unknown source such as a floppy disk. But you can also infect your system by downloading an infected file from the Internet, an online service such as CompuServe or MSN, or a BBS.

Not the Only Way   You can also introduce a virus to your system by leaving an infected floppy disk in its drive during startup.

CAUTION

Once an infected file is copied to your system, it may begin destroying data right away, or it may simply lie in wait. Even if nothing weird happens to your PC after you download a file, that doesn't mean that your PC is completely safe and virus-free. For example, some viruses, such as one called "Friday the 13th," don't begin their dirty work until they are "triggered" by a particular date (in this case, a Friday that falls on the 13th of the month). When the trigger date for such a virus matches the date within your computer, that virus comes to life and begins doing whatever it was programmed to do—such as destroying data.

Avoiding Viruses

What do viruses have to do with the Internet? As you learned in Lesson 19, the Internet is not a secure system. Basically, anyone with an Internet account can connect to just about any Internet server and upload an infected file. Although most servers routinely check for viruses before making a file available for download, you can't always be sure. If you download files from the Internet, you run the risk of infecting your PC.

However, you can easily avoid computer viruses (and the trouble they cause) by following these simple rules:

- **Download files into a temporary directory.** If you make it a habit to download all your files into a particular directory, such as C:\DOWNLOADS or C:\TEMP, you can easily check all files for viruses (using a virus detection program) *before* you use them.

- **Maintain a recent backup copy of your important files.** If you regularly back up your data onto a floppy disk or a tape, you can copy the files back to your system if the original files accidentally become damaged by a computer virus.

TERM

Back Up To copy your files onto a floppy disk or tape so that you have spares in case you lose the original files. If something happens to the original files that renders them useless, you can *restore* (copy back) the backed up files. Restoring is a process that decompresses the files stored on the backup disk or tape, and copies them back onto the hard disk.

- **Check disks for viruses before you use them.** Run all foreign floppy disks through a good virus detection program. This means *all* floppy disks that you didn't create, including disks you get from coworkers, friends, or the guy off the street.

- **Protect your disks from infections by write-protecting them.** If data can't be copied to a floppy disk, the disk can't become infected. So if you loan out your disks, protect them from infections that might exist on other systems by flipping the write-protect tab. Be sure to write-protect your installation disks, too.

- **Run a virus-detection program all the time.** Most virus protection programs come with a utility that you can run in the background as you are doing your work. That way, even if you slip up, your system is protected because it's being monitored 24-hours a day.

Penalty on the Play   The only drawback against running a virus detection program all the time is that doing so will slow down your system considerably. Also, some programs are real alarmists, warning you whenever any system file is changed (which often happens if you run Windows or install a program).

CAUTION

- **Never leave a disk in the drive**. If you leave an infected disk in its drive and then start your PC, the virus can move from the disk to your PC. To avoid this problem, make sure you remove disks from their drives whenever you power down.

What About Zipped Files?   You should scan compressed files before you unzip (decompress) them. McAfee's antivirus program can scan zipped files easily, or you can use WinZip to run your antivirus program from within WinZip.

TIP

If you suspect that you may have acquired a computer virus, run a good detection program right away—before you do anything else.

Creating an Emergency Disk

Because some computer viruses can render your PC helpless (unable to start or *boot*), you should protect yourself by creating an emergency (bootable) diskette. Follow these steps:

1. First, format a bootable disk. In Windows 95, start Explorer, right-click the disk icon, and select **Format**. Run a Full format and make sure you select the **Copy system files** option. If you use Windows 3.1, start File Manager, open the **Disk** menu, and select **Format Disk**. Then make sure the **Make System Disk** option is selected.

2. Copy your PC's configuration files, C:\CONFIG.SYS and C\AUTOEXEC.BAT, onto the bootable disk. If you use Windows, you should also copy the files C:\WINDOWS\WIN.INI and C:\WINDOWS\SYSTEM.INI.

Keep Your Disk Updated!   If you make changes to any of your configuration files (or if you install a program that changes them), recopy those files onto your emergency disk.

CAUTION

3. Write-protect your emergency disk and keep it in a safe place.

If a virus prevents your PC from starting properly, insert your emergency disk into drive A and restart the PC. You can then run a virus detection program to remove the virus and (hopefully) return your PC to operating condition.

Using an Antivirus Program

There are many antivirus programs that you can use to remove a virus from your system. I recommend McAfee Virus Protection Tools, available for download at many software sites on the Internet. You might want to purchase Norton Anti-Virus, available wherever software is sold. In any case, be sure to get an antivirus program that is compatible with the version of Windows you use.

Free Antivirus Program   If you use Windows 3.1 and DOS 6.x, you'll find the Microsoft Anti-Virus program in your DOS directory. (This program is not compatible with Windows 95.)

TIP

After you've installed your antivirus program, follow these steps to check your system for viruses and remove them:

1. If you suspect a virus is at work, stop whatever you're doing and exit any programs you're currently running.
2. Restart your PC using your emergency disk.
3. Start your virus program and use it to scan for viruses (see Figure 20.1).

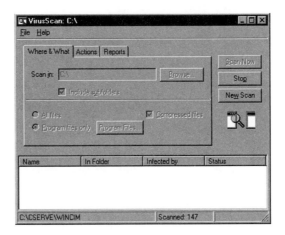

Figure 20.1 Use your antivirus program to scan the hard disk for viruses.

4. If the antivirus program detects a virus in a particular file, have the program "clean" the file. The cleaning process removes the virus from the file and makes the file usable. (At least, most of the time.)

Protect That Data! Some infected files are so damaged that they can't be cleaned (fixed). In such a case, a recent backup is your only protection. You should perform backup regularly to prevent the loss of valuable data.

CAUTION

In this lesson, you learned about viruses and how to protect your system from them.

Netscape News

The Basics of Using Netscape News

In this lesson, you will learn how to use Netscape's built-in newsreader.

What Are Newsgroups?

Bulletin boards (the cork kind that you can quickly cover with notices, ticket stubs, and whatnots) are pretty much all over the place: at work, in your kid's classroom, at the grocery store, and even at the library. They all serve the same purpose: to provide a central spot for the exchange of information.

On the Internet, bulletin boards are called *newsgroups*. Each newsgroup focuses on a particular interest. No matter how strange or seemingly insignificant your interests or hobbies might be, there's almost definitely a newsgroup that addresses it. For example, you'll find newsgroups on everything from adoption to Star Trek to body piercing.

TERM   **Usenet**   Short for *user's network*, Usenet defines the standards by which information is exchanged within a newsgroup.

You read the messages posted in a newsgroup just as you might scan through the brochures, notices, and want ads posted on a local bulletin board. You can then add your own comments or questions. Later, other people come along and read your messages, and they can reply to your posting, offering advice, opinions, or answers as appropriate.

Setting Up Netscape News

To read the messages posted in an Internet newsgroup, you need a newsreader program. Luckily, Netscape comes with its own newsreader, Netscape News, built right in.

To use Netscape News, you first have to tell it the name of your Internet provider's news server. Hopefully, you already have this information. If not, give your provider a call first to get it. Then follow these steps:

1. Open the **Options** menu and select **Mail and News Preferences**.

2. Click the **Servers** tab to see the options shown in Figure 1.1.

Type the name of your service provider's news server here.

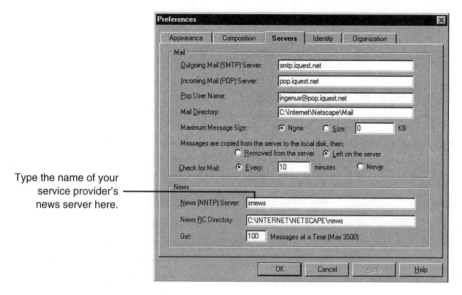

Figure 1.1 Setting up Netscape News.

3. Type the name of your Internet provider's news server in the **News (NNTP) Server** text box.

4. (Optional) In the **NEWS RC Directory** text box, change the folder in which Netscape stores your list of newsgroups.

5. (Optional) Change the value in the **Get** box to increase the number of messages Netscape reads at one time. (You might find that you waste time if you download more than the 100 most recent messages.)

6. Click **OK** to enter the settings. You're now ready to use Netscape News.

Displaying the List of Available Newsgroups

Although there are more than 10,000 newsgroups on the Internet, your service provider probably subscribes to only the top 1,000 or so. When you start Netscape News, it downloads a list of available newsgroups from your service provider. You can then *subscribe* to any of the newsgroups you find listed there.

Subscribe To gain access to the messages in a newsgroup. After you subscribe to a newsgroup, its messages are downloaded to your PC so that you can access them.

To display the available list of newsgroups, follow these steps:

1. Connect to the Internet and start Netscape.

2. Open the **Window** menu and select **Netscape News**.

3. If necessary, click the plus sign in front of your service provider's folder. Netscape News displays only the newsgroups to which you've already subscribed. (At this point, there aren't any.)

What Are These Messages? You may already have a few text messages from your service provider. To view any of these messages, click it.

4. Open the **Options** menu and select **Show All Newsgroups** to display the list of available newsgroups.

5. Because the process of downloading the list of newsgroups may take more than a few minutes, you'll see a warning asking you if you want to continue. Click **OK**.

After a few minutes, Netscape News displays your provider's list of available newsgroups (see Figure 1.2). See the next section to learn how to subscribe to the newsgroups that interest you.

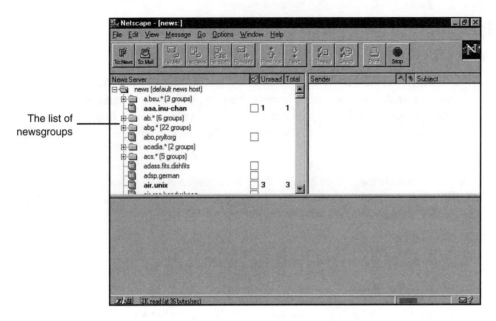

The list of
newsgroups

Figure 1.2   Netscape News displays a list of available newsgroups.

Subscribing to Newsgroups

When you find a newsgroup that interests you, you *subscribe* to it so you can
read the messages that are posted to it. How can you tell which newsgroups
you're interested in? As you may have noticed, newsgroups use abbreviated
names such as comp.lang.basic, which can make it difficult to figure out what
a particular group is about. This list of common abbreviations should help:

alt	Alternative topics (unusual stuff, possibly offensive)
comp	Computer related topics
misc	Miscellaneous topics
news	Newsgroup related information
rec	Recreational topics—hobbies, sports, and so on
sci	Science topics
soc	Social issues
talk	Discussions focused on controversial topics (talk show information)

Most of those topics are further divided into subtopics. For example, the comp group consists of many computer-related newsgroups, such as comp.dcom (data communications) and comp.ai (artificial intelligence). In addition, these sub-groups are often divided into specialized groups, such as comp.dcom.fax, which focuses on sending computer data via fax or fax modem.

When you find a newsgroup you want to review, you subscribe to it by clicking the box that appears after the newsgroup's name. A check mark appears next to each group to which you subscribed (see Figure 1.3). When you subscribe to a newsgroup, Netscape News downloads the messages in that group. You can then read and reply to those messages, which you'll learn about in Lesson 2. You can cancel your subscription to a newsgroup by clicking its check box again.

I'm Not Sure Whether I Want to Subscribe   To preview the messages in a group before you decide to subscribe, just click the newsgroup's name. Its messages appear in the second pane. You can even view the contents of the messages in a group before you subscribe (see Lesson 2 for details).

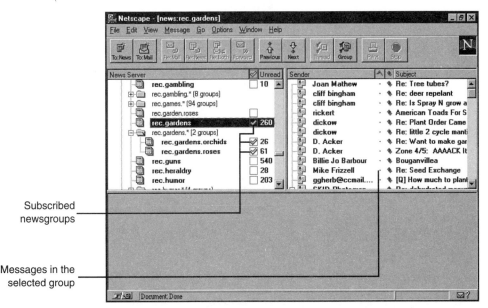

Subscribed newsgroups

Messages in the selected group

Figure 1.3 Netscape News downloads the messages in the subscribed newsgroup.

Just the Ones I Want, Please   After subscribing to a few newsgroups, you can set Netscape News so that it displays only the subscribed news-groups. To do so, open the **Options** menu and select **Show Subscribed Newsgroups**. The shorter the newsgroup list is, the easier it is for you to locate information you want.

In this lesson, you learned how to set up Netscape News and subscribe to newsgroups. In the next lesson, you'll learn how to read and reply to newsgroup messages.

Reading and Responding to Newsgroup Messages

In this lesson, you'll learn how to read and reply to newsgroup messages.

Reading a Message

To view the messages in a particular newsgroup, click the newsgroup's name. A list of the messages in that newsgroup appears. You do *not* have to subscribe to a newsgroup in order to view its messages and reply to them. Subscribing simply allows you to limit the newsgroup list to those that you like.

When you select a newsgroup, its messages appear in the panel on the right side of the screen, as shown in Figure 2.1. To display the contents of a message, click the message. Netscape News displays its contents in the lower pane. If necessary, you can access an earlier message to which your message relates by clicking one of the numbers next to **References**.

New Heading   As you can see in Figure 2.1, at the top of the message, News displays a heading area with information about the message, its sender, and so on. By default, News displays the headings shown in the figure. You can display other heading information by opening the **Options** menu, selecting **Show Headers**, and selecting **All**. You can display less information than what's shown by opening the **Options** menu, selecting **Show Headers**, and selecting **Brief**.

Hey, It's Empty!   Next to the name of each newsgroup are two numbers. The first is the number of messages you haven't read yet, and the second is the total number of messages in that newsgroup. (You may have to adjust the size of the first pane in order to see both numbers.) If you do not see any numbers at all, there are no messages in that particular newsgroup.

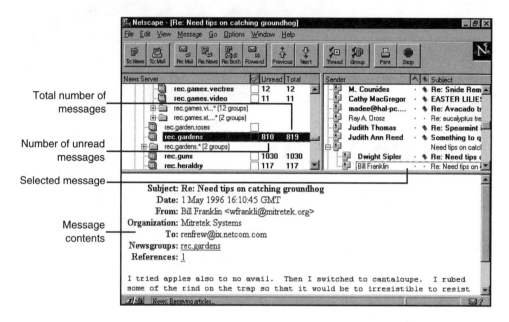

Total number of
messages

Number of unread
messages

Selected message

Message
contents

Figure 2.1   Reading a message.

Messages in a newsgroup do not appear in chronological order; instead, they follow a *thread*. A thread is a collection of messages that follow a particular discussion. A thread starts when someone replies to a comment or question. Then someone else comes along, reads the first message, reads the reply, and adds his comments. When he tacks his comments onto the reply, a single thread forms, connecting the three messages. As additional comments or questions are added, it creates a continuous discussion that anyone can trace by following the thread of the conversation. Netscape News marks a thread by indenting later comments that form the thread under the original comment that started it all.

TERM   **Thread**   A collection of newsgroup messages that follow a particular discussion.

TIP   **In Order**   You can sort messages in a newsgroup in a number of ways. To change the sort order, open the **View** menu, select **Sort**, and select **by Date**, **by Subject**, **by Sender**, or **by Message Number**.

After you read one message, you can click another one to view it. Alternatively, you can use one of these options from the Go menu to jump from one message to another more easily:

Next Message	Displays the next message in the list.
Previous Message	Displays the previous message in the list.
First Unread	Displays the first unread message in the list.
Next Unread	Displays the next unread message in the list. (You can also click the **Next** button to view the next unread message.)
Previous Unread	Displays a previous unread message in the list. (You can also click the **Previous** button to view a previous unread message.)

Flagging a Message

If you're short on time but you know you want to read a message you've come across, you can flag the message for later viewing. To flag a message, follow these steps:

1. Select the message you want to flag.

2. Open the **Message** menu and select **Flag Message**. The message appears with a small red flag in front of its name.

Fast Flag You can also flag a message by clicking in the flag column (the one marked with a red flag).

To return to a flagged message, open the **Go** menu and select **First Flagged**, **Next Flagged**, or **Previous Flagged**. When you select **First Flagged**, for example, the first flagged message in the newsgroup list is highlighted so that you can read it. If you select **Next Flagged**, the highlight moves to the next flagged message in the list.

If you want to unflag a message, select it, open the **Message** menu, and select **Unflag Message**. You can also click the red flag in front of a message to remove it (unflag the message).

Searching for a Message

You can search for a particular message based on its description. To do so,
follow these steps:

1. Click inside the message pane.

2. Open the **Edit** menu and select **Find**.

3. Type some text to search for and click **Find**. Netscape News searches the
list and highlights messages that match your search criteria.

Replying to a Message

Before you post any message to a newsgroup, make sure that you've taken the
time to familiarize yourself with the focus of its discussions. In addition, you
should read all the messages in a thread so that your comments don't repeat
what's already been said.

Read the FAQs You should search for messages with the letters "FAQ,"
which is short for frequently asked questions. In these messages, you'll find
answers for the most commonly asked questions within that newsgroup. Make
sure you always read the FAQs before posting a question, to avoid duplicating
an earlier effort.

When you're confident that you have something new (and relevant) to say, you
can post a public or private reply. A public reply appears with the other messages in the newsgroup. A private reply is basically an e-mail message sent
directly to the originator of the message.

Follow these steps to reply to a message:

1. Select the message to which you want to reply by clicking its name.

2. Open the **Message** menu and select **Post Reply** (to post a public reply),
Mail Reply (to e-mail your reply), or **Post and Mail Reply** (to post a public
reply and send an e-mail message).

3. The text of the original appears, preceded by a > mark (see Figure 2.2). In
order to keep your message short, you should repeat only the parts of the
original message that the reader needs to get the gist of it. Select and delete
the extraneous parts of the original message.

4. Type your reply after the original message's contents (see Figure 2.2).

5. Click **Send** to send your reply. If you decided to post your reply instead of mailing it, your reply appears with the other messages in the newsgroup. At that point, it is available for viewing.

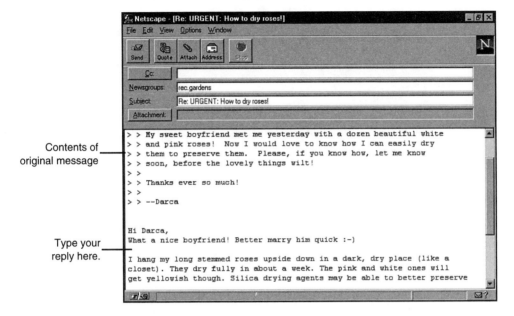

Contents of original message

Type your reply here.

Figure 2.2 Posting a reply.

CAUTION

Watch What You Say! Do not use CAPITAL LETTERS in your message. On the Internet, using CAPS is considered shouting. Also, if you want to avoid getting *flamed* (verbally abused), don't insult anybody personally or attack a particular topic as being "too silly." Instead, keep your comments pertinent to the topic being discussed and avoid repeating what has already been said.

Starting a New Thread

If you you'd like to introduce a new topic to a newsgroup, you can do that by starting your own thread (discussion). Before you start a new thread, make sure that your topic has not yet been covered under some other thread.

When you're ready to start a new thread, follow these steps:

1. Click the newsgroup to which you want to add your thread.

2. Open the **File** menu and select **New News Message**.

3. In the **Subject** text box, type a subject for your discussion (see Figure 2.3).

Type a subject.

Type your comment or questions here.

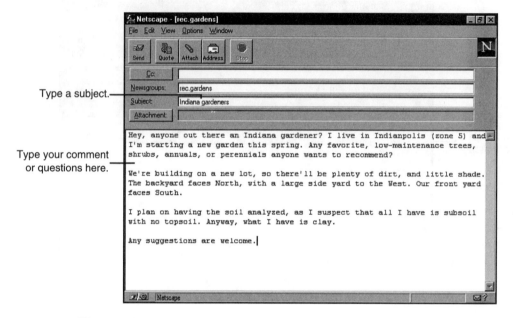

Figure 2.3   Posting a new thread.

4. Type your comment or question in the large text box.

5. Click **Send**, and your message becomes available for viewing. Check back every so often to see where your new thread goes.

In this lesson, you learned how to read and reply to newsgroup messages. In the next lesson, you learn how to attach files to your newsgroup messages and how to download files that other people have attached to their messages.

Attaching and Detaching Files in Newsgroup Messages

In this lesson, you'll learn how to attach files to your newsgroup messages, and how to download files that other people have attached to their messages.

Understanding Attached Files

Not everything you find within a newsgroup is text discussion. Often, a user will upload (send) a file to the newsgroup to share its contents with other readers. For example, in a music-related newsgroup, members might trade MIDI sound files. A photography group might trade graphic files instead. Of course, once you download such a file from the newsgroup, you must have the appropriate program to view its contents. For example, to view a graphic file, you might use a graphic viewer such as LView.

Being able to use a file downloaded from a newsgroup is only part of the story. The real story starts when the file is uploaded to the newsgroup. You see, the Internet was really designed for the transmission of textual data—data that consists of letters and numbers without fancy text enhancements such as bold, italics, and underline. But data files, such as graphic and sound files, are not simple text files; they contain special codes and not just text. So in order to transmit such files over the Internet, you have to convert into text (ASCII) using a process called *uuencoding*. The process of uuencoding converts the information in a data file into ASCII (plain text). At the other end, the recipient (or in this case, the recipient's newsreader program) decodes the file, converting it back into usable data.

If uuencoding sounds very complex, that's because it is. In some cases, you need a special uuencoding program to encode your files before you upload them to the Internet. For the most part, though, uuencoding a file for uploading is handled automatically by Netscape News. However, when downloading a file, you may have to decode the file manually, depending on the file's type (as you'll see in the next section).

Which Uuencoder Should I Use?   Because you'll need a uuencoder to decode some of the files you grab from a newsgroup, you should get a copy of WinCode, a popular uuencoding program. You'll find WinCode at various software sites on the Internet. See Lesson 11 of Part 1 for information on downloading files from the Internet.

Downloading Attached Files

Many files that you find in newsgroups are divided into parts because a lot of newsgroup servers limit the size of messages. In such a case, you'll find references like these in the descriptions for several messages:

eagle.gif (0/3)

eagle.gif (1/3)

eagle.gif (2/3)

eagle.gif (3/3)

In the 0/3 file, you'll find a description of the eagle.gif graphic. The other three files make up the eagle.gif file itself; it's divided into three parts.

There's Only One File!   Sometimes a file is small enough that it can be contained in one message. So don't fret if you don't find multiple messages for a single file as described here.

To download (receive) a file attached to a newsgroup message, double-click the first part of the file (the one with $1/x$ in the description). Netscape News automatically grabs all the parts of the file and decodes it.

If the file is a GIF or a JPEG graphic, the contents of the file appear in the message area, as shown in Figure 3.1. To use the file in a program, right-click it and select **Save this Image** from the shortcut menu. Netscape News saves the file to disk, where you can load it in the appropriate program.

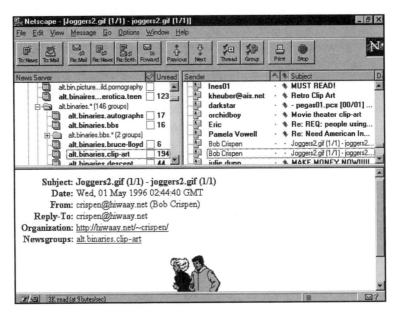

Figure 3.1 The contents of the file appear in the message area.

If the file is not a graphic, it appears in its uuencoded form, as shown in Figure 3.2.

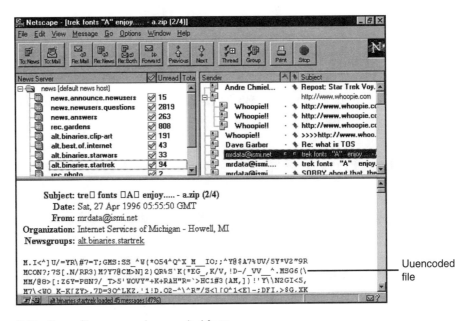

Uuencoded file

Figure 3.2 Some files appear in encoded form.

To use this file, you have to save it to disk and then decode it. Follow these steps:

1. Open the **File** menu and select **Save As**.

2. Select a directory in which to save the file, and then type a name for it using the .UUE extension (as in FILE01.UUE).

3. If the file was broken into parts (if it appears as more than one message in the newsgroup window), repeat steps 1 and 2 for each file part (each message).

4. Once you have all the parts saved to disk, start WinCode.

5. Open the **File** menu and select **Decode**.

6. Change to the directory that contains the uuencoded file(s).

7. Select the file(s) you want to decode, as shown in Figure 3.3. If the file is split into several parts, select all of them.

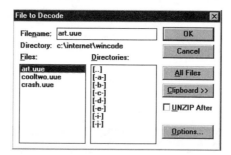

Figure 3.3 Select the file you want to decode.

8. Click **OK**, and WinCode decodes the file. You can now load it into the appropriate program for use.

Uploading Files to a Newsgroup

In addition to downloading files from newsgroups, you can upload (send) files. To upload a file to a newsgroup, you simply attach the file you want to share to your newsgroup message.

When you attach your file and send the message, Netscape News automatically uuencodes the file for transmission. As you learned earlier, the file is decoded at the user's site when he downloads your file from the newsgroup.

To upload (send) a file to a newsgroup, follow these steps:

1. Follow the usual steps for posting a message (described in Lesson 2).
2. Before you click the Send button, click **Attachment**.
3. Click **Attach File**.
4. Select the file you want to send with your message and click **Open** (see Figure 3.4).

Figure 3.4   Select the file you want to attach to your newsgroup message.

5. The name of the file you selected appears in the Attachments dialog box. Make sure the **As Is** option is selected, and then click **OK**.
6. Click **Send** to send your message. Netscape News automatically uuencodes the file, splits the file into several messages if necessary, and then sends them.

In this lesson, you learned how to download and upload files in newsgroups.

Netscape Mail

Setting Up Netscape Mail

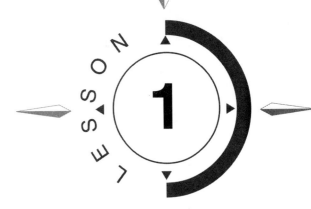

In this lesson, you'll learn how to configure Netscape's e-mail program, Netscape Mail.

What Is E-Mail?

E-mail (short for *electronic mail*) is the process by which messages are sent electronically from one PC to another. E-mail can be transmitted over network cables from one person to another on the same company network, or it can be sent to a person located further away by use of a *modem*.

Before the advent of electronic mail, businesses used either the snail-like postal service to send their correspondence or some high-priced delivery service. But with e-mail, you can send information across the U.S. or across the world in a relatively short time—from a few minutes to a few hours, depending on Internet traffic.

Modem Short for *modulator-demodulator*, a modem is a device that translates computer information into sound and then transmits those sounds over conventional telephone lines. The modem at the receiving end translates the sounds back into computer data.

Netscape includes its own e-mail program called Netscape Mail. With Netscape Mail, you can send e-mail to anyone else on the Internet and to people who use any of the popular online services such as CompuServe and America Online. You'll learn how to send and retrieve e-mail messages using Netscape Mail in upcoming lessons.

Configuring Netscape Mail

Before you can use Netscape Mail, you'll need to get some information from your Internet service provider. You need to know the following things:

- The address of your Internet provider's POP (Post Office Protocol) server
- The address of your Internet provider's SMTP (Simple Mail Transfer Protocol) server
- Your specific e-mail address
- Your password for receiving mail (which is probably the same as your Internet logon password)

To configure Netscape Mail, you'll complete five dialog box screens. Luckily, you don't have to make many changes to the information on those screens.

Completing the Appearance Screen

Follow these steps to begin configuring Netscape Mail:

1. Start Netscape Navigator. (You do not need to connect to the Internet in order to configure Netscape Mail.)

2. Open the **Options** menu and select **Mail and News Preferences**.

3. Click the **Appearance** tab to see the options shown in Figure 1.1.

4. (Optional) Change the settings of any of the following options as necessary.

Messages and Articles are shown with   You can use a variable width font if you like. A fixed width font displays each character using the same amount of space, which might be important if you're reading a message whose characters seem "misaligned." Otherwise, you may find a variable width font easier to see, especially if your monitor is not very big.

Text beginning with > (quoted text) has the following characteristics   Usually, the text of an original message appears preceded by > marks in a reply. This text is typically displayed in italics, but you can also change that, as well as the size of the text.

When sending and receiving electronic Mail   If you use Windows 95, you can select to use Microsoft Exchange for your e-mail needs, instead of Netscape Mail.

Pane Layout   The Netscape Mail window is divided into three panes. Normally, the two main panes appear side by side. You can rearrange the main panes so that they appear top to bottom, or you can stack all three panes.

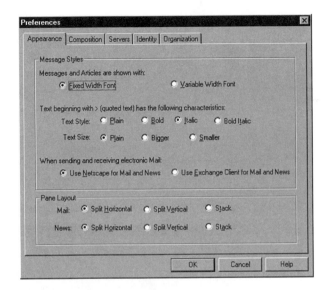

Figure 1.1 Configuring the Appearance screen.

Don't close the Preferences dialog box; you still have several screens to complete.

Completing the Composition Screen

With the Preferences dialog box open, follow these steps to continue configuring Netscape Mail:

1. Click the **Composition** tab, and you'll see the options shown in Figure 1.2.

2. (Optional) Change the settings of any of the following options as necessary to suit your needs:

When Composing Mail and News Messages   Leave this one set to Allow 8-bit. Don't change this option unless someone encounters consistent problems when receiving your messages intact.

By default, email a copy outgoing message to   If you want to send a copy of all your e-mail messages to some other e-mail address, enter that address here.

By default, copy outgoing message to the file   Netscape Mail automatically saves copies of your e-mail messages in a file that's stored in the Netscape/Mail/Sent directory. If you want the file saved in another location, specify a directory path here.

169

Automatically quote original message when replying   This is turned on by default. Turn it off if you don't want to follow the convention of including a copy of the original message in your reply.

Don't click OK just yet; it's time to complete the information on the Servers screen.

I Don't Want to Include All of the Message   If you don't want to include all of the original message in your reply, or if you don't want to include any of it in a particular reply, you should leave this option checked and just delete all or part of the copied text.

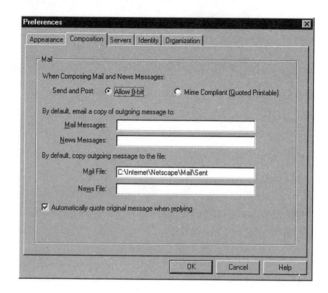

Figure 1.2 Configuring the Composition screen.

Completing the Servers Screen

In the Preferences dialog box, complete the Servers screen by following these steps:

1. Click the **Servers** tab to see the options shown in Figure 1.3.

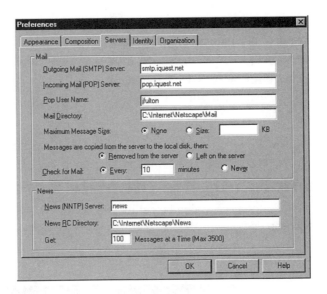

Figure 1.3 Configuring the Servers screen.

2. Enter the addresses of your service provider's outgoing and incoming mail servers in the appropriate text boxes.

3. In the **Pop User Name** text box, enter your e-mail name (the part of your e-mail address that comes before the @ sign).

4. (Optional) Change any of the following options to suit your needs:

Mail Directory Enter a new path in this text box if you want to change the directory in which Netscape Mail saves your incoming messages. (You change the directory for your outgoing messages on the Composition screen.)

Don't Change the Maximum Message Size For the most part, you should *never* change this setting. If you set a limit here, you won't be able to receive messages that are larger than the limit.

CAUTION

Messages are copied from the server to the local disk By default, this option is set to **Left on the server** so that if you accidentally delete a message from your hard drive, you can go back to the server and retrieve a

copy of it. Once you get used to using Netscape Mail, you should set this
option to **Removed from the server**, which deletes messages from your
Internet provider's hard disk after you receive them.

Check for Mail   Check the **Every** option and type an interval (such as 10)
in the text box if you want Netscape to automatically check for your e-mail
whenever it's running.

Don't click OK yet. You still have two screens to complete.

Completing the Identity Screen

With the Preferences dialog box still open, follow these steps to complete the
Identity screen:

1. Click the **Identity** tab to see the options shown in Figure 1.4.

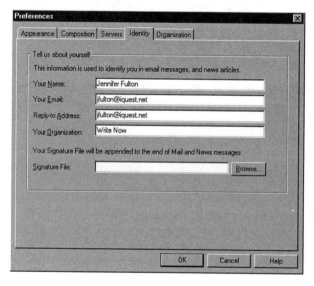

Figure 1.4   Configuring the Identity screen.

2. Fill in the **Your Name** text box.

3. Enter your full e-mail address in the **Your Email** text box.

4. (Optional) Fill in any of the following information that you want to provide:

Reply-to Address   If you want to include your e-mail address in your newsgroup postings, enter it in this text box.

Your Organization   If you want to include your company's name with your e-mail messages, enter that name here.

Signature File   If you want to attach a signature file with your e-mail messages, type the path to that file in this text box. (Or click **Browse**, select your signature file, and click **Open**.)

Signature File   A text file that usually includes your name and some kind of logo or picture. A signature usually consists of spaces and other characters such as x, I, and - that form a particular pattern, like this:

```
J Byrd   x
     =  ~xxx
        | |
        ^^
```

To create a signature file, open Notepad or Wordpad, type your name, and then create a simple picture. Save the file as SIGN.TXT. Then return to the Identity tab of the Preferences dialog box and select the file.

Completing the Organization Screen

Follow these steps to complete the final screen for configuring Netscape Mail.

1. Click the **Organization** tab to see the options shown in Figure 1.5.

2. (Optional) If you want Netscape Mail to remember your e-mail password so that you don't have to type it in each time you check your mail, check the **Remember Mail Password** option.

3. (Optional) If you want replies to your messages to appear under your original message within the message list (an arrangement that's called *threading*), check the **Thread Mail Messages** option.

4. (Optional) In the Sorting area, select the **Subject** or **Sender** option next to Sort Mail by if you want to change the sort order. (By default, Netscape Mail sorts messages by date.)

5. Congratulations, you're done configuring Netscape Mail! Click **OK**.

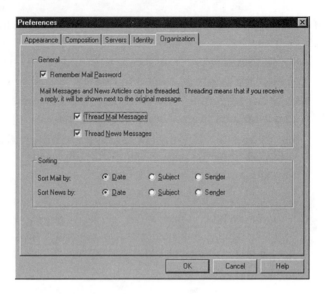

Figure 1.5   Configuring the Organization screen.

Not Just Mail   You probably noticed there are some options that pertain to Netscape News (which is covered in Part 2) on the Organization tab. Feel free to change these options as necessary.

If you weren't sure which options to choose as you were making your selections throughout this lesson, just keep in mind that you can return to the Preferences dialog box at any time.

In this lesson, you learned how to configure Netscape Mail. In the next lesson, you'll learn how to send e-mail messages.

Sending
E-Mail Messages

In this lesson, you'll learn how to send e-mail messages with Netscape Mail.

Understanding E-Mail Addresses

After you've configured Netscape Mail, you're ready to send or receive messages. You'll learn about receiving e-mail in the next lesson. But before you learn how to send an e-mail message, you need to learn about e-mail addresses and how they work.

You can send e-mail to anyone who's connected to the Internet directly or anyone who's connected indirectly through an online service such as CompuServe or America Online. To send an e-mail message to someone, you have to know his e-mail address. An Internet e-mail address looks something like this:

jnoname@que.mcp.com

The part of the address before the @ sign is the person's user name (the name by which he is known to his home system). Most user names consist of the person's first initial and last name run together, as in *jnoname*. The at symbol (@) separates the user name from the second part of the address, which is a location. The example address above is that of Que Corporation (the publisher of this book), which is part of Macmillan Computer Publishing. Therefore, part of the location is *que.mcp*. The last part of the location (*.com*) tells you that que.mcp is a commercial (business) venture. Other endings you will see include .edu (educational), .net (an Internet server), and .mil (military).

All together, the example address tells the Internet system to send messages with this address to jnoname, located at que.mcp.com, which is some type of business or commercial enterprise.

Watch That Case!   When entering an e-mail address, be careful to use upper- and lowercase letters *exactly* as they are given to you. If someone tells you that his address is SAMBeldon@imagineTHAT.com, you must type the address exactly that way. He will not receive his mail if you send it to sambeldon@imaginethat.com because that is a completely different (or nonexistent) address.

CAUTION

E-mail addresses are a little different for persons connected to the Internet indirectly, such as through CompuServe or The Microsoft Network. In such cases, the person's e-mail location is his online service. The following list shows you the e-mail address format for each of the most popular online services.

Online Service	Sample Address
CompuServe	71354.1234@compuserve.com
America Online	joeblow@aol.com
Prodigy	joeblow@prodigy.com
The Microsoft Network	joeblow@msn.com

Creating and Sending E-Mail Messages

Once you have an e-mail address, you can start sending out e-mail messages. If you have several e-mail messages to send, you should create them offline (that is, while you're not connected to the Internet). This saves you from paying online charges while you're creating your missives. When you finish creating a message, you save it in your Outbox. Then, when you're ready to send all of your messages, you connect to the Internet and send everything in the Outbox at once.

Only Text Please   A basic e-mail message contains only text. If you want to include a file (such as a spreadsheet, chart, graphic, or word processing document) with your e-mail message, see Lesson 6 for help.

CAUTION

Creating and Sending E-Mail Messages

To create an e-mail message, follow these steps:

1. Start Netscape Navigator. (You do not need to connect to the Internet in order to create e-mail messages.)

2. Open the **File** menu and select **New Mail Message**.

Quick Message   You can click the **To: Mail** button on the Netscape Mail toolbar to quickly create a message, rather than using the File menu.

3. Click in the **Mail To:** text box and enter the recipient's address. To enter a second address, separate it from the first address with a comma, as in **jfake@mcp.com,jblow@iu.edu**.

4. (Optional) To send a copy of your message to a third party, enter that address in the **Cc:** text box.

5. (Optional) Open the **View** menu and select any of the following options to have Netscape Mail display a text box for it. (By default, Netscape Mail displays only the Mail To:, Cc:, and Subject: fields.) Then complete the additional fields you selected.

From   Displays your real name

Reply To   Includes your e-mail address

Mail Bcc   Sends a blind carbon copy

Newsgroups   Posts a message to a newsgroup

Followups To   Includes a different e-mail address for followups to your message

Fast Addressing   Netscape Navigator lets you save and reuse the addresses of people to whom you send e-mail often. See Lesson 5 for details.

6. Enter a subject in the **Subject:** text box.

7. Click in the message area and type your message (see Figure 2.1).

177

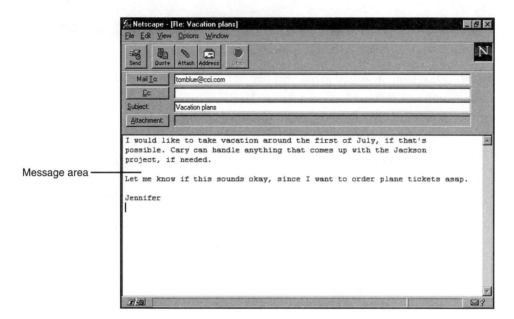

Message area ————

Figure 2.1   Type your e-mail message in the message area.

Getting Attached   You can attach a file to send with your message if you want. See Lesson 6 for instructions.

8. To send your message now, first, connect to the Internet. Then click the **Send** button. (Alternatively, you can defer delivery until you've created all the messages you want to send. Don't click Send; instead, see the next section for help.)

9. Repeat steps 2 through 8 to create additional e-mail messages.

Messages sent over the Internet often take a rather circuitous route to their destination. So your e-mail message may take anywhere from a few minutes to a few hours to reach its intended party. Even so, e-mail is a lot faster than regular mail.

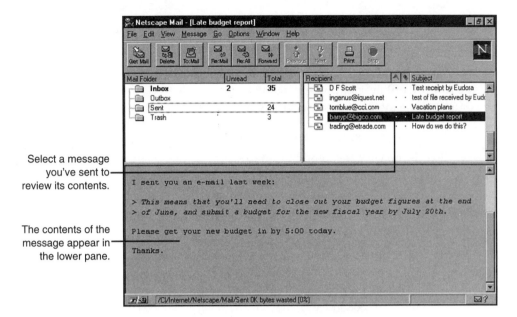

Select a message
you've sent to
review its contents.

The contents of the
message appear in
the lower pane.

Figure 2.2 You can review any message you've sent.

Once your messages have been sent, they are moved from the Outbox to the
Sent folder. (The first time you send messages, the Sent folder is automatically
created.) To view a message you've sent, click the **Sent** folder to open it, and
then click the message you want to view. It appears in the bottom pane, as
shown in Figure 2.2.

Not Really Sent   If a message cannot be delivered because the address is
invalid, you'll receive a message from your service provider's mail program
letting you know. So after you send messages, you should check your Inbox (as
explained in Lesson 3) to see if you've been notified that any of your messages
didn't reach their destination.

CAUTION

Many Web pages include a button you can use to send messages to the Web
page's owner (usually known as the Webmaster). When you click such a button,
Netscape automatically displays the Netscape Mail New Message window so
you can type your message. (The address of the Webmaster is automatically
inserted for you.) When you finish creating the message, follow the steps above
to send your comments to the Webmaster.

Sending E-Mail Messages at a Later Time

You can create messages and save them for sending at a later time. This allows you to work offline, creating several messages and sending them later, after you connect to the Internet. To delay sending your messages, follow these steps:

1. Create your message as usual.

2. Before you click the **Send** button to send your message, open the **Options** menu and select **Deferred Delivery**.

CAUTION

Deferred Delivery   When you turn on the Deferred Delivery option, all of your messages from that point forward will be stored in the Outbox whenever you click Send. They will *not* be delivered until you tell Netscape Mail to deliver what's in the Outbox. To change Netscape Mail so that it delivers your mail immediately when you click the Send button, open the **Options** menu and select **Immediate Delivery**. Of course, if you're not connected to the Internet when you click Send, you'll get an error when Netscape Mail tries to deliver your mail.

3. Click the **Send** button, and Netscape Mail places your message in the Outbox for delivery at a later time.

4. Create and save additional messages as needed.

5. When you're ready to send your messages, connect to the Internet in the usual manner.

6. Start Netscape if needed.

7. Open the **File** menu and select **Send Mail in Outbox**.

Copying Text from Other Messages

You can copy text from another message or any document file using the Edit, Copy and the Edit, Paste commands. The following steps teach you how to copy and paste data into your messages.

1. Open the message or document that contains the text you want to copy to your message, and select the text.

2. Open the **Edit** menu and select either **Copy** (to copy the text) or **Cut** (to move it).

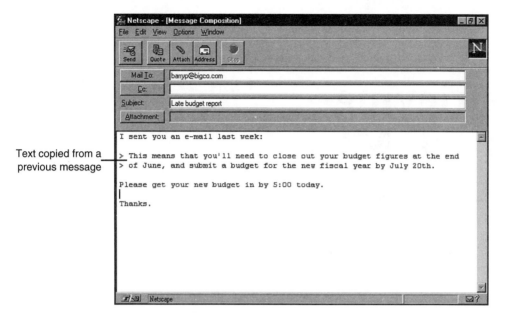

Text copied from a previous message

Figure 2.3 You can make copied text appear as a quotation.

3. Start **Netscape Mail** and open a new message window by clicking the **To: Mail** or **Re: Mail** button.

4. Click in the message area where you want the copied text to appear.

5. Open the **Edit** menu and select **Paste**. If you want the recipient to know that the copied text came from another document, select **Paste as Quotation** instead of Paste. The text appears with > marks in front of it, which indicates that it came from another source (see Figure 2.3).

Fast Copy Because Netscape supports drag and drop, you can use a shortcut to the steps above. To do so, open a new message window. Then open an old message, select the text you want to copy, and drag it into the new message window.

In this lesson, you learned how to send e-mail messages. In the next lesson, you'll learn how to retrieve and read messages sent to you.

Retrieving Your E-Mail Messages

In this lesson, you'll learn how to retrieve messages sent to you over the Internet.

Retrieving an e-mail message is like going to your mailbox and checking for mail. When you find mail in your mailbox, you take it out, open it, and read it. Netscape Mail does basically the same thing: it goes to your electronic mailbox (located on your Internet provider's computer), checks for mail, and brings back anything it finds.

Normally, Netscape Mail checks for new mail only when you start it. However, while Netscape Mail is running, you can initiate the checking process again whenever you want. Or if you prefer to do things simply, you can configure Netscape Mail to check for mail automatically at regular intervals.

Password-Protected   You'll need your e-mail password to retrieve your mail. This is usually the same password that you use to log on to the Internet. If you're not sure what your password is, or if your logon password doesn't work, contact your service provider for help.

CAUTION

After Netscape Mail retrieves your mail, you open each message to read it. You can print an open message if you want, or you can save its contents in a text file. You can also reply to the message by sending an e-mail message back to the originator.

Retrieving Your E-Mail

To retrieve your e-mail, follow these steps:

1. Connect to the Internet in the usual manner and start Netscape Navigator.

2. Open the **Window** menu and select **Netscape Mail**. The Password Entry Dialog dialog box appears (see Figure 3.1).

Figure 3.1 Enter your e-mail password.

3. Enter your password and click **OK**. Netscape Mail checks for mail. If you have new messages, Mail copies them to your system and places them in the Inbox. If you don't have any messages, you'll see a dialog box telling you so.

No Password Needed You can configure Netscape to allow you to check your mail without having to enter your password each time. (You will still have to enter the password the very first time you use Netscape Mail, though.) See Lesson 1 for details.

To view your new messages, see the section "Opening an E-Mail Message" later in this lesson.

Retrieving Mail While the Program Is Running

As I mentioned earlier, Netscape Mail usually checks for mail only once, when you start it. To check for new mail at any time when you're in Netscape Mail, use one of the following methods:

- Click the **Get Mail** button.
- Open the **File** menu and select **Get New Mail**.
- Click the envelope icon at the right end of the Netscape status bar.

When you select one of these options, Netscape Mail checks for new mail, placing new messages you've received in your Inbox or notifying you that you don't have any new messages.

TIP

Save Money After you retrieve your e-mail, when you're ready to read through it, disconnect from the Internet so you won't pay connect charges while you view your messages.

Checking Your Mail Automatically

You can easily configure Netscape Mail to check for mail at regular intervals when Netscape is running. When it finds new mail, Netscape Mail notifies you by displaying an exclamation point (!) next to the envelope icon on the status bar. You can then decide whether to retrieve it or not.

Follow these steps to set up Netscape Mail to check for e-mail automatically:

1. Open the **Options** menu and select **Mail and News Preferences**.

2. Click the **Servers** tab.

3. Enter a time interval in the **Check for Mail Every __ minutes** text box.

4. Click **OK**.

CAUTION

Error! If Netscape Mail doesn't know your password (because you aren't using the Remember Mail Password option), or if you haven't yet opened the Netscape Mail window (so you can enter the password), Netscape will try to check periodically for mail, but it will fail. When this happens, a question mark appears next to the envelope icon at the right end of the Netscape status bar.

Opening an E-Mail Message

Your new mail is placed in the Inbox. To view the messages, click the **Inbox** folder. Messages appear in the list on the right. Unread messages appear in bold text and are marked with an envelope icon, as shown in Figure 3.2. Click the message you want to open, and its contents appear in the bottom pane. If necessary, scroll down to read the complete message.

Click here to flag
important messages.

The envelope icon marks
an unread message.

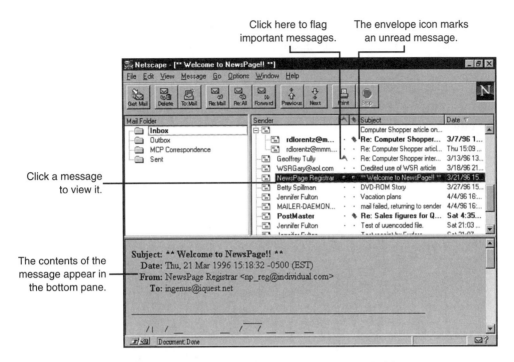

Click a message
to view it.

The contents of the
message appear in
the bottom pane.

Figure 3.2 Unread messages in the Inbox appear in bold.

Order, Please By default, Netscape Mail displays messages in the order in which they were received. You can select a different sort order using the **View**, **Sort** command. If you want Netscape Mail to use a different sort order all the time, you can configure it to do so. See Lesson 1 for help.

Can't See Enough? If you're having trouble viewing part of a message, or the message list, you can adjust the size of any of the three panes by dragging its border.

To view the next message in the list, simply click it. You can quickly open the next unread message by clicking the **Next** button or the previous unread message by clicking the **Previous** button.

If you read a message that you want to note for some particular reason, you can flag it so that you can easily find it again. To do so, click within the flag icon column (next to the message header) in the message pane. A flag icon appears, marking the message.

If you want to print the open e-mail message, click the **Print** button or open the **File** menu and select **Print**.

Files Attached If a file is attached to your message, you must follow the steps in Lesson 6 to retrieve the file.

CAUTION

To save the contents of the message in a text file, open the **File** menu and select **Save As**. The Save As dialog box appears. Change to a different folder if necessary, type a name for the new file, and click **OK**.

Responding to E-Mail Messages

You can reply to or forward any message you receive. When you reply to a message, Netscape Mail automatically fills in the address of the originator in your new message. All you have to do is type your reply and then send the message. You can reply to all the recipients of the original message (using the **Reply to All** command) or just the sender.

When you reply to a message, Netscape automatically includes the text of the original message for reference. As explained in Lesson 1, you can customize Netscape Mail so that the original text is not included if you want. Or, if you like to include the original text most of the time, you can just delete any text you don't want to include in a particular reply.

You'll learn how to forward a message in just a minute. To reply to a message, follow these steps:

1. Click **Inbox**, and the contents of the Inbox appears.
2. Click on the message to which you want to reply.

If It's Already Open... If the message you want to reply to is currently open, skip to step 3.

TIP

3. Open the **Message** menu and select **Reply** or **Reply to All**. Netscape Mail updates the appropriate header information, filling in the Mail To:, Cc:, and Subject: lines as necessary. The text from the original message appears in the message area. When you reply to a message, each line of the original message is marked with an arrow (>) as shown in Figure 3.3.

Quick Reply   To reply to a message quickly, you can click the **Re: Mail**, or **Re: All** buttons at the top of the Mail window as a shortcut to step 3.

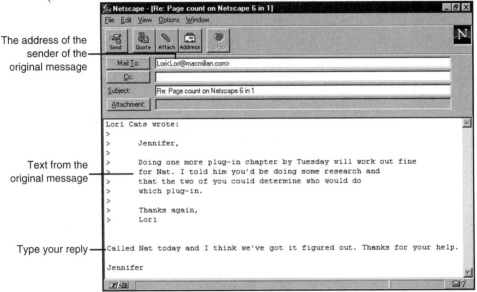

The address of the sender of the original message

Text from the original message

Type your reply

Figure 3.3   Replying to an e-mail message.

Delete That!   If you want to delete any of the lines from the original message, just select them and press **Delete**. In addition, if you want to respond to a message point-by-point, you can type your reply in-between the lines of the original message. Place the cursor at the end of an original line and press **Enter** to create a blank line on which you can type.

4. Type your message under the copy of the original message.

5. Send your message as usual by clicking the **Send** button.

Forwarding a Message Instead

When you forward a message to someone else, Netscape Mail sends a copy of the original message to the person you indicate and allows you to add your own message if you want. You can forward the original message as a quotation (by using the **Forward Quoted** command), in which case the contents of the original message are preceded by > symbols.

Follow these steps to forward a message to someone else:

1. Click **Inbox**, and the contents of the Inbox appears.
2. Click on the message you want to forward. If the message you want to forward is currently open, skip to step 3.
3. Open the **Message** menu and select **Forward** or **Forward Quoted**. Notice that, when you forward a message, its text is not copied into the window. That's because a copy of the original message is sent as an attachment to this message.

 Quick Forward   To forward a message quickly, click the **Forward** button at the top of the Mail window as a shortcut to step 3.

4. Type your message.
5. Send your message as usual by clicking the **Send** button.

In this lesson, you learned how to retrieve messages, open them, and reply to them. In the next lesson, you'll learn how to organize your incoming and outgoing e-mail messages.

Organizing Your E-Mail

In this lesson, you'll learn how to organize the e-mail messages you send and receive.

Arranging Your Messages

By default, Netscape Mail arranges your e-mail messages in the order in which they were received (by date). This arrangement may not be very useful if you're trying to locate a single message in a long list, especially if you can't remember exactly when you received it.

Mail provides you with four options you can use to determine the sort order. To arrange your e-mail, select the folder whose messages you want to arrange. Then open the **View** menu, select **Sort**, and choose from the following options:

By Date	Sorts messages by the date on which they were created.
By Subject	Sorts messages by subject.
By Sender	Sorts messages according to who sent them.
By Message Order	Sorts messages by the date on which they were received.

These options are grouped as option buttons: when you select one, you automatically deselect all the others. In other words, you can't use these options in combination, such as By Sender arranged within Date.

If you select By Date, messages are sorted by the date on which they were created. The options in the next list work in conjunction with the option you chose above. For example, if you select By Date and then select Ascending, Netscape Mail arranges messages by date, beginning with the oldest message and ending with the newest message.

Again Re-sorts messages in the selected folder, using the current sorting option.

Thread Messages Displays connected messages in a thread, so that responses to a particular message appear indented under the original message.

Ascending Sorts messages in ascending order. If you sort messages by date, older messages appear at the top of the list, and newer messages appear at the bottom. If you sort messages by subject, those whose subjects begin with the letter A are listed first, and those subjects that begin with Z are placed at the end of the list. If you do not select this option, messages are automatically arranged in descending order.

TIP **New Messages on Top** To sort your list so that new messages appear at the top, make sure the **Ascending** option is *not* selected.

You can also sort your messages by clicking the buttons at the top of the message list, as shown in Figure 4.1. To sort messages by date, click the **Date** button; to sort by sender, click the **Sender** button.

Click here to arrange messages by sender.

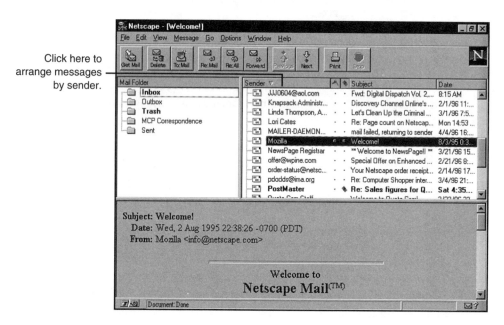

Figure 4.1 Messages arranged by sender.

Searching for a Message

To locate a particular message, you can search for a keyword in its header (subject line), or you can search for certain text within a particular message.

CAUTION

Can't Do That   You can't search for a keyword in the text of all messages at one time, only in a single message. You can, however, search all messages for a keyword in the subject line.

To search for a message, follow these steps:

1. Select the folder you want to search.

2. If you want to search the text *within* a particular message, select that message now. If you want to search the headers of all the messages in the folder, don't open a message.

3. Open the **Edit** menu and select **Find**. The Find dialog box appears (see Figure 4.2).

Type the text to search for.

Select what you want to search.

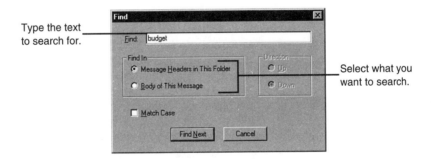

Figure 4.2 Searching for a message.

4. Type the text you want to search for in the **Find** text box.

5. To search all the messages in the current folder, select **Message Headers in This Folder**. To search within the text of the current message, select **Body of This Message**.

6. (Optional) If you select Body of This Message, you can search from the bottom of the message to the top by clicking the **Up** option in the Direction area.

7. (Optional) If you want to match your text *exactly* (capitalization and all), click **Match Case**.

8. Click **Find Next**. Netscape Mail searches the list and highlights the first match it finds. To continue your search, press **F3.**

CAUTION

Empty-Handed If Netscape Mail doesn't find a match, you'll see a message telling you so. Click **OK** to remove the message from the screen.

Creating Folders

Once you start using Netscape Mail, it's easy to accumulate a number of messages in a short time. With all this correspondence building up, you're quickly going to need some way to organize it.

By default, all incoming messages are placed in the Inbox folder. Likewise, outgoing messages (messages you send) are placed in the Sent folder. As you'll see in a moment, you can create additional folders in which you can group related messages.

Although there's no limit to the number of folders you can create, you won't want to create so many that they become unmanageable. After you create the folders, you can copy or move messages from the Inbox into your folders.

To create a folder, follow these steps:

1. Open the **File** menu and select **New Folder**.

2. Type a name for your new folder. (You can include spaces.)

3. Click **OK**. Your new folder appears in the folder list along with the other folders, arranged in alphabetical order (see Figure 4.3).

Your new folder is ready to use. You can now copy or move messages into this folder following the steps in the next section.

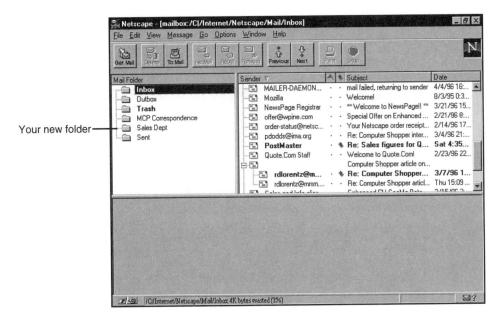

Your new folder

Figure 4.3 Your new folder appears in the folder list.

Unwanted Folders You can delete a folder you no longer want. First delete or move any messages that are in it. Then select the folder, open the **Edit** menu, and select **Delete Folder**.

Selecting Messages

In order to copy, move, or delete a message, you must select it first. When you select a message, its name becomes highlighted. You can select just one or several messages at a time, using the following methods:

- To select one message, click it.
- To select multiple adjacent messages, click the first message in the group, press and hold the **Shift** key, and then click the last message. Those two messages and all the messages in-between become highlighted.

- To select messages that are not listed next to each other, press and hold the **Ctrl** key and click each message you want to select. Figure 4.4 shows multiple nonadjacent messages selected.

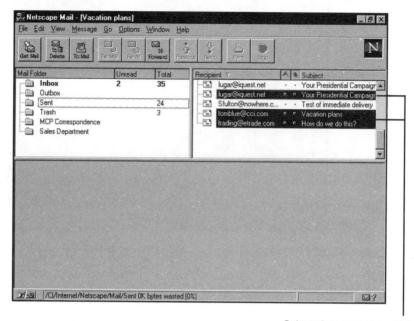

Selected messages are highlighted.

Figure 4.4   You can select any messages you want.

The Edit menu offers three additional options for selecting messages:

Select Thread   When messages are connected by subject, they are shown in a thread. In a thread, the messages that pertain to the original message (such as replies and followups) appear indented under the first message. Choose this option to select the original message and any additional threaded messages.

Select Flagged Messages   As you learned in Lesson 3, you can flag messages of particular note by clicking in the flag column next to the message name. If you choose this option, you can quickly select those flagged messages.

Select All Messages   This option selects all the messages in the current folder.

Copying, Moving, or Deleting Messages

To copy messages, simply select them, press and hold the **Ctrl** key, and then drag the messages to the folder to which you want to copy them. To move messages instead, select them and just drag them to their new home. When you drag the mouse, a small box appears next to the mouse pointer (see Figure 4.5); that box represents the messages you're moving. When you release the mouse button, the messages appear in the new location.

Drag selected messages to the folder to which you want to move them.

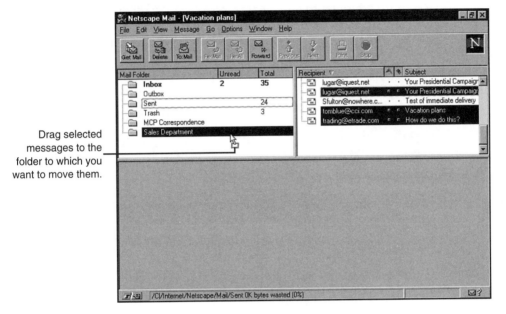

Figure 4.5 To move a message to a new folder, simply drag it.

 Another Way If drag-and-drop is not your thing, you can use the commands on the Message menu to move or copy messages from one folder to another. Just select your messages, open the **Message** menu, select either **Copy** or **Move**, and then select the folder into which you want to place your messages.

To delete messages, select them and press **Delete**. The messages disappear from the list and are placed in the Trash folder. If you accidentally delete a message, you can move it from the Trash folder back into a regular folder. When you're sure that the Trash folder contains only messages that you want to get rid of permanently, open the **File** menu and select **Empty Trash Folder**.

Compressing Folders

When you add messages to a folder, it gets bigger. However, when you delete a message or remove a message from a folder, the folder does not change in size. (Think of the folder as a row of chairs. When a person vacates his chair, the chair is not removed, so the row stays the same size.) Because empty space remains where messages used to be, you are essentially wasting space on your hard drive.

You can compress a folder to remove this wasted space. When you compress a folder, its contents are rearranged so that there are no empty spaces between messages. The resulting folder takes up less room on your hard disk. As you might think, you can read and use the messages in a compressed folder as you would normally.

To compress a folder, follow these steps:

1. Select the folder you want to compress.

2. Open the **File** menu and select **Compress Folder**. The messages are rearranged so that empty spaces are removed.

In this lesson, you learned how to arrange your messages, locate a particular message, and delete unwanted messages. In the next lesson, you'll learn how to create an address book of people to whom you frequently send messages.

Managing Addresses with an Address Book

In this lesson, you'll learn how to save the e-mail addresses you use frequently so that you don't have to retype them.

Creating an Address Book

E-mail addresses are often complex combinations of long user names and bizarre domain names, such as jkasterask@EDS.decMeca.bzzark.com. If you get any part of the address wrong, your e-mail goes nowhere. The best defense against unruly e-mail addresses is to enter them once into an address book so you can reuse them as needed. Luckily, Netscape Mail provides you with an address book that's ready to use.

Before you start adding addresses, you'll want to personalize your address book by giving it a proper name. Follow these steps:

1. Open the **Window** menu and select **Address book**.
2. Right-click the address book and select **Properties** from the shortcut menu.
3. Right now, your address book is called Address Book. Click in the **Name** text box (in front of the word **Address**), and type your name so that it reads, for example, Jennifer Fulton's Address book (see Figure 5.1).

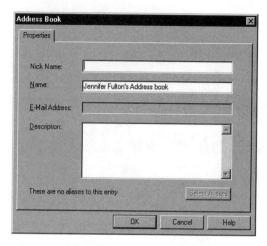

Figure 5.1   Give your address book a proper name.

4. Ignore the Nick Name and Description fields for now. (They don't really serve any useful purpose in this context, but you'll learn more about them in just a moment.) Click **OK**.

You can create smaller mailing lists within your address book. For example, if you wanted to keep your personal addresses in a private area of the address book, you could create a mailing list called Personal Addresses. Each mailing list appears on-screen as a subsection of the main address book, as shown in Figure 5.2.

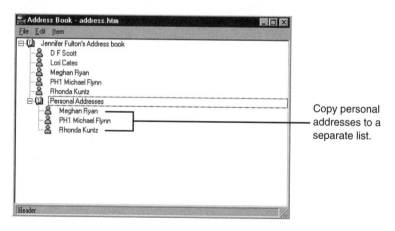

Figure 5.2   Create a separate mailing list for personal e-mail addresses.

To create a mailing list within your address book, follow these steps:

1. Open the **Item** menu and select **Add List**.

2. In the **Name** text box, replace the words New Folder with the name of your new address book.

3. (Optional) Again, there's no need to use the Nick Name field in this context. However, you can enter a description in the **Description** text box for your new mailing list.

4. Click **OK**. Your new mailing list appears underneath the main address list (see Figure 5.2).

After you add an address to your address book, you can add a copy (or *alias*) of it to your new mailing list. For example, you can add everyone you know to the main address book, and then copy your personal addresses to your personal mailing list. To copy an address to a mailing list, select it and drag it to the list.

Alias   Any copy of an e-mail address that you create within your address book. When you make a change to the original entry, Netscape Mail automatically changes the copy accordingly.

Adding an Address

You can add an address to your address book in several ways. To add an address *manually*, follow these steps:

1. Open the **Item** menu and select **Add User**. The Properties screen appears (see Figure 5.3).

2. In the **Nick Name** text box, enter a short nickname for this person (using no capital letters and no spaces). You can later enter this name in the Mail To: text box of the Message window, and the user's address will appear.

3. In the **Name** text box, type the person's full name (you can use capital letters and spaces as appropriate).

4. In the **E-Mail Address** text box, enter the person's e-mail address.

5. Type any additional information, such as the person's phone number or mailing address, in the **Description** text box.

6. Click **OK**, and the user is added to the main address book.

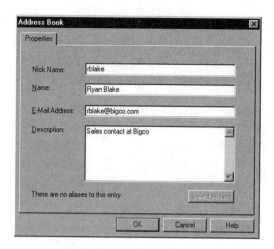

Figure 5.3   Adding an address to the Address Book.

Quick Entry   You can add the address of anyone who has sent you an e-mail message by selecting that message, opening the **Message** menu, and selecting **Add to Address Book**.

As I mentioned earlier, you can move copies of particular entries into smaller mailing lists. Having smaller lists of related entries makes it easier to locate the person you're looking for. To copy an entry to a mailing list, click the entry and drag it there.

Get a Move On   You might try to move addresses from the main list into a smaller mailing list, such as a personal list. You won't be able to do that. Netscape Mail only allows you to copy entries, not to move them. This means that all of your entries will be found in the main list, while only those you've copied will appear in smaller mailing lists.

Using Your Address Book

Now that you have your addresses neatly organized into an address book, you need to know how to use them to send e-mail messages. Follow these steps to find out:

1. Open the **File** menu and select **New Mail Message**. A blank message window appears.

2. Click in the **Mail To:** text box and type the *nickname* of the person to whom you want to send your message (see Figure 5.4). When you click in another field, the person's e-mail address appears.

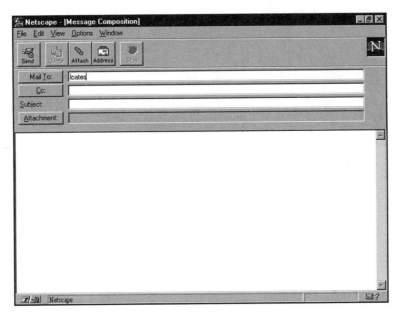

Figure 5.4 Type the nickname of the person to whom you want to send your message.

3. If the person doesn't have a nickname, or if you can't remember it, click the **Mail To:** button and select him from the list in the Select Addresses dialog box shown in Figure 5.5. Then click the **To:** button. Repeat to add additional persons to the Mail To: list. When you're done, click **OK**.

4. (Optional) Repeat step 2 or step 3 for the **Cc** and **Bcc** fields if necessary.

5. Enter a subject, type your message, and send it as usual.

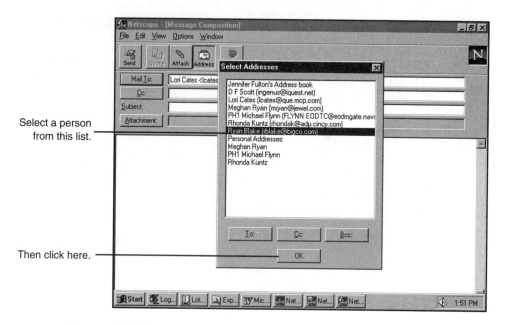

Select a person
from this list.

Then click here.

Figure 5.5 You can select a person from the Select Addresses dialog box.

Displaying Your Address Book As a Web Page

A quick way to send e-mail messages to a lot of people is to display your address book as a Web page. On a Web page, each entry appears as a link (see Figure 5.6). When you click a link, the Message window appears, with the address of the person you selected already entered. All you have to do is type a subject and create your message, and your e-mail is ready to send.

To open your address book as a Web page, follow these steps:

1. Open the **File** menu and select **Open File in Browser**.
2. Change to the Netscape directory.
3. Select the **ADDRESS.HTM** file and click **Open**. Netscape displays your address book as a Web page.

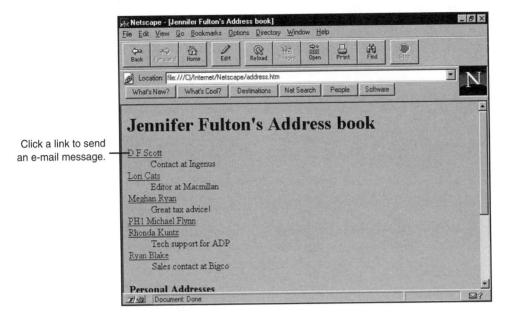

Click a link to send an e-mail message.

Figure 5.6 Display your address book as a Web page for quick access.

To send an e-mail to anyone listed on the address Web page, click that person's link.

Changing an Address

If someone switches jobs and changes his e-mail address, you'll need to change his entry in your address book. Thankfully, changing an address is easy.

1. Open the **Address Book** by opening the **Window** menu and selecting **Address Book**.
2. Right-click the entry you want to change.
3. Select **Properties** from the shortcut menu.
4. Make changes to the entry as needed, and click **OK** when you're finished. If you have copied the entry to other parts of the address book, those aliases will automatically be updated as well.

Deleting an Address

If you have an entry in your address book that you no longer need, you can remove it by following these steps:

1. Open the Address Book by opening the **Window** menu and selecting **Address Book**.

2. Select the entry you want to remove.

3. Press **Delete**.

4. If the entry has been copied to other parts of the address book, you'll see a warning telling you that the copy (alias) will also be deleted. Click **OK**.

In this lesson, you learned how to add, copy, and delete Address Book entries. In the next lesson, you'll learn how to attach files to an e-mail message.

Attaching Files to E-Mail Messages

In this lesson, you'll learn how to send files with an e-mail message and how to download files from messages you receive.

Sending a File with a Message

You can send just about any type of file over the Internet with an e-mail message. For example, you might send someone a spreadsheet file, a sound file, or a report complete with graphic images.

Of course, sending a file with a message doesn't do any good unless your recipient can actually do something with it. Your recipient needs some way of reading the contents of the file. For example, if you send a Lotus 1-2-3 spreadsheet file as an e-mail message, your recipient must have a copy of Lotus 1-2-3 (or some other program that can read 1-2-3 files) in order to view and use the information in the file.

As you know by now, e-mail messages that you create with Netscape Mail can contain only text—no fancy fonts, text enhancements (such as bold), or graphics. Therefore, all messages sent over the Internet are expected to include plain text only.

When you send an attached file over the Internet, that file has to be converted into ASCII (text codes). Likewise, when your recipient gets the file, it needs to be converted back to its original format before it can be used. There are several ways to convert files for transmittal over the Internet, each of which has its pros and cons.

Common Methods for Converting a File for Transmission

Many e-mail programs handle the problem of sending a file over the Internet by placing a MIME (Multipurpose Internet Mail Extension) header in the e-mail message just before the file's data to show that what follows is not text. The MIME header also indicates the file's type (such as a bitmap graphic or a word processing document). This process works okay as long as the recipient's e-mail program recognizes the MIME header and sends the data that follows the header to the indicated program for translation. For example, if the MIME header indicates that the attached file is a bitmap, the e-mail program automatically sends the file for translation to a program that can handle bitmap files (such as Paint). So, if you receive a MIME encoded message that contains a bitmap, Netscape Mail will wake up your Paint program (or whatever program is associated with bitmaps), and Paint will translate the encoded bitmap and display it in the Paint window.

Unfortunately, if the recipient of such a message uses an online service, it's unlikely that his e-mail program will be able to make sense of the MIME coding. For example, WinCIM (the e-mail program used on CompuServe) does not recognize MIME information. So if you were to send a MIME-encoded file to a CompuServe address, the recipient would not be able to use it.

The most dependable process for sending files over the Internet is called uuencoding. The process of uuencoding converts the information in the file into ASCII (plain text) so that it can be sent over the Internet. At the other end, the recipient (or the recipient's e-mail program) decodes the e-mail message, converting the attachment back into a usable file.

You can uuencode any file yourself with a uuencoder such as WinCode. Fortunately, though, when you attach a file to a Netscape Mail message, it is automatically uuencoded. So you don't have to do the uuencoding yourself.

Yet Another Way Another method of sending files over the Internet is BinHex. The theory behind BinHex and uuencoding is much the same, but the methods and results are somewhat different. BinHex is a method used often among Macintosh computers, but it's not very common in the Windows arena.

Including a File in an E-Mail Message

To send a file in an e-mail message, follow these steps:

1. Open the **File** menu and select **New Mail Message**.
2. Complete the **Mail To** and **Subject** fields as usual.
3. Click the **Attachment** button. The Attachments dialog box appears.
4. Click **Attach File**.
5. In the dialog box that appears, locate and select the file you want to send, and then click **Open**. You're returned to the Attachments dialog box, and the file name you selected appears at the top of the list as shown in Figure 6.1.

The file you want to attach ——

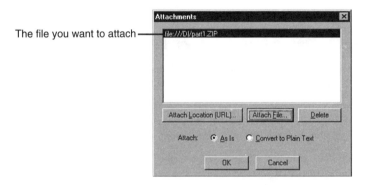

Figure 6.1 Select the file you want to attach to your message.

6. (Optional) Repeat steps 4 and 5 to attach additional files to your message.
7. Click the **As Is** option button and click **OK**. You're returned to the Message window. The name of your file appears in the Attachment text box.
8. (Optional) To include a message (information about the file's contents, for example), type it in the message area.
9. Send the e-mail in the usual manner.

Just as you can send a file, you can send a copy of the Web page you are currently viewing in Netscape Navigator. To do so, follow steps 1–3 above. Then click **Attach Location (URL)**, verify that the address you see in the box is the address of the Web page you want to send, and click **OK**. Then proceed with steps 6–9. To send the fully formatted Web page (so that the user can view it with Netscape or a similar Web browser), make sure you click **As Is** in step 7. To send the Web page as simple text, click **Convert to Plain Text** instead. After clicking **OK** in step 7, you'll need to wait a few minutes as Netscape captures the contents of the Web page you want to include. Once it's done (you can tell by looking at the status area at the bottom of the message window), then you can send your message.

Pictures, Too? When you send a Web page to someone, keep in mind that the graphics included in the page are not always sent with it. For better results, use Netscape to view the page first, and then send it using Netscape Mail.

CAUTION

Using a File Sent with a Message

If you receive a message with a uuencoded file attached to it, you have to use WinCode (or a similar program) to extract the file and decode it so it is ready to use. Of course, you also have to have the program you need to open the file. For example, if someone sends you an Excel spreadsheet file, you'll need a copy of Excel (or a program that reads Excel files) in order to open and use the spreadsheet.

If someone sends you a file using MIME or BinHex encoding, you'll need to retrieve that file using an e-mail program that supports MIME and BinHex. Fortunately, all Internet e-mail programs (including Netscape Mail) do.

When you receive a message with an attachment, it will look similar to the one shown in Figure 6.2. (If you received a uuencoded file, skip to the next section.)

To use the file, follow these steps:

1. Open the message that contains the file by clicking it.
2. Click the **Attachment** link. If a program is associated with this file's extension, then Netscape will automatically launch that program. The program will then display the contents of the file within its window.

Good Association You set up an association between a program and a particular file extension using options on the Helper tab of Netscape's General Preferences dialog box. See Part 4 Lesson 1 for details.

TIP

3. If no program is currently associated with the file's extension, you'll see the dialog box shown in Figure 6.3. Click the **Save File** button to save the file to the hard disk. Then select a directory in which to save the file and click **Save**. Once the file is saved to your hard disk, you can load the file into the appropriate program anytime you want.

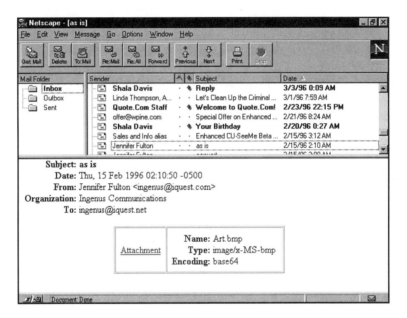

Figure 6.2   A file attached to an e-mail message.

Figure 6.3   You can save an unassociated file to the hard disk for later use.

If somebody sends you a uuencoded file in an e-mail message, it will look similar to the one shown in Figure 6.4. However, in order to be able to use the file, you'll have to get and install a good uuencoder, such as WinCode. (You can find WinCode and similar applications at the Stroud's site located at http://www.cwsapps.com.)

Figure 6.4   Use a uuencoding program to decode your file.

After installing WinCode, follow these steps to decode and save your attached file:

1. Open the message that contains the file by clicking it.

2. Click the **Attachment** link. The Save As dialog box (similar to the one shown in Figure 6.3) appears.

3. Click the **Save File** button, select a directory in which to save the file, and then click **Save**.

4. Start WinCode.

5. Open the **File** menu and select **Decode**.

6. Change to the directory that contains the uuencoded file.

7. Select the file you want to decode (see Figure 6.5).

8. Click **OK**, and WinCode decodes the file. You can load it into the appropriate program for use.

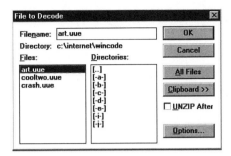

Figure 6.5   Select the file you want to decode.

In this lesson, you learned how to attach files to Netscape Mail messages and how to open files attached to messages you receive.

Netscape Plug-Ins and Helper Applications

Using In-Line Plug-Ins and Helper Apps

In this lesson, you'll learn the difference between in-line plug-ins and helper applications.

What Is a Plug-In?

A *plug-in* is a special program that extends the capabilities of Netscape Navigator. For example, you can add plug-ins that enable you to visit virtual reality Web sites to listen to live radio broadcasts over the Net or to carry on a near-to-live "conversation." There are many plug-ins for Netscape that you can download from various sites throughout the Internet—you'll learn how to download the most popular plug-ins in upcoming lessons. Once you download a plug-in and install it, Netscape uses the plug-in's capabilities as if it were built-in. Figure 1.1 shows a document Netscape can display with the help of a plug-in called Acrobat Amber Reader.

Plug-ins can work in one of three ways: embedded in a Web page frame, expanded to fill the whole Netscape window, or hidden from view (running in the background). A lot of plug-ins work either in hidden or in full window mode, as you'll see in upcoming lessons. However, regardless of which mode a plug-in uses, its functions appear fully integrated to you, the user. In other words, you don't have to learn any special commands to use the plug-in; once you install it, the plug-in's capabilities become a part of Netscape.

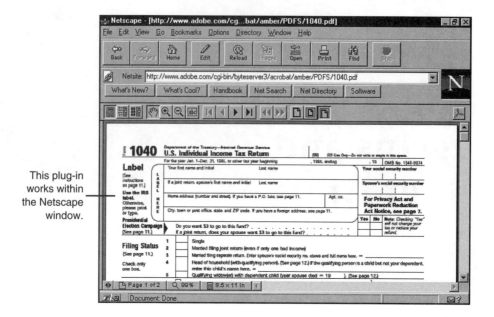

This plug-in works within the Netscape window.

Figure 1.1   A plug-in like Acrobat Amber Reader extends the capabilities of Netscape.

Installing Plug-Ins

Plug-ins are designed to work seamlessly with Netscape Navigator. Because of that, installing plug-ins is as simple as installing Navigator. You'll find the details for downloading and installing specific plug-ins in upcoming lessons.

Twins?   Many programs are available in both a plug-in and a helper app format. When selecting which format to use, keep this in mind: a plug-in works invisibly—within the Netscape window—so it might be easier to use and understand. However, helper apps are more versatile, because you can use them with any compatible file (outside of Netscape).

Keep in mind that if you have a plug-in (such as Live3D) and a helper app (such as WebSpace) that both handle the same file type (such as vrml), Netscape will use the plug-in before it will use the helper app. To tell Netscape to use the helper app instead, you have to uninstall the plug-in.

For now, here are the basic steps that you'll need to follow to install a plug-in:

1. Open File Manager or Explorer and double-click the plug-in file. The installation program starts.

2. Follow the on-screen instructions.

3. At some point during installation, you'll be asked to select the directory in which Netscape is stored (see Figure 1.2). You might want to create a new directory within the /Netscape/Plugins directory, in order to keep all your plug-ins in one place. In any case, select the directory you want to use and click **OK** to return to the main dialog box. Setup copies the plug-in's files into its directory.

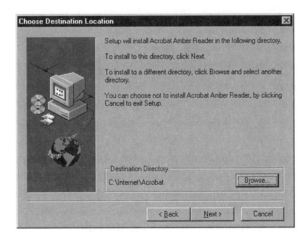

Figure 1.2   You can change the directory into which the plug-in is installed.

4. When you see a message telling you that installation is complete, click **OK**.

As you can see from these steps, you do not have to do anything to tell Netscape that the plug-in exists. The installation process takes care of any configuring that's necessary. So once the plug-in is installed, it's ready to use. Anytime you point Netscape to a file type that the plug-in supports, Netscape automatically calls on the plug-in's capabilities to display the file's contents.

Popular Plug-Ins to Try

As you'll see in upcoming lessons, there are many popular plug-ins for Netscape Navigator. This section tells you about some of the more popular plug-ins you might want to try.

CAUTION

Which Windows?   Keep in mind that some of these plug-ins are available only for Windows 95, and not for Windows 3.1.

TIP

Where Do I Get the Plug-Ins?   Although most of these plug-ins are covered in upcoming lessons (including how to download and install them), some, because of their limited applicability, are not. The location of these programs is noted in the description so you can download them if you like.

Acrobat Amber Reader by Adobe   This version of the popular Acrobat Reader lets you view, navigate, and print Portable Document Format (PDF) files within the Navigator window. PDF is a format used over the Internet to produce printer-independent, formatted documents that can be reprinted at the user's end *exactly* as they were created. Acrobat Amber Reader is located at http://www.adobe.com/Amber/Download.html.

ASAP WebShow by Software Publishing Corporation   With WebShow, you can view and print graphically rich reports and presentations created with ASAP WordPower. ASAP WebShow is located at http://www.spco.com/asap/asapwebs.htm.

Astound Web Player by Gold Disk   This plug-in plays multimedia documents created using Astound or Studio M, which can include sound, animation, graphics, and video. Some documents are even interactive! And Astound Web Player is fast because it downloads each slide in the background while you're viewing the one before it. Astound Web Player is located at http://www.golddisk.com/awp/index.html.

Carbon Copy/Net by Microcom   With Carbon Copy/Net, you can control a remote PC through the Internet, running applications, copying and deleting files, and even editing documents—just as if you were using your own PC. (The remote PC must also have Carbon Copy/Net installed and must be ready to receive your call.) With Carbon Copy/Net, you can provide remote support for your product, perform demos in remote locations, and access remote resources such as programs and data. Carbon Copy/Net is not available for Windows 3.1. Carbon Copy/Net is located at http://www.microcom.com/cc/ccdnload.htm.

Chemscape Chime by MDL Information Systems   Whether you're a scientist or just interested in science, you can use Chemscape Chime to view 2-D and 3-D chemical structures within an HTML page or table. Chemscape is located at http://www.mdli.com/chemscape/chime/download.html.

CoolFusion by Iterated Systems   With CoolFusion, you can view standard video (AVI) files almost live, using a process called *streaming*, in which the video file appears as it's being received (without a time-gap). CoolFusion is not available for Windows 3.1. CoolFusion is located at http://www.iterated.com/coolfusn/download/cf-loadp.htm.

CMX Viewer by Corel   You can use CMX Viewer to view vector graphics. CMX Viewer is not available for Windows 3.1. CMX Viewer is located at http://www.corel.com/corelcmx/.

Crescendo PLUS by LiveUpdate   This plug-in enables you to listen to MIDI files without a time-delay, using a process called *streaming*. Crescendo PLUS is located at http://www.liveupdate.com/midi.html.

DWG/DXF Plug-In by SoftSource   With DWG/DXF Plug-In, you can view AutoCAD (DWG) and DXF drawings *dynamically*. This means that you can manipulate them by panning or zooming the drawing, and hiding or displaying layers—right on the Web page! DWG/DXF Plug-In is not available for Windows 3.1. DWG/DXF Plug-in is located at http://www.softsource.com/softsource/lpugins/npdwg32.exe.

EarthTime by Starfish Software   EarthTime displays the local time and date for eight geographic locations—all within the Netscape window. With its animated map, you can also see which countries around the world are in daylight and which are in darkness at the current point in time. This can be helpful if you're doing Internet business with people all over the world. EarthTime is not available for Windows 3.1. EarthTime is located at http://www.starfishsoftware.com/getearth.html.

Envoy by Tumbleweed Software   You can view documents created with Envoy software exactly as they were designed—complete with multiple fonts, graphics, and complex layouts. Envoy is located at http://www.twcorp.com/plugin.htm.

FIGLeaf Inline by Carberry Technology/EBT   FIGLeaf Inline provides expanded graphic support for CGM, GIF, JPEG, PNG, TIFF, CCITT GP4, BMP, WMF, EPSF, Sun Raster, RGB, and other popular formats. FIGLeaf Inline also enables you to rotate images 90, 180, 270, or 360 degrees, and to view multipage files. FIGLeaf Inline is not available for Windows 3.1. FIGLeaf Inline is located at http://www.ct.ebt.com/figinline/download.html.

Formula One/NET by Visual Components   With Formula One/NET, you can create Excel-compatible spreadsheets with live charts, buttons and controls, and links to URLs. Formula One/Net is located at http://www.visualcomp.com/f1net/download.htm.

Fractal Viewer by Iterated Systems   This plug-in enables you to view fractal images (such as digitized photographs) that have been compressed using Iterated's Fractal Image Format. You can zoom, stretch, flip, and rotate images, and specify the amount of image detail you prefer. Fractal Viewer is located at http://www.iterated.com/fracview/download/fv-loadp.htm.

InterCAP Inline by InterCAP Graphics Systems   You can use InterCAP Inline to view, zoom, pan, magnify, and animate Computer Graphics Metafiles (CGM) vector graphics. InterCAP Inline is not available for Windows 3.1. InterCAP Inline is located at http://www.intercap.com/about/DownloadNow.html.

KEYview For Windows by FTP Software   With this plug-in, you can view, print, convert, and manage nearly 200 different file formats (including Microsoft Word, WordPerfect, Microsoft Excel, EPS, PCX, and even compressed files) from inside Netscape Navigator. KEYview For Windows is not available for Windows 3.1. KEYview For Windows is located at http://www.ftp.com/mkt_info/evals/choice.html.

Lightning Strike by Infinet Op   You can use Lightning Strike to compress your Web pages. Lightning Strike is located at http://www.infinop.com/html/extvwr_pick.html.

Live3D by Netscape   Live3D is probably the best Virtual Reality (VR) viewer because it's designed by Netscape. Live3D is located at http://comprod/products/navigator/live3D/download_live3D.html.

Look@Me by Farallon   With this plug-in, you can view a remote Look@Me user's screen through the Net in *real time*. (You can't, however, control the other PC remotely.) This is great for reviewing presentations or providing training and support. Look@Me is not available for Windows 3.1. Look@Me is located at http://collaborate.farallon.com/www/look/download.html.

MovieStar by Intelligence At Large   This plug-in enables you to view QuickTime movies in Netscape. MovieStar is not available for Windows 3.1. MovieStar is located at http://www.beingthere.com.

OLE Control by NCompass   With OLE Control Plug-In, you can embed OLE controls in your Web pages as applets. OLE Control Plug-In is not available for Windows 3.1. OLE Control is located at http://www.excite.sfu.ca/Ncompass/nchrome.html.

OpenScape by Business@Web   You can create interactive Internet applications with OpenScape and Visual Basic. OpenScape is not available for Windows 3.1. OpenScape is located at http://www.busweb.com/download/f_down.html.

PreVU by InterVU   With PreVU, you can watch MPEG videos in almost-live mode, using a process called *streaming*. (Streaming enables you to view a video file even while it's still being downloaded.) PreVU is not available for Windows 3.1. PreVU is located at http://www.intervu.com/download.html.

QuickServer by Wayfarer Communications   QuickServer enables you to create high-performance intranet and Internet apps using QuickServer and Visual Basic, PowerBuilder, C++, or Java. QuickServer is not available for Windows 3.1. QuickServer is located at http://www.wayfarer.com/demonstration/index.htm.

QuickSilver by Micrografx   With QuickSilver, you can view and edit object-oriented graphics created with Micrografx products. QuickSilver is not available for Windows 3.1. QuickSilver is located at http://www.micrografx.com/office/offdownload/offdownload.html.

QuickTime   This plug-in makes it possible for you to experience multi-media video and sound in a near-live format. QuickTime is located at http://www.apple.com.

RealAudio by Progressive Networks   With RealAudio, you can listen to live or on-demand audio files in real-time. RealAudio is located at http://www.realaudio.com.

Shockwave for Director by Macromedia   Shockwave for Director enables you to view multimedia presentations created with Director. Shockwave for Director is located at http://www.macromedia.com.

Sizzler by Totally Hip   You can view Sizzler animations before they are completely downloaded, using a process called *streaming*. Sizzler is located at http://www.totallyhip.com/sizzler/6_sizz.html.

SVF Plug-In by SoftSource   With this plug-in, you can view SVF images such as CAD drawings and other complex graphics. You can pan and zoom an SVF image, and you can hide and display layers. SVF Plug-In is not available for Windows 3.1. SVF is located at http://www.softsource.com/softsource/plugins/npsvf32.exe.

ToolVox by Voxware   ToolVox enables you to add high-quality real-time audio to your Web pages. ToolVox is located at http://www.voxware.com/download.htm.

VDOLive by VDONet   This plug-in lets you view VDO compressed video images *fast*. VDOLive is located at http://www.vdolive.com/download/.

VR Scout by Chaco Communications   This plug-in enables you to play VR (Virtual Reality) worlds. VR Scout is not available for Windows 3.1. VR Scout is located at http://www.chaco.com/vrscout/plug.html.

VRealm Browser by Integrated Data Systems   This is another VR (Virtual Reality) viewer. VRealm Browser is located at http://www.ids-net.com/ids/downldpi.html.

Wavelet Image Viewer by Summus   With Wavelet Image Viewer, you can quickly view Wavelet graphic images, and you can control the amount of detail Netscape shows. Wavelet Image Viewer is located at http://www.summus.com/download.htm.

WIRL by VREAM   This plug-in is a VR (Virtual Reality) viewer. WIRL is not available for Windows 3.1. WIRL is located at http://www.vream.com/3dl1.html.

Word Viewer Plug-In by Inso Corporation   You can use Word Viewer Plug-In to view, copy, or print any Microsoft Word 6.0 or Microsoft Word 7.0 document on the Web. Word Viewer Plug-In is not available for Windows 3.1. Word Viewer Plug-In is located at http://www.inso.com/plug.htm.

What Is a Helper Application?

A helper application is like a plug-in, in that it also extends the capabilities of Netscape. However, a helper application goes about it in a different way.

Unlike a plug-in, whose functionality interacts seamlessly with Netscape (so much so that the plug-in almost seems to be built into Netscape), a helper application works independently of Netscape. A helper application specializes in handling specific file types, such as ZIP or WAV files, for example. When Netscape encounters one of these file types, it launches the appropriate helper app and lets it display what's in the file. The helper app then deciphers and displays the contents of the file inside its own window—*not* within the Netscape window (see Figure 1.3). You might think of this process in terms of football: when the quarterback (Netscape) runs into trouble, he passes the ball to the wide receiver (the helper app), who then carries it into the end zone.

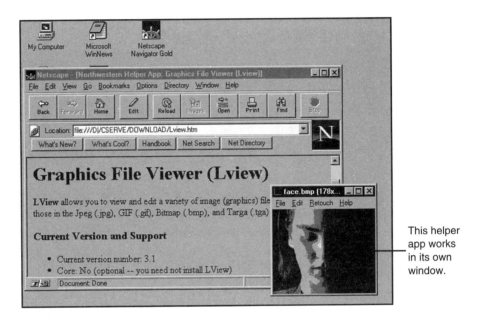

This helper app works in its own window.

Figure 1.3 A helper app displays the contents of the file in its own window.

Because a helper application runs in its own window, it can be used separately from Netscape. This flexibility allows you to use the helper application in other scenarios. For example, you can install WinZip as a helper app so that Netscape automatically launches it whenever it encounters a zipped (compressed) file. You can then view the contents of the zipped file before you download it. But because WinZip is not integrated into Netscape, you can also use it independently to zip and unzip your own files.

Which to Choose? Some plug-ins discussed in the upcoming lessons are also available as helper applications. Remember that a helper app can be used independently of Netscape, and it might contain some additional features that can prove useful. Taking that into consideration, choose the type of program (in-line plug-in or helper app) that best suits your needs.

You can even use a helper app in place of Netscape's viewer. For example, Netscape is perfectly capable of displaying simple graphic images such as JPEG, GIF, and XBM files. If you want to be able to manipulate those images, though, you might prefer to use a helper app such as LView instead.

Installing Helper Apps

Netscape can understand many file types, including HTML (the format used on most Web pages) and the graphic file types JPEG, GIF, and XBM. To display the contents of other file types, Netscape requires the expertise of a helper app.

On the Internet, each file is identified by its MIME type. MIME (Multipurpose Internet Mail Extensions) is a system that organizes various file types into groups, listing similar file types together as the same MIME type. Netscape keeps a list of MIME types in its Preferences dialog box.

When Netscape attempts to display a file, it first looks at the file's MIME type. If the MIME type is one that Netscape itself can handle, the process continues as usual. If Netscape determines that the MIME type is associated with a particular helper app, Netscape automatically launches that helper application and turns the file over to it for display.

CAUTION

What If I Don't Install a Helper App?   If Netscape encounters a file type that it can't handle, and for which you have not assigned a helper app, it displays an error message asking you what you want to do. You can choose to install the helper app at that time, to not display the file, or to save the file to your hard disk for viewing at a later time.

How does Netscape know when you've installed a helper app for a particular file type? Netscape keeps track of MIME types in its Preferences dialog box. There you'll see a list of the various MIME types and the helper applications (if any) that are associated with them (see Figure 1.4). To let Netscape know that you want it to launch a certain helper app when it encounters a particular file type, you need to add the name of your helper app in the appropriate place on this list.

Sometimes, the helper app's installation program takes care of the process of adding its name to this list. Other times, you have to do that manually.

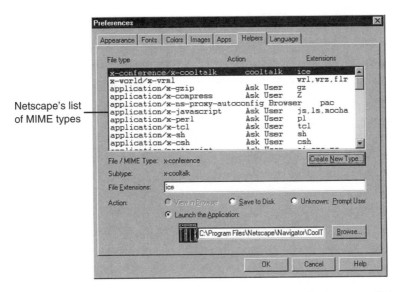

Netscape's list of MIME types

Figure 1.4 Netscape keeps track of MIME types in its Preferences dialog box.

The specifics for installing many popular helper apps are covered in upcoming lessons. But this gives you an idea of the general steps you must follow to install a helper app to the MIME list manually.

1. Use the helper app's install program to copy its file onto your PC's hard disk.

2. Start Netscape (you do not need to connect to the Internet).

3. Open the **Options** menu and select **General Preferences.**

4. Click the **Helpers** tab.

5. In the **File type** list, select the file type you want to associate with the helper app (see Figure 1.4).

CAUTION

Missing Type If you don't see the file type you need, you can add it by clicking the **Create New Type** button, entering the **MIME Type** (such as video, audio, image, or application), entering the **MIME** Subtype (such as RealAudio or QuickTime), and clicking **OK**.

6. If necessary, add additional file extensions to those listed in the **File Extensions** text box. (Separate file extensions with a comma.)

7. Click **Launch the Application**.

8. Click **Browse**, select the program's starter (executable or .EXE) file, and click **Open**.

9. Click **OK**. The next time Netscape encounters a file with the extension(s) you specified, it will pass that file to the associated helper app for viewing.

Popular Helper Apps to Try

You'll learn about several helper apps in upcoming chapters, but for now, here are a few of the more popular ones:

Where Do I Find These Helper Apps?   A lot of these helper apps are covered in upcoming lessons (including how to download and install them). However, some, because of their limited applicability, are not covered. The location of these programs is noted in the description so you can download them if you like.

Acrobat Reader   This older version of the Acrobat Amber Reader by Adobe enables you to view and print Portable Document Format (PDF) files in a separate window. Acrobat Reader is located at ftp:// ftp.adobe.com.

AVI Pro   This helper app plays MPEG video clips with AVI Pro. AVI Pro is located at ftp://gatekeeper.dec.com/pub/micro/msdos/win3/ desktop/avipro2.exe.

eShop Plaza   With eShop Plaza, you can shop on the Internet within a secured environment (so nobody can steal your credit card numbers). eShop Plaza is located at http://www.eshop.com/test-plaza/s_2.cgi.

GhostScript   You can print PostScript documents on a non-PostScript printer. GhostScript is located at ftp://ftp.cs.wisc.edu/pub/ghost/.

LView Pro   With this helper app, you can view many types of graphic files, including JPEG, BMP, TRG, PCX, PGM, PPM, PBM, TIFF, and GIF files. LView Pro is located at http://world.std.com/~mmedia/lviewp.zip.

Netscape Chat   Netscape Chat is one of many IRC (Internet Relay Chat) clients. With Netscape Chat, you can carry on a typed conversation with one (or several) friends over the Internet. Netscape Chat is located at ftp://ftp20.netscape.com/pub/chat/.

Netscape SmartMarks   This helper application enables you to organize and update your bookmarks with automatic updates. Netscape Smart-Marks is located at http://www.firstfloor.com/form-bin/evalform16.

MPEGPlay MPEGPlay enables you to view MPEG video files with MPEGPlay. MPEGPlay is located at ftp://gatekeeper.dec.com/pub/micro/msdos/win3/desktop/.

PolyView for Win95 You can view a variety of graphic files, including BMP, GIF, JPEG, PNG, and TIFF files with PolyView for Win95. PolyView is located at http://solid.inav.net.

QuickTime With QuickTime, you can experience incredible multimedia video and sound in a near-live format. QuickTime is located at http://www.apple.com.

RealAudio This helper app enables you to listen to live or on-demand audio files presented in real-time on the Net. RealAudio is located at http://www.realaudio.com.

TrueSpeech With TrueSpeech, you can listen to near-live audio transmissions over the Internet. TrueSpeech is located at http://www.dspg.com.

VMPEG Lite You can view MPEG video files with VMPEG Lite. VMPEG Lite is located at ftp://papa.indstate.edu/winsock-l/Windows95/Graphics.

WebSpace WebSpace enables you to visit 3-D worlds with this VR (virtual reality) viewer. WebSpace is located at http://www.sd.tgs.com/~template/WebSpace.

WHAM Use WHAM to play and edit audio files, such as AU, AIFF, IFF, VOC, and WAV files. WHAM is located at ftp://gatekeeper.dec.com/pub/micro/msdos/win3/sounds/wham133.zip.

WinCode WinCode handles all your e-mail encoding needs, including MIME, uuencoding, and BinHex. WinCode is located at http://www.globalone.net/users/snappy/snapp/index.html.

WinZip WinZip compresses and decompresses zipped (PKZIP) and LHArc files. WinZip is located at ftp://ftp.winzip.com.

WPlany WPlany is a simple sound player that plays AU, IFF, SND, VOC, and WAV sound files. WPlany is located at ftp://ftp.ncsa.uiuc.edu/Mosaic/Windows/Viewers.

In this lesson, you learned the difference between in-line plug-ins and helper applications. You also learned the names of many popular plug-ins and helper apps you might want to try. In the next lesson, you'll learn how to download and install Netscape Chat, a popular IRC (Internet Relay Chat) helper application.

Netscape Chat

L E S S O N 2

In this lesson, you'll learn how to install and use the Netscape Chat helper application.

What Is Netscape Chat?

Netscape Chat is one of several popular IRC (Internet Relay Chat) clients. With it, you can carry on a conversation with one or several persons over the Internet by simply typing what you want to say. Using Netscape Chat is similar to participating in the chat rooms you typically find on popular online services such as America Online, CompuServe, The Microsoft Network, and Prodigy.

You might be thinking, "So what's the big deal? How is that any different from sending an e-mail message?" Well, with Netscape Chat, you can experience near-to-live conversations in which you type messages and replies on-screen and the other person sees your answer almost immediately. Chatting on the Internet is like a cross between e-mail and conventional long-distance, but it's much more economical than a phone call. For the cost of a relatively cheap Internet connection, you can talk to your friends in Italy or to a coworker in Japan.

Because even the low cost of textual conversation might not be enough to sell some people on Internet Relay Chat, Netscape Chat takes this model one step further. Netscape Chat enables you to share not only textual conversations with your coworkers, but also multimedia files such as a sound file, graphics file, or video file. You can even share Web pages and their contents with your coworkers or friends. For example, you can send someone a copy of a particular Web page, or a graphics file, or whatever, and then have a discussion about it.

CAUTION

Can She Use the File?   The recipient must have a means of displaying the contents of any file you send. For example, if you send a graphics presentation file, the recipient must have a copy of a graphics presentation program such as PowerPoint in order to use the file.

To use Netscape Chat, you connect to a *chat server*, which processes the on-going conversations. If you're in a private conversation with another person, your transmissions are routed between only the two of you. If you're carrying on a conversion in a chat room, your transmissions are copied and sent along to other occupants of the room. You can enter several chat rooms at once (to carry on simultaneous conversations) if you want. Conversations within each room appear in separate windows.

TERM

Chat Room   You enter into a conversation on a chat server by opening a channel called a chat room. Conversations carried on within an individual room are copied to everyone else on the same channel (in the same room).

Downloading Netscape Chat

In this section, you'll download Netscape Chat from its FTP site. You can use an FTP program such as WS_FTP, or you can use Netscape Navigator. I find that using my Web browser is much easier than using an FTP program, so that's how I do it.

TIP

Not Freeware   Netscape Chat, like many software programs you'll find on the Internet, is shareware. Shareware works under the concept of "play before you pay." If you decide to keep Netscape Chat after trying it out, you need to register it and pay a small fee. Use the **Help**, **Registration** command to register Netscape Chat.

To download a copy of Netscape Chat, follow these steps:

1. Connect to the Internet and start Netscape.
2. Type **ftp://ftp20.netscape.com/pub/chat** in the **Location/Go to** text box and press **Enter**.
3. Click the file you want to download. The Windows 3.1 file includes the number **16**; the Windows 95 version includes the number **32** (see Figure 2.1).

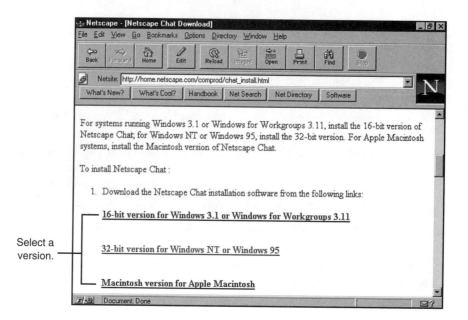

Select a
version.

Figure 2.1 Select the version of Netscape Chat that you want to use.

Read All About It If you want to read about Netscape Chat (or any other IRC client) before you download it, click the **Full Review** link at the top of the left column.

4. Select the folder into which you want to download Netscape Chat. (You might want to download your file into a TEMP directory so you can check it for possible viruses. See Part 1 Lesson 17 for help.)

5. Click **Save**. You can watch the progress of the download. When it's done, you're returned to the Stroud's Web page.

6. Close Netscape Navigator and disconnect from the Internet so that you won't waste online time while you set up Netscape Chat.

Installing Netscape Chat

After you've downloaded a copy of Netscape Chat, you have to install it. Follow these steps to install the 32-bit (Windows 95) version of Netscape Chat:

CAUTION

Windows 3.1 Users If you are installing the 16-bit Windows 3.1 version of Netscape Chat, note that these steps will vary a bit. For example, when you double-click the downloaded file, the setup program does not begin automatically. Instead, the zipped file expands into the current directory. Once it's expanded, you'll see a file called SETUP.EXE. Double-click that file to begin installation.

1. Open Explorer and change to the directory that contains the Netscape Chat file.

2. Double-click the Netscape Chat file.

3. You'll see a warning message telling you that you're about to install Netscape Chat. Click **Yes** to continue. The file expands, copying its contents into the current directory.

CAUTION

All Mixed Up? Unless you want the Netscape Chat files mixed in with other files in the current directory, you should move the downloaded file into its own directory (such as Chat) before you expand it.

4. The installation program starts. Click **Next>** to continue.

5. The Choose Destination Location dialog box appears, giving the name of the directory into which Netscape Chat will be installed (see Figure 2.2). To use the suggested directory, click **Next>**. To change the directory, click the **Browse** button, select another directory, click **OK**, and then click **Next>**.

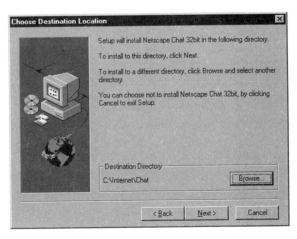

Figure 2.2 Choose the directory into which Netscape Chat is installed.

6. The Netscape Chat files are copied to the hard disk. When you see a message asking if you would like to review the README.TXT file, click **Yes**. A text editor opens and displays the README.TXT file, as shown in Figure 2.3.

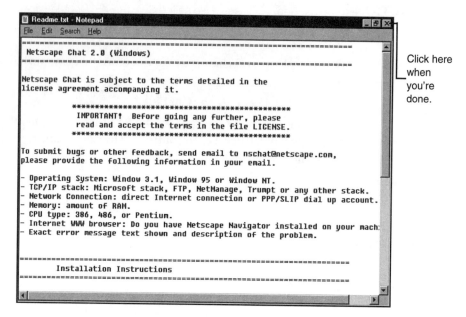

Click here when you're done.

Figure 2.3   It's always a good idea to review the README.TXT file.

7. Close the text file when you finish reviewing it.

8. When setup is complete, you'll see a message telling you so. Click **OK**.

Configuring Netscape Chat as a Helper Application

Well, you're about halfway there. Now that Netscape Chat is installed, you need to configure it as a helper application. To do that, follow these steps:

1. Start Netscape Navigator. (You don't need to connect to the Internet.)

2. Open the **Options** menu and select **General Preferences.**

3. Click the **Helpers** tab.

4. Click **Create New Type**, and the Configure New Mime Type dialog box appears, as shown in Figure 2.4.

Figure 2.4   You can configure Netscape Chat as a helper app.

5. Enter **application** in the **Mime Type** text box, and enter **x-nschat** in the **Mime SubType** text box. Click **OK**, and you're returned to the Preferences dialog box.

6. In the **File Extensions** text box, type **nsc**.

7. Click **Browse**.

8. In the dialog box that appears, change to the Netscape Chat directory, select the **NCHPER.EXE** file (if you use Windows 3.1) or the **NSCHAT.EXE** file (if you use Windows 95), and click **Open**.

9. In the Preferences dialog box, click **OK**.

Netscape Chat Basics

Once you've installed Netscape Chat, it's pretty much ready to go. But before you jump in, you need to locate either a Netscape Chat server or an IRC server to which to connect. (You'll need an exact address of a chat server in order to get Netscape Chat up and running.) Luckily, Netscape provides a list of the more popular ones, as shown in Table 2.1.

Table 2.1   Popular IRC and Netscape Chat Servers

Country	Address	Port
United States	iapp.netscape.com	6667
United States	davis.dal.net	7000
United States	groucho.dal.net	7000
United States	skypoint.dal.net	7000
United States	cin.dal.net	7000
United States	xanth.dal.net	7000

Country	Address	Port
United States	mindijari.dal.net	7000
United States	uncc.dal.net	7000
United States	phoenix.dal.net	7000
United States	austin.tx.us.undernet.org	6667
United States	manhattan.ks.us.undernet.org	6667
United States	milwaukee.wi.us.undernet.org	6667
United States	pittsburg.pa.us.undernet.org	6667
United States	sanjose.ca.us.undernet.org	6667
United States	rochester.mi.us.undernet.org	6667
United States	tampa.fl.us.undernet.org	6667
United States	washington.dc.us.undernet.org	6667
United Kingdom	liberator.dal.net	7000
Finland	xgw.dal.net	7000
Europe	caen.fr.eu.undernet.org	6667
Europe	gothenburg.se.eu.undernet.org	6667
Europe	oxford.uk.eu.undernet.org	6667
Canada	montreal.qu.ca.undernet.org	6667

Before you start, you need to learn one more thing. You will find group rooms (in which everyone talks to everyone else) and auditoriums (in which you talk to the moderator, who gives you permission to speak if appropriate). You can also carry on a private conversation with someone in a chat room if you like.

Now you're ready to chat. Follow these steps:

1. Connect to the Internet.
2. Start Netscape Chat. The Server Connection dialog box appears, as shown in Figure 2.5.
3. In the **Host** text box, type the address of the chat server you selected. (The address of Netscape's chat server is iapp.netscape.com, if you want to use that.)

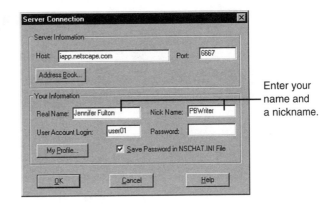

Enter your
name and
a nickname.

Figure 2.5 The Server Connection dialog box.

Changing Servers Later To display this dialog box later, start Netscape Chat, open the **File** menu, and select **Connect**.

4. In the **Port** text box, enter the port for the chat server you selected. (The port for Netscape's chat server is 6777.)

For Future Reference You can save your favorite chat servers in the Address Book. To do so, click the **Address Book** button, and then enter the address and port of the server you want to save. Use a colon to separate the address and the port number (as in davis.dal.net:7000). Click **Add** to add the address. Once you have entries in your Address Book, you can use them by clicking the **Address Book** button in the Server Connection dialog box, selecting the server you want to use, and clicking **OK**.

5. Type your real name in the **Real Name** text box.

6. Type a nickname in the **Nick Name** text box. You'll be known to others by this nickname, not by your real name.

7. If you know that the server to which you plan to connect requires a login id and a password, enter the information you were given.

8. Click **OK**.

9. After you connect to the chat server, the Quick Join dialog box appears (see Figure 2.6). To join the newbie room, click **Join**. To see a list of other rooms, click **List**.

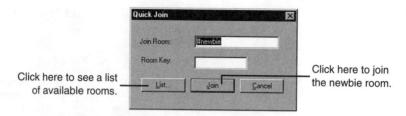

Click here to see a list of available rooms.

Click here to join the newbie room.

Figure 2.6 The Quick Join dialog box.

10. Select a room or auditorium from those listed, and click **Join**. The room window for the selected conference appears.

Be Creative! You can create your own room (conference) by typing a name for the conference in the **Join Room** text box and clicking **Join**. To invite someone to join you, click the **People** button, select someone from the list, and click **Invite**.

TIP

What's the Key? Some rooms (conversations) are private and require a key. If you know the keyword and want to join, enter the keyword in the **Room Key** text box before you click Join.

CAUTION

11. Chat your life away. For details on *how* to chat, see the next section.

12. To leave a room, open the **Commands** menu and select **Leave Room**.

13. You'll see a message asking if you want to save a transcript of the conversation. Click **Yes** or **No**. The transcription file is saved to the Netscape Chat directory.

Carrying On a Conversation

When you enter a room, you see a room window similar to the one shown in Figure 2.7. A list of participants appears in the left panel. The conversation stream appears in the large panel, and the name of the person speaking appears in brackets (as in <Jennifer>).

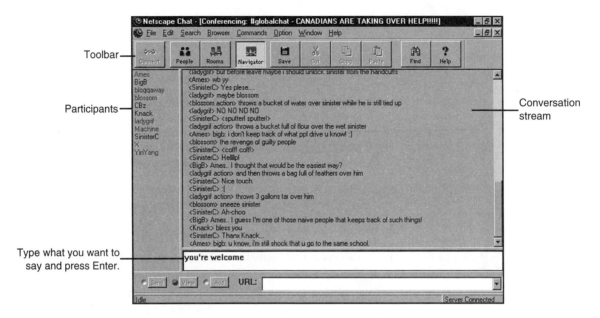

Toolbar

Participants

Conversation stream

Type what you want to say and press Enter.

Figure 2.7 A room window.

To enter into the conversation, type your message in the lower panel and press **Enter**. When you press Enter, Netscape Chat sends your comment to everyone in the room, and it appears in the conversation stream. To send a message to one particular person only, select his or her name from the list before you press Enter.

Only in Moderation When you enter an auditorium, you can only speak to the moderator. If you want to address the audience, you must ask permission. To do that, send a message to the moderator, and then open the **Privilege** menu and select **Request Microphone**. If the moderator grants your request, a microphone appears next to your nickname.

Keep in mind that comments appear in the order in which they are received. Usually, by the time something is said and you comment on it, several additional comments have appeared. This makes following the gist of the conversation a bit difficult at first. For this reason, you may want to observe the conversation for a few minutes before you join in.

Sometimes it's easier to follow a conversation if you ignore some of the people in the group. If you want to ignore someone, right-click that person's name and select **Ignore** from the shortcut menu.

Sending a Web Page To send a Web page to the participants of a conversation, enter the URL (address) of the Web page in the **URL** text box at the bottom of the window and click **Send**. (You can use Netscape Navigator first to locate a particular Web page if necessary.) To send a Web page to a particular person, select that person from the list before you click Send.

Usually, Web pages that are sent to you are automatically displayed. To manually view a Web page whose address appears in the URL toolbar, select it from the URL list and click the **View** button.

If you want to carry on a private conversation, click the **Show People** button in the Chat toolbar. Select a person from the list and click **Talk**. A Personal Conversation window opens, and you can chat in the usual manner. To end the conversation, open the **Commands** menu and select **Leave Room**.

In this lesson, you learned how to use the Netscape Chat helper application. In the next lesson, you'll learn how to use Acrobat Amber Reader.

Acrobat Amber Reader

In this lesson, you'll learn how to use Acrobat Amber Reader.

What Is Acrobat Amber Reader?

Acrobat Amber Reader is the plug-in version of the popular Adobe Acrobat helper application. You can use either program to view and print PDF (Adobe Portable Data Format) files. PDF allows documents to be saved in a way that preserves their text formatting, such as fonts, text enhancements (bold, italics, and so on), columns, tables, graphs, and such. Once a file is converted to PDF format, it can be downloaded and printed on any printer, exactly as the creator intended it to look.

You'll find PDF files at many Web sites, such as the FedWorld site (where you can download PDF versions of any IRS tax form) and the PC Week site (where you can download a version of the magazine in PDF format.) But to view and print a PDF file, you'll need a copy of Acrobat. In this lesson, I'll show you how to download and install Acrobat Amber Reader (an in-line plug-in). If you prefer a helper application instead, you could download and install Adobe Acrobat.

Downloading Acrobat Amber Reader

There are many places on the Internet from which you can download Internet software, such as Acrobat Amber Reader. So, if you run into trouble downloading from the Acrobat site, you can try a general software site such as Stroud's or Tucows, as explained in Part 1 Lesson 11. You can use an FTP program to download software, or you can use Netscape Navigator. Usually, using Netscape is much easier than using an FTP program, so that's what I use.

Nothing's Free   Acrobat Amber Reader is similar to many software programs that you find on the Internet, in that it's shareware. Shareware works under the concept of "play before you pay." If you decide to keep Acrobat Amber Reader after trying it out, you need to register it and pay a small fee. See the README.TXT file included with the other program files for more information.

To download a copy of Acrobat Amber Reader from the Acrobat site, follow these steps:

1. Connect to the Internet and start Netscape.

2. In the **Location/Go to** text box, type **http://www.adobe.com/acrobat/amber/download.html**. Then press **Enter**.

3. Scroll down the page until you find the version of Acrobat Amber you need, and read about Acrobat's system requirements.

4. When you're ready to download the file, click the **Download** link (see Figure 3.1).

Click here to download.

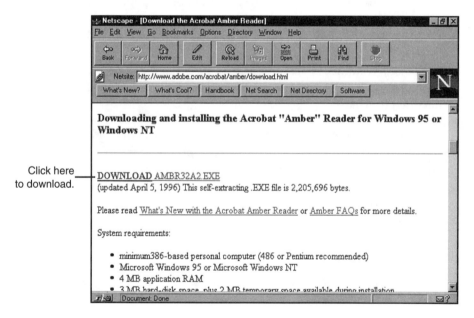

Figure 3.1   Select the version of Acrobat Amber Reader you want to download.

5. Select the folder (directory) into which you want to download Acrobat Amber Reader. (You might want to download the file into a TEMP directory, where you can check it for possible viruses before installing it.)

6. Click **Save**, and the download begins. When the download is complete, you're returned to Acrobat's Web page.

7. Close Netscape Navigator and disconnect from the Internet so you don't waste online time while you set up Acrobat Amber Reader.

Installing Acrobat Amber Reader

After you've downloaded a copy of Acrobat Amber Reader, you need to install it. Follow these steps to install the 32-bit (Windows 95) version of Acrobat Amber Reader.

CAUTION

Windows 3.1 Users When installing the 16-bit Windows 3.1 version of Acrobat Amber Reader, you'll find that these steps vary a bit. For example, when you double-click the downloaded file, the setup program might not begin automatically. Instead, the zipped file expands into the current directory. After it has expanded, you'll see a file called SETUP.EXE. Double-click that file to begin installation.

1. Open Explorer and change to the directory that contains the Acrobat Amber Reader file.

2. Double-click the **Acrobat Amber Reader** file.

3. You'll see a warning message telling you that you're about to install Acrobat Amber Reader. Click **Yes** to continue. The file expands, copying its contents into the current directory.

CAUTION

All Mixed Up? Unless you want the Acrobat Amber Reader files mixed in with other files in the current directory, you should move the downloaded file into its own directory (such as Amber) before you expand it.

4. The installation program starts. Click **Next>** to continue.

5. Read the Adobe license agreement and click **Yes** to continue.

6. By default, Acrobat Amber Reader is installed in the directory called /Acrobat/Reader. To use the suggested directory, click **Next>** (as shown in Figure 3.2). To change the directory, click the **Browse** button, select another directory, click **OK**, and then click **Next>**. For example, you might want to place all your plug-ins in separate subdirectories under the /Netscape/Plugins directory (as in /Netscape/Plugins/Amber).

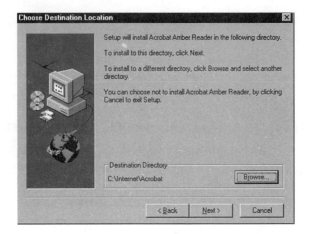

Figure 3.2 You can change the directory into which Acrobat Amber Reader is installed.

7. The Acrobat Amber Reader files are copied to the hard disk. You'll see a message asking if you would like to review the README.TXT file. To do so, leave the **Display Acrobat Amber Reader Readme** check box selected, as shown in Figure 3.3.

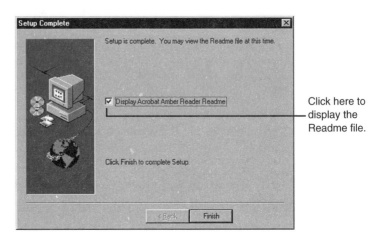

Click here to display the Readme file.

Figure 3.3 Be sure to review the README.TXT file.

CAUTION

Can't Find Netscape Navigator If setup can't find the directory into which you've installed Netscape, you'll get an error message. If that happens, select the correct directory and click **Next>**.

8. Click **Finish**. If you chose to view the Readme file in step 7, it appears now.

9. Close the Readme file when you finish reviewing it.

10. You'll see a message telling you that setup is complete. Click **OK**.

That's it! Acrobat Amber Reader is installed and linked to Netscape Navigator.

Acrobat Amber Reader Basics

Because Acrobat Amber Reader is a plug-in application, it works invisibly with Netscape. When you encounter a PDF file on a Web page, Netscape automatically turns over the problem of displaying that file to the Acrobat Amber plug-in. The contents of the file appear within the Netscape window (see Figure 3.4).

Acrobat Amber works within the Netscape window.

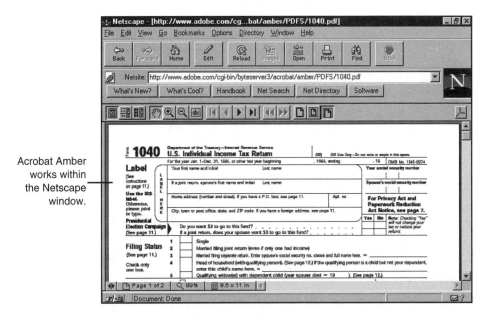

Figure 3.4 Acrobat Amber Reader displays the PDF file within the Netscape window.

To test your new plug-in, you'll need to find a PDF file. Adobe has a test site you can visit (http://www.adobe.com/acrobat/amber/amexamp.html) that has links to many PDF documents. To try out Acrobat Amber Reader on the Adobe test site, follow these steps:

1. Connect to the Internet and start Netscape Navigator.

2. Type the address **http://www.adobe.com/acrobat/amber/amexamp.html** in the **Location/Go to** text box and press **Enter**.

3. Click the link of a file you want to view as shown in Figure 3.5. A small file like the IRS 1040 form is perfect for our example. Acrobat Amber Reader displays the tax form in the Netscape window.

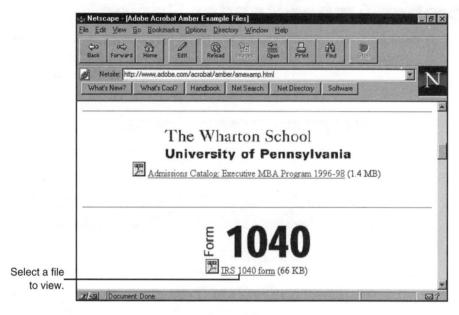

Figure 3.5 The Acrobat Amber Reader test site.

4. (Optional) Use the buttons on the toolbar (see Figure 3.6) to print, zoom, or page through the file as necessary.

5. When you finish viewing or printing the file, don't close the window; it's the Netscape window, and doing so will close Netscape. Instead, move to a different Web site by using the Back or Forward button or by entering a new URL in the Location/Go to text box.

Zoom in Move from page Display Make document fit
and out to page 100% view in window

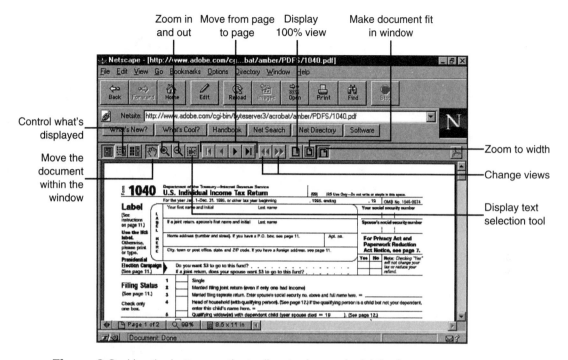

Control what's
displayed

Move the
document
within the
window

Zoom to width

Change views

Display text
selection tool

Figure 3.6 Use the buttons on the toolbar to view and print the form.

I Want to Keep a Copy! The PDF file is *not* copied to your PC's hard disk
when you display it. If you want to keep a copy of the file, you must open the
File menu, select **Save As**, and click **Save** to save the file. If you use Windows
95, you can also right-click and select **Save As** from the shortcut menu.

In this lesson, you learned how to install and use the in-line plug-in Acrobat
Amber Reader. In the next lesson, you'll learn how to install and use Shockwave
for Director.

Shockwave for Director by MacroMedia

In this lesson, you'll learn how to get Shockwave and how to use it to view multimedia presentations over the Web.

What Is Shockwave?

Shockwave is a plug-in created by MacroMedia, whose Director program is the leading tool for putting together multimedia presentations. With Director, you can combine still pictures, animations, and sounds, and include point-and-click interaction. If you play CD-ROM-based adventure games or use a CD-ROM reference program, odds are good that you've been using a Director presentation.

Shockwave lets you view Director presentations over the Web. (You *don't* need a copy of Director, unless you want to design your own presentations.) A Web site designed for use with Shockwave can present video and sound without your having to request each animation and sound file. It also allows you to use more complex interactivity than simple HTML links allow.

Downloading Shockwave

You can download Shockwave from MacroMedia's Web site by following these steps:

1. Type **http://www.macromedia.com/Tools/Shockwave/sdc/Plugin/ index.html** in Netscape's **Location/Go to** text box and press **Enter**. This takes you to the Macromedia Cool Tools Web site.

2. Click the Plug-In Center link to open the Plug-In Center Web page, which describes the Shockwave plug-in. Then scroll down the page to the drop-down list box for selecting an operating system (see Figure 4.1). Click the drop-down arrow and select your operating system from the list.

Select your operating system from this drop-down list.

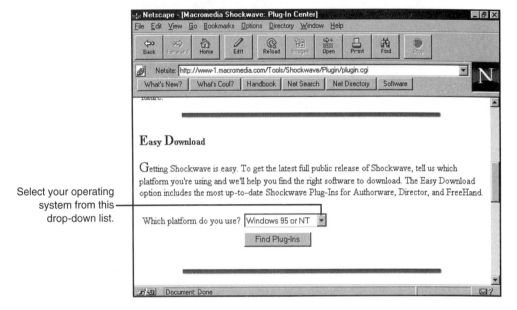

Figure 4.1 Scroll down the page to locate the platform drop-down list.

3. Click the Find Plug-Ins button.

4. The Web page that appears next is a license agreement form. It contains standard legal information that comes with many software programs. Click the Accept button to continue.

5. On the next Web page that appears, scroll down until you see a list of sites from which you can download Shockwave (see Figure 4.2) and click one of those sites.

The Road Less Traveled You're usually better off *not* clicking the first one. Many people automatically click the first one, which quickly becomes tied up and slows down the site.

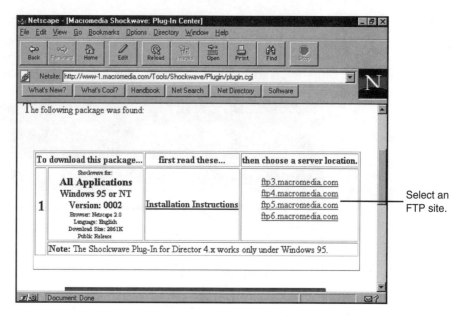

Figure 4.2 Choose an FTP site to download the program from.

6. From the Save As dialog box shown in Figure 4.3, choose a temporary directory in which to store the downloaded file (you probably have one named C:\TEMP or C:\TMP). Then click the **Save** button, and the download begins.

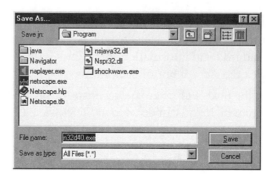

Figure 4.3 Choose a destination for the downloaded file.

7. When the download is complete, you're ready to install the program. Close Netscape and disconnect from the Internet.

Installing Shockwave

The Shockwave program you downloaded in the previous section actually contains three Shockwave plug-ins: Shockwave for Director, Shockwave for Authorware, and Shockwave for Freehand. Work through the steps in the next section to extract the setup files for all three plug-ins. In the rest of this lesson, however, we'll focus on configuring and using only the Shockwave for Director plug-in.

Crowded Disk?   When you need to clear some disk space, you should always look in your TEMP directories for files that have been there for some time and that you no longer need.

Extracting the Setup Files

To extract the setup files, follow these steps:

1. In Windows 95, click the **Start** button and select the **Run** command. In older versions of Windows, pull down File Manager's **File** menu and select the **Run** command.
2. Click the **Browse** button to navigate your file system.
3. Locate the directory with the downloaded file in it, and click the name of the file.
4. Click the **Open** button to return to the Run dialog box.
5. Click **OK** to start the installation, and the WinZip Self-Extractor dialog box appears (see Figure 4.4).

Figure 4.4   Type the path to your temporary directory in this dialog box.

6. Type the path for your temporary directory in the **Unzip To Directory** text box and click **Unzip** (see Figure 4.4).

7. The names of the installation program files appear at the bottom of the WinZip dialog box as they are unzipped. When they've all been extracted, a smaller dialog box appears telling you how many files were unzipped. Click **OK**, and then click the **Close** (X) button.

Running the Setup Program

When you finish extracting the files, you need to run the setup programs to finish installing Shockwave. Each plug-in has its own setup file and will have to be installed separately. In this lesson, we'll concentrate on setting up and using Shockwave for Director. However, you can follow these same steps to run the setup programs for the other plug-ins.

It's a good idea to read the README.TXT file that you unzipped in the previous steps before you finish installing. You'll find the file in the temporary directory where you unzipped the files (Windows 95 users can just double-click the README file name in Windows Explorer). If that file contains any specific new directions that differ from these, the steps in the README file supersede any of these given to you here.

Follow these steps to run the Setup program for shockwave for Director:

1. In Windows 95, click the **Start** button and select the **Run** command. In older versions of Windows, pull down File Manager's **File** menu and select the **Run** command.

2. Click the **Browse** button, and locate the temporary directory to which you saved the extracted Shockwave files. You'll find three files there—one for each plug-in. Open the Director folder and select the **SETUP.EXE** file.

3. Click the **Open** button to close the Browse dialog box. Then click **OK** in the Run dialog box to run the setup program. The installation program starts.

4. First you'll see a dialog box full of boring legal stuff. Read this (you don't want to agree to something without knowing what you're agreeing to!) and click **Yes** to continue the installation.

5. When the next screen of information appears, click the **Next** button. You'll see a dialog box in which the Install Shockwave Director and Read README.TXT option boxes are checked (see Figure 4.5).

6. Click the **Read README.TXT** box to remove the check mark.

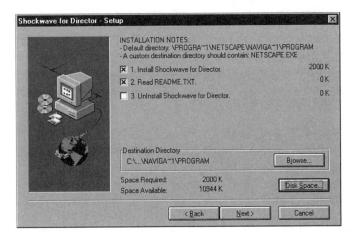

Figure 4.5   Choose a destination directory for the Shockwave plug-in.

7. Then click the **Browse** button, and the Choose Directory dialog box appears (see Figure 4.6).

Figure 4.6   Specify the directory you keep Netscape in.

8. In the Choose Directory dialog box, select the drive and directory in which your Netscape program (NETSCAPE.EXE) is stored and click **OK**. (The setup program needs this information to know where to put certain files so Netscape can find them.) You're returned to the main dialog box.

9. Click the **Next** button. The setup program starts putting the files in place, and a meter appears, displaying the progress of the installation.

10. When the installation is complete, the message **Completed the installation** appears in a dialog box. Click **OK**. Now Shockwave for Director is ready to go!

Shockwave Basics

Shockwave enables you to see multimedia presentations with sound, video, and point-and-click interactivity. To help you understand this better, let's check out one such presentation. Follow these steps.

1. In Navigator's **Location/Go to** text box, type the URL **http:// www.macromedia.com/Gallery/Shockwave/Credits/2lane.html** and press **Enter**. This opens a page from Macromedia's interactive gallery (see Figure 4.7).

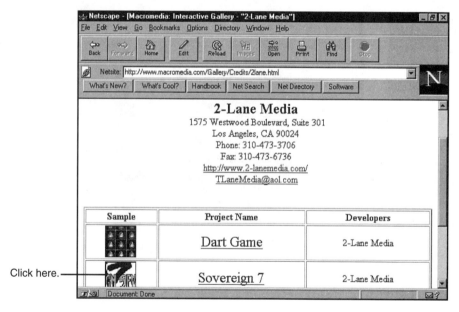

Figure 4.7 Choose a Shockwave presentation from this Web page.

2. Click the **Sovereign 7** link or graphic, and a page with a large Sovereign 7 logo appears.

3. Click the logo. A large frame displays a MacroMedia log while the presentation downloads to your hard disk (it will be stored in your Netscape

Cache directory). The status bar keeps you up-to-date on how much has downloaded so far. (This particular presentation is approximately 350K.) When the download is complete, the presentation starts.

4. A short animated ad for Sovereign 7 (a comic book series) appears in the frame, and then the animation stops to display the image shown in Figure 4.8. Move your mouse pointer across the image, and notice that when it passes over each character, that character's name appears in the bottom center of the image.

Figure 4.8   The cast of characters for Sovereign 7.   Click on this character.

5. Click on the guy eating hamburgers in the lower-right corner of the picture. A description of the character appears (see Figure 4.9). Click the **S7** logo in the upper-left corner to return to the bar scene.

6. Click the arrow in the lower-left part of the frame, and your view pans across the bar until you see a whole other group of characters in another part of the bar.

7. Click the **Exit** sign at the left side of the image, and the presentation restarts.

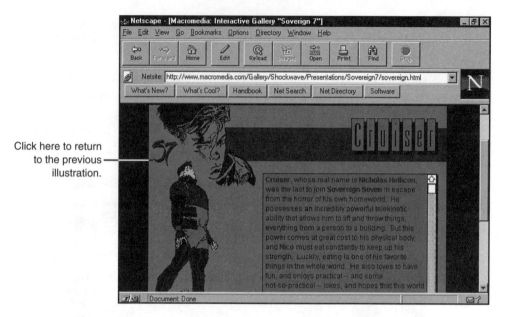

Click here to return to the previous illustration.

Figure 4.9   Get the inside story on Sovereign 7's characters.

If clicking Exit doesn't get you out of the presentation program, how do you leave it? The answer is that you don't really have to, any more than you have to leave the viewer that displays a GIF picture on a Web page. This presentation is just part of the Web page. So you can use any of the standard Netscape tools to move to another page, or you can log off of the Web and quit Netscape altogether.

This is just a very simple Shockwave presentation. Much more complex things are possible with Shockwave, including arcade games, short movies, and more! And be sure to install the other Shockwave plug-ins (Shockwave for Authorware and Shockwave for Freehand) for a greater selection of Web presentations.

Save on Connect Charges   While some Shockwave presentations link to other presentations, most are self-contained. Once the presentation is downloaded to your hard disk, you can disconnect from the Web and continue viewing the presentation without running up your Internet bill!

Shockwave Sites

You can find a number of good Shockwave presentations by starting from the MacroMedia Gallery page, or you can look them up in the directory at http://www.macromedia.com/Tools/Shockwave/Gallery/Vanguard/directory.html. In addition, you might want to try some of the pages listed in Table 4.1.

Table 4.1 Pages with Shockwave Content

Site	URL
Astro game astro.html	http://www.pineapple.co.jp/tango/astro/
Daily Tortoise game	http://www.sirius.com/~jtaylor/shockwave/shockwave.html
Demolition Graphics	http://www.halcyon.com/flaherty/movie1.html
Eadweard Muybridge	http://www.linder.com/muybridge.html
Art Exhibit Educational Demos	http://www-leland.stanford.edu/~dmiller/
Etch-A-Sketch toy simulator	http://members.aol.com/dkimura/etch.html
FaceMaker	http://users.aol.com/jrbuell2/ShockFace.html
Fortune Cookie	http://www.nets.com/lebow/fortune.html
Gary Rosenzweig's Arcade	http://www2.csn.net/~rosenz/shock.html
Hollywood Online	http://hollywood.com/movies/shocked.html
Kids Web	http://www.pacificcolor.com/gary/
Michael's Haunted House	http://yip5.chem.wfu.edu/yip/haunted_house/mhhmain.html
Nando.net games	http://www2.nando.net/nandox/shock.html
Paper Circus	http://www.em.com/circ.htm
Pop Rocket games	http://www.poprocket.com/shockwave/
Toru's Arcade	http://sharedcast.hccs.cc.tx.us/toru.htm
Tulane University guide	http://www.bentmedia.com/bentmedia/dtulane/Shockwave.html
Velma Apparelizer	http://headbone.com/text/dressvelshock.html
Virtual Drums	http://www.cybertown.com/virtdrum.html

In this lesson, you learned how to download, install, and view a presentation with Shockwave. In the next lesson, you'll learn about the VDOLive plug-in.

VDOLive by VDONet

In this lesson, you'll learn how to get the VDOLive plug-in and use it to view video displays over the Web.

What Is VDOLive?

VDOLive is a plug-in created by VDONet. Its goal is to allow you to view movies that you might find on some Web sites. VDONet lets you see these movies in real-time so you don't have to wait for them to download before you can start watching them. This not only makes for faster viewing, it also limits the amount of open disk space you need for a long movie.

VDONet claims that their product can receive 10 to 15 frames per second on a standard 28,800 bps modem—an impressive rate. For a Web site to provide a VDOLive movie, it must have VDONet's server software, which the owner has to pay for. However, the viewing software is free and is available over the Web (as are most plug-ins).

Downloading VDOLive

You can download VDOLive from VDONet's Web site, using the following steps:

1. Connect to the Internet and start Netscape.
2. In the **Location/Go to** text box, type **http://www.vdolive.com/download/** and press **Enter**.
3. Click the **VDOLive Video Player** link, as shown in Figure 5.1.

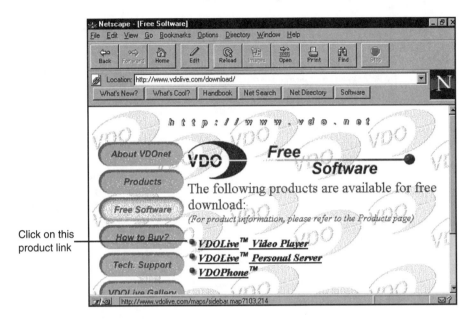

Click on this
product link

Figure 5.1 The VDOLive page has several products you can download, including VDOLive Video Player.

4. The next Web page lists the available product platforms. Click the product version you want to download, such as Windows 95 (see Figure 5.2).

5. On the next Web page, you'll find a short list of FTP sites from which to download the software. Click the name of the site you want to use.

6. In the Save As dialog box that appears, choose a temporary folder or directory to store the downloaded file in (such as a TEMP directory). Click **OK**, and the download begins. (Be sure to note the name of the file you're downloading and the directory or folder you're saving it to. You'll need both names later to install VDOLive.)

7. When the download is complete, close or minimize Netscape Navigator and disconnect from the Internet.

You're now ready to install the plug-in. It's always a good idea to log off the Internet while you install programs so you don't waste valuable online time.

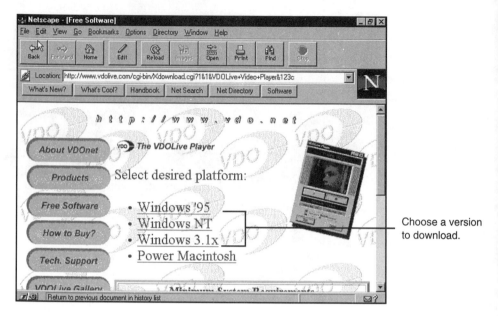

Figure 5.2   Choose a version of VDOLive that will work with your computer.

Installing VDOLive

You can run theVDOLive program directly to install the software. Unlike other plug-ins, it does not need to be dearchived (or extracted) first. Follow these steps to install VDOLive:

1. In Windows 95, click the **Start** button and select the **Run** command. In older versions of Windows, pull down File Manager's **File** menu and select the **Run** command.

2. Click the **Browse** button and locate directory with the downloaded file in it. Then click the name of the file.

3. Click the **Open** button to return to the Run dialog box.

4. Click **OK** to start the program, and the opening screen appears.

5. Click **OK** in the Welcome! dialog box to start the installation.

6. The installation program locates your copy of Netscape and displays a dialog box indicating where it found that file. If, for some reason, you have multiple copies of Netscape on your computer and you want to install VDOLive on a different version, select the directory that houses that version now. Otherwise, click **OK**.

7. When the license agreement appears, read it over. (Yes, it's boring, but using this software indicates that you agree to the terms of this document—and it's good to know what you're agreeing to.) Click **OK** to continue.

8. VDOLive displays a dialog box asking for confirmation of your name and e-mail address (which it got from the Netscape registration file). Click **OK** to continue.

9. Another dialog box appears, asking where you want to put your VDOLive files (see Figure 5.3). This will default to some standard program file directory, but you probably don't want it there. It's a good idea to organize all your plug-ins in a subdirectory of the directory that contains Netscape. If you already have a plug-ins directory, select it, and a new directory called "vdoplay" is created in that directory. If you don't have a plug-ins directory, edit the **Destination Directory** field to include it (the end of your directory path should read **\Programs\plugins\vdoplay**), and a plug-ins directory is created for you. Click **OK**.

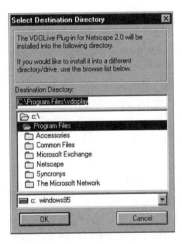

Figure 5.3   The VDOLive installer asks you to designate a location for the program files.

10. As files are copied to their appropriate directories, a meter shows you the progress. When all the files are in place, a dialog box asks you **Do you want to add icons to the Program Manager?** (For Windows 95 users, this means that they will be added to the Start menu.) Click **OK**.

You Might As Well...   Go ahead and have the icons added to Program Manager or the Start menu. You can always delete them later if you decide you don't need them.

11. Next the program asks which Program Manager group you want the icons in. If you want them in a new group, click **OK**. If you want to add them to an existing group, click the group name and click **OK**.

12. A final dialog box tells you that installation is complete.

If you check out the program group where you indicated the icons should go, you will find that you now have not only an icon for the player, but also an icon for uninstalling the program if you no longer need it, some sample HTML files, a Help file, and a Release Notes file. The Release Notes contain any additional information that you need about this revision of the software, so you should read them.

VDOLive Basics

Once you have VDOLive installed, it's time to start watching some videos! To test your new VDOLive Video Player, load up the demo page by selecting its icon or by opening the **Start** menu and clicking **VDOLive demo page**. You can also test the player by opening the **test.htm** file in the VDOLive folder or program group window. When the page loads, you'll see a little area on-screen with a test pattern image in it (see Figure 5.4).

After a few seconds, a line appears under the image saying **Connecting....** This indicates that the VDOLive player software on your system is connecting with the special VDOLive server software on the Web server. When the connection is established, this status line changes to **Requesting** and then **Loading...** as it preloads some information (it is *not* loading the whole video). A percentage counter tells you how much of that information is loaded.

When the counter hits 100%, the video begins. The status line splits into two parts: the left part displays how much time has passed in the video (in minutes and seconds), and the right side shows a reception level both as a percentage and as a colored meter. The more green on the meter or the higher the percentage, the more of the video you are getting. At lower percentages, the image is slightly jumpy. At very low percentages, you'll hear significant skips in the sound.

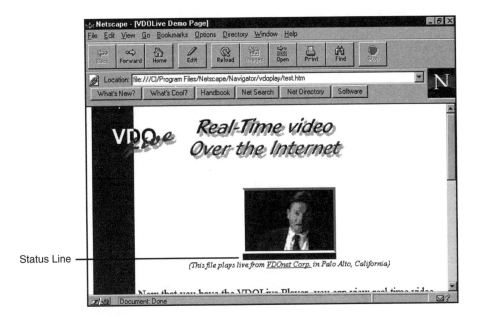

Status Line

Figure 5.4 The VDOLive demo page.

The limiting factor in watching the video is the communications speed. Theoretically, you should be able to get 100% reception from a 28,800 modem. If you're seeing significantly lower figures and you want to watch and listen to a certain video more cleanly, you might try viewing it at a time when the Internet and the server are likely to be less busy.

Some Videos Need a Nudge Not all VDOLive videos start automatically. For some you have to click the video display area to start them.

Setting Options

A site can contain two types of videos. One is *embedded*, which means that the video is included on an HTML page. The other is *stand-alone*, which means the page contains a link that points directly to the video. When viewing stand-alone videos, you can choose whether to view them using a separate VDOLive window or using a Netscape viewer. The VDOLive window is better because it gives you more control.

When you view an embedded video, you have easy access to a menu that lets you control the video and set the options for the VDOLive window. To set options for the VDOLive window, follow these steps:

1. Right-click on the video display area, and a menu appears.

2. This menu contains the commands Play (which starts a stopped video) Stop (which stops playing a video), Setup (which lets you set options), and About (which opens a window of information about your system). Select **Setup**, and the Setup dialog box shown in Figure 5.5 appears.

3. Click the **Show Session Statistics** box to put a check in it. When turned on, this replaces the reception display in the VDOLive window with more detailed information about how much video and audio is being lost.

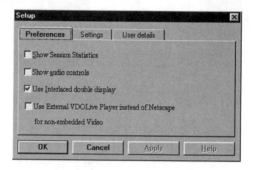

Figure 5.5 VDOLive's optional settings.

4. If you're using Windows 95, check the **Show audio controls** check box. Otherwise, leave it empty. When you check this box, volume controls appear in the VDOLive window—but the controls only work with Windows 95.

What Do I Do About the Third One?   The third option lets you control how the display is drawn when you ask to see the video double-sized. This is an option you can experiment with, but for the most part, you'll leave it as it is.

5. Put a check in the last option box to tell the system that you do want to use the VDOLive window for non-embedded videos.

6. Click **OK** to save these options and close the Setup dialog box.

Using the VDOLive Window

The VDOLive window is a complete console with a full set of easily accessible controls. This makes it a better choice to use for viewing movies that aren't embedded. Viewing it in a Netscape window may make the product seem more a part of Netscape, but it really doesn't gain you anything.

To view a sample video, follow these steps:

1. Enter **http://www.vdolive.com/vdofiles/hike2.vdo** in Netscape's **Location/Go to** text box and press **Enter**. The .vdo extension identifies this as a VDOLive video. A standard VDOLive background design appears in the Netscape window, and the VDOLive Player window opens, as shown in Figure 5.6.

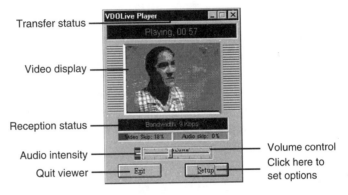

Figure 5.6 The VDOLive Player window.

2. When the connection is made, the video starts playing. Right-click on the transfer status to see a list of different status information you can display. Choose **Frames/Sec** to see just how often the image is being updated.

3. Double-click in the video screen. The window resizes itself, doubling the size of the image (see Figure 5.7). Notice that the image doesn't actually become more detailed when it gets larger, so the quality of the image degrades.

4. When you're done with the video window, click **Exit**

Figure 5.7   An enlarged image looks more grainy than a smaller one.

Figure 5.6 shows the video with the Session Statistics option on. Notice that you can see the actual data bandwidth (the higher the better, topping out at the speed of your modem) as well as the percentage of the video and audio being lost (the lower the better). Figure 5.7 shows the video with the Session Statistics option off. There you see just the reception percentage summary, like you saw on the embedded video.

Other VDOLive Sites

The number of VDOLive sites is growing rapidly. VDOLive seems to be popular with news and information organizations (as seen in Figure 5.8). However, other sites have more artistically oriented movies (such as Figure 5.9), and new sites are popping up all the time with other uses.

Still, VDOLive movies are not yet so common that you're likely to run into them while casually surfing the Web. Table 5.1 lists a handful of movies you might want to check out.

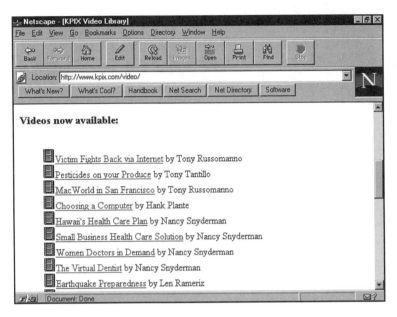

Figure 5.8 A menu of videos available from KPIX, San Francisco's TV Channel 5.

Figure 5.9 This is a shot from the video for David Broza's song "Together," which raises funds for Unicef, the United Nations Children's Fund.

Table 5.1   VDOLive Sites

Site	URL
Brainworks	http://www.brainworks.net
CBS Up To The Minute	http://uttm.com
Church of the SubGenius	http://bob.upx.net/slack
David Broza/UNICEF	http://www.vdolive.com/broza/broza.htm
Full Digital	http://urban1.fulldigital.com/vdo
Grolier's Club Internet	http://www.clubinternet.com/vdolive/index.html
Hollywood Network	http://www.hollywoodnetwork.com/vdolive
InterneXperts	http://www.InterneXperts.com
KPIX TV channel 5 (San Francisco)	http://www.kpix.com/video/cnet.vdo
Marshall	http://www.marshall.com/pub/tis/dsp/pdc80.htm
netradio	http://www.netradio.net/video.html
netvideo	http://www.netvideo.com/netvideo/netstream.html
NowTV	http://NowTV.com
phuture.com	http://www.phuture.com/vdo.html
Postering	http://www.ran.es/postering
Preview Vacations	http://www.vacations.com/Multimedia/VDOLive
Sawyer Brown	http://www.acton.com/country/sawyerbrown.html
Talk 101	http://www.talk-101.com
WCVB NewsCenter 5	http://wcvb.com/aw/tv5/page/tv5/video
Yard Productions Inc.	http://www.yrd.com/yrd/vdos/

In this lesson, you learned to download and install VDOLive and use it to view video clips. In the next lesson, you will learn about the EarthTime plug-in.

EarthTime by Starfish Software

In this lesson, you'll learn how to get EarthTime and how to use it to check the time in different places of the world.

What Is EarthTime?

EarthTime is a plug-in from Starfish software that provides a quick way of checking the time in other parts of the world—which can be very handy if you're involved in international communication over the Web. There's also a built-in database of information about international cities, which you can use to pull up their populations, their locations, or other vital information quickly. It also offers quick conversion between various types of measurements (converting miles to meters, for example).

The full registered version of EarthTime costs $19.95. Before you shell out those shekels, however, you can download a free trial version that will work for a month. EarthTime is also available as part of another program from Starfish called Sidekick '95.

Downloading EarthTime

You can download the trial version of EarthTime from Starfish's Web site, using the following steps:

1. Start Netscape, type **http://www.starfishsoftware.com/getearth.html** in the **Location/Go to** box and press **Enter**.

2. Read through the Starfish Web page. At the top is information on purchasing the full version. Toward the bottom, you'll find a list of sites from which you can download the trial version file (see Figure 6.1). Click one of the listed sites.

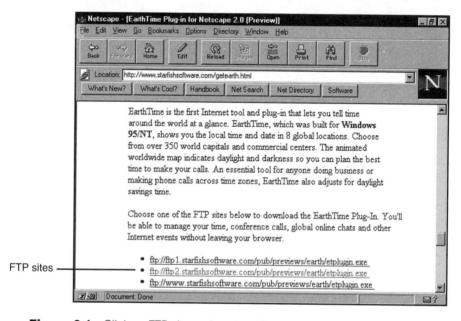

Figure 6.1   Click an FTP site to download EarthTime.

3. Netscape displays the Save As dialog box shown in Figure 6.2. Choose a temporary directory to store the downloaded file in (you probably have one named C:\TEMP or C:\TMP).

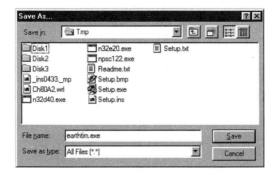

Figure 6.2   Choose a location on your hard drive for the downloaded file.

4. Click the **Save** button, and the download begins. The file name will be etplugin.exe. A meter appears, indicating the progress of the download; when the download is complete, the meter disappears.

This file is one megabyte in size. Under ideal conditions, it will take approximately 10 minutes to download using a 14,400bps modem. During the Internet's usual busy times, you can expect it to take 15–20 minutes. Of course, it will take less time with a faster modem and more with a slower one.

Installing EarthTime

The earthtim.exe file that you downloaded is an installation program. To run it, follow these steps:

1. Exit Netscape and make sure that you do not have any browser windows open. Exit any other programs that you do not need running.

2. If you're using Windows 95 or Windows NT 4, click the **Start** button and select the **Run** command.

If you're using Windows NT 3.51, open Program Manager's **File** menu and select the **Run** command.

3. In the Run dialog box, click the **Browse** button to navigate your file system.

4. Using the Browse dialog box (shown in Figure 6.3), locate the directory that contains the downloaded file and click the name of the file.

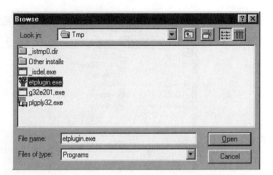

Figure 6.3   Locate the etplugin.exe file and select it.

5. Click the **Open** button to return to the Run dialog box, and click **OK** to start running the installation program.

6. When the Starfish Installation Launcher window asks **Do you want to continue?**, click **OK**. You'll see a couple of progress meters as the program breaks the etplugin.exe program into a number of smaller files needed for the installation and performs some additional setup tasks.

7. Eventually, the Welcome Setup window appears. Click **Next** to continue.

8. The User Information dialog box (see Figure 6.4) asks for your name and company name. The program might have already filled in one or both of these fields with information it got from Windows. Fill in the fields, if necessary, and click **Next**.

It's Required!   You cannot continue with the installation until there is something in both the Name and the Company fields.

CAUTION

9. Select a program folder for the EarthTime icons. By default, the program creates a new folder for them. If you want them in any other folder, click that folder name. Click **Next**.

10. A Software Licensing Agreement dialog box appears. If you continue to install the software, you're agreeing to this, so you should read it over. When you finish it, click **Yes**.

11. Another dialog box appears, asking you to verify the location of both your Netscape plug-ins folder and your choice of program folders. Click **Next**, and the actual installation begins.

Figure 6.4 The User Information dialog box.

12. First a meter appears, showing you the progress of the installation. Then you'll see the Setup Complete dialog box. Leave the check boxes as they are, and click **Finish**.

13. An editor or word processor opens and displays a README file. Read its contents, and then close the editor. You should now see the EarthTime Plug-in icon on your desktop (see Figure 6.5).

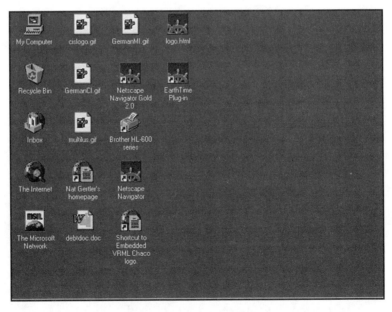

Figure 6.5 The EarthTime icon appears on your desktop.

EarthTime Basics

Double-click the **EarthTime Plug-in** icon on your desktop to start Netscape and automatically start EarthTime. Notice that because all of the information is on your hard disk, you don't have to make an Internet connection. When EarthTime starts, it displays a dialog box letting you know how much of your 30-day trial is left. Just click the **OK** button to get past that.

The first time you start EarthTime, you'll see the dialog box shown in Figure 6.6. EarthTime displays the time for eight cities at once. You pick those cities from the EarthTime Settings dialog box using the controls listed below.

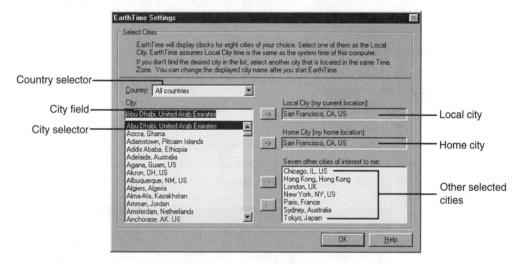

Figure 6.6   The EarthTime Settings dialog box.

- **Country**   Select a country from the **Country** drop-down list. (Which country you select determines which cities will appear in the City drop-down list. If you select "All countries," every city in the database will be listed in the City list.)

A Shortcut   You don't have to scroll to the country or city you need. With the list open, type the first letter in the name of the country or city you want, and the list moves directly to the countries or cities that start with that letter.

- **City**   Type the name of the city you want, or click the **City** drop-down arrow to see an alphabetical list of cities and click the city you want. The selected city appears in the City field.

Can't Find a City?   If you cannot find the city you're looking for, pick a nearby city in the same time zone.

- **Local City**   This field contains the name of whatever city you're nearby now. Click the right arrow (->) next to **Local City** to copy the city from the City field to this field.

- **Home City**   This field contains the name of the city you consider home. (If you're not traveling, this should be the same as the Local City.) Click the right arrow (->) next to **Home City** to copy the city from the City field to this field.

- **Seven other cities...**   This area lists the selected cities you want EarthTime to display clocks for. To add the city in the City field to this list, click the right arrow button (**->**). To remove a city from this list, click the city's name and click the left arrow button (**<-**).

The OK button remains grayed out until you pick enough cities because EarthTime must display eight cities at a time. When you've picked eight cities, click the **OK** button. EarthTime displays the times for those cities in a screen similar to Figure 6.7. The bright area of the map is the part of the world where it is currently daytime, and the dark area is where it's night.

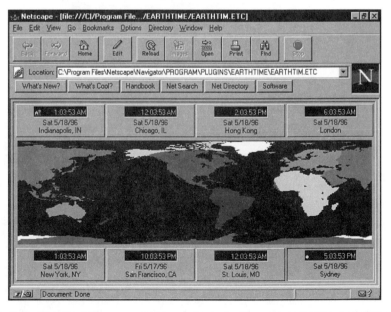

Figure 6.7   The EarthTime screen shows times for the selected cities and shows you where it is currently daytime.

273

Your home city should be in the horizontal center of the map. However, you can change that focus. Right-click anywhere on the map and select **Center map here** from the shortcut menu. EarthTime redraws the map, using the point you clicked as the center.

One of the clocks above or below the map has a picture of a person on it; that represents your local city's clock. Similarly, one clock has a house on it; that represents your home city's clock. In addition, some of the clocks might show little diamonds, which means that the city is currently under daylight savings time.

Changing City Settings

Right-click one of the clocks, and you'll see a menu like the one shown in Figure 6.8. This shortcut menu contains controls you can use to change the city on the clock, to make it the local or home city, to make it the map's center, or to change the look of the clock.

Figure 6.8   This shortcut menu lets you change settings for the selected city.

Viewing Facts About a City

You can right-click a clock and select the **Facts about the City** command to learn about the selected city. EarthTime displays a dialog box like the one in Figure 6.9. This includes information that is fairly permanent (such as the city's native language and form of currency), as well as calendar-related information such as sunrise and sunset times for a given day.

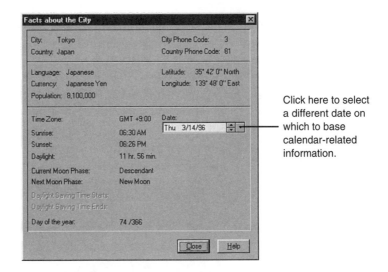

Click here to select a different date on which to base calendar-related information.

Figure 6.9 You can view facts about the selected city.

When this dialog box first appears, all of the calendar-related information is for the current day. However, you can use the date-selection tools to pick another date. For example, you might change the date so you can find out what the phase of the moon will be on Halloween or when daylight savings time starts in Denmark in 1998.

What If Eight Isn't Enough? If you need information for a city you don't have a clock for, right-click any clock, select the **Change City** command, select the city you want, and click the **Facts about the City** button. Once you have the facts you need, click the **Close** button and then the **Cancel** button. The clock still displays the city it originally did!

Converting Measurements

You can also use EarthTime to convert measurements that are relevant in one part of the world to measurements that will work in another. For example, you might want to know how many kilometers are equal to 37 miles.

To use the measurements conversions, follow these steps:

1. Right-click any clock.

2. Select the **Conversions** command from the menu.

3. The Conversions dialog box appears (see Figure 6.10). Click the **Categories** drop-down arrow and select the type of measurement you're working with. (For example, if you want to figure out how many kilometers there are in 37 miles, select **Length**.)

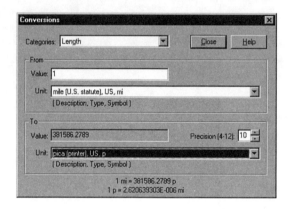

Figure 6.10 EarthTime's conversion feature.

4. In the From section, type the value you know into the **Value** field. (In this example, you would type **37**.)

5. Click the **Unit** drop-down arrow and select the units for that value (such as **miles**).

6. In the To section, click the **Unit** drop-down arrow and select the unit you want to convert to (such as **kilometers**). The number you are looking for immediately appears in the To section's Value field!

Marking EarthTime If EarthTime looks like a handy tool that you'd like to use often, press **Ctrl+D** to create a bookmark. Then, anytime you're using Netscape, EarthTime is available from your Bookmarks menu!

In this lesson, you learned how to download and use the EarthTime plug-in. In the next lesson, you learn about TrueSpeech.

TrueSpeech
by DSPG

In this lesson, you'll learn how to get TrueSpeech and how to use it to listen to audio recordings over the Web.

What Is TrueSpeech?

TrueSpeech is a program that enables you to listen to recorded audio over the Web. Although Netscape has a built-in audio player, it requires you to download the whole sound file before you can listen to it. With TrueSpeech, however, you listen to the audio as it arrives, which is much better for long recorded pieces. Because it uses compressed audio files, the files can usually be transferred as quickly as they are read and there's less of a chance of the Net falling behind, causing a gap in the sound.

The TrueSpeech player program is currently available on an indefinite trial basis. The version currently available combines both a helper and a plug-in. Some sites will require the plug-in, which shows its controls as part of the Web page. Most sites, however, will *only* work with the helper, which opens a separate window for the audio controls. It's good that most sites are set up to work with the helper, which gives you a better set of controls than the plug-in.

To use TrueSpeech, your computer will need a Windows-compatible sound card and speakers (or headphones).

Downloading TrueSpeech

You can download TrueSpeech from DSPG's Web site, using the following steps:

1. View the Web page at **http://www.dspg.com/allplyr.htm** using Netscape. On this page, you will find buttons for downloading versions of TrueSpeech for different operating systems (see Figure 7.1).

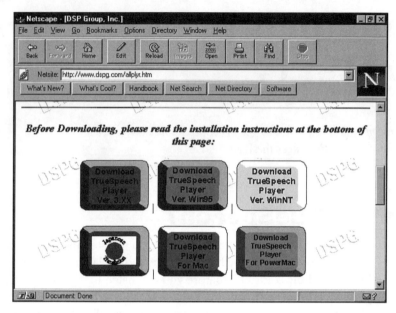

Figure 7.1   Choose the version of TrueSpeech that works with your operating system.

2. Click the button that corresponds to your operating system. This takes you to a page with some installation instructions.

3. Once again, click a button to indicate your operating system.

4. Look over the legal agreement for the software at the top of the next page. Below that (on the form shown in Figure 7.2), fill in your name, e-mail address, and any other information you want DSPG to have.

5. When you finish filling in the form, click the **Download Software** button. Netscape displays the Save As dialog box (see Figure 7.3). The file name will be something like TSPLY95.EXE.

6. Choose a temporary directory to store the downloaded file in (you probably have one named C:\TEMP or C:\TMP), and click the **Save** button. The download begins. A meter appears, showing you the progress of the download. When the download is complete, the meter disappears.

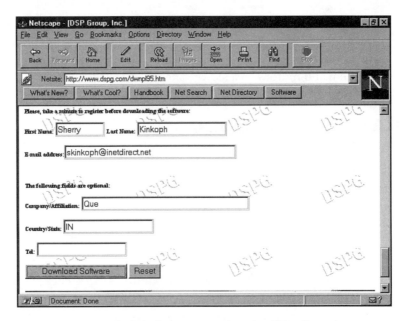

Figure 7.2   You must register before you can download TrueSpeech.

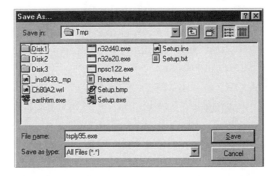

Figure 7.3   Choose a location for the file.

What's in a Name?   In the file name TSPLY95.EXE, TS stands for TrueSpeech, PLY stands for player, and what follows that is an indication of the Windows version you're using (such as 95 for Windows 95).

279

This file is about 3/4 of a megabyte. Under ideal conditions, it will download in approximately 7 minutes using a 14,400bps modem. Under normal conditions, expect it to take 10–14 minutes. It will, of course, take less time with a faster modem and more with a slower one.

Installing TrueSpeech

The program is delivered as a self-extracting archive file that contains the setup program. Your computer needs the setup program only when you install the program. Because you stored such files in a temporary directory, they are set aside for you to delete them later.

The first thing you need to do is to extract the setup files from the archive. To do so, follow these steps:

1. If you're using Windows 95 or Windows NT 4, click the **Start** button and select the **Run** command.

   If you're using Windows 3.1 or Windows NT 3.51, pull down Program Manager's **File** menu and select the **Run** command.

2. In the Run dialog box, click the **Browse** button.

3. In the dialog box that appears, select the directory with the downloaded file in it, and click the name of the file. Click the **Open** button to return to the Run dialog box.

4. Click **OK**, and an MS-DOS window opens, running the self-extracting archive program (see Figure 7.4). Each file is listed as it is extracted.

5. If the program tells you that one of the file names already exists and asks whether to overwrite it, press **y** to continue. The files in your temporary directory are probably there from installing some other program, and while they may have the same name, they aren't the same files. Because they're in your TEMP directory, you can be fairly certain that you don't need them anymore and it's safe to overwrite them.

6. When the program finishes extracting files, the word **Finished** appears on the title bar. Click the **Close** (X) button to close the MS-DOS window. (If the MS-DOS window is in full-screen mode with no title bar, press **Alt+Enter**, and a title bar will appear.)

Figure 7.4 Files are listed in an MS-DOS window as they are extracted.

After you extract the setup files, it's time to run the setup program. Follow these steps:

1. Close Navigator and any programs that you have open that you don't need.

2. If you're using Windows 95 or Windows NT 4, click the **Start** button and select the **Run** command.

   If you're using Windows 3.1 or Windows NT 3.51, pull down Program Manager's **File** menu and select the **Run** command.

3. Click the **Browse** button, and select the **SETUP.EXE** file from the Browse dialog box. (You should still be in your temporary directory, assuming you haven't used the Run command since the previous procedure.)

4. Click the **Open** button to close the Browse dialog box; then click **OK** in the Run dialog box to run the setup program.

5. A TrueSpeech title screen appears, and then a meter appears showing the progress of the setup program. Once that is complete, a setup background fills the screen, and a Welcome dialog box appears. Click the **Next** button to continue.

6. When you are asked to choose the directory to install the program files in, click the **Browse** button.

7. In the Choose Directory dialog box (see Figure 7.5), navigate to your Netscape program directory and add **tsplay** to the end of the path name. This tells it to create a new directory in the program directory to store the TrueSpeech player program. Click **OK**.

281

Figure 7.5   Create a new directory called tsplay in which to store TrueSpeech.

8. Another dialog box appears to ask if you want to create a new directory. Click the **Yes** button.

9. You are returned to the Choose Destination Location dialog box, where you clicked the Browse button. Click the **Next** button to continue.

10. Select a program folder for the TrueSpeech icons. By default, setup creates a new folder for them. If you want them in any other folder (such as the folder where you keep Netscape), click that folder name. Click **Next**.

11. Next you're asked which browser you are using TrueSpeech with. Click the **Netscape Navigator** check box to select it and click **Next**. The installation begins, and a meter shows the progress of the installation.

12. When you are asked to enter the Netscape Navigator path, click the **Browse** button.

13. Again, a Choose Directory dialog box appears. Navigate to your main Netscape directory (probably C:\Netscape or D:\Netscape). Click **OK**.

14. You are returned to the Choose the Netscape Navigator Path dialog box, where you clicked the Browse button. Click the **Next** button to continue.

15. When the installation is complete, a dialog box appears asking if you want to read the README file now. Click **Yes**.

16. An editor or word processor opens and displays the README file. Read through it; it may contain information on new features. When you finish, close the editor.

17. A dialog box appears telling you that the **setup is complete**. Click **OK**. The TrueSpeech player program opens a window like the one in Figure 7.6, and a recorded message plays through your speakers.

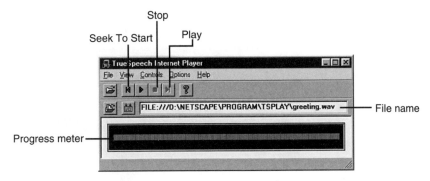

Figure 7.6 TrueSpeech starts and plays a greeting.

TrueSpeech Basics

The TrueSpeech player has the capability to play both TrueSpeech compressed files (file names that end with .tsp) and uncompressed wave-format files (.wav). Both .tsp and .wav Web links transfer files that end in .wav; when Netscape sees a link that ends in .tsp, it knows to request the .wav file and then play it as compressed audio. Originally, the player only sets itself up for the compressed files; see the section "Playing Noncompressed Files" to learn about setting up TrueSpeech to play .wav files.

To see TrueSpeech at work, get online and follow these steps:

1. Close the TrueSpeech player if it is still open from the installation process.
2. In Netscape Navigator, go to the sample sounds page at **http://www.dspg.com/tsampl85.htm**. This page includes a list of links for recordings.
3. Click any link. A file transfer meter appears, followed by the TrueSpeech Player helper window. The two numbers at the bottom of the player indicate (respectively) how many bytes of the recording have been downloaded and how many bytes the recording has total. After a few seconds, the recording should start playing.

While the recording is playing, notice the lines on the progress meter (see Figure 7.7). The width of the progress meter represents the length of the recording. The single green line indicates how much of the recording has been downloaded and decompressed so far, and the bluish-green lines that build from the left indicate how much of the recording has played so far.

283

Amount played   Amount downloaded

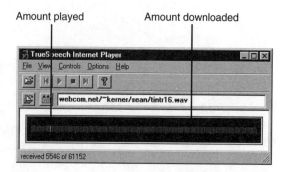

Figure 7.7   The meter tells you how much of the recording has been downloaded and how much has been played.

If the bluish-green lines catch up to the green line before the green line gets all the way to the end, it means that you've heard all the sound that has downloaded so far. Unfortunately, this can happen when the Internet is slow. If it does, the player pauses until it gets more data, and then it plays until it runs out of data again.

Use the **Stop** button to stop the sound from playing, the **Play** button to resume the sound, and the **Seek To Start** button to stop playing and reset the bluish green lines to the beginning, so that next time you hit the **Play** button it plays over from the start. These functions are also available as commands on the Controls menu.

Playing Noncompressed Files

To set up the player to also play noncompressed .wav files, follow these steps:

1. Open Netscape's **Options** menu and select **General Preferences**. A Preferences dialog box appears.

2. Click the **Helpers** tab to see the options shown in Figure 7.8.

3. Scroll through the File type list and select the **audio/x-wav** entry.

CAUTION

You Don't Need This   If a path name appears in the field at the bottom of this tab, you already have a .wav player selected. To leave that one configured, click the **Cancel** button.

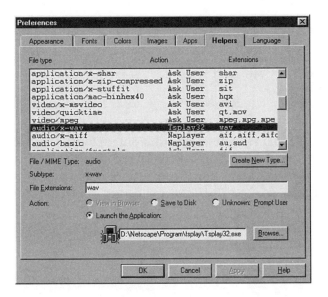

Figure 7.8 The Helpers tab in the Preferences dialog box.

4. Click the **Browse** button, and a directory dialog box appears.

5. Locate the tsplay directory that you created when installing TrueSpeech and select the **tsplay16.exe** or **tsplay32.exe** file (whichever you have).

6. Click the **Open** button to return to the Preferences dialog box.

7. The file name you selected is now listed at the bottom of the dialog box. Click **OK**.

When you use the TrueSpeech player to play uncompressed .wav files, it waits until the entire file has been downloaded before it starts to play.

Where Can I Find More? To find Web sites with TrueSpeech files, check out http://www.dspg.com/cool.htm, which is where DSPG keeps its guide to sites.

Using the TrueSpeech Plug-In

The plug-in version of TrueSpeech is used only on those rare sites that are specifically designed to use it. To see it in action:

1. If the TrueSpeech helper window is open, close it by clicking the **Close** (X) button. (The plug-in may not work correctly if the helper is still open.)

2. Go to **http:/www.dspg.com/plugin.htm** using Netscape. As the page loads, sound will begin playing. The plug-in can automatically play sound, without waiting for a link to be clicked.

3. On the Web page, find the controls seen in Figure 7.9. Once the sound has played once, try using the **Play** button to restart it and the **Stop** button to stop it. (The Help button will load helpful information from one of DSPG's Web pages.)

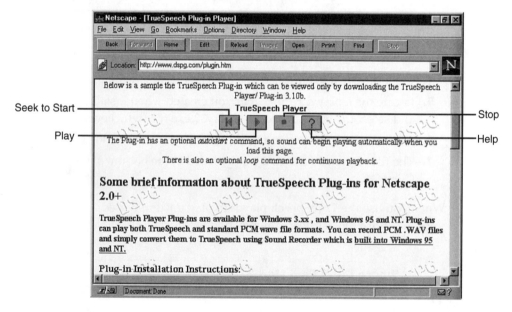

Figure 7.9 TrueSpeech plug-in controls.

In this lesson, you learned about TrueSpeech. In the next lesson, you learn about StreamWorks.

StreamWorks
by Xing

*In this lesson, you'll learn how to get the StreamWorks helper application
and how to use it to view video and listen to audio over the Web.*

What Is StreamWorks?

StreamWorks is designed to work with *streaming* information, information that
is constantly coming across the Web and that has no fixed beginning or end.
StreamWorks is different from many Web audio and video products, which are
designed to work only with pre-existing files that have a definite beginning and
end. Examples of streaming information available on the Web include radio and
TV broadcasts, which some stations put out over the Web as well as through the
airwaves.

Because the StreamWorks software requires something more than a simple file
transfer, any server with a Web page containing StreamWorks audio or video
presentations must also have special StreamWorks server software that can
handle it. The receiving software that this chapter covers is considered the
StreamWorks *client* software.

StreamWorks' video capabilities are really designed to work with high-speed
Internet connections, such as ISDN and T-1. The typical dial-in modem user will
see no more than one frame out of each second of video—just a sampling from
the stream of data that passes by. Its handling of audio, however, is much less
speed-dependent.

The version of StreamWorks covered in this chapter is a helper, not a plug-in, so
it has to open a separate window to display its video. There is a plug-in version
in the works, but it was not available as of the time of this writing. The basic
functions should be much the same as what is described here though, and if
you occasionally check the Xing Technologies Web page, you should see an
announcement of where to get the plug-in when it becomes available.

Downloading StreamWorks

You can download the StreamWorks client software from Xing's Web site, using the following steps:

1. Start Netscape and go to the Web page at **http://www.xingtech.com/ streams/info/reg_client.html**. This page contains the form shown in Figure 8.1.

2. Fill out this form as part of the registration process. (And when you get to the Comments field, tell 'em I sent you!)

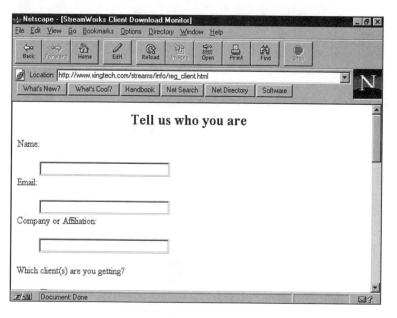

Figure 8.1 Before you download StreamWorks, you need to register.

3. When you finish filling in the form, click **OK**.

4. A new page appears, telling you about StreamWorks. Toward the bottom is a set of links for different sorts of computers with which you might want to use StreamWorks. Click the **PC with Windows** link.

5. This page includes a simple guide to installing StreamWorks. Click the **CLICK HERE** link to download.

6. In the Save As dialog box, choose a temporary directory to store the downloaded file in (you probably have one named C:\TEMP or C:\TMP), and then click the **Save** button. The STREAMWK.EXE file begins downloading, and a meter shows you the progress of the download.

The STREAMWK.EXE file is approximately 1 1/4 megabytes. Under ideal Internet conditions on a 14,400bps modem, it should take about 13 minutes to download. Under typical conditions, it should take between 20 minutes and half an hour. A faster modem will take less time, and a slower one will take more time.

Installing StreamWorks

The file that you downloaded for the helper is an installation program, which must first break itself apart into a number of installation-related files, then it performs the installation.

To run the installation program, follow these steps:

1. Exit Netscape and make sure you do not have any browser windows open. Exit any other programs that you do not need.
2. If you're using Windows 95 or Windows NT 4, click the **Start** button and select the **Run** command.

   If you're using another version of Windows, pull down Program Manager's **File** menu and select the **Run** command.
3. In the Run dialog box, click the **Browse** button.
4. In the Browse dialog box, select the directory with the downloaded file (STREAMWK.EXE) in it, and click the name of the file. Click the **Open** button to return to the Run dialog box.
5. Click **OK** to start the installation program. A WinZip Self-Extractor dialog box appears with Xing Technology contact information in it.
6. This WinZip program breaks STREAMWK.EXE into a bunch of smaller files needed for installation. Click **OK**.
7. In the next WinZip Self-Extractor dialog box (see Figure 8.2), type the path for your temporary directory in the **Unzip To Directory** field, but *don't* change any other options. Then click **Unzip**.

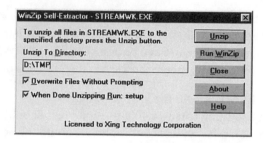

Figure 8.2 Type the path to your temporary directory in this dialog box.

8. The names of the installation program files appear at the bottom of the WinZip dialog box. When all of these have been extracted, a smaller dialog box appears telling you how many files were unzipped. Click **OK**.

9. A StreamWorks image appears in the center of the screen, and then a meter appears, indicating that the installation program is being set up. Once the installation program is set up, it starts to run, filling the whole screen with an image and opening a Welcome dialog box. Click the **Next** button to continue.

10. The program displays a checklist of the Web browsers you have on your system (see Figure 8.3). This includes Netscape Navigator and any other browsers you might have. Click to remove the check mark next to any browser that you *don't* want configured to run StreamWorks. When you're satisfied with the list, click **Next**.

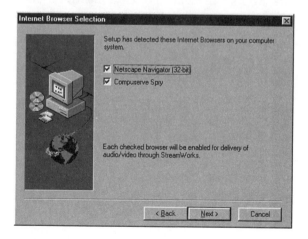

Figure 8.3 Deselect the browsers you don't want to run StreamWorks with.

11. You'll see some information about other browsers that StreamWorks will work with. Click **Next**.

12. The Component Selection dialog box proposes a destination directory for the files. Click the **Browse** button.

13. In the Choose Directory dialog box, enter the path for your Netscape Program directory in the **Path** field (you can use the disk drive and directory controls if you want). Then add **\streamwk** to the path name to create a new directory just for StreamWorks.

14. A Setup dialog box asks if you want to create the directory. Click **Yes**.

15. Back in the Component Selection dialog box, click the **Next** button. The installer begins installing StreamWorks as you requested, and a progress meter shows you how it's going.

16. When you get the message **the installation is complete**, click **OK**.

17. You're asked if you want to delete the setup files from the temporary directory. Click the **Yes** button.

StreamWorks Basics

Before you try StreamWorks online for the first time, it's a good idea to configure your modem speed and get a look at the program. To do so, follow these steps:

1. Start the StreamWorks helper app. If you use Windows 95 or NT 4, click the **Start** button, point to **Programs**, point to **Xing StreamWorks**, and click **StreamWorks**. If you use another version of Windows, open File Manager, select the **Xing StreamWorks** folder, and double-click the **StreamWorks** icon.

2. Read the license agreement that appears. (It's all legal stuff that you are agreeing to if you use the program.) Then click the **Accept** button.

3. The next window provides information about the program. Click **OK**, and the StreamWorks program window shown in Figure 8.4 opens.

TIP

You're Only Bothered Once The windows referred to in steps 2 and 3 appear only the first time you run the program.

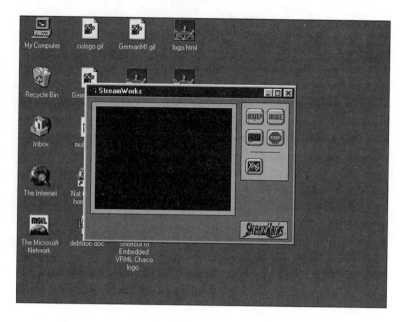

Figure 8.4   The StreamWorks program window.

4. Click the **Setup** button. The StreamWorks Setup dialog box appears (see Figure 8.5).

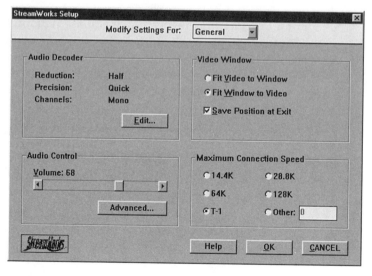

Figure 8.5   Tell StreamWorks how fast your modem is.

5. In the Maximum Connection Speed area, select the speed of your modem.

6. Adjust the **Volume** slider down to about 50 to keep the audio from being too loud. Then click **OK**.

7. If a dialog box appears telling you that the bandwidth will be slightly less than your modem speed, click **OK**.

8. Click the StreamWorks window's **Exit** button to exit StreamWorks.

More Options You can click the **Edit** button in the StreamWorks Setup window and pick stereo and higher-quality audio for people with fast computers and modems. You can click the **Modify Settings For** drop-down arrow and pick other setup-related dialog boxes, in which you can do such things as assign buttons to certain online "stations."

Now that you have, your viewer configured, get online and test it out!

1. Connect to the Internet, start Netscape, and go to the page at **http://www.xingtech.com/streams/testdrv/testdrv.html**. This page has a list of available audio and video feeds, sorted by the bit rate (the rate at which the data gets sent over the Net).

2. Select the first item on the list: **LIVE VIDEO**. A file transfer meter appears briefly, followed by the StreamWorks program window.

3. After a few seconds, the display resizes itself to fit the video being sent. Then the picture appears (see Figure 8.6), and the sound starts. Watch the video for a while.

Figure 8.6 StreamWorks picks up a live video feed.

4. Click the symbol in the upper-left corner of the StreamWorks window and select **Diagnostics** from the menu that appears. The Network Diagnostics window appears (see Figure 8.7). If the number of Lost Video Packets or Lost Audio Packets is more than zero, it means you're not getting all the data that's being sent because your modem or the Internet isn't fast enough. This can cause choppy sound and images. (The Network Throughput value tells you how quickly the data is actually coming through.)

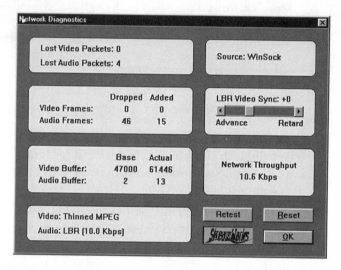

Figure 8.7   Check the Network Diagnostics dialog box for lost packets.

5. Click **OK** to close the Network Diagnostics dialog box.

6. Click the StreamWorks **Stop** button to stop receiving the video.

7. On the Netscape window, click one of the low bit-rate entries marked **LIVE AUDIO to hear an example of StreamWorks audio.** The StreamWorks window comes to the front again, and an **Audio Only** symbol replaces the video window (see Figure 8.8).

8. Listen to the audio for a while. When you finish, click the **Stop** button.

If you have a high-speed connection, you should try some of the higher bit-rate communications to see what StreamWorks is capable of. You may run into a situation, however, in which your modem is fast enough but your computer can't keep up because decoding the compressed video takes so much work

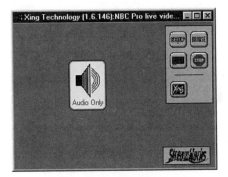

Figure 8.8 You can opt to receive only the audio part of the transmission.

There's no reason you can't continue to surf the Web while StreamWorks is running. This means that you can listen to your favorite online radio station while you're on the Web. (Of course, that radio station will be competing for your modem's time with the Web pages you're pulling up. As a result, the Web pages will appear more slowly, and the sound may occasionally skip.)

Xing Technologies offers a list of available StreamWorks sites. Check their Web page at http://www.xingtech.com/streams/index.html to learn about everything from bluegrass music stations to Finnish TV broadcasts available over the Net!

In this lesson, you learned to use StreamWorks to receive audio and video over the Web. In the next lesson, you'll learn how to get and use VR Scout.

VR Scout by Chaco

In this lesson, you'll learn how to get VR Scout and how to use it to view virtual reality scenes over the Web.

VR Scout is a program that lets you view and navigate through three-dimensional objects and scenes called *worlds*. Instead of just looking at still images of a computer-designed house, for example, or watching a video that takes you on a certain path through the house, you can control your own path and pick the angles from which you view the objects.

The 3-D worlds that you interact with are stored in computer files using *Virtual Reality Markup Language*, also known as *VRML*. VRML is an industry standard, and VR Scout is one of a number of Netscape plug-ins that you can use to view VRML scenes. Other VRML viewers covered in this book include WebSpace, WorldView, Live3D, and VRealm Browser.

VR Scout is free for students and teachers. Anyone else can use it free for 30 days but is then obligated to either pay for it or stop using it. Figure 9.1 shows the VR Scout plug-in in use.

There are three versions of VR Scout, and which one you need depends on which operating system and which version of Netscape you are using. The examples in this chapter use the plug-in version, which works only if you are using Windows 95 or Windows NT to run the 32-bit version of Netscape Navigator 3.0 or Netscape Navigator Gold. If you're using an older version of Windows, an older (before version 2.0) or 16-bit version of Netscape, or one of certain non-Netscape browsers, you'll need a VR Scout helper app instead of a plug-in. The helper app is like a plug-in, except that you set it up differently, and when you view a VRML scene, it opens its own window instead of running in the Netscape window.

Figure 9.1 The plug-in version of VR Scout displays the scene in the Netscape window.

Be Sure Your Hardware Is Adequate To use VR Scout, your system must have at least 8 megabytes of memory. You also need an 80386 or better processor with a math coprocessor. All Pentiums have math coprocessors built-in, as do 486DX chips. However, 486SX chips and 80386 chips do not, so if you have one of those, you need a separate coprocessor chip on your computer's motherboard.

Downloading VR Scout

You can download VR Scout from Chaco's Web site using the following steps:

1. Start Netscape and go to the Web page at **http://www.chaco.com/vrscout/**.

2. This Web page gives you links for the plug-in version of the software and two different helper *(external viewer)* versions (one for systems with 3-D accelerators, the other for ones without). Click the link for the version you need.

3-D or Not 3-D?   If you don't know whether you have a 3-D accelerator, you probably don't.

3. Read through the page that appears, which contains information on the current revision of the VR Scout.

4. Toward the bottom of this page is a list of sites from which you can download VR Scout. Click the link for a site on your continent.

5. In the Save As dialog box (see Figure 9.2), choose a temporary directory to store the downloaded file in (you probably have one named C:\TEMP or C:\TMP).

Figure 9.2   Choose a directory into which to download VR Scout.

6. Click the **Save** button, and the download begins. The file name will be something like NPSC122.EXE. (The 122 stands for the revision number—in this case, 1.22.)

The size of the VR Scout file varies somewhat depending on the version you choose, but it will be in the range of 3 megabytes. On a 14,400bps modem under ideal conditions, it will take about half an hour to download this file. In the real world, expect it to take 45 minutes to an hour on a 14,400 modem, less time on a faster modem.

Installing VR Scout

The file that you download for the VR Scout plug-in is an executable program that installs the plug-in. To run it, follow these steps:

1. Exit Netscape and make sure that you do not have any browser windows open. Exit any other programs that you do not need.

Potential Problem If you have a file named Disk1 in your temporary directory, you must delete it before starting the installation. Open up Explorer, select the file, and press the **Delete** key to delete it.

CAUTION

2. If you're using Windows 95 or NT 4, click the **Start** button and select the **Run** command.

If you're using Windows 3.1 or NT 3.51, open Program Manager's **File** menu and select the **Run** command.

3. In the Run dialog box, click the **Browse** button.

4. The Browse dialog box appears (see Figure 9.3). Select the directory with the downloaded file in it, and click the name of the file. Then click the **Open** button to return to the Run dialog box.

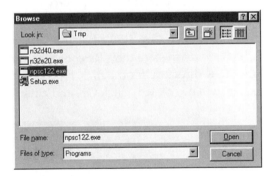

Figure 9.3 Indicate which directory holds the file you downloaded.

5. Click **OK** to start the installation program. The WinZip Self-Extractor dialog box shown in Figure 9.4 appears.

6. Click the **Unzip** button, but *don't* change any of the options.

7. The names of the installation program files appear at the bottom of the WinZip dialog box. When all of the files have been extracted, a dialog box appears, telling you how many files were unzipped. Click **OK**.

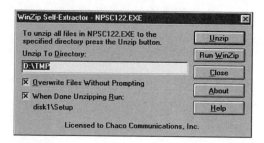

Figure 9.4   The WinZip Self-Extractor dialog box.

8. A VR Scout image appears in the center of the screen, and then a meter appears indicating that the installation program is being set up. When the installation program starts to run, it covers the whole screen with an image and opens a Welcome dialog box. Click the **Next** button.

9. Read over the legal information that appears (it's something you're agreeing to if you continue to install the program). Then click the **Yes** button.

10. When the Choose Destination Directory dialog box appears, click the **Browse** button.

11. In the Choose Directory dialog box (see Figure 9.5), select the directory in which you want to store the VR Scout files and click **OK**. (If you want to create a new directory for the files, type a directory path for it, and the new directory will be created. Click **OK** and click **Yes**.)

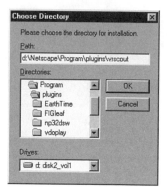

Figure 9.5   Choose a directory in which to store the unzipped VR Scout files.

12. You are returned to the Choose Destination Directory dialog box. Click the **Next** button to continue.

13. The next dialog box (called Select Components) asks which browser you are using. Netscape should already be selected; click **Next** to move on.

14. When you are asked for the location of your Netscape plug-ins directory, an unexpected directory name might appear. If it is the wrong directory or if you don't already have a plug-ins directory, click the **Browse** button and repeat step 11. Click the **Next** button.

15. Select a program folder for VR Scout icons. By default, the program creates a new folder for them. If you want them in any other folder, click its name. Click **Next** to move on.

16. The next dialog box asks for confirmation of the information you entered in steps 10–15. Click the **Next** button. The installation starts, and a meter shows you the progress of the installation.

17. An Information dialog box tells you that it is going to install Microsoft's Reality Lab rendering engine. Click **OK**. (If you have already installed that piece of software for some other reason, skip steps 18 and 19.)

18. The Reality Lab will take a while to install. When it is done, a dialog box tells you that the installation was successful. Click **OK**.

19. Another meter appears while some final installation work is being done, and then the Setup Complete dialog box appears. Click the **Finish** button.

20. Notepad, WordPad, or a word processor automatically opens and displays a README file. Read over the file for important new information. Then exit the program.

Now, you're ready to use the plug-in!

Installing the helper application is very similar, except that it skips a few steps. The first time you run Netscape with the helper installed and come across a VRML file, Netscape asks you which program you want to use to view VRML files. Select VR Scout from the dialog box that appears.

VR Scout Basics

VR Scout supports two file formats. Standard VRML files end in .wrl (which stands for *world*). Compressed VRML files end in .wrl.gz (the gz stands for *geometric ZIP*). If you see two links—one that takes you to a .wrl file and one that takes you to a .wrl.gz file of the same world—pick the .gz file. It loads much faster.

To try out one of those files, follow these steps:

1. Start Netscape.

2. Enter **http://www.chaco.com/vrml/chaco3c.wrl.gz** in the **Location/Go to** text box and press **Enter**. Netscape displays the dialog box shown in Figure 9.6.

Figure 9.6 Netscape thinks it won't understand this file. Don't worry, it will!

3. Click **OK**. VR Scout starts and displays a control panel with some flashing lights. When the entire file has been transferred, the lights disappear, and the world logo appears (see Figure 9.7).

Save on Connect Charges When the entire file has been downloaded, you can disconnect from the Internet and stop running up your Internet bill, if you have one.

Figure 9.7 A 3-D version of Chaco's logo, which is based on the Sun Dagger in Chaco Canyon National Park.

4. Click the word **Headlight**. The word stops glowing, and the object becomes dark. The VR Scout headlight is like a miner's hat that lights up whatever you're looking at. Click **Headlight** again to light the object up.

5. Click **Walk**, and that word turns green. This is one of three modes by which you can travel through the world:

- In *Walk mode*, you're standing vertically, but you can look in other directions.

- In *Fly mode*, you tilt and turn at angles like you would in an airplane, and you move in the direction you're facing.

- In *Examine mode*, you stand still and move the world around you.

6. Point to the main screen, press and hold down the left mouse button, and push the mouse forward. A crosshair appears where you first pressed the button, and a line runs from the center of the crosshair to where the pointer is now, as seen in Figure 9.8. You start moving toward the logo.

7. Think of the line as a joystick. Pushing it above the crosshair makes you go forward, pulling it down makes you go backward, and dragging it left or right makes you go, well, left or right! In addition, you can hold down the **Shift** and **Control** keys to use more complex controls, as shown in Table 9.1. Explore this world for a while!

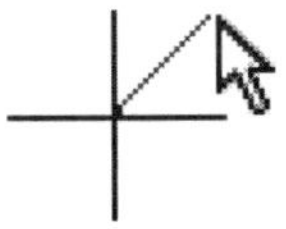

Figure 9.8   VR Scout's on-screen crosshairs.

8. Click the word **Reset** to go back to where you started.

9. Click **Fly**, and you enter Fly mode. The controls for Fly mode are listed in Table 9.1. Explore the world this way.

Careen in the Canyon   For a real challenge, try flying within the spiral of the logo!

303

Table 9.1   Walk and Fly Mode Controls

Direction	Action	With Shift Key	With Control Key
Up	Move forward	Move straight up	Look up
Down	Move backward	Move straight down	Look down
Left	Turn left (flying only)	Slide left	Tilt left
Right	Turn right (flying only)	Slide right	Tilt right

10. Right-click in the main screen. The shortcut menu offers you some additional controls and functions (including a help function). This is especially useful when you're exploring a virtual world that's embedded into an HTML page because the control panel doesn't appear for embedded worlds.

Once you have the hang of moving around this fairly simple world, you should check out some of the more complex worlds that are available online. To find a list of links to sites with VRML content, go to **http://www.chaco.com/vrml/**.

In this lesson, you learned about VR Scout. In the next lesson, you'll discover VRealm Browser, another virtual reality browser.

VRealm Browser by Integrated Data Systems

In this lesson, you'll learn how to get VRealm Browser and how to use it to view virtual reality presentations over the Web.

What Is VRealm Browser?

VRealm Browser brings Web browsing into 3-D, allowing you to explore three-dimensional scenes that people have created and published on the Web. These scenes, called *worlds*, are created using the standard *Virtual Reality Markup Language* (VRML). Figure 10.1 shows an example VRML scene viewed through VRealm Browser.

There are different VRML browsers out there; this book also covers WebSpace, World View, Live 3D, and VR Scout. Each product has somewhat different controls and works at its own speed. You should try out several browsers to see which works best on your machine and which controls you are most comfortable with.

Just as some Web browser manufacturers have created extensions to the HyperText Markup Language, some virtual reality program manufacturers have created their own extensions to the Virtual Reality Markup Language. As a result, you can experience some virtual worlds with VRealm Browser that you cannot experience with other viewers (or at least not in the same way). Likewise, you will not be able to experience some worlds, at least not fully, with VRealm Browser.

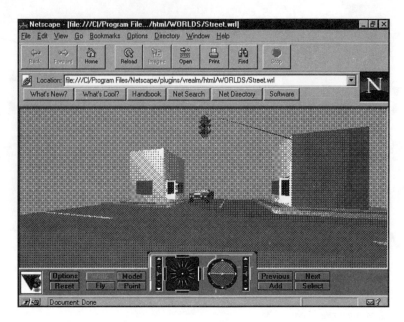

Figure 10.1   You don't have to come to a full stop at a virtual reality stop light. Virtually stopping is acceptable!

VRealm Browser is available for download for a free two-month trial. The program requires a fairly powerful computer, with at least a 90 megahertz Pentium processor, 16 megabytes of RAM, and a 256-color display. It can be run on a less powerful computer (I used a 486DX2-66 processor and 12 megabytes of RAM), but it will be slower, and it may not be able to handle large worlds.

Downloading VRealm Browser

The first step toward using VRealm Browser is to get the software. It's available for download from the Integrated Data Systems Web site. As of the time of this writing, the plug-in version would work only with Windows 95 and NT, but other versions were in the works. To get VRealm Browser, follow these steps:

1. Start Netscape and go to the Web page at **http://www.ids-net.com/ids/ downldpi.html**. On the page that appears, read the information about the plug-in. (This is where you'll find out if there is a version you can use if you're not running Windows 95 or NT.)

2. Click the **Continue download** link at the bottom of the page.

3. Read through the licensing agreement, which you must agree to in order to use the software. At the bottom, click **ACCEPT**.

4. Fill in the registration information in the form shown in Figure 10.2. Then click the **Process** button at the bottom.

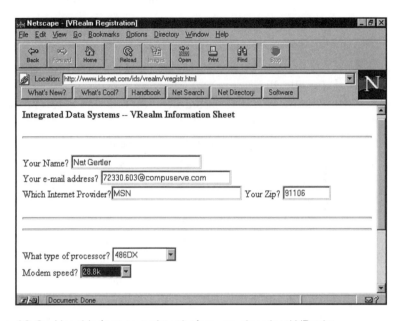

Figure 10.2 Use this form to register before you download VRealm.

5. On the new page that appears, there is a list of sites you can download the file from. Click the link for one of them. Netscape displays the Save As dialog box.

6. Choose a temporary directory to store the downloaded file in (you probably have one named C:\TEMP or C:\TMP).

7. Click the **Save** button, and the download begins. The file you receive will be called something like vrpgb04.exe. (The b04 indicates the revision number of the plug-in; in this case, it's beta version 04.)

This file is approximately 3 megabytes in size. Under ideal conditions, a 14,400bps modem will download this in about half an hour. Given normal Web conditions, you should expect it to take 45 minutes to an hour. (It will download faster on a faster modem or over a network connection.)

Installing VRealm Browser

The downloaded file contains an installation program and all the files needed for VRealm Browser—all compressed into one. To break out the separate files and install them in their appropriate places, follow these steps:

1. Exit Netscape and make sure that you do not have any browser windows open. Exit any other programs that you do not need.

2. If you're using Windows 95 or NT 4.0, click the **Start** button and select the **Run** command.

   In Windows NT 3.51, pull down Program Manager's **File** menu and select the **Run** command.

3. In the Run dialog box, click the **Browse** button.

4. In the Browse dialog box, select the directory that contains the downloaded file, and click the name of the file. Then click the **Open** button to return to the Run dialog box.

5. Click **OK** to start the installation program.

6. A dialog box tells you that this will install VRealm Browser and asks **Do you wish to continue?** Click the **Yes** button.

7. The program breaks out the separate files, and a meter shows its progress. When that's finished, a large Setup window with a Welcome dialog box appears. Click the **Next** button.

8. The Choose Destination Location dialog box asks you where you want to put the VRealm files. Click the **Browse** button.

9. In the Choose Directory dialog box (see Figure 10.3), select the path for your Netscape Program directory, and add **\plugins\vrealm** to the end of the path name. Click **OK**, and you're returned to the previous dialog box.

10. The next dialog box tells you that that directory does not exist and asks if it should be created. Click **Yes**.

11. A very similar dialog box appears, asking where you want the program files stored. Simply click the **Next** button, and the program begins installing the files in their proper directories. A meter appears to show you the progress of the installation.

12. When all the files are installed, you'll see the Verifying Netscape Version dialog box. Click **OK**.

Figure 10.3 Create a subdirectory within your Netscape Program directory for storing the VRealm files.

Make Sure You're Current   Netscape and its plug-ins and helper apps are constantly being revised. Make sure you have the latest version of Netscape and the latest version of the plug-in or helper app. Otherwise, the plug-in or helper app might not work smoothly with Netscape.

13. A dialog box appears, telling you **Setup is complete**. Click **OK**.

14. When asked if you want to read the README file, click **Yes**. The setup window closes, and a word processor or editor opens, displaying the README file.

15. Read the README file (it may have some new information). When you finish, leave the editor.

By installing this program, you are essentially naming it as your default VRML viewer. The next time you try to view a VRML file, VRealm Browser automatically starts. If you install any other VRML viewer after this one, it becomes your default viewer.

VRealm Browser Basics

Included among the VRealm files are some VRML worlds that you can use to learn about navigating virtual reality without the delay or cost of dialing in to the Internet. To explore one of those worlds, follow these steps:

1. Start Netscape *without* hooking up to the Internet. Depending on your Internet provider and software, you might have to cancel a dial-in attempt, or you might even have to connect and then log off.

2. Open the **File** menu and select the **Open File** command (Netscape Gold users will select **Open File in Browser**). The Open dialog box appears.

3. Go to the **Netscape Program** directory (which is probably already selected by default) and double-click the **plugins** folder. The contents of the plugins folder appear.

4. Double-click the **vrealm** folder to move into that folder. From there, double-click the **html** folder to move into it, and then double-click **Worlds** to move into the folder you really want (finally!).

5. (Optional) If you do not see any files here, don't panic! Click the **Files of type** drop-down arrow and select **Vrealm(vrml) (*.wrl)** from the list that appears. Some VRML world files should now be listed.

6. Double-click the **Bridge.wrl** file name. After a short loading time, a starship bridge with a VRealm control panel across the bottom should appear in your Netscape window (see Figure 10.4).

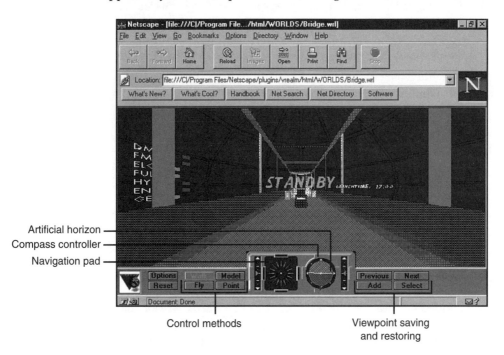

Figure 10.4 The starship bridge and control panel.

7. Click the **Walk** button to enter Walk mode. When you explore objects, you will stay on the surfaces. If you walk off of a surface, you will fall off of it; if you walk into something, you will automatically climb over it.

8. Click the top part of the circle in the navigation pad to step forward in the world. Figure 10.5 shows the navigation controls and tells how to use them.

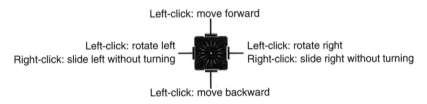

Left-click: move forward

Left-click: rotate left   Left-click: rotate right
Right-click: slide left without turning   Right-click: slide right without turning

Left-click: move backward

Figure 10.5 Navigational pad commands in Walk mode.

9. Double-click at the top of the circle to enter Continuous Movement mode so that you don't have to command each individual step one at a time. In this mode, moving your pointer around the navigation pad without clicking steers you.

10. Head down the bridge until you see your viewpoint rise, as if you were climbing on top of something in your path—which is in effect what you are doing. Click once on the navigation pad to get out of Continuous Movement mode.

11. Click the **Add** button to store your current position. A dialog box opens and asks for a description of the position. Type **Right here!** and click **OK**.

12. Click the **Fly** button to go into Fly mode. In Fly mode, you do not have to stay on the floor; the controls are designed to let you move around in a more three-dimensional sense (see Figure 10.6).

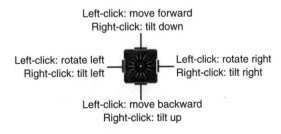

Left-click: move forward
Right-click: tilt down

Left-click: rotate left   Left-click: rotate right
Right-click: tilt left   Right-click: tilt right

Left-click: move backward
Right-click: tilt up

Figure 10.6 Navigational pad commands in Fly mode.

13. Explore the world for a while in Fly mode. Double-clicking still puts you in Continuous Movement mode. Keep an eye on the artificial horizon. The white line is where the world's horizon is, relative to you.

14. When you're not in Continuous Movement mode, click the **Select** button. A dialog box opens, in which you can choose from any previously stored viewpoint.

15. Double-click **Right Here!**, and you'll instantly be transported back to where you were when you stored that viewpoint.

16. Point to the red line on the *compass controller* (the circular rim around the artificial horizon). Hold down the mouse button and drag the red line around the circle. The display appears to rotate. This red line indicates the compass direction you're facing; you can drag or click it into place.

17. Right-click on the scene itself. The shortcut menu that appears offers many of the commands that you have buttons for, along with a few others (see Figure 10.7).

Figure 10.7   Right-click on the scene to access a shortcut menu with many navigational commands.

This gives you an idea of VRealm Browser's capabilities. Other topics you may want to explore include altitude controls, Model mode (which lets you move objects instead of moving yourself), and other viewing modes. Use the Help file to investigate these and other available features. You can open the Help file from its own icon in the VRealm Plug-In Folder or from the shortcut menu.

In this lesson, you learned about VRealm Browser. In the next lesson, you'll learn how to get and use WebSpace.

WebSpace by Template Graphics Software

In this lesson, you'll learn how to get the WebSpace helper program and how to use it to view virtual reality scenes over the Web.

What Is WebSpace?

The real world is three dimensional; you can move back and forth, up and down, left and right. The World Wide Web is usually quite two dimensional, as you scroll up and down (and sometimes side to side) through flat images on a flat screen. There are pockets of three-dimensionality on the Web, however. These are designed 3-D scenes, called *worlds*, which are stored in files using the *Virtual Reality Markup Language* (VRML).

In order to be able to view these worlds, you need a piece of software called a *VRML browser*. These browsers display the scene on your monitor, letting you move through it as if you were walking or flying through the world. WebSpace is one such browser. Other VRML viewers covered in this book include VR Scout, WorldView, Live3D, and VRealm Browser.

Unlike most of those VRML viewers, which are plug-ins, WebSpace is a helper application. The advantage to this is that it will work with a number of different Web browsers, if you have reason to use a browser other than Netscape. The disadvantage is that you cannot use WebSpace to view VRML worlds in the Netscape window; the program opens its own viewing window.

WebSpace is available for a variety of computers and operating systems. However, there is not a version currently available for 16-bit versions of Windows

(Windows 3.1 and below, including Windows for Workgroups). To run this program, you will need Windows 95 or Windows NT. Your computer will have to have at least 8 megabytes of memory, a display mode of at least 256 colors, and a 486-or-better processor running at 66 megahertz or faster. Higher numbers on any of these things (especially RAM) will let you move more smoothly through worlds.

WebSpace in Windows 95   As of the time of writing of this book, WebSpace was released for Windows NT 3.5 and 3.51 but was still considered beta for Windows 95. Before installing and running WebSpace, check the Help page at http://www.sd.tgs.com/WebSpace/Help/for information about whether WebSpace is running properly in Windows 95 and with your version of Netscape.

CAUTION

WebSpace is free for noncommercial use. If you want to be able to get technical support, however, you'll have to register it, for $49 US.

Downloading WebSpace

The first step toward using WebSpace is to get the software. It's available for downloading from the Template Graphics Software Web site. To get it, follow these steps:

1. Go to the Web page at **http://www.sd.tgs.com/~template/WebSpace/index.htm** using Netscape.

2. On this page, you'll find links to download WebSpace for various computers and operating systems (see Figure 11.1). Click the link for your version of Windows.

MIPS?   There are links for Windows versions marked with **MIPS** at the end. These require special hardware. Unless you specifically know you have a MIPS system, click one with **Intel** at the end.

CAUTION

3. Netscape displays the Save As dialog box. Choose a temporary directory to store the downloaded file in (you probably have one named C:\TEMP or C:\TMP).

4. Click the **Save** button, and the download begins. The file you are receiving will be called something like WEBSPC10.EXE, where 10 stands for revision 1.0. A meter shows you the progress of the download.

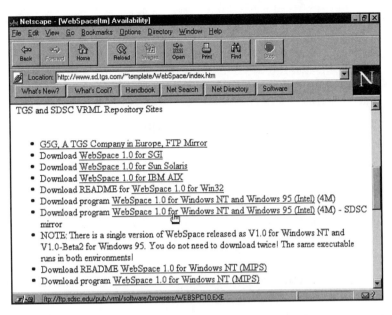

Figure 11.1 Pick the version of WebSpace that's appropriate for your computer's operating system.

This file is a huge one, weighing in at about 4 megabytes. Under ideal conditions, a 14,400bps modem will take around 45 minutes to download this. Given normal Web conditions, you should expect it to take an hour to an hour and a half. (It's because of files like these that people get faster modems!)

Installing WebSpace

The program is delivered as a self-extracting archive file, which contains the setup program. You'll only need the setup program when you first install the program. Because you stored these files in a temporary directory, however, they are set aside so you can easily delete them later.

Need Some Space? Anytime you need to clear some disk space, you should look in your TEMP directories and delete any files that have been there for a while and are no longer needed. (Windows does use this space for files that currently running programs are using, but it will not let you delete those.)

First, you need to extract the setup files from the archive. To extract those files, follow these steps:

1. Clean out unneeded files from your temporary storage directory. Specifically, delete any files or directories in there named Disk1, Disk2, Disk3, or Disk4.

2. In Windows 95 or NT 4.0, click the **Start** button and select the **Run** command.

   In older versions of Windows or Windows NT, open Program Manager's **File** menu and select the **Run** command.

3. In the Run dialog box, click the **Browse** button.

4. In the Browse dialog box, select the directory that contains the downloaded file, and click the name of the file. Then click the **Open** button to return to the Run dialog box.

5. Click **OK**. An MS-DOS window opens, running the self-extracting archive program (as shown in Figure 11.2). Each file is listed as it is extracted.

Figure 11.2   You can watch the files being extracted in this MS-DOS window.

6. If the program tells you that one of the file names already exists and asks whether to overwrite it, press **y** to continue. (These are probably files left from the installation of some other program. And while they may have the same names, they aren't the same files. Because they're in your temporary directory, you can be fairly certain you won't need them anymore and can overwrite them.)

7. When the program finishes extracting files, the MS-DOS window disappears.

Now that you have all the files and installation directories in place, it's time to install the program. To do so, follow these steps:

1. Close any open programs. This procedure will involve restarting Windows, so you may lose any work you have in progress in any programs that you don't close.

2. In Windows 95 or NT 4.0, click the **Start** button and select the **Run** command.

   In older versions of Windows or Windows NT, open Program Manager's **File** menu and select the **Run** command.

3. Click the **Browse** button. The Browse dialog box should still be pointing to your temporary directory, if you haven't done anything since the previous procedure. Double-click the **Disk 1** folder to look into that folder, and then select the **SETUP.EXE** file.

4. Click **Open** to close the Browse dialog box. Then click **OK** in the Run dialog box to run the setup program. A small dialog box appears telling you to wait a while.

5. Eventually, a Setup window appears with a dialog box full of legal information. Read through this document so you know what you are agreeing to, and then click the **Accept** button.

6. In the Welcome dialog box that appears, click **Next**.

7. If you get the dialog box shown in Figure 11.3, click the **Yes** button to install a special Microsoft driver that this product needs. (If this box doesn't appear, your system already has this driver.)

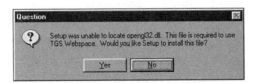

Figure 11.3 Click Yes to install the special Microsoft driver.

8. The Choose Destination Directory dialog box appears. Click the **Browse** button.

9. In the Choose Directory dialog box, select your Netscape plugins directory. At the end of the **Path** field, type **\WebSpace** as shown in Figure 11.4. (If you don't already have a plugins directory, select your Netscape Program directory and add **\plugins\WebSpace**.) Click **OK**.

Figure 11.4   Create a new subdirectory called WebSpace.

10. A dialog box asks **Do you want the directory to be created?** Click **Yes**.

11. Back in the Choose Destination Directory dialog box, click the **Next** button.

12. By default, the installation program creates a new folder for the WebSpace icons. To use the suggested folder, click **Next**. To use any other folder, click its name and then click **Next**. The files are copied into place, and a meter shows the progress of the procedure.

13. When all of the files have been copied, a dialog box asks **Do you want Setup to modify AUTOEXEC.BAT for you?** Click the **Yes** button.

14. The changes are made to AUTOEXEC.BAT. Then a dialog box appears to tell you that the modification has been done. Click **OK**.

15. Another dialog box tells you that Setup is complete. You must restart the system before running the installed programs. Click **OK**, and the setup window goes away.

16. Restart your system. If you use Windows 95 or NT 4.0, click the **Start** button, select the **Shut Down** command, select the **Restart the computer** option, and click **Yes**. If you use an older version of Windows NT, exit Windows and press **Ctrl+Alt+Delete**.

When your computer starts back up, your system can find WebSpace. However, Netscape still isn't aware of it, so we have to tell it how and when to use this helper program. To do that, follow these steps:

1. Start up Netscape.

2. From the **Options** menu, select **General Preferences**, and click the **Helpers** tab to see the Preferences dialog box displayed in Figure 11.5.

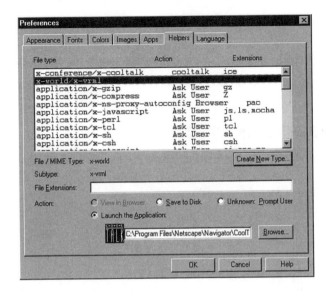

Figure 11.5 Use the Helpers tab to choose an application for viewing VRML files

3. Search the list for an entry with the file type **x-world/x-vrml**. If you find it, click it and skip to step 5.

4. If you don't find the entry, you'll have to create it. Click the **Create New Type** button, and a dialog box appears. Type **x-world** into the **MIME Type** field and **x-vrml** into the **MIME SubType** field. Click **OK**, and the dialog box disappears.

5. Type **wrl,wrz,flr** into the **File Extensions** field on the **Helpers** tab.

6. Click the **Browse** button and a File Navigation dialog box appears, starting in your Netscape Programs folder. Move down through the following folders: **plugins**, **Webspace**, and then **Program**.

7. When you see a file called **WebSpace.exe**, click it. Then click the **Open** button to close this dialog box.

8. Click **OK** to close the Preferences dialog box.

If you already have a VRML plug-in installed, you will have to repeat this procedure every time you start Navigator and want to use WebSpace. (This is because Netscape assumes that if you have a helper and a plug-in that do the same thing, you want to use the plug-in.) However, if you decide you want to use WebSpace as your primary VRML browser, you should uninstall the plug-in. (There should be an uninstall program in the plugins directory or on the Start menu in Windows 95.)

Uninstalling Plug-Ins   If you have trouble running WeSpace, try uninstalling all VRML plug-ins and reinstalling WebSpace. Then repeat the helper app setup in Netscape.

CAUTION

WebSpace Basics

Now that you have installed and configured WebSpace, you can finally take it out for a spin. The Template Graphics Software folks were kind enough to include some sample files on their disk, so you won't have to get on the Internet to give it a try. To use one of the sample files, follow these steps:

1. In Netscape Navigator's **Location/Go to** text box, enter the path to your Netscape program directory. Then add **\plugins\webspace\data\vrml\kitchen.wrl** to the end to point to a particular *world* file (which is what .wrl stands for).

2. Netscape tells you that it is starting an external program, and then a WebSpace window opens. If it is not in front of your Netscape window, shuffle your windows to find it.

3. WebSpace shows a black window for a while, and then it displays the image shown in Figure 11.6. Click the **Maximize** button (the button *next* to the X button) to expand this window to full-screen.

4. Point to the on-screen joystick and hold the left mouse button down. The pointer turns into an arrow with a little **V** next to it. (On slower machines, it may take a little while for the pointer to change or for other controls to respond. Be patient.)

5. Still holding down the mouse button, push the mouse forward. This pushes the joystick forward. You will start moving toward the wall you see in front of you. Keep going forward until you pass through the wall, at which point, you'll be inside a virtual reality kitchen!

6. Use the mouse to drag the joystick left (to turn left), right (to turn right), and back (to back up). Look around the kitchen by turning different directions.

7. Release the mouse button, point to the tilt knob at the right end of the joystick, and hold down the mouse button again. Now when you push the mouse forward, you tilt upward, and when you pull it back, you tilt downward.

8. Click the **Seek** tool, and your pointer turns into a crosshair. Click on something in the world, and you start moving toward it.

9. Point to the up arrow on the arrow pad and hold down the left mouse button. The pointer turns into a hand, and you start moving straight up. The left, right, and down arrows work similarly.

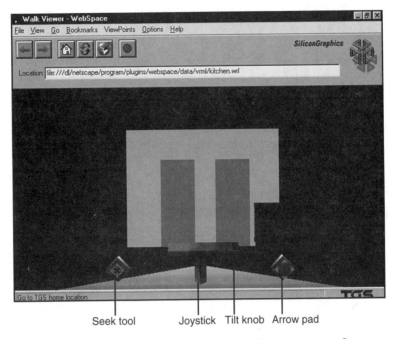

Seek tool   Joystick Tilt knob Arrow pad

Figure 11.6 The WebSpace window. Are you ready for an adventure?

This is just WebSpace's Walk mode. It also has an Examine mode, which lets you rotate the world while you stand still. To learn more about this and other WebSpace functions, use the Help menu. Be prepared, though: the Help information doesn't appear in the WebSpace window. It appears in the Netscape window as the current document!

In this lesson, you learned about WebSpace. In the next lesson you learn to get, install, and use WorldView.

WorldView by Intervista

In this lesson, you'll learn how to get the WorldView helper application, and how to use it to view virtual reality scenes over the Web.

What Is WorldView?

WorldView is a VRML browser, a program that lets you look at 3-D scenes (called *worlds*) from the perspective of someone in the scene. These are stored as VRML-format files that you can load from the Web or from a disk. Other VRML browsers covered in this book are Live3D, WebSpace, VRealm Browser, and VR Scout.

As of this writing, WorldView is available only as a helper application, rather than a plug-in. The main disadvantage of a helper application is that it has to open its own window to display the world; you can't see the world as part of a Web page in the Netscape window. The biggest advantage of a helper application is that it can work with other Web browsers; if for some reason you switch from Netscape to Mosaic or Internet Explorer (for example), you can still use the same helper application.

A plug-in version is in the works and may be available by the time you go to download WorldView. At that point, you can choose whether you'd rather have a plug-in or a helper app. This chapter describes how to get and use the helper, but getting and using the plug-in will be similar.

The Windows version of WorldView works only with Windows NT (revision 3.51 or higher) and Windows 95. The hardware requirements are somewhat less than those for some other browsers; you need a 486 or better processor running at 50 megahertz or faster, with eight megabytes of RAM. This configuration would be a little slow, particularly for scenes that are complex or have *texture mapping*.

Texture Mapping Designs put on faces of computer-rendered objects, rather than just flat color. With texture mapping, a desk can have a wood grain finish, for example, or a car can have a license plate with text, rather than just a single-colored rectangle.

WorldView is free for students and educators. Everyone else gets it free for 90 days, after which they must register and pay for it, or get rid of it.

Downloading WorldView

The first step toward using WorldView is to get the software. It's available for downloading from the Intervista Web site. To get it, follow these steps:

1. Go to the Web page at **http://www.webmaster.com/vrml/** using Netscape.

2. Toward the bottom of this page is a list of versions of WorldView that are planned, as seen in Figure 12.1. The Windows version that does *not* specify Netscape is the helper application. Click that link.

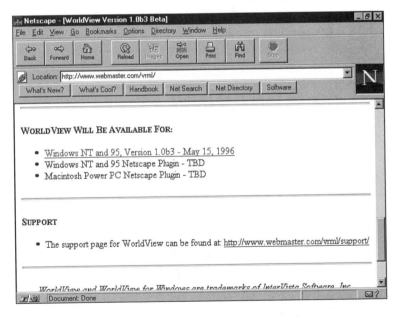

Figure 12.1 Click the link for the WorldView helper application.

Is There a Plug-In Yet?   On this page, you'll also see whether the plug-in is available, so you can choose to download it if you want it.

3. This takes you to another page with a numbered list of items. First on that list is a link marked **Download WorldView for Windows NT and 95**. Click that link.

4. Netscape displays the Save As dialog box. Choose a temporary directory to store the downloaded file in (you probably have one named C:\TEMP or C:\TMP).

5. Click the **Save** button, and the download will begin. The file you are receiving will be called WRLDVW32.EXE (the 32 stands for 32-bit operating system, which is what Windows 95 and NT are). A meter shows how the download progresses.

The file is a whopping 4 1/2 megabytes. Under ideal conditions, a 14,400 modem will take around 40 minutes to download this. Given normal Web conditions, you shouldn't be surprised for it to take from 1 to 1 1/2 hours. (You'll likely get the fastest times if you try to download it before people on the East Coast go to work, or after the people on the West Coast go to sleep.) A faster modem should cut down considerably on the download time.

Installing WorldView

The program is delivered as a self-extracting archive file, which contains the setup program. The setup program is needed only when you're first installing the program. By storing the archive and installation programs in a temporary directory, they are set aside where you can delete them later.

First, you need to extract the setup files from the archive. To do so, follow these steps:

1. In Windows 95 or Windows NT 4, click the **Start** button and select the **Run** command.

   In Windows NT 3.51, pull down Program Manager's **File** menu and select the **Run** command.

2. In the Run dialog box, click the **Browse** button.

3. In the dialog box that appears, locate the directory that contains the **WRLDVW32.EXE** file, and click the name of the file.

4. Click the **Open** button to return to the Run dialog box.

5. Click **OK**. An MS-DOS window opens, running the self-extracting archive program (as shown in Figure 12.2). Each file will be listed as it is extracted.

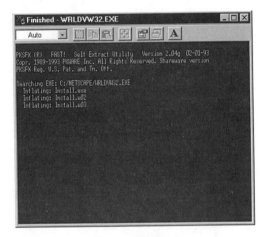

Figure 12.2 The MS-DOS window lists each file as it is extracted.

6. If the program tells you that one of the file names already exists and asks whether to overwrite it, press **y** to continue. It's probably the same name as a file left over from the installation of some other program. Because it's in your temporary directory, you can be fairly certain you don't need it anymore and it's safe to overwrite it.

7. When the program finishes extracting files, the MS-DOS window says **Finished** at the top. Click the **Close** (X) button on the title bar to get rid of this window.

Now that you have all the files in place, it's time to install the program by following these steps:

1. Close any open programs that you don't need.

2. In Windows 95 or Windows NT 4, click the **Start** button and select the **Run** command.

   In Windows NT 3.51, pull down Program Manager's **File** menu and select the **Run** command.

3. Click the **Browse** button. The dialog box that appears should still be pointing to your temporary directory, if you haven't done anything since the previous procedure. Select **INSTALL.EXE** and click the **Open** button to close the Browse dialog box.

4. Click **OK** in the Run dialog box to run the installation program. A big blue window opens, and a Welcome dialog box appears in front of it.

5. Click the **Next** button. The Select Destination Directory dialog box shown in Figure 12.3 appears.

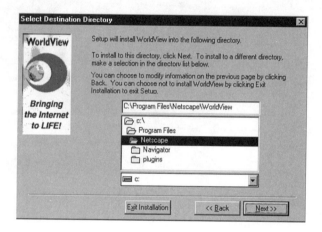

Figure 12.3   Create a subdirectory for the WorldView program.

6. In this dialog box, locate your Netscape Program folder. If you have a plugins folder with it, select that. The path listed above the folder selector will automatically add **WorldView** to the path you selected. This is the name of the directory it is creating. Click the **Next** button.

7. You will be asked if you want to store backup copies of any files the installation changes. The Yes option is already selected for you. Click the **Next** button.

8. The Select Backup Directory dialog box appears. Click the **Next** button, and the backup directory will be created as a subdirectory of the WorldView directory.

Save Space   Once you've decided to keep WorldView, you can delete the backup directory to save space.

9. You will now be told **WorldView can be added to the Start menu**. The **Yes** option is already selected, so click **Next**.

10. When the Ready to Install! dialog box appears, click the **Start Install** button. The installation begins, and a meter shows you its progress.

11. When WorldView is completely installed, an Install Microsoft Reality Lab dialog box appears. (If it doesn't, you already have the right version of this 3-D driver installed; you can skip to the end of this procedure.) Click the **Next** button.

12. A dialog box asks you to wait, and the WorldView installation window is replaced by a Reality Lab setup window. A dialog box appears asking you to select a driver, and listing some options. Make sure **Software driver** is selected and click the **Next** button.

13. The Reality Lab installation begins. A meter shows the progress of the installation. When all the files are in place, a dialog box tells you **Reality Lab has been installed successfully**. Click **OK**.

WorldView has now been set up. You can run it as a stand-alone application, if you want, to view worlds stored on disk or that you already know the full URL for. If you want Netscape to automatically use WorldView to display any worlds you find while surfing the Web, however, you'll need to inform Netscape of that. To do so, follow these steps:

1. Start Netscape.

2. From the **Options** menu, select the **General Preferences** command, and click the **Helpers** tab to get the dialog box displayed in Figure 12.4.

3. Search the list for an entry with the file type **x-world/x-vrml**. If you find it, click it and skip to step 5.

4. If you don't find the entry, you'll have to create it. Click the **Create New Type** button, and a dialog box appears. Type **x-world** into the **MIME Type** field and **x-vrml** into the **MIME SubType** field. Then click **OK**, and the dialog box disappears.

5. Type **wrl,wrz,flr** into the **File Extensions** field on the **Helpers** tab (if the entry is not already there).

6. Click the **Browse** button and a File Navigation dialog box will appear, starting in your Netscape Programs folder. If you see a **WorldView** folder, double-click it to enter it. Otherwise, double-click the **plugins** folder, and then double-click the **WorldView** folder.

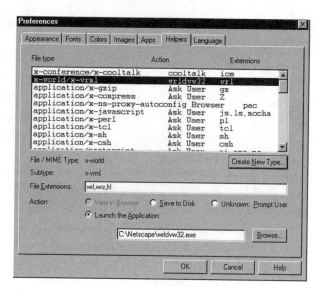

Figure 12.4   Use the Preferences dialog box's Helpers tab to configure WorldView as your VRML browser.

7. When you see a file called **WrldView.exe**, click it. Then click the **Open** button.

8. Click **OK** to close the Preferences dialog box.

If you already have a VRML plug-in installed, you will have to repeat this procedure every time you start Navigator and want to use WebSpace. (This is because Netscape assumes that if you have a helper application and a plug-in that do the same thing, you want to use the plug-in.) Therefore, if you decide you want to use WorldView as your VRML browser, you must uninstall the plug-in. (There should be an uninstall program in the plugin's directory.)

WorldView Won't Run?   If you have trouble running WorldView, make sure Windows is set up to display 256 colors. To check in Windows 95, right-click a blank area of the Windows desktop, click **Properties**, click the **Settings** tab, and make sure 256 appears in the **Color Palette** text box.

WorldView Basics

Now that you've installed and configured WorldView, you can use it to do some world-viewing. The installation routine stored some worlds on your hard disk, so you don't have to get on the Web to test it out. To use one of the sample files:

1. Pull down Netscape's **File** menu, and select the **Open File** command. (Netscape Gold users will choose the **Open File in Browser** command.)

2. The Open dialog box appears, displaying the contents of your Netscape Program directory. Double-click the **plugins** folder icon to move into that folder. From there, double-click the **WorldView** folder, double-click the **Worlds** folder, and then double-click the **Basic** folder.

3. Click the **Files of type** drop-down arrow, and a list of file types appears. Click **All files (*.*)** to see a list of all the files in the current directory.

4. Double-click the icon for **vrml.wrl**, which is a world file (that's what .wrl stands for).

5. Netscape tells you that an external program is starting, and then a WorldView window opens. If it is not in front of your Netscape window, shuffle your windows to find it.

6. WorldView shows a spinning globe while the file loads, and then it displays the world shown in Figure 12.5. Click the **Maximize** button (the button *next* to the X button on the title bar) to expand this window to full-screen.

The URL Is Different Notice that the URL in the Worlds field isn't the same URL you entered in Netscape. Netscape sometimes gives the helper a copy of the file, instead of telling the program the file's URL. This can cause problems with worlds that use information from more than one file.

7. To be sure you get the whole world, enter the URL right into WorldView's **Worlds** field.

8. Click the **Navigation** button to enter World Navigation mode.

   Point to the main screen, hold down the mouse button, and push the mouse forward. You start to move toward the object. Release the button, and you stop.

   Try the same thing again, only this time pull the mouse back (which will make you back up), or to the left or right (which will make you turn).

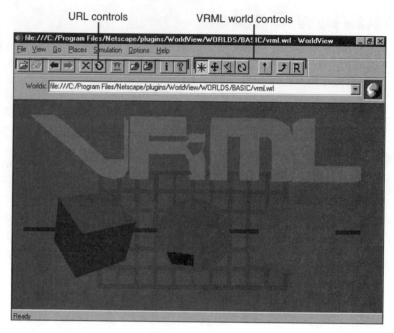

Figure 12.5   The WorldView window.

9. Click the **Restore view** button, and the scene returns to its original location.

10. Click the **Inspect** button, and try holding down the mouse button and dragging the mouse around the screen again. The viewer stands still, but the scene rotates in the direction of the mouse movement.

11. Click the **Tilt** button and drag. This tilts the viewer in the direction of the pointer movement.

12. Click the **Go to** button. The pointer turns into crosshairs.

13. Click part of the scene, and the viewer zooms toward that point, until it is centered on the screen, a fixed distance away.

14. Click the **Pan** button and drag the mouse. The scene moves in the same direction as the pointer.

If you're finding the object movement is too slow or jerky, right-click the scene. A shortcut menu appears, from which you can select the **Simulation** command. Then pick **Quality**, **Quality When Moving**, and **Good**, (see Figure 12.6). This simplifies the drawing that is done when the object is moving, and allows the image to be updated more often.

Figure 12.6 Use the cascading menus to change how the world appears.

To learn more about WorldView, pull down the **Help** menu and select the **Tour Guide** command. The help information shows up in the Netscape window instead of the WorldView window.

In this lesson, you learned about the WorldView helper application. In the next lesson, you'll learn how to get the FIGleaf Inline plug-in, and how to use it to view a variety of graphic formats and manipulate graphics.

FIGleaf Inline by Carberry Technology

In this lesson, you'll learn how to get the FIGleaf Inline plug-in and how to use it to view and manipulate graphics in a variety of formats.

What Is FIGleaf?

FIGleaf Inline improves Navigator's capability to handle graphics. On its own, Navigator has the capability to display only JPEG and GIF format graphics. With FIGleaf installed, you can view these other formats as well:

BMP	(Windows Bitmap)
CGM	(Computer Graphics Metafile)
G4	(CCITT Group 4 Type 1)
PBM	(Portable Bitmap)
PGM	(Portable Greymap)
PNG	(Portable Network Graphics)
PPM	(Portable Pixmap)
Silicon Graphics RGB	(Red, Green, Blue)
SUN	(SunRaster)
TG4	(CCITT Group 4 Type 2)
TIFF	(Tagged Image File Format)
WMF	(Windows Metafile)

In addition, you can view the preview headers (simplified versions of the pictures) stored in EPS (*Encapsulated PostScript*) files. FIGleaf also enables you to flip and rotate images and zoom in for a more detailed view. Figure 13.1 shows a figure that I blew up with FIGleaf Inline. This feature works on JPEG and GIF graphics, as well as the formats previously listed.

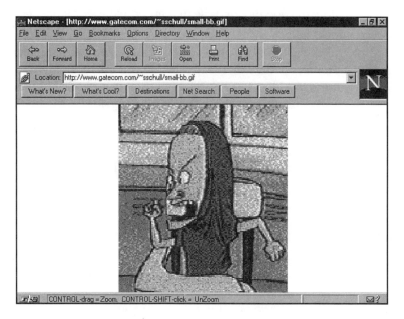

Figure 13.1 FIGleaf gives you complete control to manipulate downloaded images.

Taking It Lightly A junior version of this program, called FIGleaf Inline Lite, is also available. The difference is that it adds only CGM and TIFF to the list of supported file formats, and it doesn't let you manipulate GIF files.

FIGleaf requires Windows 95 or NT to run. (A Windows 3.11 version is in the works.) FIGleaf is available for a 60-day free trial. After that, you pay $19.95 to purchase it.

Downloading FIGleaf Inline

The first step toward using FIGleaf is to get the software. It's available for download from the Carberry Technology Web site. To get it, follow these steps:

1. Go to the Web page at **http://www.ct.ebt.com/figinline/download.html** using Netscape.

2. About midway down the page, you'll see a list of sites where FIGleaf Inline is stored. Click the link for the site nearest you.

3. Netscape displays the Save As dialog box. Choose a temporary directory to store the downloaded file in (you probably have one named C:\TEMP or C:\TMP).

4. Click the **Save** button. The download begins, and a meter shows the progress of the download. The file you are receiving will be called something like FINL10.EXE (the FINL stands for FIGleaf Inline, and the 10 represents the revision—in this case, version 1.0).

This file is about 1 1/2 megabytes. Under ideal conditions, a 14,400 modem will download this in approximately 15 minutes. Given normal Web conditions, however, it could reasonably take 20 to 30 minutes. It will take less time on a faster modem, more on a slower one.

Installing FIGleaf Inline

Carberry has made installing FIGleaf a fairly simple process, as such things go. To install it on your system, follow these steps:

1. In Windows 95 or NT 4.0, click the **Start** button and select the **Run** command.

    In an older version of Windows NT, open Program Manager's **File** menu and select the **Run** command.

2. In the Run dialog box, click the **Browse** button.

3. In the dialog box that appears, select the directory that contains the downloaded file, and then click the name of the file. Click **Open** to return to the Run dialog box.

4. Click **OK**, and a meter appears, showing the progress as the downloaded file is broken down into separate files. When that's done, another meter appears while the installation program sets itself up.

5. When the installation program runs, it displays a Software Licensing Agreement dialog box. Read through this heavy legal stuff (you're about to agree to it), and then click the **Accept** button.

6. A Welcome dialog box appears. Click the **Next** button.

7. The next dialog box suggests a storage directory for the files. The one it suggests, however, is not the standard one for plug-ins. To keep all your plug-ins in one place, click the **Browse** button.

8. The Choose Directory dialog box appears (see Figure 13.2). The suggested directory will be a FIGleaf subdirectory to your main Netscape directory (on most Netscape installations, the path ends in Netscape\FIGleaf). Click just before **\FIGleaf**, and the cursor appears there.

9. Type **\Program\plugins** and click **OK**.

10. A dialog box appears asking **Do you want the directory to be created?** Click the **Yes** button.

11. The directory you specified appears as the proposed one. Click the **Next** button, and the files are copied into the directory. A meter shows the progress of the copy procedure.

12. When all of the files are in place, a dialog box asks **Do you want to view the README page now?** Click the **Yes** button.

Figure 13.2 Store FIGleaf in your plugins subdirectory.

13. Another dialog box tells you **Setup is complete**. Click **OK**, and the setup program goes away.

14. Two Netscape windows open: one displaying the readme file from the hard disk and the other one trying to get a page over the Web. Do whatever you need to do to complete the Internet connection.

15. When you're connected to the Web, a page with a registration form appears (see Figure 13.3). Fill it out to register your copy for the trial period.

16. After you fill out the form, click the **Send User Info** button, and the information is sent to Carberry Technologies.

17. A dialog box appears on your screen, warning you to wait until the next page is complete before you log off or leave. Click **OK**.

18. When the words **Thank You** appear in a graphic at the top of the new page, the transfer is complete. Click the **Close** (X) button on the title bar to close the window. You can disconnect from the Web now.

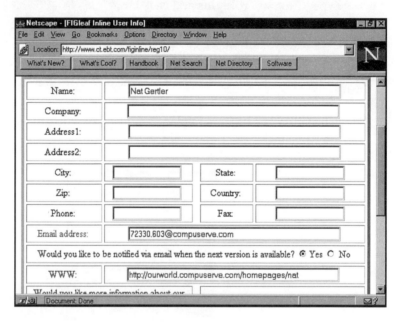

Figure 13.3   Register your new plug-in program.

The other Netscape window (the one with the readme file) should still be open. Take a quick look at this to make sure there's no obviously urgent new information for the current revision. The readme file is the main Help file for the program. A FIGleaf Inline icon appears on the Start menu's Programs menu; you can click it to access the program quickly when you need it.

FIGleaf Inline Basics

You will use FIGleaf in the three specific situations described here, and it functions in slightly different ways for each.

- When you load a standard HTML Web page with a GIF or JPEG image on it.

- When you load a Web page designed to be used with FIGleaf with any of the supported file types.

- When you directly load any of the supported file types from their own URLs instead of as part of a Web page.

Luckily, the FIGleaf installation leaves you with files on the hard disk that you can use to try out all three situations.

GIF or JPEG Images on a Standard Web Page

Follow these steps to take a look at the basic image manipulation functions of FIGleaf:

1. Open the FIGleaf README file. If you just followed the installation procedure, it should still be on your screen. If not, enter the path to your Netscape Programs directory in Netscape's **Location\Go to** text box, followed by **\plugins\FIGleaf\README.htm**. Then press **Enter**.

2. The top frame fills with a GIF image. Right-click this image and select **View Image (helphead.gif)** from the shortcut menu that appears (see Figure 13.4).

3. Netscape now displays only the logo on-screen, and the URL points to the GIF file. Right-click the image to access the menu of FIGleaf commands shown in Figure 13.5.

4. Select the **Rotation** command, and then select **180°** from the menu that appears. The image turns upside down.

5. Right-click to get the menu again, and select **Vertical Flip**. This creates a mirror-like reflection of the image, so the picture is right-side up again—but it's backward!

6. Press and hold down the **Ctrl** key, point to the upper-left corner of the now backward **F**, and hold down the mouse button. The pointer turns into a magnifying glass.

7. Drag the mouse to the lower-right corner of the leaf symbol. As you do, a box of dotted lines appears, indicating the area you're selecting. Release the mouse button.

8. FIGleaf displays a close-up of that part of the image (see Figure 13.6). Try the selection process again, this time selecting the red word **FIGleaf** that appears over the leaf.

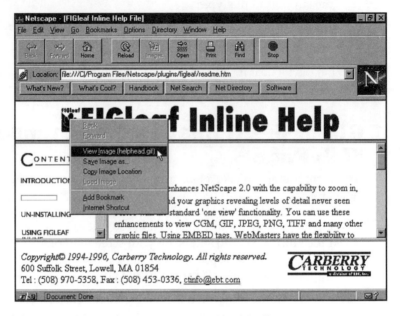

Figure 13.4 Use FIGleaf to view an image in the Help file.

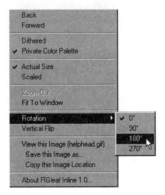

Figure 13.5 The FIGleaf shortcut menu.

9. The word **FIGleaf** is now very large (each dot is about as big around as your pinky). Press and hold the **Ctrl** and **Shift** keys, and click the image. The display reverts to the previous level of enlargement.

10. **Ctrl+Shift+Click** again to return to the normal size image. Open the **Go** menu and select the **Back** command to go back to the README page.

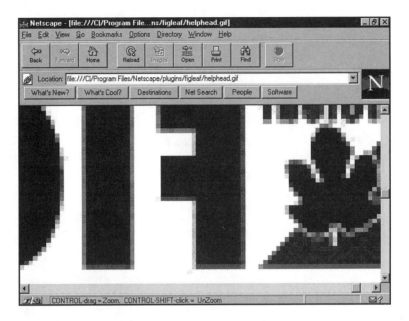

Figure 13.6 A close-up view of the manipulated image.

All of the image manipulation (the flipping and the enlargement) is for current online viewing only. When you go back to the README page, you'll see that the image is still in its original size and orientation. Even if you selected the Save Image command while viewing the enlarged, reversed image, it still saves the original image.

Loading a Graphic Directly

If you have a URL for a graphic file that's in one of the supported graphic formats, you can just enter that URL into Netscape's Location/Go to text box. Netscape automatically uses FIGleaf to display the file. Then you can manipulate it as necessary using steps 4 through 10 of the previous exercise.

Images on Pages Designed for FIGleaf

When a Web page is specifically designed for use with FIGleaf, you can get all of the same capabilities that you get when you call up the graphics file directly—

339

without ever leaving the page. You can view graphics in all the formats, and you can enlarge and manipulate them. However, you are limited in that you can only work in the space that the graphic takes up.

To try this function of FIGleaf, follow these steps:

1. Open the FIGleaf README file. If you just followed the previous procedure, it should still be on your screen. If not, type the path to your Netscape Programs directory in Netscape's **Location/Go to** text box, followed by **\plugins\FIGleaf\README.htm**. Then press **Enter**.

2. In the frame marked **Content**, click **WHY USE VECTOR GRAPHICS?** (You may have to scroll down to find it.) A discussion of vector graphics appears in the adjoining frame.

3. Scroll through the frame until you see two nearly identical images side by side, as shown in Figure 13.7. It's a little hard to make out, but it's a landscape picture of the Space Shuttle, ready to launch, against the dawn sky.

Figure 13.7   Side-by-side pictures of the Space Shuttle.

4. Point to the picture on the left, press and hold the **Ctrl** key, and use the mouse to select a small rectangle that includes the top half of the launch tower. That section becomes enlarged, and scroll boxes appear at the edge of the image so you can scroll around and see the whole image enlarged (see Figure 13.8).

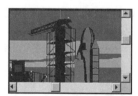

Figure 13.8   The enlarged Space Shuttle shot.

340

5. Right-click the image to access the shortcut menu of FIGleaf commands.

6. Select the **Vertical flip** command, and a mirror-image appears.

7. **Ctrl+Shift+Click** on the image, and it returns to normal size but remains flipped.

Notice that when you enlarge the image, you can see important details that you couldn't see when it was smaller. That wasn't true in the previous exercise. That's because the file you enlarged there was a GIF file, which stores the image as a bunch of dots (exactly what you normally see on-screen). File formats that store images as dots are called *raster* formats. GIF and JPEG are both raster formats.

The file you just enlarged, however, was stored as a CGM file, which is a *vector* file format. This means that the image is described in the file as a combination of lines, curves, and shapes. When you enlarge it, the picture shows as much detail as the screen will display in that mode, and lines that were too small to see in the original size now become visible.

In this lesson, you learned about the FIGleaf Inline plug-in. In the next lesson, you'll learn how to get the Crescendo plug-in and how to use it to listen to MIDI music stored on the Web.

Crescendo by LiveUpdate

In this lesson, you'll learn how to get the Crescendo plug-in and how to use it to listen to music stored on Web pages in MIDI format.

Understanding MIDI

Crescendo is a plug-in that lets you listen to music stored as MIDI files on Web pages. *MIDI* (Musical Instrument Digital Interface) stores music in a way that's very different from that of the digitized sound recordings that other audio plug-ins play.

The MIDI file doesn't contain a recording of a performance of the music. Instead, it is the computer equivalent of sheet music: a list of which notes are played, by which instruments, and in what order (see Figure 14.1). Your sound card knows how to re-create the sounds of many different instruments. When Crescendo feeds this MIDI information to your sound card, the sound card performs the music.

MIDI has advantages and disadvantages when compared to digitized audio. You don't get any vocals with MIDI. Standard PC speech synthesis is certainly not developed enough to synthesize a good singer! You also don't get the nuances of a fine artist's performance from a MIDI file; you merely get the notes in the right order. What you hear may be very different from what the person who created the file heard, because the final sound depends heavily on how your sound card generates the music. (Cards that have *wave tables* tend to sound much better than the cheaper sound cards that merely synthesize the instruments. Also, the original composer may have been using professional-quality MIDI-controlled electronic instruments, which sound better yet.)

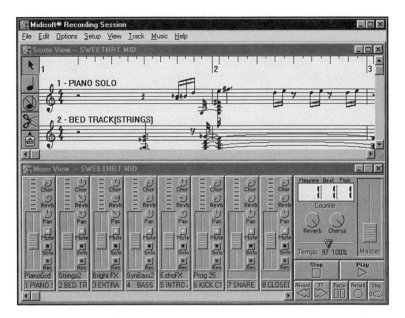

Figure 14.1 An example of a MIDI file as viewed by the MIDI editing program Midisoft Recording Session.

Wave Table The digitized sounds of various instruments stored on a sound card. When a card with a wave table plays the sound of the instruments, it's producing an actual recording of the instruments instead of a mathematically designed computer simulation.

The capability to vary the sound is actually one of MIDI's strengths, however. Because you have the sheet music, you can change how it is interpreted. You'll need separate MIDI editing software to do so (Crescendo is just a player, not an editor), but once the file is on your disk, you can change which instruments play which parts, you can change the tempo, or you can rearrange the notes.

Compose Yourself If you want to create your own MIDI music or edit other people's music, you will need a MIDI editor program, which is often called a *sequencer*. Popular sequencers include Powertracks and Dr. T's.

The biggest advantage of MIDI for Web use, however, is file size. The tune loaded in Figure 14.1, for example, has 16 instruments playing for almost a full minute. Yet the file is less than 13 kilobytes. It can be downloaded in one-twentieth of the time it would take to download a typical low-quality digitized sound that you might find on the Web; it can be downloaded in less than one-five-hundredth of the time that it would take to download pure CD-quality audio.

Crescendo is available for Windows 3.1, Windows 95, and Windows NT, as well as for the Macintosh. You need to have a sound card to use Crescendo.

There is an enhanced version available called Crescendo Plus, which doesn't have to wait until the file is finished downloading before it starts playing. That version costs more, though, so I'll show you how to get the shareware version. If you want Crescendo Plus, you can look into upgrading later. Registering the shareware version costs $9.95; buying the Plus version costs $19.95.

The Crescendo file itself is quite small, a mere 10 kilobytes. Therefore, download time is insignificant, no matter what speed your modem runs at.

Downloading Crescendo

Crescendo is available for download from LiveUpdate's Web site. To get your copy, follow these steps:

1. Go to **http://www.liveupdate.com/dl.html** using Netscape.
2. In the form that appears, fill in your name and e-mail address and click the **Submit** button.
3. Scroll down to the bottom of the page until you see the OS logos shown in Figure 14.2. Click the logo for your operating system.
4. At the bottom of the new page is a list of download sites. Click one of them, and Netscape displays the Save As dialog box, which points to your Program directory.
5. If you don't already have a plugins folder, click the **New Folder** button and type **plugins** as the folder name.
6. Double-click the **plugins** folder icon to indicate that you want the file stored there.
7. Click the **Save** button, and the download begins. The file you are receiving will be called either MIDI16.EXE (for 16-bit versions of Windows) or MIDI32.EXE (for Windows 95 and NT).

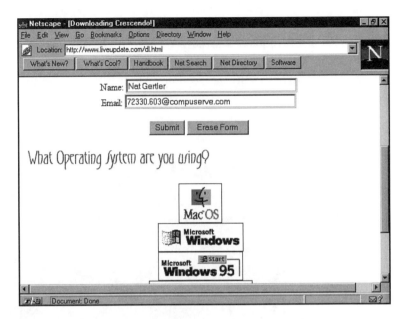

Figure 14.2 Choose the version that works with your operating system.

Some downloading information appears for a brief time. When that display disappears, the download is complete. You can disconnect from the Internet now, but installation is so quick that you might not want to bother doing so because you'll have to get back on the Net to try it out.

Installing Crescendo

Being a rather simple product, Crescendo installs quickly and easily. All it does is expand a single file from the compressed form that you downloaded. To start that process, follow these steps:

1. Exit Navigator.
2. In Windows 95, click the **Start** button and select the **Run** command.

   In older versions of Windows, open Program Manager's **File** menu and select the **Run** command.
3. In the Run dialog box, click the **Browse** button.
4. In the dialog box that appears, select the plugins directory and click the name of the file (which should be something like cres32b.exe).
5. Click the **Open** button to return to the Run dialog box.

6. Click **OK** to start the installation program. The WinZip Self-Extractor dialog box appears (see Figure 14.3). Self-Extractor will decompress the zipped files to the current folder unless you choose a different folder.

7. Click **Unzip** to start the decompression. After a short time, WinZip indicates that the files have been successfully decompressed.

8. Click **OK**. The installation program opens a Readme file in WordPad. Read it, and then exit WordPad.

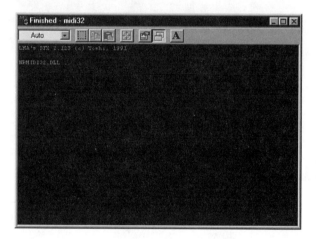

Figure 14.3   This window appears after the file has expanded.

If you want to, you can now delete the MIDI16.EXE or MIDI32.EXE file from the plugins directory.

Crescendo Basics

Basics are really all there is to Crescendo. It's a useful and fun utility, but it is not at all complicated. To test Crescendo, follow these steps:

1. Head to **http://www.liveupdate.com/crescendo.htm** using Navigator.

2. When the page is fully loaded, a control panel appears in the upper-right corner (see Figure 14.4). Click the **Play** button to start playing the recording. Drag the slider below the buttons to increase or decrease the volume.

3. Click the **Stop** button (see Figure 14.5) to stop playing the MIDI file at any time.

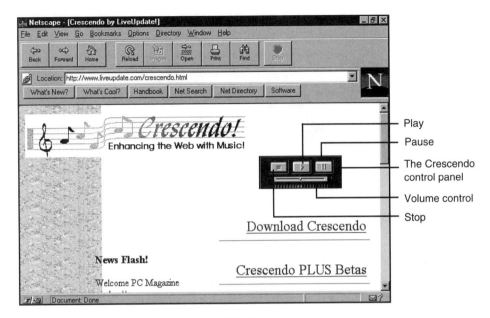

Figure 14.4 The control panel lets you play MIDI files.

Click this button to stop.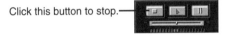

Figure 14.5 You can stop the music at any time.

4. Click the **Pause** button (the rightmost button on the control panel) to pause or resume play.

 Embedded Tunes Some embedded tunes play automatically; as soon as the page loads, the tune starts playing. To start other tunes, however, **TIP** you have to click the Play button.

5. Scroll down the page and click the **Experience Crescendo!** link. A page with a list of MIDI tunes appears, and a randomly chosen tune begins to play. (Each time you connect to this page, a different tune starts playing.)

6. Scroll down the page and click one of the links to load the MIDI file. The Netscape window is empty except for the control panel in the upper-left corner (see Figure 14.6). If the file doesn't start playing, click the **Play** button.

7. Click the **Stop** button to stop the music.

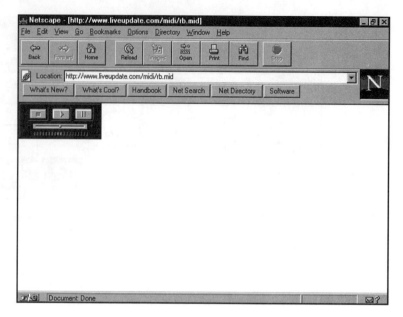

Figure 14.6   The window is blank except for the control panel.

More MIDI

There are tens of thousands of MIDI scores available on the Web. Some are great, some are horrible, and some will sound good only if you have a good sound card. (As a rule, music that's designed for play on the computer will sound okay on a cheap sound card, but transcriptions of music intended for performance will really only sound good on a high-quality sound card that uses wave table synthesis).

You cannot play all MIDI files off of the Web. There are two main reasons for this:

- The MIDI files have been compressed—as you can tell by the .zip file extension. Compressing makes sense for a file that someone will download and listen to later because it reduces the download time. However, Crescendo (and other MIDI players) can't understand such a file until it has been run through a decompression program such as WinZip. As MIDI capability becomes a more common Web browser feature, fewer MIDI files will be zipped. But those that are out there for a long time to come will be zipped.

- The file is in the proper form and has an extension of .mid or .midi, but the server on which it is stored does not know what those extensions stand for. If you click a MIDI file and end up with a Navigator window with a small amount of garbled text, this is the problem. The server has to be able to tell Navigator that this is a MIDI file in order for Crescendo to be able to pick it up.

Despite these problems, there are plenty of good sites with Crescendo-friendly MIDI files. Here are just a few (many of which have links that will lead you to others):

- http://www.pensacola.com/~sunstar/jukebox.html has the MIDI Jukebox, a selection of popular songs available at the push of a button (see Figure 14.7).
- http://www.prs.net/midi.html is the site of The Classical MIDI Archives, a gargantuan collection of long-haired music that contains more than 1,800 MIDI files (see Figure 14.8).

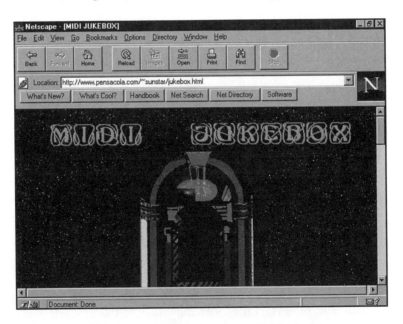

Figure 14.7 High-tech emulates lower-tech with the MIDI Jukebox.

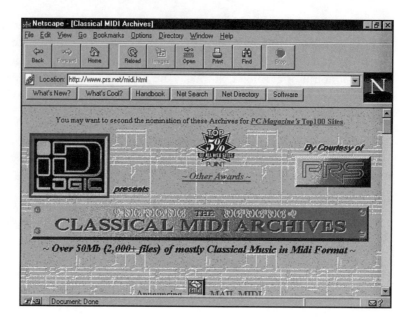

Figure 14.8   The Classical MIDI Archives offer hours of pleasure for the classical music fan.

- http://www.metronet.com/~caw/midi/ is the #Midi Page, which has some modern selections.
- ftp://ftp.cs.ruu.nl/pub/MIDI/SONGS/ is a constantly growing archive with hundreds of tunes in various categories.
- http://www.eeb.ele.tue.nl/midi/ doesn't have much in the way of actual tunes. What it does have, however, are some good articles about MIDI. If listening to some of these files makes you curious about what these files are and how you can make them, this is a good source for information.
- http://www.dzp.pp.se/midi/ is the home of The MIDI Music Pages, a good source for rock and pop music.
- http://math.idbsu.edu/gas/midi is the Gilbert and Sullivan Archive. In addition to files for the music of this classic musical theater team, this site also offers text files with the words to the songs. If you've ever tried to dope out the lyrics to "The Major General's Song," you'll enjoy this.

In this lesson, you learned how to use Crescendo to play MIDI music files over the Web. In the next lesson, you'll learn how to get RealAudio Player and use it to receive near-live radio transmissions over the Web.

RealAudio Player

In this lesson, you'll learn how to use RealAudio Player.

What Is RealAudio Player?

RealAudio Player is a program through which near-to-live audio transmissions are sent over the Internet. Think of it as radio on the Internet.

But don't confuse it with radio transmissions, because unlike live radio, RealAudio Player produces only near-to-live transmission. This means that when you listen to a RealAudio transmission, there's a small delay between the time that the sound signal is sent and the time that you actually hear it—about two seconds or so. In other words, it's almost "live."

To hear a RealAudio broadcast, you'll need a copy of RealAudio Player. In this lesson, you'll learn how to install the RealAudio Player and how to use it. By the way, there are other programs that can perform near-to-live transmission of sound over the Internet, but RealAudio Player is, by far, the most popular.

How does near-to-live sound transmission differ from regular sound transmission over the Net? Well, normally, when you encounter a sound file, such as an .AU or .VOX file, on a Web page, Netscape has to receive the entire sound file and save it to disk before launching a sound player application, which reads the sound file in its entirety and, finally, starts playing it. Since many sound files are large (256K or so), this means you'll spend a lot of time online before you can hear the sound.

RealAudio Player cuts a lot of time out of this audio transmission process. When you encounter a Web page with a RealAudio Player sound file, RealAudio Player begins decompressing it after it receives just the first few thousand bytes.

It then starts playing the decompressed portion; meanwhile, the rest of the sound file is still being transmitted. Also, you can save a RealAudio Player transmission as a file if you want, but you don't have to in order to hear it just once.

How Do I Create a RealAudio Sound File? If you create your own Web pages and you'd like to include a RealAudio Sound file, you can easily convert a conventional .AU or .WAV file using the RealAudio Encoder program you can download from the RealAudio Web site.

Downloading RealAudio Player

In order to install RealAudio Player, your PC must have at least a 486/33 MHz CPU, with 8MB of RAM, 2MB of free hard disk space, a sound card, and at least a 14.4 Kbps Internet connection. (If you use a 28.8 Kbps connection, you'll need at least a 486/66 MHz CPU.)

RealAudio Player comes in two versions: as a helper application (which runs outside the Netscape window as a separate program) and as a plug-in (which runs invisibly, within Netscape). The choice is yours.

Which One Should I Choose? Unless you have a big need for a helper application that you can use without Netscape to play sound files, choose the plug-in version of RealAudio Player. It works automatically once installed, and it takes up less space on your hard disk.

You download RealAudio from the RealAudio Web site, located at http://realaudio.com. During the download process for RealAudio Player, you'll complete a form with your name, address, and computer information. This form gives the RealAudio developers information about their users so they can fine-tune their product. In addition, you'll need to apply for a password that RealAudio will send you via e-mail, which you'll need in order to visit the RealAudio site and play a test sound file. Once you download RealAudio Player, you'll install it, which is described in the next section.

To download RealAudio Player (the plug-in version), follow these steps:

1. Connect to the Internet and start Netscape.

2. In the **Location/Go to** text box, type **http://www.realaudio.com** and press **Enter**.

3. Click **RealAudio Player**, as shown in Figure 15.1.

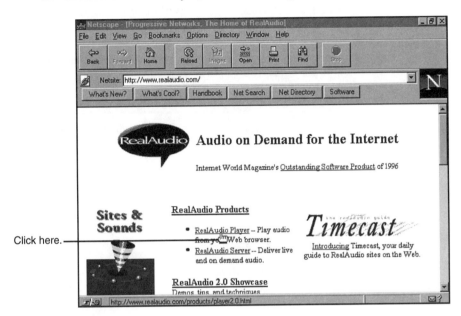

Click here.

Figure 15.1 The RealAudio Player Web site.

4. Click **Download the Free RealAudio Player**.

5. Complete the form for downloading RealAudio by typing in your name, organization, address, and so on (see Figure 15.2).

6. Select your operating system, processor, and Internet connection speed from the drop-down list boxes provided.

7. When you're ready, click **Go to download and instructions page** to download RealAudio Player.

8. You'll see a warning; click **Continue**.

9. Click a download site.

10. Select a folder in which to save the file, and then click **Save**. You may want to save the file into a TEMP directory so that you can check it for possible viruses before installing it.

Remember to Get a Password Before you log off the Internet, apply for a RealAudio password by jumping to the password request page, located at http://www1.realaudio.com/get_password.html. Enter the appropriate information and click **Sign me up!** You'll receive your password via e-mail in a few days.

CAUTION

11. After the file is downloaded to your PC, disconnect from the Internet so that you can install RealAudio Player without racking up connect-time charges.

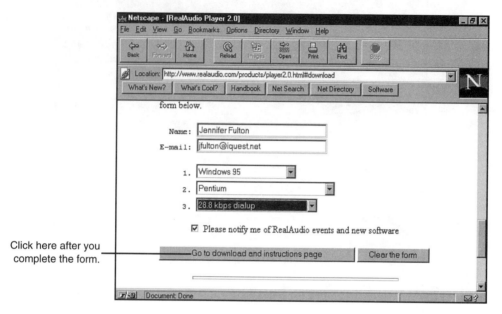

Click here after you complete the form.

Figure 15.2 Complete the RealAudio download form.

Installing RealAudio Player

RealAudio Player comes in two forms: a helper application which works outside of Netscape as an independent program, and as an in-line plug-in, which works within Netscape, enabling it to recognize and play RealAudio transmissions whenever you encounter them.

During the process of installing the RealAudio Player, it automatically ties itself into your Web browser. This allows your Web browser to activate the RealAudio player whenever it encounters a RealAudio page on the Web. However, the way in which RealAudio Player is used by Netscape depends on whether you install the helper app, or the in-line plug-in version. If you install the helper app, then when a RealAudio file is found, Netscape turns it over to the RealAudio program, which opens its own window and plays the file. If you install the plug-in, when a RealAudio file is found, the RealAudio program automatically begins playing it without opening a separate window.

Not So Fast! After downloading and installing RealAudio Player, you'll need to wait until you receive your password via e-mail. The process takes a few days. The password is needed to listen to most RealAudio sound files at the RealAudio demo site.

Installing RealAudio As a Plug-In

To install RealAudio Player as a plug-in in its default directory C:\RAPLAYER, follow these steps (if you want to install RealAudio as a helper app and change its directory, follow the steps in the next section):

1. Start File Manager or Explorer and change to the directory in which the RealAudio file is stored.

2. Double-click the **RealAudio** file.

3. Read the license agreement and click **Accept**.

4. Next, enter your **Name** and **Company** and click **Continue,** as shown in Figure 15.3.

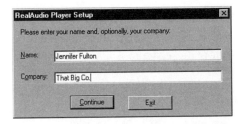

Figure 15.3 Enter your name and company name.

5. Click **OK** to confirm your name and company information.

6. Select your modem speed from the list and click **OK**.

7. Click **Express setup**.

355

Which Directory?   If you want to install RealAudio into a specific directory, such as /Netscape/Plugins/RealAudio, you'll need to select **Custom setup** in step 7.

8. Next, you're asked for the name of the directory that contains Mosaic. Since you use Netscape instead of Mosaic, click **Cancel** instead.

9. You'll see a message telling you when RealAudio Player is installed. Click **OK** to continue.

10. RealAudio Player starts and plays a test file, as shown in Figure 15.4. After it's complete, click the **Close** button.

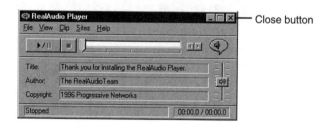

— Close button

Figure 15.4   RealAudio Player tests your configuration by playing a file.

Installing RealAudio As a Helper Application

To install RealAudio Player as a helper application, or to change its default directory, follow these steps:

1. Start File Manager or Explorer and change to the directory that contains the RealAudio file.

2. Double-click the **ra32_20.EXE** file.

3. Read the license agreement and click **Accept**.

4. Enter your name and your company and click **Continue** (see Figure 16.3).

5. Click **OK** to confirm your name and company information.

6. Select your modem speed from the list and click **OK**.

7. Click **Custom setup**.

8. Enter the name of the directory in which you want RealAudio Player placed and click **Continue**.

9. When you're asked if you want to link RealAudio Player with Netscape, leave the first check box selected, as shown in Figure 15.5.

If you don't want to add the RealAudio Web site to your bookmarks list, you can deselect the second check box. Click **OK** when you're through making your selections.

Leave this option selected. ──

You can deselect this
option if you want. ──

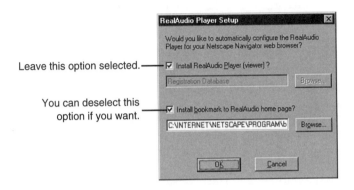

Figure 15.5 Linking RealAudio to Netscape.

10. Next you're asked if you want to install RealAudio as a plug-in. Since you want to install it as a helper app, click **No**.

11. You'll be asked if you want to link RealAudio Player to Mosaic. Since you use Netscape, deselect both check boxes (see Figure 15.6). Then click **OK**.

Deselect both of
these options. ──

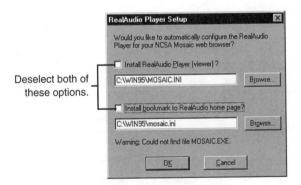

Figure 15.6 Because you use Netscape, deselect both check boxes in this dialog box.

12. When you see a message telling you that RealAudio Player is installed, click **OK**.

357

13. RealAudio Player starts and plays a test file. After it's complete, click the **Close** button.

RealAudio Player Basics

RealAudio Player is easy to use. When you connect to a Web site with a sound file, your Web browser automatically launches RealAudio Player to play it.

There are several Web sites that use RealAudio Player, and more appear every day. The best place to start is to simply visit the RealAudio Web site, located at http://www.realaudio.com. The site contains links to other Web sites that feature RealAudio sound files (files that end in .RA or .RAM), such as the National Public Radio Web site and the ABC Internet Hourly News site.

To visit the RealAudio site and play a test file, follow these steps:

1. Connect to the Internet and start Netscape.

2. In the **Location/Go to** text box, enter the address **http://www.realaudio.com** and press **Enter**.

3. Click **Sites and Sounds**. This will take you to a page listing many RealAudio Web sites, as shown in Figure 15.7.

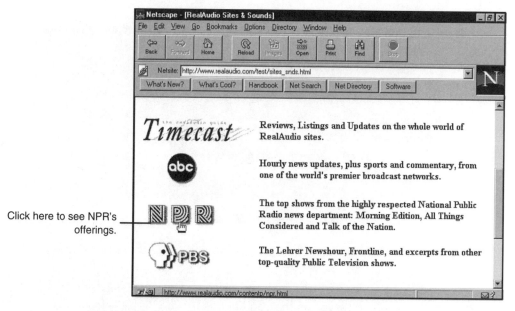

Click here to see NPR's offerings.

Figure 15.7 The RealAudio Web page contains links to many RealAudio test sites.

4. Click the **NPR** logo. You're taken to a page that lists many NPR RealAudio sites.

5. Click **Morning Edition**.

6. Select a file from those listed, as shown in Figure 15.8. The length of the audio transmission (in minutes) appears in parentheses.

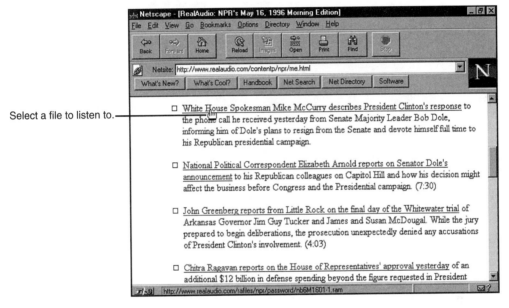

Select a file to listen to.

Figure 15.8 Select the RealAudio file you want to hear.

7. Fill in the **User Name** and **Password** text boxes in the dialog box that appears.

8. Click **OK**, and the RealAudio Player automatically launches. The elapsed time appears in the lower right-hand corner.

9. (Optional) To pause the transmission at any time, click the **Pause** button, as shown in Figure 15.9. To resume the transmission, click the **Play** button.

10. (Optional) Use the **Volume** slider to increase or decrease the volume, or click the **Stop** button to stop the transmission at any time.

You can continue to use your Web browser to visit other non-RealAudio sites. The RealAudio transmission continues as you work. When the transmission ends, the RealAudio player automatically closes.

Stop button

Pause and Play button

Volume Control

Figure 15.9 You can pause the transmission if you like.

I Want to Stop! You don't have to play the entire audio transmission if you don't want to. Simply click the **Close** button to close RealAudio Player.

In this lesson, you learned how to install and use RealAudio Player. In the next lesson, you'll learn about PreVU, an MPEG video player.

PreVU MPEG Video Plug-In Player

In this lesson, you'll learn how to play MPEG videos using the PreVU plug-in for Netscape.

What Is PreVU?

MPEG video is a format for storing a full-motion color video "movie" with a soundtrack together in a single file. That's the good part. The bad part is that MPEG video files are typically very large.

Most MPEG viewers work like this: when you click a link that points to an MPEG file, the entire file is downloaded to your hard disk, and then the viewer begins to play it. MPEG files, even for the shortest videos, are quite large and you can end up waiting a long time for them to download before you start to view them.

Using a process called *streaming*, PreVU lets you see the contents of the MPEG video *as you're downloading it*, albeit at the speed of the download (which is generally slower than the playback speed). This gives you the opportunity to cancel the download if the video contains nothing you particularly want or need. Once the file is downloaded, of course, the playback continues at normal speed. In addition, PreVU provides controls for starting and stopping the video as needed.

Because PreVU is an in-line plug-in, you view the video within the Netscape Navigator window, so that the movie remains an integral part of the Web page. With other MPEG viewers, you typically view the MPEG video within a separate window, outside of the Web page. This makes the whole experience a bit disconnected.

What If I Have a Video File Saved on My Hard Disk? Because PreVU is an in-line plug-in, it can't act as a stand-alone program; in other words, you can't launch PreVU without Netscape. But, if you want to view an MPEG video file from your hard drive, simply start Netscape, and then drag-and-drop the video file into the Navigator workspace. The video will then play at normal speed (since it's not being downloaded.)

What About MPEG-2 Video? MPEG-2 is a more highly compressed video format than regular MPEG, complete with stereo soundtracks. Because MPEG-2 is so very different from regular MPEG format, it is not supported by the current version of PreVU.

CAUTION

Downloading PreVU

In theory, PreVU can be installed on any system that can run Netscape Navigator. In reality, on some systems, its performance may be limited. For optimal performance, your PC should have at least a 486 66 MHz CPU. Also, for at least moderately smooth viewing during the downloading of a video file, your modem should be no slower than 14.4Kbps. With this latest version of PreVU, if your PC is equipped with a sound card, you will be able to hear what you see (that is, if the video has sound).

Nothing in Life Is Free Nothing in life is free, including PreVU. If you decide to keep PreVU after installing it, you need to register it and pay a small fee. The next section explains how.

CAUTION

In the next section, you'll learn how to install PreVU following the download. To download PreVU, follow these steps:

1. Connect to the Internet and start Netscape.

2. In the **Location/Go to** text box, type **http://www.PreVU.com/ download.html** and press **Enter**. You'll be taken to the download page (not the home page) of PreVU's Web site.

3. System requirements for PreVU may change without notice. To double-check whether your system can accommodate PreVU, click **PreVU's system requirements**, as shown in Figure 16.1.

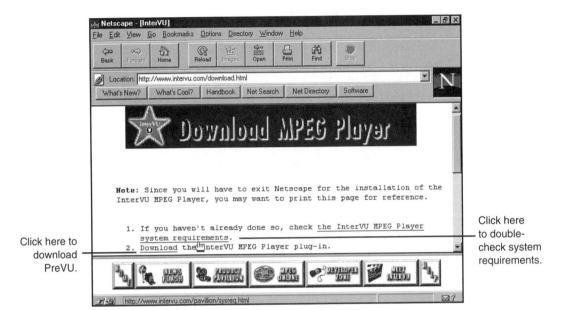

Click here to download PreVU.

Click here to double-check system requirements.

Figure 16.1 InterVU's main download page.

4. Current system requirements will be listed here. If your PC meets these standards, click Navigator's **Back** (left-arrow) button to continue the download. If your PC is lacking the requirements, you can still download PreVU, although it may not function properly (if at all).

5. Click **download** (see Figure 16.1), and a license agreement appears.

6. Read the license agreement, and then click **I Agree** at the bottom of the page. A form appears, asking for your name and e-mail address.

7. Complete the form and click **Download MPEG Player**. If you have Netscape security options set, a confirmation dialog box appears; click **Continue**.

8. Click the **Download** link. A dialog box appears, prompting you to select the folder in which you want to place the downloaded file.

9. Select a folder in which to save the file, and then click **Save**. You may want to download the file into a TEMP directory, in order to check it for possible viruses before actually installing it.

363

10. After the file is downloaded to your PC, disconnect from the Internet so you can save on connect charges while you install PreVU.

Installing PreVU

Like most other in-line plug-ins, PreVU automatically ties itself into Netscape during the installation process. This allows Netscape to activate PreVU whenever it encounters an MPEG video on the Web.

Another interesting side note is that, unlike most other installation programs, PreVU's setup does not allow you to select the directory where PreVU will be installed. Instead, it is installed into its default directory, where Netscape Navigator will know to find it.

CAUTION

What If I Have More Than One Netscape Navigator on My System? As silly as that might sound, you can possibly be evaluating/ comparing both Navigator and Navigator Gold on the same system. As a Navigator plug-in, PreVU can only be installed for one copy of Navigator—or rather, on one copy at a time. If you want PreVU to work for both copies, you'll need to install it twice.

Here's what you do: Run the copy of Navigator for which you want to install PreVU first; then exit the program and run the PreVU installation program. Once you're done, run the *other* copy of Navigator and exit. Having an entry in a file located in the Windows directory tells the PreVU installer that, for all intents and purposes, that second copy is the "active" copy. Run the installation program a second time, follow the same instructions, and PreVU will work for both copies.

Once you've downloaded the PreVU installation program, follow these steps to install it on your system:

1. Start File Manager or Explorer and change to the directory where you downloaded the PreVU file.

2. Double-click the **PreVU** file (its file name should be something like iv0_952.exe). The PreVU Installation program starts (see Figure 16.2).

3. Click **OK** to begin the setup process, and the standard license agreement appears.

4. Read the license agreement and click **OK**. Next, you're shown the directory into which PreVU will be installed.

5. As mentioned earlier, you can't change this directory, so just click **OK**. The installation program begins copying files to the PreVU directory.

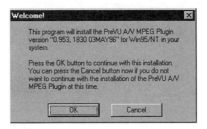

Figure 16.2 PreVu is ready to install itself.

CAUTION

What If PreVU Has Found the Wrong Version of Netscape?
If the setup program has identified the wrong version of Netscape (assuming you have two different versions), click **No, I must ABORT THIS INSTALLA-TION and run a different copy of Navigator!** Start and exit the version of Netscape you want to link PreVu to, and then start the installation process again.

6. If you want to add PreVU to your Windows 95 Start menu, click **Yes**.

7. Take note of how to uninstall PreVU in case you want to remove it later. When you're ready, click **OK**. The Test PreVU MPEG dialog box appears, asking if you want to view a Help page and a video (which of course, you do).

8. If you want to test PreVU with an MPEG video now, click **Yes**. Netscape Navigator will automatically be launched—you don't have to be connected to the Internet. The preview page appears, as shown in Figure 16.3.

9. The test video is located at the bottom of the preview page. Scroll down until you see the US Navy Blue Angels in a video frame.

10. Click the green arrow button at the bottom of the frame to start the video (see Figure 16.4). This MPEG video is already on your disk, so you won't be downloading it, just testing to see if it plays. The video will stop automatically.

11. You're finished installing PreVU. Close the Netscape window.

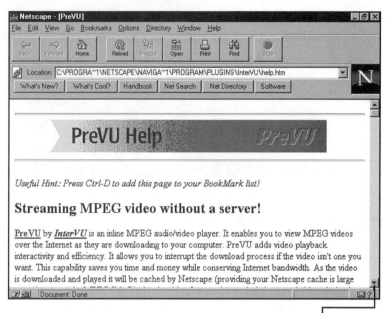

Figure 16.3 The PreVU test page.

Scroll down to
see an MPEG test file.

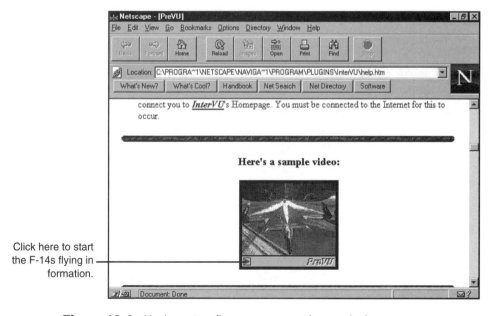

Click here to start
the F-14s flying in
formation.

Figure 16.4 You're not surfing anymore; you're *soaring*!

PreVU Basics

Like most in-line plug-ins, there's not much to running them. Click a link to an MPEG file, and Netscape automatically launches PreVU.

If you were using some other MPEG video viewer and you clicked a link, you'd have to wait until Netscape Navigator downloaded the entire video, after which the MPEG video player would finally begin playing it. Between clicking the link and starting to play the video, there can be an interval of anywhere up to a half-hour of thumb twiddling.

However, with PreVU installed, you can view the video almost as soon as your system begins to receive it. Of course, this early preview is not perfect. It runs in a slower-than-real mode, so the video seems a bit jerky at times. In addition, during the preview, sound is omitted. Once the file is completely downloaded, you can play it, complete with sound, at real speed.

So, if you're anxious to try out your new toy, follow these steps to connect to the demo page on the PreVU Web site:

1. Connect to the Internet and start Netscape.

2. In the **Location** text box, type **http://www.PreVU.com/demo.html** and press **Enter**. PreVU's demo page appears.

3. Scroll down to see a list of demos as shown in Figure 16.5. Click any link to play the associated demo. An opening frame appears.

4. Begin downloading the video by clicking the green right-arrow **Play** button.

5. PreVU begins playing the portion of the video it has downloaded thus far in regular time (but without sound). When PreVU gets to the part it hasn't downloaded yet, it pauses. PreVU then plays the next frames of the video as they become available. During playback, to cancel the downloading of the video at any time, click the red square **Stop** button.

6. When the video finishes downloading, the Disk button will appear just to the right of the Stop button on the PreVU control panel, as shown in Figure 16.6. If you want to save the video on your hard disk, click this button. Select a directory in which to save the file; then click **OK**.

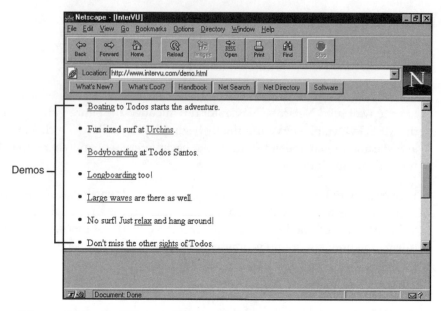

Figure 16.5 PreVU's test drive page.

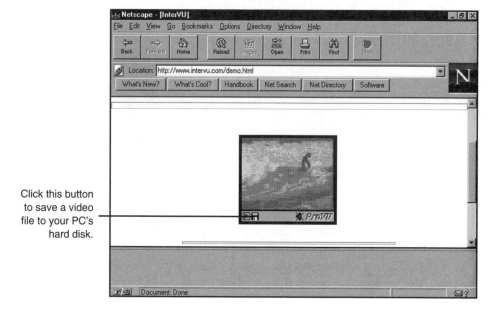

Figure 16.6 Click the Disk button to save the video permanently.

Playing Saved MPEG Video Files

Although PreVU is not a stand-alone program, it can play MPEG files you've saved to your hard drive. Follow these steps to get PreVU to play a saved MPEG video:

1. Open Explorer or File Manager, and change to the directory that contains the MPEG video file you want to play.

2. Start Netscape Navigator. (You do not need to connect to the Internet.)

3. Resize the Netscape window, if necessary, so that you can see File Manager or Explorer.

4. Drag the MPEG file into the Netscape Navigator window (where the Web pages are generally displayed) and drop it (release the mouse button). PreVU plays the video, as shown in Figure 16.7.

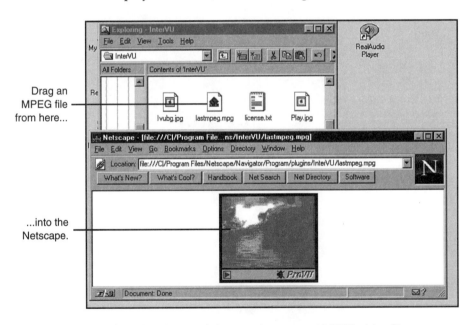

Drag an MPEG file from here...

...into the Netscape.

Figure 16.7 Use drag-and-drop to play a saved MPEG video file.

Where Are the Rewind and Fast Forward Buttons? PreVU provides only basic controls such as Play and Stop. Playback is at standard MPEG speed, and you can't adjust that. Also, you cannot resize the playback frame. If you need more control over the video playback, consider using Apple's QuickTime viewer, which plays back both QuickTime and MPEG videos with many, many more controls.

In this lesson, you learned how to install and use the PreVU plug-in to play MPEG video files.

Using HTML and the Netscape Extensions to Create Web Pages

Getting Started with HTML

In this lesson, you learn what HTML is, and you learn how to create your first HTML file and open the file for viewing in Netscape.

What Is HTML?

HTML stands for HyperText Markup Language. HTML is used to define the location and description of elements on a Web page (or other hypertext document). An HTML encoded document includes the text you want to display, information on how that text should be formatted (such as whether the text is a headline, whether it should be centered, and so on), the names of the pictures that will appear (but not the pictures themselves), and other important information. When you connect to a Web page, your Web browser (such as Netscape Navigator) "builds" the Web page in memory according to the HTML instructions, and then it displays the assembled Web page on-screen.

How Is an HTML File Organized?

An HTML file is a plain ASCII text file that contains only letters, numbers, spaces, and punctuation. You can edit an HTML file with any text editor (such as Notepad or WordPad, which are included with Windows) or any word processor that has a "save as text" feature (which includes most modern word processors such as Microsoft Word and WordPerfect). HTML file names usually end in the extensions .HTM or .HTML, so that computers and humans can recognize them as HTML files.

Automated HTML Coding Some text editors were designed for creating just Web pages. For example, HoT MetaL and HotDog offer shortcuts for creating and testing your page, which saves you time. In addition, Netscape Navigator Gold includes a specially designed Web page editor, which you'll learn how to use in Part 6.

Two basic types of information appear in an HTML file: *text* and *tags*. The words that appear on the Web page are the text. The tags are the special commands that tell the browser how to format the lines of text and how to include other elements on the page. The tags in an HTML file are easy to spot because they appear inside angled brackets as shown here:

```
One word will appear in <B>bold</B> type.
```

In this line, <B> and </B> are the tags. The first tag means "start bold type," and the second tag means "end bold type." So when that line appears on a Web page, it looks like this:

```
One word will appear in bold type.
```

Who Decided What the Tags Mean?

HTML isn't actually a language per se, it's more of a document type definition (DTD), or an adaptation of another language. That other language is SGML (Standard Generalized Markup Language). SGML is deceptively simple; all it really does is define markup tags, stating that they begin with a < and end with a >. HTML defines what each specific tag is supposed to do.

The original HTML language was designed by Tim Berners-Lee of CERN, the European Laboratory for Particle Physics. The language is maintained by two groups: the Internet Engineering Task Force (IETF), which is made up of representatives from software developers, and the World Wide Web Consortium (W3C), a group based at MIT. Think of these groups as a sort of United Nations of software developers and manufacturers—all of which have similar stakes in Web technology. The IETF and W3C periodically revise HTML (sometimes working jointly, but more often each working on its own agenda) to add new functionality to the language structure, as well as to address the concerns of manufacturers and many Web users (often adding new tags and eliminating tags that are not being used). The current official version of HTML is 2.0, but W3C is currently drafting a proposal for version 3.2, which has advanced features including provisions that would make HTML documents more easily interpreted by database management systems.

Netscape and Microsoft have designed their Web browsers to understand not only the standard HTML tags, but additional tags as well—some of which just aren't part of the official HTML yet, and some of which may never be. The good thing about the additional tags, called *extensions* (as in the Netscape Extensions and the Microsoft Extensions) is that they allow more complex and useful Web pages. The bad thing is that you can't properly view Web pages that are designed around them unless you have a browser that understands these extensions. (To the Web browser manufacturer, this has historically been a good thing because it encouraged people to use their browsers instead of the competition's.) With the promised widespread adoption of HTML 3.2 (whose specifications were drafted with the assistance of both Netscape and Microsoft) however, these extensions might become a thing of the past.

Starting a Web Page

In order to see how an HTML page is built, let's just go ahead and start making one! Start up a text editor and open a new blank document. I'll walk you through building the document.

Many HTML pages begin with an identification command, which is called a *prologue*. For example, you might see a prologue like this:

```
<!DOCTYPE HTML PUBLIC "-//IETF//DTD HTML//EN//2.0">
```

This prologue lets the Web browser know that this is an HTML document, built around specification 2.0. This line is not very important because if the line isn't there, the browser will assume it's true anyway.

A complex HTML document is comprised of elements, which are parts of a document in much the same way chapters and appendixes are elements of a book. A simple HTML document has only one element—itself. Therefore, to tell the browser that a document is going to be more complex and will have formally distinguished elements, you need the tag <HTML>.

The first formal element of a document that contains the <HTML> tag is the head element, whose beginning is marked with the <HEAD> tag. The head element contains identifying information about your Web page, such as its title and its place in a sequence or database. Many Web pages have just one line in the head element, such as

```
<TITLE>A very empty Web page</TITLE>
```

where the words between the <TITLE> tag and the </TITLE> tag are a title for the page. This is the title that Navigator and other Web browsers put on the title bar so you can tell where you are. It's also the name you'll see when this page is stored in your bookmark or history file.

Uppercase or Not?   You don't have to type tags in uppercase letters; the <title> tag works the same as the <TITLE> tag. But if you type them in all uppercase, it's easier to distinguish the tags from the text when you're working in your HTML file.

Notice that when the <TITLE> tag showed the start of the title, the end tag was the same, only with a slash after the first bracket. This is similar to the relationship between the tag to start bold text, <B>, and the tag to end it, </B>. Now that you have all the header information that you really need, you need a tag that indicates the end of the head element. As you probably guessed, that tag is </HEAD>. (Later, you'll add the end to the <HTML> section, which contains an </HTML> tag.)

The element following the head is the body element of the HTML document, the material that will appear on your page. As you might expect, the body element begins with this tag:

```
<BODY>
```

If you're not going to have anything actually in the document, you can follow the <BODY> tag immediately with the tags indicating the end of the body of the document and the end of the HTML material.

```
</BODY>
</HTML>
```

As your first test of HTML document structure, you can put all of this together to create a Web page that has the formal element structure of a complex HTML document—with none of the contents. Type the following HTML code into your word processor or Windows Notepad, and you'll have a complete, but blank, HTML document.

```
<!DOCTYPE HTML PUBLIC "-//IETF//DTD HTML//EN//2.0">
<HTML>
<HEAD>
<TITLE>A very empty Web page</TITLE>
</HEAD>
<BODY>
</BODY>
</HTML>
```

Create a directory called **htmldocs**, and (using a Save as Text or Text Only option if you're using a word processor) save this file as a plain text file with the file name **blank.htm**. That way, whenever you need to start a new HTML document, you have a blank one that you can just fill in!

Viewing Your HTML File

Even though Netscape is called a Web browser, you can use it to view HTML documents stored on your hard disk. To view your newly created HTML document, follow these steps:

1. Start Netscape. If it starts to dial your modem to connect to the Internet, cancel it; there's no need for you to be tying up the phone line or racking up Internet charges while you do this.
2. Open the **File** menu and select **Open**.
3. Select your HTML file and click the **Open** button. Netscape loads the file and displays it, just as it would if the file were a page on the Web (see Figure 1.1).

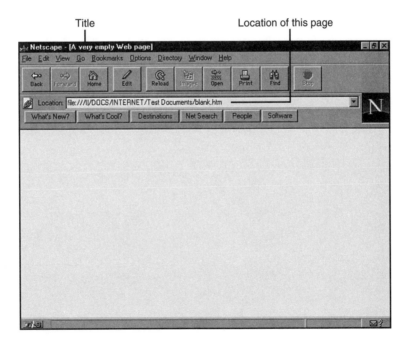

Figure 1.1 Here's your blank HTML page!

Windows 95 If you're using Windows 95, you can start your Web browser and display the file quickly by clicking the **Start** button, selecting **Run**, entering the full path to your file, and pressing **Enter**.

Leave your Web browser open for the next lesson.

In this lesson, you learned about HTML, created a simple HTML file, and viewed it in your Netscape browser. In the next lesson, you'll learn to format text within an HTML file.

Dealing with Text

In this lesson, you learn to enter text in your Web page and format it.

In Lesson 1, you created a basic HTML document. We'll work through this lesson using that document. If you don't still have that document open, start Netscape, press **Ctrl+O**, and select the file to open. Netscape displays your document on-screen.

Adding Text to Your Page

In your text editor, put your cursor between the <BODY> and </BODY> tags and start typing. You can type any characters you want, except the characters " < > and &. Navigator treats these characters as if they were always part of HTML code (which you don't want other viewers to see). So don't use them in regular text. However, you can insert special codes in place of those characters. Each code tells the Web browser to display the symbol the code represents instead of the code itself. You make these substitutions so that Web browsers don't confuse the text characters with the characters that start special HTML commands.

Code	Description
"	Displays a quotation mark (")
<	Displays the "less than" sign, which is an open angle bracket (<)
>	Displays the "greater than" sign, which is a close angle bracket (>)
&	Displays an ampersand (&)

To add text to your Web page, follow these steps:

1. Type the following text in your HTML document on a line between the
   <BODY> and </BODY> tags.

   ```
   About this page:
   I am writing this page because Nat Gertler told me to. He's one of
   the authors of this book I'm reading, but he's also a great guy,
   &amp; really doesn't deserve the nickname &quot;muffinhead&quot;.
   ```

2. Save the page (as you learned in Lesson 1), giving it the name **test1.htm**.
   Make sure you don't overwrite the file blank.htm; you want to keep it to
   use as a template each time you start a document.

3. Bring Netscape to the front by clicking the **Netscape** button on the taskbar
   (in Windows 95) or by pressing **Alt+Tab** until you see the Netscape
   window (in Windows 3.1).

4. Select the **File**, **Open** command, choose the **test1.htm** file, and click the
   Open button. The browser loads the page from the disk and displays it.
   Figure 2.1 shows the new Web page displayed in Netscape.

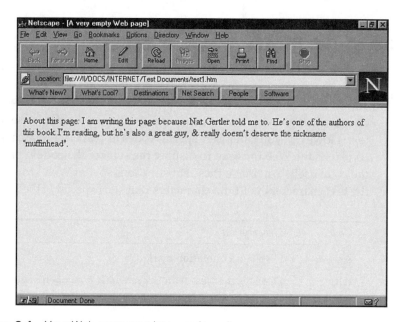

Figure 2.1   Your Web page now has words on it.

Notice that the lines all run together, regardless of where you started new lines. With the exception of one specific case (described shortly), Web browsers *always* ignore the carriage returns. If you want to start a new line of text, you have to use formatting tags (set off with < and >), which you'll learn about in "Adding Line Breaks and Paragraphs" later in this lesson.

Formatting the Page Layout with HTML Tags

HTML provides a number of tags that enable you to place your text where you want so you can organize it for logic and readability. The more you understand these tags, the more readable you'll be able to make your Web page, and the better your Web page visitor will be able to understand you.

Adding Line Breaks and Paragraphs

The first thing you'll want to do after you enter your text is break it up so that it doesn't run together in one big block. There are two ways to do this. The first is to use the tag <BR>, which stands for *break*. Whenever the Web browser sees that tag, it starts a new line. For example, suppose you type this text:

```
Once upon a time, there was a space bunny.<BR> His name was Horatio.
```

In your browser, it will appear like this:

```
Once upon a time, there was a space bunny.
His name was Horatio.
```

The other method is to use the <P> tag, which stands for *paragraph*. The exact shape of a paragraph (its indentation and so on) isn't standard, so you might be able to customize it in your Web browser. The <P> tag has a matching end tag (</P>) that you can use, but it is not required. A line with <P> tags might look like this:

```
<P>This is a paragraph.</P>
```

The main difference between <BR> and <P> is that <P> adds a blank line after the text, where <BR> does not. However, you can create that effect by using two <BR> tags in a row.

Centering Text

The <CENTER> and <CENTER/> tags tell Netscape to center any enclosed text horizontally across the page. (It also centers pictures, which you'll learn about in Lesson 4.) This tag is a Netscape extension, so it's not in HTML 2 or even in the proposed HTML 3 specification (in which centering will be incorporated as an attribute to the <P> tag, as in <P align=center>). However, it's a tag that most Web browsers currently recognize.

1. In your editor, put a <CENTER> command right after the <BODY> tag, and put a </CENTER> tag right before the </BODY> tag.

2. Save the file.

3. Click Netscape's **Reload** button to see how that changes your page's appearance.

Web Browsers Ignore Beginning Spaces Typing spaces before the first word of a paragraph will not make the first line appear indented. Netscape ignores all spaces before the first character on the line.

Separating Lines

Sometimes you want to visually separate one section of text from another. If you were writing a book, for example, you could start a new section by starting a new page. When you're creating a Web page, you can produce the same effect by adding a horizontal line across the page.

The tag that adds a separator line is <HR>, which stands for *horizontal rule*. When a browser finds that tag in an HTML file, it draws a line under the current line of text and starts remaining text after that line. Netscape has created an extended version of the <HR> tag. By adding *attributes* to the tag, you can shape the length, width, position, and color of the line.

Attribute An additional setting that you can include in the tag, which changes the effect of the tag in some way. You add an attribute, set off by spaces, after the name of the tag but before the closing bracket.

You can use the following attributes with the `<HR>` tag:

- `NOSHADE` makes the line black. Example: `<HR NOSHADE>`
- `SIZE` changes the thickness of the line. This attribute always needs a measurement of the line thickness, measured in pixels (the little dots that make up the screen). Example: `<HR SIZE=10>`
- `WIDTH` changes how far across the screen the line goes. (If you don't use the `WIDTH` attribute, the line will go all the way across.) `WIDTH` needs to be set equal to a value that's measured either in number of pixels or in percentage of the screen width. Examples: `<HR WIDTH=200>` or `<HR WIDTH=80%>`
- `ALIGN` tells Netscape where to start a line that doesn't go all the way across; therefore, it is really only used with `WIDTH`. `ALIGN` also needs a more detailed setting, but its settings are words, not numbers. Use `LEFT`, `RIGHT`, or `CENTER` to align the line flush against either side of the screen or to center it. Example: `<HR WIDTH=50% ALIGN=RIGHT>`

To try both the simple and complex forms of the `<HR>` tag, add the following lines after the text lines in your HTML file:

```
<HR>
<HR NOSHADE SIZE=12 WIDTH=30% ALIGN=RIGHT>
```

On-screen, your lines should look something like those in Figure 2.2. If you were using a Web browser that did not support the Netscape extensions, the lines would look identical.

Formatting Special Blocks of Text

If you look through this book, you'll see that while a lot of the text is in standard paragraph form, a lot of it isn't. You have headlines (like the one right above this paragraph) and lists (like the index in the back of this book). The same is true of Web pages. HTML has the capability to handle text in a number of ways other than standard paragraph form.

Headlines

The folks who designed HTML allowed for six different sizes of headlines, which you indicate using the tags `<H1>` through `<H6>`. To add some different types of headlines to your document, type the following text and tags into your HTML file:

```
<H1>The Epic Adventures of Horatio Space Bunny!</H1>
<H2>Series One</H2>
<H3>Book I</H3>
<H4>Chapter 1</H4>
<H5>Section (1)</H5>
<H6>First word: Once...</H6>
```

The standard line created with the <HR> tag

A line created with the <HR> tag and attributes

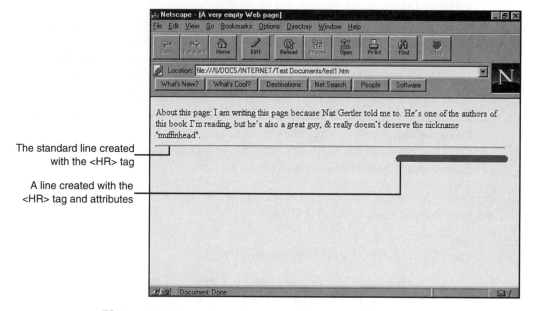

Figure 2.2   Two different horizontal lines.

When you look at the file with Netscape, you can see that each headline starts on a new line, and there is a fair amount of space between headlines. These general settings are part of the HTML specifications for the <H1> through <H6> heads.

The actual sizes of the headlines depend on which browser you use to view them, as well as the user's configuration. You can't assume that the person who is viewing your Web page will see the same size letters you see in your Web browser. The only thing that you can really assume is that an H1 headline will be at least as big as an H2, and an H2 will be at least as big as an H3, and so on. (In most cases, the higher the number, the smaller the headline, but sometimes you will run into cases where the last few sizes are the same.) In addition, some people are still accessing the Web with terminals that don't have graphical capabilities, in which case, all lettering throughout the page looks the same. However, those people make up a small percentage of the Web-surfing public, and their numbers are dwindling.

Lists

Often, you will want to display information in a list. Whether that information is the names of your pets, steps for building a nuclear reactor, or a glossary of movie terms, HTML has a way to display your list. HTML supports five types of lists, each of which is shown in Figure 2.3.

- *Unordered lists* display each list element on a separate line, which is usually indented and begins with a bullet. The tag for unordered lists is <UL>.

- *Ordered lists* also display each element on a separate line, but each line begins with a number instead of a bullet character. (You don't have to enter the numbers yourself; Netscape does that automatically.) The tag for ordered lists is <OL>.

- *Menu lists* are for items no longer than one line of text. Depending on the browser, each item may or may not have a bullet in front of it. Menu lists are usually indented. The tag for menu lists is <MENU>.

- *Directory lists* are for very short items (no longer than 20 characters each) such as file names or employee lists. Some browsers put a bullet in front of each one, and some automatically put the lists into columns. The tag for directory lists is <DIR>.

- *Definition lists* are for items in which you have a short entry (such as a word being defined) followed by a possibly longer entry (such as a definition). The tag for definition lists is <DL>.

Unordered, ordered, menu, and directory lists are put together very similarly. The first line of a list starts with the proper list tag, which is followed by an <LI> tag and the first list item. Then each consecutive line contains an <LI> tag followed by the text for the entry. After the last list element, the closing tag for that sort of list appears on a separate line. As an example, enter the following list between the </CENTER> and </BODY> tags in your file. (It goes after the <CENTER> tag because you don't want the list centered.)

```
Things I've got to do today:
<OL><LI>Eat donuts
<LI>Worry about my weight
<LI>Eat more donuts
</OL>
```

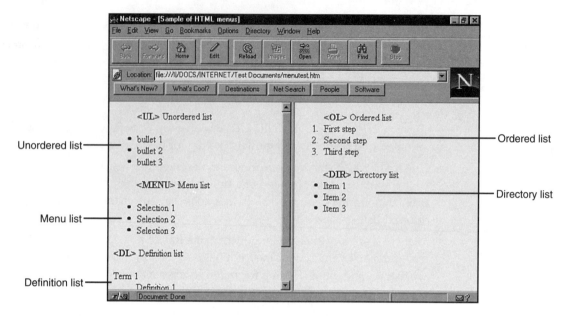

Figure 2.3   HTML offers a variety of lists.

When you save the file and open it in Netscape, you'll see that the three elements appear numbered. If you let your browser handle the numbering, you don't have to worry about renumbering the entire list if you add, remove, or rearrange entries. In addition, the browser automatically starts a new line after the list, so you don't have to worry about upcoming text getting mixed in with the last entry.

The Change-Up   You can replace these opening and closing tags with tags for one of the other types of lists to see what they look like in your browser.

The definition list has to be organized a bit differently because each list entry has two parts: the word and the definition. In a definition list, you don't use the <LI> tag. Instead, you use the <DT> tag (which stands for *Definition list Term*) and the <DD> tag (which stands for *Definition list Definition*). Type the following definition list in your file to see what it looks like.

```
<DL>
<DT>Dough<DD>Some cash, a little cash
<DT>Ray<DD>The guy who mows my lawn
<DT>Mi<DD>A name that's short for Mimi
</DL>
```

When you display your definition list, it should look something like this:

```
Dough
      Some cash, a little cash
Ray
      The guy who mows my lawn
Mi
      A name that's short for Mimi
```

Although this is called a definition list, you aren't limited to using it for definitions only. For example, you could use it for the script of a play, making the name of the character speaking a <DT> entry, and making his or her lines a <DD> entry.

Character Formatting

In Lesson 1, you learned about the <B> and </B> tags, which you can use to make text bold. HTML also provides the <I> and </I> tags that let you italicize text. To see how they work, perform these steps:

1. Enter the following line into your HTML file:

```
You can <I>mix <B>and</I> match</B> bold and italic.
```

2. Save your file.

3. Reload the Web page by clicking Netscape's **Reload** button. What you see should look like this:

```
You can mix and match bold and italic.
```

Lately, many HTML designers are turning away from the <B> and <I> tags and are using the <STRONG> and <EM> tags instead. In most Web browsers, the <STRONG> tag has the same effect as the <B> tag, and the <EM> tag (which stands for *emphasis*) has the same effect as the <I> tag. In other Web browsers, you can

387

decide how to make <STRONG> and <EM> text look. So if a user wants to, he can have emphasized words appear in a different color or a different font instead of in bold or italic. Add this line to your HTML file to see this at work:

```
I like my coffee <STRONG>strong</STRONG> and my debates
<EM>emphatic</EM>.
```

Two other ways of highlighting text have been proposed for the HTML 3 specification. The <U> and </U> tags mark text for underlining, and the <STRIKE> and </STRIKE> tags tell the browser to put a line through the middle of the text. However, because these are proposed tags right now, you can't yet count on Web browsers supporting them.

<BLINK> is a Netscape extension tag that causes your words to blink on-screen. This text effect can make it very hard for the readers to focus on other words on the page. However, <BLINK> is not recognized by many browsers.

Emphasis Everywhere!   Character formatting tags such as <B> and <BLINK> do work in headlines, lists, and other altered text.

Using Preformatted Text

The only way to make all of your carriage returns appear as carriage returns, to make sure the Web browser doesn't automatically wrap the lines when it hits the edge, and to have the browser display spaces at the beginning of a line is to use the *preformatted text tags*. Any text that appears between the tags <PRE> and </PRE> will be treated as preformatted. For preformatted text, Web browsers use a monospace font so you can line things up. (This is different from the font used for text in most graphical Web browsers, which is not monospace.)

To test some preformatted text in your Web page, follow these steps:

1. Type the following text into your HTML file:

```
<PRE>   Once upon a time I was a young man,
but then I
  ate some walnuts
    Sold some pretzels
      and juggled kittens. Or not.</PRE>
```

2. Save the HTML file.

3. Reload the Web page by clicking Netscape's **Reload** button, and the following text appears on your page, with the same spacing you gave it:

```
    Once upon a time I was a young man,
but then I
    ate some walnuts
      Sold some pretzels
         and juggled kittens. Or not.
```

Monospace   A monospace font is one in which every character is the same width. (This type of font is commonly used on typewriters.)

Using preformatted text is a good way to take information from a non-HTML file and include it in an HTML file. You can copy text out of your word processor or even your spreadsheet, paste it into your HTML document, and insert preformatted text tags—without losing line breaks and indents.

In this lesson, you learned to enter and format text. In the next lesson, you will learn to add links to your Web page.

Creating Links

In this lesson, you learn to add links to your Web page.

Adding Basic Links

What puts the hypertext into the HyperText Markup Language is the capability to create links to other documents or to other parts of the same document. This is a very powerful feature, and luckily, it is also easy to use. You can turn any text—whether it's part of a normal paragraph, a list, or even a headline—into a link.

Every link in hypertext has two parts, both of which are called *anchors*. An anchor is the endpoint of a link, regardless of whether you're linking from that point or to it. To mark a link, you use the <A> tag, which stands for *anchor*. To use it to specify the destination anchor to which the <A> anchor is linked, you'll also need to use the HREF attribute. Put the following text into your test1.htm file:

```
Click here to go to <A HREF="http://ourworld.compuserve.com/
homepages/nat/">Nat's home page</A>.
```

When you save and reload the file in Netscape, the link should look like the one in Figure 3.1.

Notice that the full URL for my home directory was enclosed in those quotes. If you are linking to a Web document that isn't on your system, you will need to include the full URL. That URL can be for a specific file or a directory. If you enter the URL of a directory without any reference to a specific file, the file will be linked to that directory's default file (usually named "index.html" or "index.htm"). If there is no such file, the server sends a picture of the contents of that directory, as though the user were linking to that directory using an FTP program.

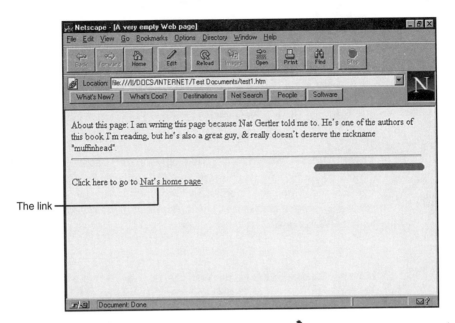

The link —

Figure 3.1   Notice how the words between the open and close tags appear under-lined and in a different color.

If, however, your destination anchor points to another file on the same system, you don't have to include the full URL. You can use a *relative* URL, which shows the path from the current document's directory to the file you're linking to. The "linked-to" file can be in one of four places in relation to the current file's directory:

- *In the same directory (or folder).* In this case, no directory information is needed. For example, if you're linking from /me/homepage/recipes.htm to the file located at /me/homepage/aspic.htm, you can use the tag `<A HREF="aspic.htm">`.

- *In a subdirectory of the current directory.* For this, you need to list the directory path after the current directory. For example, if you're linking /me/homepage/recipes.htm to /me/homepage/cookbook/aspic.htm, your tag should be `<A HREF="cookbook/aspic.htm">`.

- *In a directory above the current directory.* Two periods in a row represent the parent directory to the current directory. So to link from the page at /me/homepage/recipes.htm to the page at /aspic.htm, you would use the tag `<A HREF="../../aspic.htm">`.

- *In a directory that's not directly above or below the current directory.* You will need to use the two dots method to get up to a directory in the path of the file (which may even go all the way back to the root directory), and then you must specify the rest of the directory from there. For example, if you were linking /me/homepage/recipes.htm to /me/favorites/soup.htm, you would use the tag <A HREF="../favorites/soup.htm">.

Think Ahead   When creating links on your Web pages, try to organize a directory structure on your hard drive in the same way it's going to be organized on the system that stores your Web page. That way, you can test your relative links because they will link the same from your hard disk as they do from the Web page.

How to Slash   Because the Web is a UNIX system, the directories in a URL are separated with front slashes (not back slashes as in DOS and Windows).

Linking to a Specific Part of a Page

If you have a large Web page, you might want to create a link to a specific part of that page. For example, if you have a page of movie reviews, you might want to create a link directly to the review of *Revenge of the Space Bunny II* so that it immediately comes up on-screen when someone clicks the link. You might even want to use multiple links in a table of contents of your Web page. You can put the table at the top of the page so a reader can jump directly to the part he's looking for.

In order to link to a specific location, you must give that location a name called a *target*. To set up such a target, follow these steps:

1. Go to a line in the middle of your test1.htm file.

2. Name that spot "middle" by inserting the following tag:

```
<A NAME=middle></A>
```

You're using the anchor tag again, but it has a different attribute. The name that you give it can include any string of letters and numbers without spaces. The only requirement is that you can use each particular name only once on a Web page.

3. Immediately following the <BODY> tag, add the following line:

```
Go to the <A HREF=#middle>middle of the page</A>.
```

392

This is like a normal link, except that instead of typing a URL in quotation marks, you type the # sign followed by the location name, and you don't use quotation marks.

4. Save the file.

5. Load the file in your Web browser, and check out the link to see how it works.

Linking to a Specific Place in Another File

In order to see how you link from one file to a specific location in another, you're going to need a second HTML file. That's easy to take care of because you have a template for new HTML files on your hard drive.

First, make a copy of the file blank.htm and call it **test2.htm**. Next, open the file test2.htm and change the title from A very blank Web page to Another example page. Then follow these steps to create a link to a specific spot in a different Web page:

1. If you haven't added the "middle" anchor to the test1.htm file (as instructed in the previous task), go back and do that now.

2. In the test2.htm file, add this line (the relative URL with the # and the location tacked on) between the <BODY> and </BODY> tags:

```
Go to the middle of <A HREF="test1.htm#middle">another page</A>.
```

3. Save this file and test the link. Because you used a relative URL, this link will work anywhere that both files exist in the same directory—whether that's on your hard disk or on the Web server.

CAUTION

Graphics Hassles If you create a link to the middle of another page, when that page comes up, the graphics that appear before the destination anchor may not load. For that matter, even if you create a link to the middle of the *same* page, the graphics may stop loading when the user clicks that link. Because of this, you should use links to named locations on other pages only if those pages are text-only pages. You should use such links within the same page only if the graphics load so quickly that the user does not have a chance to click the link before the graphics appear.

Creating Mail Links

If you want someone reading your page to be able to send you e-mail, you can build a link into your Web page that will start up the user's e-mail editor and let him or her create a message for you. In order to do this, you must have an e-mail address. (Odds are good that if you are publishing Web pages, you also have an e-mail address.)

As an example, let's use my address: 72330.603@compuserve.com. To create the link, you treat the e-mail address as a special URL called a *mailto* URL. Your link will look something like this:

```
Let's send mail to <A HREF="mailto:72330.603@compuserve.com">Nat
Gertler!</A>
```

Not everyone's setup will allow him to use the mailto link. There are both hi-tech and low-tech ways to address this problem. The hi-tech way is to use the <FORM> tag to create an on-screen form. But forms are an advanced topic and are not covered in this book. The low-tech way is simply to display your e-mail address on the Web page, so readers using your Web page can copy it down and send you e-mail the old-fashioned way.

Adding Comments

You might want to keep track of certain information about your HTML file that you won't want to make visible on your Web page. For example, you may want the file to include the date that the file was last changed, a history of the changes made to the file, or explanation for some of the fancier HTML tricks you used in the file. You can do any of these things using a comment tag.

It's No Secret!   Even though comments are not visible in a Web page, anyone who can view your Web page can also look at the source of the page and see your comments. Don't put anything secret in there!

A comment tag is a bit different from most tags. Whereas most tags are made up of <, the tag name, and >, a comment tag is made up of <!—, the comment, and —>. To try out a comment tag, type the following line after the <BODY> tag in your test2.htm file:

```
<!— I made this file while I was learning HTML —>
```

Add comments to your file as much as you need to so you can understand it later. If you're not sure whether you should bother with putting in a comment, go ahead and put it in. You don't save a lot of time now by not putting it in, but you could waste a lot of time later trying to figure out what you did.

CAUTION

Don't Use Closing Brackets   Unless you have to, don't use a closing angle bracket (>) in your comments. Although the proper end mark for a comment is —>, some browsers will think the > mark is the end of the comment and will display everything after it!

In this lesson, you learned to create links to other pages and add comments to your text. In the next lesson, you will learn to add graphics to your pages.

Inserting Graphics

In this lesson, you learn about the different graphics formats and how to insert them into your Web page and use them as links.

Graphics Formats

Web browsers support two standard graphics file formats: GIF and JPEG. Most graphics programs can save in one or both of these formats. Even if your favorite tool can't save in one of these formats, it isn't hard to find a program that can convert the file format it does use into a format you need. You don't need an expensive program such as Photoshop to do this; freeware and shareware programs such as LView Pro and Graphics Workshop also provide this feature.

GIF Format

The GIF standard (Graphics Interchange Format) was developed by CompuServe as a standard format that could be read by many computers. This format can store images with up to 256 colors, and it uses *lossless compression* to keep files small. GIF files have the .gif file extension.

TERM **Lossless Compression**   A form of compression in which every pixel of the compressed picture is exactly the same as the original uncompressed image.

GIF files have a number of advantages that make them quite useful for Web pages:

- Because they are compressed, they take up less disk space.

- Most Web browsers support the GIF file format, which means that most people who visit your Web page will be able to see your images without the help of a third-party program.
- Compression makes for faster transmission (so your page comes up faster).
- GIF files can be made transparent.
- They can be interlaced.

The first two advantages are self explanatory; look at the latter two in detail.

A transparent GIF has one color that doesn't show up when the picture is displayed on the Web page. Instead, the background shows through where that color should be. This effectively lets you have pictures that do not have rectangular shapes (such as round buttons or borderless logos).

Usually, when a picture appears on-screen, the top of the picture appears first, and then the picture is filled in downward until the bottom appears. Interlaced GIFs appear full-sized but rough at first, and then the picture gets clearer with time. This way, the user gets a sense of the picture much more quickly.

For both GIFs and interlaced GIFs, each line of the picture is shown immediately when it is received over the Web. Because GIFs are generally stored with each of the horizontal lines in consecutive order, they appear from the top down. By comparison, interlaced GIFs are stored with every eighth line first, followed by the lines in-between, so a skeleton of the picture appears immediately and is then filled in.

Figure 4.1 shows pictures of an image as a normal GIF, a transparent GIF, and a partially transmitted interlaced GIF.

To create transparent and interlaced GIFs, you need a software program such as LView Pro that specializes in handling GIFs. Most programs that work with a multitude of file formats will save noninterlaced GIFs. Many such programs are available, some of which are freeware.

CAUTION

Don't Use Fancy GIF Tricks! Although your GIF editor may offer you some advanced features, you should avoid using them. A single GIF file can actually be used to hold more than one image, but Web browsers will show only the first one in the file. In addition, some popular Web browsers can't display images stored in GIF's 2-color mode. So even if you use only two colors in the file, you should use a different color mode for your graphics. Most graphics programs will save in 16- and/or 256-color mode.

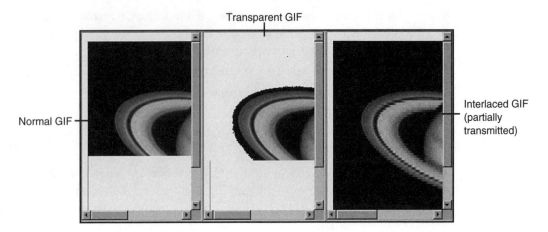

Figure 4.1   Three types of GIF files.

GIFs do, alas, have a couple of significant disadvantages. The first is a visible one: 256 colors is not enough to smoothly re-create real-life images with subtle colors, such as photos or watercolor paintings. Reducing these images to 256 colors results in a *posterizing* effect, in which there are blocky areas of individual colors, and the transition from one color to another stands out.

The other disadvantage is not so obvious, and its full impact has yet to be determined. When CompuServe developed the GIF standard, they made it an open standard so that anyone who wanted to could make a program that would read or write GIFs. After the GIF format became popular, however, it was discovered that the compression technique infringed on a patent held by Unisys. CompuServe eventually made a settlement with Unisys that covered all existing programs that handle GIFs, and that allowed for the development of new *free* programs that read and write GIFs. However, if anyone develops a new *commercial* program that reads or writes GIFs (thus making use of Unisys' patented technique), they have to pay Unisys. This makes it difficult to find a good GIF image editor.

Watch Your GIF Sizes!   The GIF format stores the image size in two places: one is with the image, and one is in the header block just before the image starts to appear. If you're using an advanced GIF editor in which you can set the sizes by hand, you might find cases in which these two sizes do not CAUTION   match. If so, you should set them both to the smaller size. Otherwise, some browsers will use one size, and some will use the other.

JPEG Format

The JPEG format was developed by the Joint Photographic Experts Group as a means of storing photographic-quality images. A JPEG picture can use any of more than 16 million colors, which results in a very accurate reproduction of an image. A JPEG image has the file extension .jpeg, .jpg, or .jpe.

JPEG uses a *lossy* compression scheme. This means that in order to make the file smaller, the JPEG format "generalizes" parts of the image that have similar adjacent colors. A relatively imperceptible part of the image's integrity is lost, in exchange for a much smaller file size. When you save a JPEG picture, you can choose just how much information to keep, on a scale from 0 to 100. If you pick a high number, you will get a picture that is hard to distinguish from the original; if you pick a low number, you'll get a rough version of the picture in a much smaller file.

Figure 4.2 shows enlarged portions from the same picture. The first figure was saved with no lossy compression; the second was saved using JPEG compression with a high information setting (80); and the third was saved using JPEG compression with a low setting (20). Notice that the stray dots and discoloration increases with compression, which makes the picture look fuzzy.

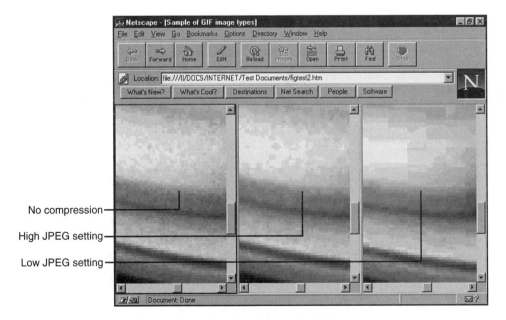

Figure 4.2 A higher setting means less compression takes place, and the picture looks better.

Most programs in which you can create pictures with more than 256 colors can save a file in JPEG format. However, they usually offer some lossless file format as well (such as PCX, BMP, or TIFF).

Preserve Image Quality   If you can spare the disk space, always save your file in a lossless format while you're working on it. (Luckily, the native format of all art programs is lossless.) Only when you're ready to add it to your Web page should you save it in JPEG format. Every time you save and reload a JPEG file, you degrade the picture a bit more, and even with a high information setting, this degradation can add up.

Unlike GIF files, JPEG images cannot be made transparent or interlaced. This means that JPEG images will always be rectangular, and they will appear on-screen either all at once if the compression ratio is high, or starting from the top and working downward as the file is transferred.

Also unlike GIF—and to the advantage of JPEG—there are no charges connected with developing software for this format, so it should maintain popular support for some time to come.

Inserting an Image

You use the <IMG> tag to insert an image in your Web page. However, you cannot use this tag without adding certain attributes. The one attribute that is absolutely required is SRC, which is used to indicate the URL of the graphics file to be displayed.

To experiment with the <IMG> tag, follow these steps:

1. You need one GIF file for this exercise. If you have one handy, make a copy of it called **agif.gif** and put it in the htmldocs directory; then skip to step 6.

2. If you don't have a GIF file lying around, you can borrow one from our Web page. To do that, type **http://www.mcp.com/que/new_users/6n1.html** in Netscape's **Location/Go to** text box and press **Enter**.

3. Right-click the first image.

4. Select **Save this Image as** from the shortcut menu.

5. Put the file in your htmldocs directory, giving it the name **agif.gif**. (Because you're also storing the .html files in this directory, you'll be able to include this image using a short relative URL.)

6. In the body of your test2.htm file, add this line:

```
<IMG SRC="agif.gif">
```

7. Open the test2.htm file in Netscape, and you should see the picture you inserted.

The HEIGHT and WIDTH Attributes

Two attributes you are likely to use with the <IMG> tag are HEIGHT and WIDTH. These Netscape extensions enable you to describe the size of the image in pixels to create two possible effects.

- If you use the HEIGHT and WIDTH attributes to specify actual size of the image, the browser sets aside the correct amount of space it needs to store the picture—before it begins downloading the image. This way, the page won't have to be rearranged when the image actually comes into view. (When you're loading a page from disk instead of from the Web, the pictures usually load so fast that you will not notice the difference.)

- If you specify a size other than the image's original size, the browser sets aside the amount of space you indicate, and when the image arrives, the browser squashes and stretches it as necessary to fit the space provided.

Try putting the HEIGHT=30 WIDTH=300 attributes in the <IMG> tag (after the file name but before the closing bracket) to see what effect it has. Figure 4.3 shows four images: the first with its actual height and width, and the other three with dimensions modified by attributes.

Preserve Image Quality The order of the attributes in a tag doesn't matter. You can put the WIDTH before the HEIGHT, or put both of them before the SRC. However, the tag name (such as IMG) always has to be first.

The ALT Attribute

Another commonly used attribute, ALT, enables you to put text into the space that the image will take up. Using ALT, you can define the image in words so that people can tell what's supposed to be there before it loads. This also gives people who are using text-only browsers (browsers that are incapable of displaying graphics) a sense of what's going on.

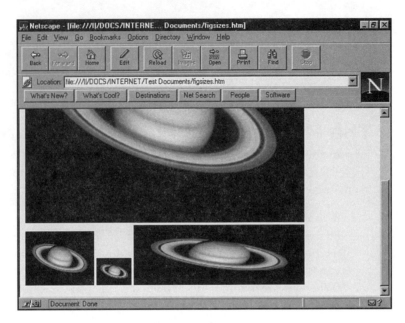

Figure 4.3   Modify the dimensions of an image using the HEIGHT and WIDTH attributes.

The format for ALT is ALT, followed by an equals sign, followed by the text in quotation marks. The complete <IMG> tag might look like this:

```
<IMG SRC="ajpeg.jpg" ALT="A picture of my cat, Vegetables.">
```

Positioning Images

You will rarely have a Web page that contains only images; usually, you will mix images and text together. When the browser places an image, it puts it into the line of text where the <IMG> tag falls. If you don't want any text on the same line as the image, you can include tags that create a new line (such as a <BR>, <HR>, <P>, or a headline) immediately before and after the image. You can then use the <CENTER> and </CENTER> tags on each side of the <IMG> tag (just as you would with text) if you want to center the image on the page.

If you do use the image on a line with text, you can use the ALIGN attribute with the <IMG> tag to control where the text shows up in relation to the image. Under the HTML 2 standard, there are three possible values for ALIGN:

- ALIGN=TOP lines up the top of the image with the top of the line of text.
- ALIGN=MIDDLE vertically lines up the center of the image with the *baseline* of the line of text.
- ALIGN=BOTTOM lines up the bottom of the image with the baseline of the line of text.

TERM **Baseline** The bottom of most letters in a line of text. Letters such as g and p have descenders, which drop below the baseline.

Try adding each of these attributes to the <IMG> tag in your test2.htm file. Then add a few sentences of text immediately after the tag, so you can see the effect it has on how your page is displayed.

The Netscape Extensions' ALIGN Values

The Netscape extensions allow for a broader range of ALIGN values, which enable you to make better-looking documents. The following list describes the common values you might use in addition to ALIGN=TOP, ALIGN=MIDDLE, and ALIGN=BOTTOM (which were covered in the previous section). Figure 4.4 shows examples of each ALIGN value.

- ALIGN=LEFT positions the image against the left side of the page. The text that follows wraps around the right side, top, and bottom of the image.
- ALIGN=RIGHT positions the image against the right side of the page and causes the words to wrap on its left, top, and bottom.
- ALIGN=ABSMIDDLE lines up the center of the image with the center of the line of text.
- ALIGN=ABSBOTTOM lines up the bottom of the image with the very bottom of the line of text. This might place the image somewhat lower on the page than ALIGN=BOTTOM would because some characters (such as the lowercase g) have descenders that drop below the baseline.

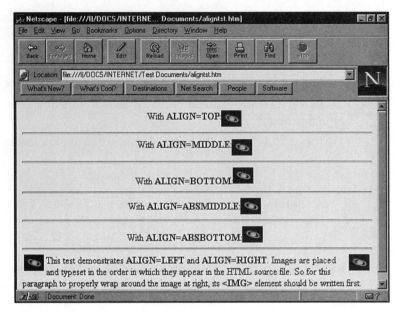

Figure 4.4 Examples of the ALIGN values.

Using Images As Links

You can use an image as an anchor for a link in the same way you would use text. To turn an image into a link anchor, follow these steps:

1. Put the <A HREF...> and </A> tags before and after your <IMG> tag like this:

```
<A HREF="test1.htm"><IMG SRC="agif.gif"></A>
```

2. Save the file.

3. Open the file in your browser, and you'll see that your image has a colored box around it, indicating that it is a link. When a user clicks the link, he jumps directly to the URL you specified in the tag.

One of the best reasons to do this is to provide a link to a larger version of the image. For example, suppose you have a large painting you want to let people look at, but you realize that not everyone is going to want to wait for the whole thing to download. You can put a very small version of the picture on your page and make it a link to the larger version of the picture. You don't even have to put the full-sized image on an HTML page because the browser can display an image directly. (Netscape Navigator users can right-click any image and select View Image from the shortcut menu to see the image in its full size. Not all Web browsers provide this luxury, though.) To see image linking at work, perform the following steps.

1. You need one JPEG file for this exercise. If you have one handy, make a copy of it and call the copy **ajpe.jpg.** Put the copy in the htmldocs directory, and then skip to step 6.

2. If you don't have a JPEG file lying around, you can borrow one from our Web page. To do that, type **http://www.mcp.com/que/new_users/6n1.html** in Netscape's **Location/Go to** text box and press **Enter**.

3. Right-click the second image.

4. Select **Save this Image as** from the shortcut menu.

5. Put the file in your htmldocs directory, giving it the name **ajpeg.jpg**. (Because you're also storing the html files in this directory, you'll be able to include this image using a short relative URL.)

6. In the body of your test2.htm file, add this line:
   ```
   <A HREF="ajpeg.jpg"><IMG SRC="agif.gif"></A>
   ```

Open that page in Netscape, and your agif.gif file appears as a link. When you click it, Netscape displays the ajpeg.jpg file.

In this lesson, you learned about graphics, and you learned how to insert a graphic into a Web page and turn a graphic into a link. In the next lesson, you will learn to change the colors of your Web page.

Setting Backgrounds and Colors

In this lesson, you learn how to change the color of your Web page's text and backgrounds.

The use of color text, color backgrounds, and even background graphics can really make your Web pages stand out. These functions are among the most popular Netscape extensions to HTML, and they have been integrated into most browsers that are currently available.

Setting Text Colors

You can set the text colors by adding an attribute to your <BODY> tag. There are four attributes, each of which sets the color for a different type of text. These attributes can be used together within the same <BODY> tag.

- TEXT sets the color of all text except that in links.
  Example: <BODY TEXT="#F70039">

- LINK sets the default color for text in links.
  Example: <BODY LINK="#F70039">

- VLINK sets the color for links that you have already visited.
  Example: <BODY VLINK="#F70039">

- ALINK sets the color for the active link (the link currently being clicked).
  Example: <BODY ALINK="#F70039">

You can set the colors for any or all of the types of text described above. If you opt not to select a color for any of those types of text, your browser assigns a color, usually according to defaults that you've chosen.

You describe a color as a set of three values, each ranging from 0 to 255. The three values (respectively) indicate how much red, how much blue, and how much green you want in the color. By mixing varying amounts of these three colors, you can create any color imaginable.

The values are two-digit *hexadecimal* values, and the group of three two-digit hexadecimal values is known as a *hexadecimal triplet*.

Hexadecimal A system of counting that is easy for computers—it would be easy for humans if we each had 16 fingers. (Don't worry, you don't really need to understand hexadecimal to work with these values.)

The first digit in a hexadecimal pair is the main one you have to worry about. It can be set to 0–9 or A–F, where the letters are higher than the numbers. If you want a lot of red in the color, set the first digit to E or F; if you want just a little, set it to 2. If you want almost none, set it to 0.

The second digit in a hexadecimal pair is for fine-tuning. Setting this digit in the red value to 1, for example, gives you just a little more red than if it's at 0. Setting the second digit all the way up to F will give you visibly more color, but not as much as you would have if you increased the first digit by one. Setting the two digits to 00 will give your color absolutely no red, while setting them to FF gives you as much red as possible.

When using a color attribute, you enter the attribute name, followed by an equals sign, a quotation mark, and a pound sign. Then you enter the red, green, and blue values with no spaces in between, followed by another quotation mark. For example, you could enter the attribute TEXT="#F7001A" to set the red level to F7 (a lot of red), the green level to 00 (no green), and the blue level to 1A (a little blue). Table 5.1 lists the values for some common colors you might use.

Table 5.1 Hexadecimal Triplets for Common Colors

Value	Resulting Color
"#000000"	Black (no color)
"#FFFFFF"	White

Value	Resulting Color
"#7F7F7F"	Gray (everything is halfway between white and black)
"#7F0000"	Burgundy or dark red (half the possible red, but with no other colors to add brightness)
"#FF0000"	Rich red
"#FFC0C0"	Pink (color is predominantly red, but contains a lot of the others to lighten it up)
"#FF00FF"	Purple (even mix of red and blue)

Back in grade school, you probably learned how to mix colors. You probably learned that the three primary colors for paints and other pigments are red, yellow, and blue, and that you can make other colors by mixing those colors. If you went to a good school, they may have also taught you that the primary colors of light are different; they are red, green, and blue. If you remember the ways that *paint* colors mix (red and green make brown, for example), but not the way that *light* colors mix (red and green make yellow), you might get confused when it comes to mixing colors on-screen.

The screen colors are made of light. If you remember that red and green make yellow, green and blue make aqua, and blue and red make purple, you can make just about any color you want. Of course, experimentation will also help. Let's try changing some of the text colors in the test2.htm file.

1. Open your **test2.htm** file with your editor.

2. Change your <BODY> tag to look like this:
   ```
   <BODY TEXT="#000000" LINK="#996600" VLINK="#6666FF">
   ```

3. Save the file.

4. Take a look at the file with your browser, and you should see white text, brown links, and blue visited links.

If you want to try out other text colors, background colors, and background patterns, check out the Web site at http://www.imagitek.com/bcs.html. It offers controls that make it easy to experiment with different combinations (see Figure 5.1).

Figure 5.1   Use these options to change background and text colors.

One of the newer Netscape extensions enables you to change the color of just part of a line of text. Try adding this line to your test2.htm file:

```
I feel queasy being <FONT COLOR="#00FF00">green</FONT>.<BR>
```

If you bring this page up in Netscape Navigator or Gold, you should see the word "green" in green. However, older versions of Netscape, as well as most other browsers, probably will not show that text color change.

Setting the Background Color

By changing the color of the page behind the text, you can set a tone for your page. A white background gives the page a business-like look; a yellow background makes the page look cheery; and a black background can create a sinister or a stylish look, depending largely on what color text you use on it.

Setting your background color is very similar to setting your text colors: it's just another attribute for the <BODY> tag. In this case, the attribute is BGCOLOR, and you use it exactly the same way as you do text attributes. To try it out, add the attribute BGCOLOR="#FFFF33" to the <BODY> tag of test2.htm. Then check to see how the page looks with a yellow background.

409

The BGCOLOR attribute for setting background color is a Netscape extension commonly supported by other browsers.

Using a Background Pattern

Although a background color is nice, if you want something even fancier, you can fill the background of your page with a picture. The BACKGROUND tag that you use to do this was created as a Netscape extension in the first release of Netscape, but it is currently scheduled for inclusion in HTML 3. Therefore, most newer browsers support this feature. Of those browsers, some support both JPEG and GIF format backgrounds (also called a *texture*), while others support only GIF. So you're a little better off using a GIF background than using JPEG.

It doesn't make any difference whether the GIF you use for your background is interlaced or transparent because the background won't appear until the whole graphic is downloaded—and there is nothing for a transparency to show. What does make a difference, however, is the size of the GIF file. Some browsers won't show the page at all until the background has been downloaded, and if that background includes a large GIF, it can take a long time. Netscape Navigator will go ahead and display foreground text while it's loading the background image, even though the BACKGROUND attribute appears within the <BODY> tag toward the beginning of the HTML source file.

To try this feature out, delete the BGCOLOR attribute from your BODY tag and replace it with BACKGROUND="agif.gif". Save the file, and then reload the page on your browser. You should see your page with a background image.

If your screen is wider or higher than the background image, your browser will repeat the image to fill up the screen. Therefore, other users who look at your page may see your image repeated a different number of times depending on their browsers. (They might have different screen widths, as well as other settings that can affect this.)

Yuck!   Most images that aren't specifically designed to be backgrounds don't work well as backgrounds; often they are too colorful for the text to be legible, or they don't look good repeated. You'll learn about picking a good background in Lesson 13, "Designing for Readability."

CAUTION

In this lesson, you learned how to change the color of your text and backgrounds. In the next lesson, you will learn how to create tables and frames.

Creating
Tables and
Frames

In this chapter, you learn to enhance your Web page with tables and frames.

Creating Tables

Tables enable you to organize information in a grid design. The table feature is to be part of HTML 3, but it has been supported for some time by various browsers.

A table is organized into columns and rows. The intersection of each column and row forms a rectangle called a *cell*. Most cells take up only the space allotted for one row and one column, but you can create cells that span multiple rows or columns. It's unlikely that all of the rows and columns will be the same size because the browser will try to compactly, but completely, fit all of your cell contents into the table.

When filling in the cells of a table, you can put in just about anything that you might put elsewhere on the page (such as text, images, links, or even other tables). And although you can also use most of the tags you would use elsewhere, some of the tags are replaced with special table attributes.

You'll use a lot of tags when you build a table, and you'll need a bunch of attributes if it's a complex table. However, you use only a few *types* of tags—you just use them over and over.

- Place the <TABLE> and </TABLE> tags at the beginning and end of the entire table section in your HTML document. (In most of the examples in this section, you'll use the BORDER attribute with the <TABLE> tag, which makes the gridlines visible.)

- Use the <TR> and </TR> tags before and after the contents of each row of the table. (TR stands for *table row*.)

- Place the <TD> and </TD> tags before and after the contents of each cell of the table. (TD stands for *table data*.)

- The <TH> and </TH> tags are the same as the <TD> and </TD> tags, except that they make the text in the cell appear in bold type. (TH stands for *table header*.)

To see these tags at work, build a text copy of one of the world's most famous table grids, the opening screen for *The Brady Bunch*. Follow these steps to create that table:

1. Open a new HTML file and name it table.htm.

2. Type the following into the body area:

```
<TABLE BORDER>
  <TR><TD>Marsha</TD><TD>Dad</TD><TD>Greg</TD></TR>
  <TR><TD>Jan</TD><TD>Alice</TD><TD>Peter</TD></TR>
  <TR><TD>Cindy</TD><TD>Mom</TD><TD>Bobby</TD></TR>
</TABLE>
```

You don't *have* to break the lines to match this example. Everything could be on one line, and it would still work the same. However, with it organized like this, it's easy to see what appears on each row.

3. Save the file and open it in your browser. You should see a table like the one in Figure 6.1.

Figure 6.1 When this lady met this fella, they formed a three-by-three intersection.

When you look at this table, you should note that by default, each column is just wide enough to accommodate the longest entry in that column. (So, thanks to "Marsha," the girls have the run of the table.)

Adding a Table Header and Different Cell Formats

Next, make a more difficult grid that shows the layout of the Brady males—before the lady met that fella—and give it a header telling what it is. This layout has "Dad" in one cell on the left that spans two-thirds of the height of the grid; the three boys' names appear in smaller cells on the right. To do this, you'll need to know the following attributes:

- COLSPAN is an attribute you can use with <TD> and <TH> to indicate that a cell takes up more than one column of the table. You use it with a value, which tells the browser to set it equal to the specified number of columns (for example, <TD COLSPAN=3>).

- ROWSPAN is just like COLSPAN except that you use it to indicate an attribute that takes up more than one row.

To see the effects of these attributes, enter the following table under the previous one:

1. Open **table.htm** with your editor.

2. Add the following table description under the previous table:

```
<TABLE BORDER>
    <TR><TH COLSPAN=2>The Brady Boys</TH></TR>
    <TR><TD ROWSPAN=2>Dad</TD><TD>Greg</TD></TR>
    <TR><TD>Peter</TD></TR>
    <TR><TD></TD><TD>Bobby</TD></TR>
</TABLE>
```

3. Save the file.

4. Open **table.htm** in Netscape. It should look like Figure 6.2.

Figure 6.2 Four men, living all together, each in separate cells.

Especially note that "Peter" ended up in the second column with "Greg" and "Bobby" even though you entered "Peter" on a row by itself. The browser knew that making the "Dad" entry two rows high would take up that space in the first column.

413

CAUTION

It Didn't Work!   If your table doesn't look like the one in the figure, check your tags carefully; with all these tags, it's easy to get a <TD> confused with a <TR> or to accidentally put a slash in front of an opening tag.

Because the "Dad" cell took up only two rows, you had to enter a blank cell in order to get "Bobby" into the second column. If you look closely, however, you'll see that the blank space next to "Bobby" looks kind of covered over; it's not just an empty grid space. That's how Netscape displays cells in which the data area is completely empty.

Aligning Cells in Tables

The names in the Brady tables show up next to the left wall of each cell, which looks a little awkward. After all, on the TV show, each person is well-centered in his/her square. Luckily, you can adjust where text falls in a cell. To do this, you'll need to know the following attributes:

- ALIGN is an attribute that you can use in the <TD> and <TH> tags (where it affects one cell) or the <TR> tag (where it affects the whole row). This controls the horizontal placement of the text within the cell. ALIGN has three possible values in an HTML 3 table: ALIGN=LEFT, ALIGN=CENTER, and ALIGN=RIGHT.

- VALIGN is like ALIGN, except that it controls the vertical placement of the text. The values are VALIGN=TOP, VALIGN=MIDDLE (the default), VALIGN=BOTTOM, and VALIGN=BASELINE (which lines up all the text in the row).

To see the effects of these attributes, edit the table as described in these steps.

1. Open **table.htm** with your editor.

2. On the Brady Boys table, replace each of the four <TR> tags with <TR ALIGN=CENTER VALIGN=MIDDLE>.

3. Save the file.

4. Open **table.htm** in Netscape. The table should now look like Figure 6.3.

Figure 6.3 A well-centered family.

Cell Blanking

If you've ever worked with a chart on a spreadsheet, you'll recall that the upper-left cell often remains blank. (This is the cell at the intersection of the left reference column and upper reference row; because it does not refer to a cell at all, it's left empty.) In an HTML table, the easy way to leave a cell blank is not to write anything between the <TD> and </TD> cell tags. With many browsers, this creates an effect in which the cell area itself appears to be filled with a border.

To test how this works, edit that ever-aging Brady table to read like the following HTML lines:

```
<TABLE BORDER>
  <TR><TH COLSPAN=2>The Brady Boys</TH></TR>
  <TR ALIGN=CENTER VALIGN=MIDDLE><TD></TD><TD>Greg</TD></TR>
  <TR ALIGN=CENTER VALIGN=MIDDLE><TD>Dad</TD><TD>Peter</TD></TR>
  <TR ALIGN=CENTER VALIGN=MIDDLE><TD></TD><TD>Bobby</TD></TR>
</TABLE>
```

When you finish, save the table as table.htm again and load it into Navigator. Figure 6.4 shows what you should see.

Figure 6.4 Giving Dad equal footing with the boys.

You'll immediately notice that the bevel effect that the browser normally adds to cells that contain text is not present in the empty cells. For most purposes, that's perfectly fine. But suppose, for consistency purposes, you need to display the bevel effect. To make a blank cell on a bordered table look beveled like the other cells, use the <PRE> tag followed by a space, all between the <TD> and </TD> tags. Although this isn't exactly proper HTML usage, it works. To test it, replace the two blank <TD> and </TD> cells in table.htm with <TD><PRE> </TD> (remember to include the space). Then save table.htm again. The result that appears in the browser should look like Figure 6.5.

Figure 6.5   Making room for a larger family.

Page Formatting with Tables

You can use tables for more than just grids of data. Because you can create columns in tables, you can use tables to create column-style text layouts. For example, the Web page in Figure 6.6 was created using a table.

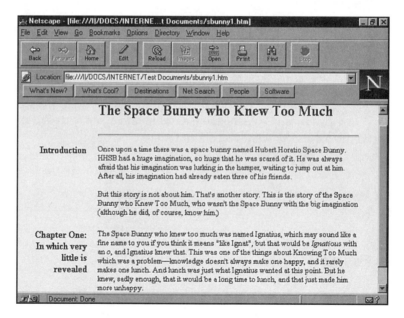

Figure 6.6   A table-based page layout.

You can create the look shown in Figure 6.6 by using a wide table. This table has three columns: a column for the titles, a column for the text, and a blank column between them. Using this blank column, you can create a nice amount of space between the titles and the text. Whenever you need to add a new title that you want to line up with the text, just start a new row.

The following listing shows the contents of the HTML file for the page shown in the figure. You don't have to type it all in, but look through it carefully to make sure you understand it.

```
<BODY BGCOLOR="#FFFFFF">
<TABLE WIDTH=90%>
<TR><TD WIDTH=90 ALIGN=RIGHT><H3>The Space Bunny who Knew Too Much
</H3><HR></TD>
<TD WIDTH=80></TD></TR>
<TR>
<TH ALIGN=RIGHT VALIGN=TOP>Introduction</TH><TD></TD>
<TD ALIGN=LEFT><P>Once upon a time there was a space bunny named
Hubert Horatio Space Bunny. HHSB had a huge imagination, so huge that
he was scared of it. He was always afraid that his imagination was
lurking in the hamper, waiting to jump out at him. After all, his
imagination had already eaten three of his friends.</P>
<P>But this story is not about him. That's another story. This is the
story of the Space Bunny who Knew Too Much, who wasn't the Space
Bunny with the big imagination (although he did, of course, know
him.)</P><TD>
</TR>
<TR>
<TH ALIGN=RIGHT VALIGN=TOP>Chapter One:<BR>In which very little is
revealed</TH><TD></TD>
<TD ALIGN=LEFT><P>The Space Bunny who knew too much was named
Ignatius, which may sound like a fine name to you if you think it
means &quot;like Ignat&quot;, but that would be <I>Ignatious</I> with
an <I>o</I>, and Ignatius knew that. This was one of the things about
Knowing Too Much which was a problem—knowledge doesn't always make
one happy, and it rarely makes one lunch. And lunch was just what
Ignatius wanted at this point. But he knew, sadly enough, that it
would be a long time to lunch, and that just made him more unhappy.
</P></TD>
</TR>
</TABLE>
</BODY>
```

Take a minute to look at the WIDTH attribute in the first couple of lines. You can use WIDTH in one of two ways:

- In the <TABLE> tag, WIDTH controls how much of the page width the entire table takes up. You set this either as a number of pixels (as in <TABLE WIDTH=300>) or as a percentage of the available screen width (as in <TABLE WIDTH=90%>).

417

- In a <TD> or <TH> tag, WIDTH controls how much of the page width that column takes up. You can also set the width using number of pixels or a percentage. If you use a percentage (as in <TD WIDTH=20%>), it refers to the percentage of the table width.

If your table does not appear on-screen exactly as you wanted it to, it will be very close.

Width Definition Placement   In tables in which the width of the cells in each column is the same for every row (which includes most tables ever made), you only have to specify column width once—using the WIDTH attribute with the <TD> and </TD> tags in the first row (even if the cell in the first row is empty).

Adding Frames

Frames enable you to divide the browser screen so that you can display different Web pages in different sections of the screen. Frames were a powerful new addition with Netscape 2.0. However, as of the time of this writing, the feature was not available on other browsers.

In order to set up frames, you need a separate HTML framing file: a file that has no <BODY> tags. Instead of <BODY> tags, it uses three tags that aren't used in normal HTML files:

- The <FRAMESET> tag sets the layout of the page. It must have one of two attributes: ROWS (for breaking the screen into multiple rows) or COLS (for breaking the screen into multiple columns). If you intend to divide the window into rows and columns, you need to use one <FRAMESET> command within another (which is called nesting). The <FRAMESET> tag requires the closing </FRAMESET> tag.
- The <FRAME> tag describes the features of a frame and denotes which separate HTML file contains the contents of that frame. The attributes that go with it are SRC (which specifies which HTML file will be displayed in the window), NAME (which gives the frame a name so that it can function as a link anchor), SCROLLING (which can be set to YES, NO, or AUTO to control how the frame scrolls), and MARGINWIDTH and MARGINHEIGHT (which enable you to set the space between the edge of the frame and the edge of the text).

- The <NOFRAME> and </NOFRAME> tags enable you to bracket information that will appear if the user doesn't have frame capabilities. (Browsers with frames will ignore this information, but browsers without frames will interpret it as standard content for the page.)

To create a Web page with frames, follow these steps:

1. Start a new HTML file by copying blank.htm and naming it **frames.htm**.

2. In frames.htm, replace the <BODY> tag with <FRAMESET ROWS="20%,80%">. This indicates that you will be splitting your browser window into two horizontal frames, of which the top one will take up the top one-fifth of the screen, and the bottom one will take up two-fifths.

3. On the next line, enter the following text:

   ```
   <FRAME SRC="test2.htm" NAME="topframe">
   ```

   This says that you're going to load the test2.htm file into the top section, which you are naming *topframe*. Giving the top section a name lets you control it separately of the other frames.

4. Specify the bottom frame similarly. Use the <FRAMESET> tag to break it into two side-by-side frames:

   ```
   <FRAMESET COLS="160,*">
   ```

TIP

Don't Use the Sign Notice that you didn't use the percent sign when specifying the width of these frames. When specifying frame size, you can give it as a percentage of the screen size, as a pixel count (which is what the 160 is), or as a share of what's remaining after all the pixel count and percentage columns are calculated. The * stands for one share. So if you use the attribute COLS="*,*,2*", the lower frame will be broken into three frames, where the first two are the same size, and the third is twice that size. Because you had only one entry with the asterisk, that share is the rest of the screen.

5. To define the two lower frames, enter the following lines:

   ```
   <FRAME SRC="control.htm" NAME="leftframe">
   <FRAME SRC="test1.htm" NAME="rightframe">
   ```

6. Close off the two <FRAMESET> tags with these tags:

   ```
   </FRAMESET>
   </FRAMESET>
   ```

419

7. Enter the following note, which will appear on the page only when the page is viewed in a browser that does not support frames:

```
<NOFRAME>
Hey there! Time to upgrade your Web browser, frameless!
</NOFRAME>
```

8. Because this file is no longer empty, you might not want its title to be "A very empy Web page." So delete the old title from between the <TITLE> and </TITLE> tags and replace it with **Frame test** page.

9. Make sure there's no </BODY> tag in the file, save the file, and then try to look at it with your browser. It should look something like Figure 6.7.

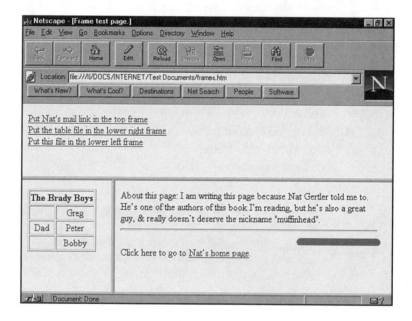

Figure 6.7   A browser window broken into three frames.

Controlling One Frame from Another

For the next test, you'll see how an HTML page within one frame can be used to access or control other frames in the browser window. To do this, you'll need to use the TARGET link attribute. By setting this attribute to the name of the frame, the link loads the new page into that frame instead of the current one.

1. Go back to frames.htm and edit the line that currently refers to blank.htm so that it reads as follows:

```
<FRAME SRC="control.htm" NAME="topframe">
```

2. Save the file again as **frames.htm.**

3. Next, open **blank.htm** and save a copy of it as **control.htm.**

4. In control.htm, delete the <HEAD> and </HEAD> element tags and everything between them.

5. Between the <BODY> and </BODY> tags, enter the following lines:

```
<A HREF="test1.htm" TARGET="rightframe">Put test file in the next
frame</A><BR>
<A HREF="table.htm" TARGET="rightframe">Put the table file in the
next frame</A><BR>
<A HREF="control.htm" TARGET="topframe">Put this table file in the
top frame</A><BR>
```

6. Save this file, and load **frames.htm** again in the browser. (If you still have the browser open from the previous task, you can just click the **Reload** button.) The file should look like Figure 6.8.

7. Click the links in the lower-left corner to see how they affect the other frames.

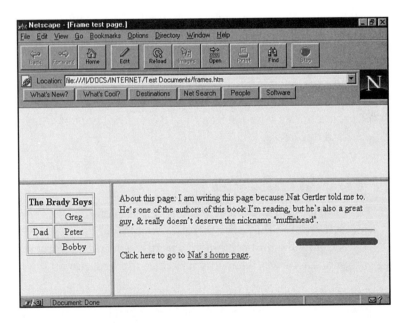

Figure 6.8 One frame can control another frame.

In this lesson, you learned to use tables and frames with your Web pages. In the next lesson, you will learn about advanced technologies such as Java, which you can use to enhance your Web pages.

Learning About Web Programming

In this lesson, you get a basic understanding of CGI and Java, two tools that are widely used to make Web pages "interact" with users.

When you decided to tackle HTML in order to create your own Web pages, you probably didn't count on having to become a programmer to do it. Well, good news; you don't. However, for all its complexities, HTML simply cannot do some things, such as search through a database of documents for the one that contains specified information, or display a scrolling stock ticker. In order to include such items in your Web pages, you're going to need to use some kind of programming language such as CGI or Java, both of which you'll learn more about in this lesson.

CGI Programming

The *Common Gateway Interface* (CGI) enables you to use a Web page as an interface that lets the user control a program running on a Web server. CGI controls how the information gets from the user to the program; the actual program can be written in any language that will run on the server.

The most common examples of CGI programs on the Web are on-screen forms. If you fill out a form and click the button that indicates you're done, you might see the information being sent to the server in a very complex URL. When the Web server processes that URL, it takes the form information out and runs it through the program named in the URL (the name probably appears just after /CGI-BIN/, the traditional directory used for storing these programs). Figure 7.1 shows a page that was created from a form sent to the Web server. Notice that the URL at the top contains the information from the form.

For example, if you go to the Web search site Yahoo!, you'll find a very simple form: one field into which you type the text you want to search for, and a button you push to start the search. If you type **kittens** into the field and click the button, your browser sends to the server a request for a URL that ends with /search?p=kittens. When the server gets that URL, its CGI program sees that URL. The CGI program knows that it has to start the program search, and that it has to tell that program that **kittens** is the value for the field the program calls P. The Search program searches its database of Web sites for the word **kittens** and creates an HTML page listing all of the sites it finds. The server then sends this page out to you.

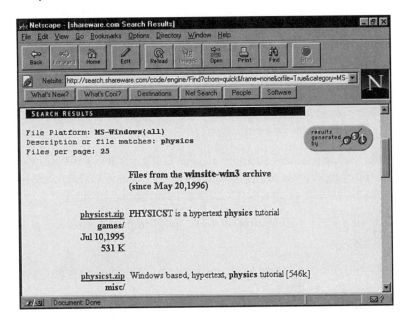

Figure 7.1 A Web page created from the information entered in a form.

Not all Web providers allow you to run CGI programs on their system. There are two main reasons for this:

- CGI programs use up processor time, which may slow down other activities carried out on the server.
- The provider runs the risk of a breach in security. If you can run programs on the provider's server, you might be able to gain access to and damage other people's files.

You should check with your Web provider before you start working on any vast CGI projects.

If you want to learn more about CGI programming, check out the book *Teach Yourself CGI Programming with Perl in a Week*, published by sams.net. It covers not only CGI, but also Perl, a popular programming language for Web applications.

Java

As you learned in Part 1 Lesson 14, Java is a new programming language that is quickly gaining popularity. While CGI programs are run on the Web server, Java programs are run on the Web user's machine, interpreted by the browser. The first Java-compatible browser was HotJava (created by Sun Microsystems, who also created the Java language). Since then, a number of major Web browser manufacturers, including Netscape and Microsoft, have elected to support Java. (However, Microsoft's Java-compatible browser is not out as of the time of this writing.)

Netscape's way of supporting Java is slightly less straightforward; Netscape supports the use of Java-like code embedded in HTML pages—a form Netscape calls *JavaScript*. (See Part 1 Lesson 14 for more details.)

Using Java or JavaScript on your own computer gives you numerous advantages:

- You don't have to worry about whether your Web server will let you run the program.
- You don't have to worry about security concerns.
- You can use real-time programs with animations and interaction; you're no longer limited to things that can be presented to the user via an HTML page.

There are certain things that can only really be done via CGI. For example, CGI is necessary for searching large databases and for storing information received from the user. However, you can use Java to create a program that gets information from the user and then uses CGI to pass that information to a program running on the server.

People are using Java applets to create a lot of fun additions to their pages. Some of them are animations such as the one in Figure 7.2. Others have little games built into their pages.

But Java programs aren't limited to just little decorative items. Java is a full-featured language (in fact, the browser HotJava was created using Java!), and you can expect to soon see Java-based spreadsheets, huge multiplayer games, and anything else that one might want on the Web.

Most computer languages are *compiled*, which means that a compiler program translates the file that the programmer created into a file of *machine language* commands that the processor chip can understand. That machine language file is all that you need to run the program. Other computer languages are *interpreted*, which means that each needed command in the programmer's file gets translated into machine language commands while the program is running.

Figure 7.2 This moving signboard simulation is a Java applet.

Java is an interesting combination of the two. The programmer's file, written in the Java language, gets compiled not into machine language, but into an intermediate language. This file with the intermediate language is stored on the Web server and downloaded to your computer when you load a page with a Java applet on it. Then the Java interpreter (which is built into Netscape Navigator) very efficiently turns these commands into machine language.

The reason for this two-step process is simple: Java programs have to be able to run on many different types of computers, which use very different machine languages and have different ways for programs to interact with the screen and the mouse. The compiler takes care of most of the translation work, making the program compact and efficient. That leaves only one—very important—last step for the user's computer to take care of.

A Java program is called an *applet* because it's a small application. There are currently two versions of Java: *alpha* and *beta*. Alpha applications are used only by older versions of the program HotJava, and they can be included on a Web page by means of the <APP> tag. Netscape Navigator understands only beta, the never version. Beta applets can be included on a Web page by means of the <APPLET> tag, which takes such standard arguments as the name of the applet and the size of the area needed on the Web page. So, if you see a page that's supposed to have an applet on it, and it doesn't seem to be running, check the HTML source code; if it has an <APP> tag, the program uses the wrong revision of Java to run on Navigator.

The Java-related language called JavaScript is an interpreted language that can be included on Web pages through use of the <SCRIPT> tag. A program written in JavaScript would look a lot like a Java program that does the same thing. The advantages to using JavaScript include the following:

- You don't need a compiler to write programs; you only need a JavaScript-compatible browser because the browser acts as the interpreter.
- With Java, the browser has to download the HTML file for the Web page, see the tag with the program name in it, and then download the Java program. With JavaScript, only the HTML file has to be downloaded because the program is in that file.

Of course, there are also disadvantages to using JavaScript.

- JavaScript programs run slower than Java programs because with JavaScript, the browser is controlling both the Web page and the Java interpreter.
- You can't hide all of your programming tricks from the user. If he wants to see how your program works, all he has to do is use Netscape's View, Document Source command!

JavaScript programs work only with Web browsers that are JavaScript-compatible. At the time of this writing, Netscape Navigator is the only one.

Java was created by Sun Microsystems in an attempt to create a C-like language that would suit the needs of online programs. To learn more about creating your own Java programs and to download the Java Development Kit (which includes all the things you need to do so), check out Sun's Web site at http://java.sun.com.

If you really want to learn more about Java and JavaScript, look for one of these other available books.

- *The Complete Idiot's Guide to JavaScript* by Aaron Weiss and Scott J. Walter (Que, ISBN 0-7897-0798-5).
- *Java By Example* by Clayton Walnum (Que, ISBN 0-7897-0814-0).
- *Java!* by Tim Ritchey (New Riders Publishing, ISBN 1-56205-533-X).
- *Teach Yourself Java in 21 Days* by Laura Lemay and Charles Perkins (sams.net, ISBN 1-57521-030-4).

In this lesson, you learned about CGI and Java, which let you run programs on the Web. In the next lesson, you'll learn to publicize your Web site to get people to come see your Web pages.

Publicizing Your Web Site

In this lesson, you'll learn various ways to publicize your Web page so that people will visit it.

URLs Are Everywhere!

If your goal in creating a Web site is simply to take pleasure in the creation, you can keep the site a secret. However, if your goal is to have people take a look at your page, you will have to let them know that it exists.

There are many ways to spread information about your Web page. More and more often now, TV and newspaper ads include the advertiser's URL. In addition, people are putting URLs on their business cards, on letterhead, and at the bottom of e-mail messages. You might even see them on T-shirts and race cars. These are all good ways to spread the word, but they cost money. The following sections show you how to get some free publicity for your Web page.

Don't Publicize Your URL Too Early If you publicize a URL before the site is in proper running condition (or before it's even up at all), people who visit it might decide the site is not worthwhile—and then they'll never return. Although your site doesn't have to be perfect, you shouldn't publicize it until it is usable and useful.

Because you want to reach people who are on the Web, one of the best ways to reach them is via the Web. There are a number of ways to have your page listed where people will find it.

Exchanging Links

No matter how esoteric in nature your site is, odds are good that sites on similar or related topics exist. If you can create a link from those sites to yours, you have a good chance of drawing in people who are surfing that link.

Arranging to create those links, particularly for noncommercial pages, is generally not hard. Find a page on which you'd like to put a link to your page, drop the owner or manager of that site an e-mail suggesting that he check out your site, and ask him to drop you a note with his reaction. At the same time, you can ask him if he wants to swap links, but it might be a good idea to wait until he drops you that note; if he responds favorably, then you can make an offer to swap links.

When you suggest the swap, you should suggest where on his pages the link would make sense, and you might even suggest the wording and the HTML code for the link. The easier you make it for him to put in the link you want (as you want it), the more likely you are to get a good placement.

Obviously, if he agrees to swap links, you have to add a link to your page that other users can click to get to his site. If you're planning to have a lot of links, you might want to create a separate page just for links. Not only does this keep you from having to figure out where to put the links, it also helps ensure that someone looking for links finds them. This doesn't mean you can't also put the same links in other relevant places on your site, of course.

Registering Your Page with Search Engines

There are dozens of different search engines and World Wide Web directories designed to help people find what they are looking for on the Web and the rest of the Internet. These systems can help steer interested people toward your site—but only if the systems know about it. A search engine or directory might find out about a Web site in either or both of two ways.

- You *register* your site by supplying the URL, the topic of your site, and other relevant pieces of information.
- The system finds your site by means of its *Web crawler program*. A Web crawler program run unmanned, searching the Web and following whatever links it finds; as it does, it looks for new Web pages it hasn't seen before and grabs the information from them.

If you want to register with a directory, go to that directory's Web site. (Try looking up *search engines* in your favorite Web directory, and you should find links to more Web directories.) If the directory accepts registrations, there should be a clearly marked link to a registration form.

A typical registration form asks you for a description of your site, a list of keywords relating to the topic of your site, the URL, and an e-mail address for the person in charge of the site. Choose your keywords carefully, realizing that you might have to put in several words that mean the same thing or overlap in concept. If you have a Web site about growing roses, for example, you should use the keywords *roses*, *flowers*, and *horticulture* because the person searching for that information could be using any of those words as his search keyword.

Registration might not produce instant results. In fact, it may be weeks before your page appears in the directory because the managers of many directories check each site that's registered before they add it to their official lists. When your page is added, you might receive e-mail telling you that the registration went through and asking you to return the courtesy by putting a link to the directory somewhere on your site. If a directory asks you to create such a link, you don't have to put it in an obtrusive location; adding it to your page of links should be fine.

Remember that you aren't limited to a single registration for your entire site. If you have pages on different topics, you should consider registering each page separately. For example, instead of requesting one entry for your home page, which covers both your guide to growing roses and your Moxy Fruvous discography, you can register the URL of each page separately with its own description and keywords. That should increase the odds that interested people will find the appropriate page.

Becoming Easy Prey for "Web Crawlers"

You can do a number of things to increase the chances that a Web crawler program will find your site. The more people there are who have links to your site, the more likely it is that your site will be found. And it's very important that you make sure every one of your pages has links that go (either directly or indirectly) to your home page. It would be a shame if the Web crawler found a link to one of your pages and that page was a dead-end. That page would be the only part of your site to be registered.

You can also do certain things to ensure that once the Web crawler does find your site, the site will show up in other people's searches.

- Make sure that the titles on your pages are descriptive of the contents of the page that people will be interested just from reading the title.
- Make sure that the first few lines of text on your page contain appropriate keywords that someone might use on a search for such a page. Because some Web crawlers record only the first few text lines, someone using the crawler's search form will only find your page if she enters one of those words. Other directories capture the whole text of your document, but later during the search, they determine whether to list your page as a "hit" based on where the user's keywords appear in the document. Those directories will recommend a document in which the words appear at the beginning before they will recommend one in which the words occur at the end.

Many of the larger Web crawler sites and search engines are commercial undertakings, and they make money by selling display ads on their pages. If you're running a commercial site, you might want to consider getting some of these ads. Generally, they let you run a small graphic with a link to your page. Some of these randomly display an ad whenever someone performs a search, while others just add the graphic to the listing of the site (much like in the Yellow Pages, where your listing is free, but you can pay extra for a fancy display).

Using Submit-It

You'll rank *Submit-It* among your best friends when you're trying to get your site registered with the search engines. Submit-It is a site at http:// www.submit-it.com that provides a single interface for helping you register with more than a dozen directories all at once. It can speed up the registration process considerably, as well as point you toward directories you might not have known about.

To submit your information to Submit-It, follow these steps:

1. Go to the page **http://www.submit-it.com** using Netscape.
2. Begin filling out the form shown in Figure 8.1, providing pertinent information about yourself and your site. Not all of the directories will use all of the information you give here; each directory uses different bits.
3. After you enter all the data, click **OK**; move on to the submitting area button to move to the next step.

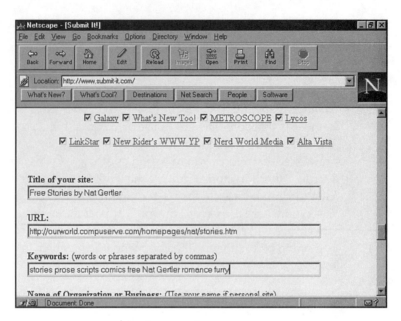

Figure 8.1   The first part of the Submit-It form.

4. You are presented with a listing of all the directories you can register with. For each directory, there will be a small description, a link to the service, and a button you click to begin the submission process. If necessary, fill in any additional form fields that apply to just that directory.

5. Before you submit to each directory, read the description and make sure that what you're registering is appropriate. If your site is about "How to adopt a kitten," for example, it probably won't get into a business-to-business directory. If you're not sure from the description whether this is a reasonable service for your site, click the link and visit the directory. Then use Netscape Navigator's **Back** button to return to Submit-It.

6. When you make each submission, you will be taken to a response screen that lets you know your submission was received. (You will be warned of any potential problems with it.) Pay attention to this screen and make sure that you don't need to do anything else.

7. When you receive confirmation, click the **Back** button to return to Submit-It so you can register with another directory. Repeat the process for each directory to which you want to submit.

In this lesson, you learned how to let people know that your Web page exists. In the next lesson, you'll learn how to target, develop, and design your Web page's information.

Choosing a
Design
Philosophy

*In this lesson, you will choose a target audience and decide how your Web
page's information will flow.*

What's a Design Philosophy?

Before you start building your page, you should have your design goal in mind.
This includes not only what your content will be, but how you will present it.
Suppose you were comparing the magazines *Ranger Rick*, *Reader's Digest*, and
Wired, for example. Although all three magazines might have an article about
the rain forest, each article reads and looks quite different from the others. The
writing style, the presentation of text, and the choice of graphics reflect the
design philosophy of each magazine.

Choosing a Target Audience

The first step toward building your design philosophy is to figure out who you
expect to visit your site. A page aimed at explaining to school children the
proper procedure for feeding Jersey cows will be very different from a page
aimed at explaining the same thing to farmers. You should evaluate the following factors about your intended audience:

- **Age** If you're designing for children, you may want to lean toward
  shorter sentences and cleaner graphics, for example. (This is a good goal
  when creating pages for adults, too, but it's vital on pages for children.)

- **Computer experience**   Less experienced users will benefit from pages that can fit on a single screen and pages that contain clearly marked links. A computer is befuddling enough for most newcomers; your page should not confuse them more.

- **Reason for visiting your site**   Someone doing research is going to want a clearly organized site he can navigate quickly, without many distractions such as decorative graphics. Someone who's just out surfing the Web to see what's cool will be attracted by graphics and links that appear be mysterious and intriguing.

- **Knowledge of you**   For the same reasons you talk differently to your friends than you do to strangers, your Web site should be different for people who do and do not know you. If it's a personal page, for example, you might include information about yourself for people who don't know you, or you might include an update of what's new for your friends. If it's a commercial site, you would want to pitch advertising-type information to new customers, but include different sorts of information for existing customers.

You'll probably determine that you expect more than one type of visitor. No problem. You can design around that, particularly with different pages for different people. But you should know ahead of time what audience you expect to be dealing with.

You should also pay attention to any e-mail responses you get regarding your Web page. While such information won't reflect your entire visitor base, it might give you some clue.

Determining the Intended Flow

If you know how a visitor is going to go through your pages, you can try to organize the information on your Web site so that it is easy to find and is seen in reasonable context. Toward that end, the first thing you have to know is where people are going to start.

Most sites have a clear home page—the online equivalent of a front door. Other sites are designed so that people interested in different topics come in via different pages, often from links on other pages. Once you know where people are entering from, your choice of what links you put on each page can control the way in which people experience your site. The simplest site has just one HTML page. This may not be an exciting site, but if you have only a small amount of information to get out, there's no reason to complicate things.

A Controlled Site

If you want to run a *controlled* site—and make sure people see exactly what you want them to see, in the order you want them to see it—you can build a linear site with no optional paths. You might think of this as a way to present a story online, or perhaps as the Web equivalent of a slide-show presentation. The user won't get the thrill of exploring different paths, but if the content is thrilling enough, that shouldn't be a problem. Figure 9.1 shows a simple diagram of what a controlled site might look like.

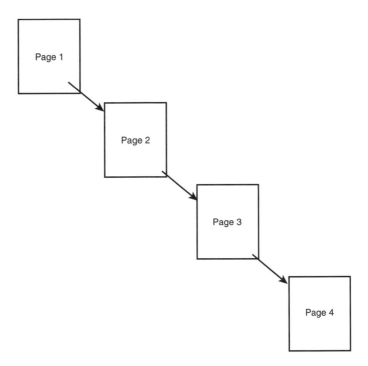

Figure 9.1 Diagram of a controlled site.

The Tree Structure

Another basic structure is a *tree* structure, in which you start at a home page (the tree's trunk) that serves as a table of contents. The links on that page take you to a number of pages (the tree's branches), each of which can be a content page or can have a more detailed table of contents with its own page links (smaller branches). Each page should have a link back to the one that it branches from, and possibly a link to the home page.

With a setup like this, it's very easy to add or remove pages because each page only has links to the page it links from and the pages it has links to. As you can see in Figure 9.2, the tree structure provides a good organized way to store large amounts of data. However, users might find it difficult to get from one piece of data to a related piece.

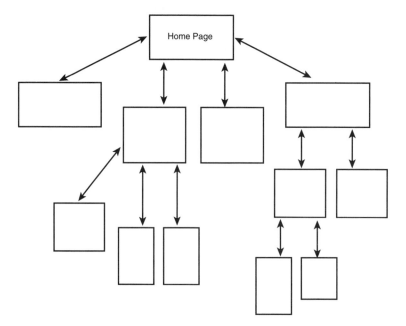

Figure 9.2 Diagram of a tree site.

An Equilateral Structure

The third basic design is an *equilateral* structure (shown in Figure 9.3), in which every page links to every other page, usually by a group of links at the top or bottom (or both) of the page. This type of structure enables quick movement from page to page. It also eliminates any worries you might have about which page the visitor is coming in on; no matter which page that is, he will be able to get to the other pages.

However, the equilateral structure has certain weaknesses.

- If it contains a large number of pages, the number of links becomes unwieldy.
- To add or remove a page, you must change all of the pages.
- You have no control over the order in which the visitor moves through the information.

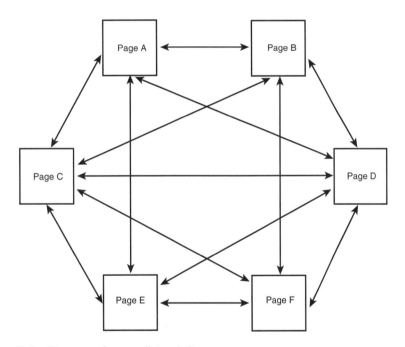

Figure 9.3 Diagram of an equilateral site.

Frames Using frames, you can create and maintain an equilateral site more easily. Split the page into two frames. Make one a small frame that always contains the links to all of the pages, and make the other a larger frame in which you see the current page. This way, you don't have to maintain links on every page!

Combining Structures

In reality, any reasonably complex site is going to draw from each of these designs, combining them in a way that makes sense for that site. For example, Figure 9.4 shows an equilateral set of pages on various topics, some of which serve as the starting page for a tree structure. In addition, some of those pages contain links that leap to otherwise unconnected pages for ease of access.

However you implement it, you should make sure that your basic structure is reasonably clear to the visitor. That way, he can easily find whatever he is looking for on the page.

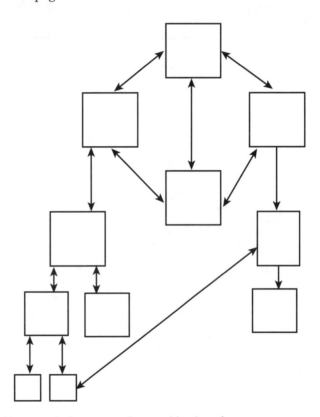

Figure 9.4 You can design a complex combination of structures.

In this lesson, you learned how to design the flow of your Web page. In the next lesson, you'll learn to find good Web pages and perhaps borrow ideas from them.

Taking Inspiration from Good Web Pages

In this lesson, you learn to look at existing Web pages to get ideas you can use on your own pages.

They Should Know Better!

While I hope this book gives you many good ideas about what to do (and what *not* to do) with Web pages, the best learning tool is not in any book. Rather, it's out there on the Web, in the hundreds of thousands of good and bad Web sites.

Luckily, you don't have to look very far on the Web to find examples of what not to do. There are horrible Web pages all over the place, and with just a little Web surfing, you can find a ton of them. You'll find pages that don't look right on your screen. You'll see pages that are hard to read either for graphical reasons or because of improper use of language. You'll even find pages that are missing graphics, and pages that have links that go nowhere. The Web gives everyone the ability to be a publisher—without giving them the talent to do it well.

It's not just individuals and small organizations that are putting up bad Web sites; major corporations are frequently guilty as well. If the designer is working on a corporate computer with a T-1 link, he may not realize what the page is like to people who are dialing in at 14,400bps. I've seen sites put up by the biggest multinational entertainment and computer companies that took so long to transmit that they were unusable.

They should know better. If you pay attention, you will.

Finding Good Web Sites

Finding good Web pages can be a little more difficult than finding bad ones, but it's far from impossible. Because of the abundance of bad sites, several organizations have shouldered the responsibility of making sure that the good and cool sites do not get lost in the shuffle. The following URLs take you to online lists of the sites considered by some people to be the best the Web has to offer.

- **http://home.netscape.com/home/whats-cool.html** is Netscape's own guide to cool sites.
- **http://www.yahoo.com/Entertainment/Cool_Links/** is Yahoo!'s cool links page. This Internet directory also displays a little sunglasses graphic next to officially cool sites in its normal listing.
- **http://www.pointcom.com/** offers a listing of the top 5% of all Web sites, sorted into a number of categories.

Plenty of other guides are available, some in the form of a service provider's list of key sites on their server, and some in the form of an individual's list of his personal favorite sites.

How Cool Is Cool?   Of course, what makes a site "good" or "cool" is very subjective. You might have to bop around a bit until you find a list that tends to steer you in the right direction.

Figure 10.1 shows Point Communications' guide to cool sites. Notice, however, that the text on the graphic isn't clear on a 16-color display. Even the experts in good Web pages can't always make their own pages all things to all people.

Seeing How It's Done

One of the nice things about HTML is that nothing is a secret. If you see a page with a particularly interesting feature, and you want to know how it's done, you can find out. To view the HTML codes that make up a particular Web page, follow these steps:

1. Display the page on-screen in Navigator.

2. Open the **View** menu and select the **Document Source** command. Navigator opens up a window and displays the HTML source for that page.

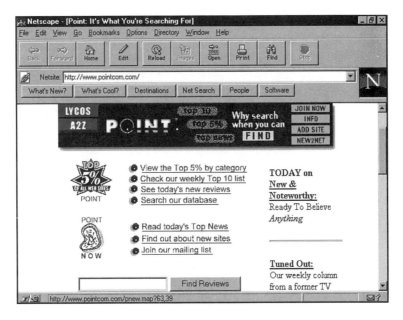

Figure 10.1 The Point's guide to cool sites.

The HTML source display doesn't display just the ASCII text. It also highlights the following types of elements to make them more easily distinguished.

- Keywords (exclusive parts of the HTML language) appear in bold purple.
- Quoted values within tags appear in blue.
- Attributes appear in bold black.
- Comments appear in italics.

If you can follow the flow of the text in the document, you shouldn't have any problem locating the section of code that generates the effect you are interested in. The tags are right there—you just have to know how to read them.

Learning to Identify Strange Tags

This section provides an example with which we can put this through the paces. First, go to the fine online bookstore **http://www.amazon.com**. There you'll see links that use mixed sizes of lettering. Figure 10.2 shows a headline in which some of the letters are bigger than others.

P̲ERSONAL N̲OTIFICATION: A T̲RULY C̲OOL S̲ERVICE

Figure 10.2 Mixed letter sizes within a headline.

This is something you haven't seen before. You've learned how to make a whole line bigger by making it a headline, but in headlines all the letters in the entire line are the same size. Here, individual letters are larger than others. Something else must be going on.

If you display the document source, you should find the segment of code that produces the text shown in Figure 10.2. You can see in Figure 10.3 that the pair of Netscape extension tags <FONT SIZE=+2> and </FONT> surrounds each of the larger letters. There's the trick to making letters larger. The normal size for characters in Netscape Navigator is considered 0; therefore, SIZE+2 makes text two sizes larger. Only the text between the <FONT> and </FONT> tags is resized.

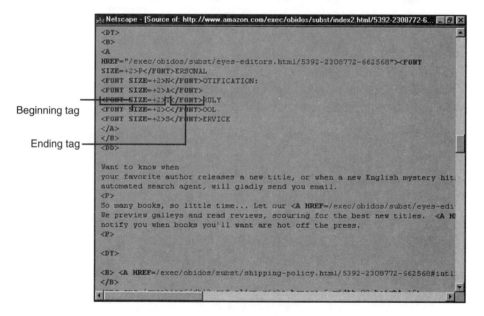

Figure 10.3 The HTML code for the mixed-size lettering links.

This section of the book doesn't cover all of the HTML tags and attributes, but you have learned about the ones that are used to make up the majority of all Web sites. Therefore, if you find a tag that you don't recognize, or if the tag is familiar but its attributes are not, you can guess it's probably not pure HTML, which means it's an extension. If it works with your Netscape browser, it's a Netscape extension.

A Reference at Your Fingertips! In the back of this book is an appendix listing all of the tags and attributes that Netscape supports, as well as a short description of each. Check it out!

Netscape was kind enough to provide a page at http://www.netscape.com/ assist/net_sites/html_extensions.html that lists all of their extensions. If you bring up that page (see Figure 10.4), you'll find the description of the <FONT> tag.

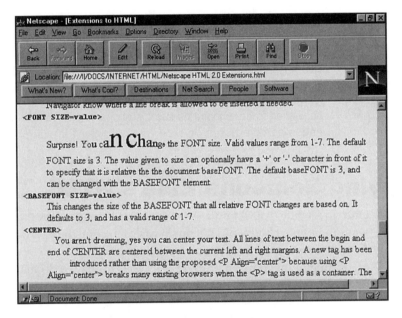

Figure 10.4 Tag descriptions from the Netscape site.

As this description shows, you can set your font to any of seven different sizes. Your default font (whatever it may be) is considered size 3; the smallest font you can get is 1; and the largest is 7. You can create larger or smaller letters by using any of the following tags:

- <BASEFONT=x>, where x is a number from 1 to 7. Paired with </BASEFONT>, this creates a separate element inside of <BODY> . . .<BODY>, whose default size is set to a value other than 3.

- <FONT SIZE=x>, where x is a number from 1 to 7. This makes all the text between this tag and the </FONT> tag size x. Outside of these tags, the font size is either the default or the size created by a <BASEFONT> tag.

443

- <FONT SIZE=+*y*>, where *y* is a number. This makes the text between this tag and the </FONT> tag *y* sizes larger than the current size.

- <FONT SIZE=–*y*>, where *y* is a number. This makes the text between this tag and the </FONT> tag *y* sizes smaller than the current size.

This section showed you one example of how you can learn from someone else's HTML code. There are many others ways. Whenever you look at a good page, pay attention and try to think about how it was created. If you can't figure it out, take a look at the code.

CAUTION

CGI-BIN?   There are some aspects of a Web page that you won't learn much from. For example, a link with /bin/ or /cgi-bin/ in the path tells you that a CGI-BIN program is being used, but it doesn't tell you how that program works. You would need to see the source code to see how it works. And even if you knew, you might have to rewrite the program for your own server (unless you happened to be running the same sort of server as the site where that Web page was stored).

Copying Someone Else's HTML Tags

Once in a while, you'll find a set of tags that is so complex that you really don't want to retype it bit by bit. It's much easier to copy the text right out of someone else's page, strip out everything that made it unique to his needs, and rebuild it by putting in the things that make it fit your needs. To do that, follow these steps:

1. Bring up the page in Netscape.

2. Open the View menu and select the Document Source command. Navigator opens a window and displays the HTML source for that page.

3. Select the text you want to copy (point to the first character, hold down the left mouse button, and drag the mouse to the last character). The text you select appears in white characters on a blue background.

4. Press **Ctrl+C**.

5. Open the editor with which you're editing your page.

6. Place the cursor where you want to add the copied text. Then press **Ctrl+V**, and the text appears.

CAUTION

The Ethics of Borrowing Code Back in grade school, you learned to use an encyclopedia to research a report. You probably also figured out that you could create a report just by copying paragraphs right out of the encyclopedia—but that was plagiarism and it was wrong. The same concepts apply to HTML documents: it is one thing to learn the structure of tags and organizational concepts from someone else's page, but it's another thing to reuse large chunks of HTML code in your own pages without permission (both ethically and legally, as there are copyright concerns at work).

If you find yourself reusing a large, barely modified section of someone else's code, or effectively copying something that made that person's page unique, you've crossed over a line. If you're ever in doubt, it's best just to ask permission. People will usually be happy to grant permission, but it really is their right to say yes or no.

In this lesson, you learned how to find cool pages, look at their HTML code, and borrow ideas. In the next lesson, you'll learn how to make your page easy to access and view.

Web-Friendly Design

In this lesson, you learn how to make sure your Web page works correctly and is accessible to as many people as possible.

Being Browser-Compatible

With the millions of Netscape users out there, it is easy to forget that there is also a huge number of folks using other browsers. If you want everyone to be able to access your page, you have to avoid the assumption that they have Netscape Navigator.

The first step toward this is to make sure your Web site is not dependent on browser-specific extensions. If you design your site in such a way that a person can only navigate from one page to another using navigational information in a frame, for example, users of Mosaic, Internet Explorer, and all the dozens of other browsers won't be able to get around your site.

Does this mean that you shouldn't use any of the Netscape Extensions? Not at all! You just have to understand what will happen when a non-Netscape browser encounters one of those extensions. There are three prime possibilities:

- Despite the fact that it's not Netscape, the browser will understand the tag. Many other browsers are programmed to understand the most popular Netscape extensions (such as the <CENTER> tag).

- The browser will not recognize the tag and will simply ignore it. Browsers know that anything in angle brackets is a tag, so they're smart enough not to put the unrecognized tag on the screen as text.

- The browser will recognize the tag, but will not recognize the attribute within the tag. In this case, the browser will just act as though the attribute isn't there at all.

If the unrecognized tag or attribute is necessary for your page to work, you have a problem. If it just helps the page look better, providing a visual bonus in some way, it's not going to cause problems if it's not understood.

Image Attribute Problems

Suppose you want to design a page with an illustration on the right that the text wraps around. You would use the Netscape extension attribute ALT=LEFT in an <IMG> tag placed on a line above the text itself. The result in Netscape would look something like Figure 11.1.

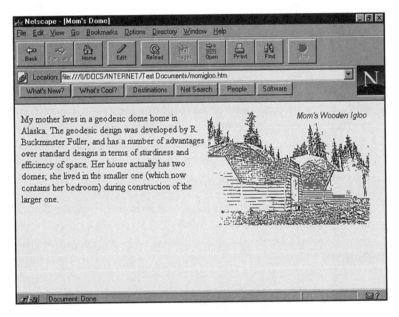

Figure 11.1 Text wrapped around an image in Netscape.

If a browser that doesn't understand the ALIGN attribute displays this page, it ignores the ALIGN=LEFT attribute and puts the image at the current location of the cursor. Figure 11.2 shows the same page as it would look in an incompatible browser that didn't understand ALIGN.

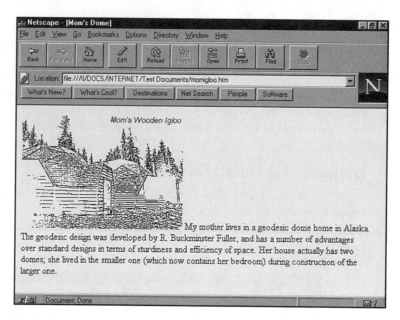

Figure 11.2   The same page as it looks without internal alignment.

Although it may not look as well-planned and constructed, this page is still perfectly usable. However, the same incompatibility can cause confusion and make your effort seem lackluster under slightly different circumstances. If you look closely at Figure 11.3, you'll see that the incorrect placement of the image messes up the intended message of the page.

If you're not sure how your page will look in a browser that doesn't understand the tags and attributes in question, there's a simple way to find out. Just remove those tags and attributes and see what your page looks like in Netscape without them.

Tags Within Tags

One other issue to pay attention to is how different browsers treat multiple simultaneous text formatting. For example, consider the following line of HTML code:

```
Some things are <B>bold <I>and</I> others are not</B>.
```

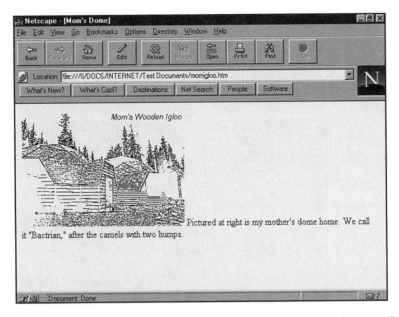

Figure 11.3   The "at right" in the text ain't right when viewed with an incompatible browser because the image doesn't end up on the right.

Some browsers will display that line as

```
Some things are bold and others are not.
```

However, some browsers are unable to mix some formatting characteristics and will have to turn off one type of characteristic to display another. In those browsers, the same line might look like this:

```
Some things are bold and others are not.
```

Or even like this:

```
Some things are bold and others are not.
```

With that in mind, if you want to be able to predict what your page will look like, you should avoid nesting or overlapping text highlights.

Frames

One Netscape feature that you can make use of without worrying about the outcome in non-Netscape browsers is frames. The implementation of the frames feature includes the ability to create material that will only be seen by nonframe browsers.

For example, on my own home page, I use a narrow frame that includes an index of links to all of the main pages of my site (see Figure 11.4). However, in the same file, I also include a <NOFRAMES> tagged section that displays a standard list of links (see Figure 11.5). As a result, people without frames can still navigate the site.

Figure 11.4   Nat's home page as it looks in Netscape.

All in all, to make sure your site is not too browser-specific, it is a good step to test your site with as many different browsers as possible.

Nongraphical Browsers

In these days of Web pages full of font tricks, graphical links, and eye-searing backgrounds, it is easy to assume that everyone surfing the Web is doing so with a powerful, picture-friendly computer. That assumption is wrong.

Many people use nongraphical terminals to access the Web. This is most common on college campuses, where the students may be using terminals attached to larger computers as opposed to using personal computers. The Web looks very different to these people, as Figure 11.6 attests.

Figure 11.5 Nat's home page as it looks in a browser that does not support frames.

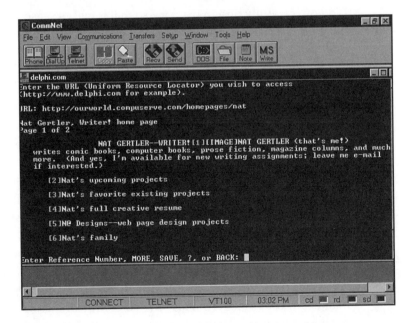

Figure 11.6 Nat's home page again—this time without graphics.

There are also people out there who are using graphical browsers but have the automatic loading of graphics turned off. For the most part, these are people who have only slow Internet access. This group includes people in more rural areas of the U.S., who may not have available the array of high-speed local dial-in access points that more urban folks do. It also includes people in many foreign countries, where the general level of technology is lower.

There are even some people browsing the Web whose main method of access is not the screen. There are blind Web surfers out there who use special tools that turn the words of the Web into either Braille or speech. You can choose to deal with these low-resolution citizens of the Web in one of three ways:

- You can ignore these people. This is a particularly viable option if what your page is about is so graphical in nature that there is no way to represent it in text. It's a particularly bad choice, however, if the academic audience is one of your target groups.

- You can make a completely separate version of your site that is designed to be text-only, and then include a link (a text link, of course) that lets these people access that page from your home page.

- You can carefully design the page so that it makes sense whether or not the pictures are visible.

This last option is a lot easier than you might guess. If you follow these guidelines, you should be well on your way.

- Avoid using graphics with vital words or large amounts of words on them. It's a bad idea to be sending all those words as a picture anyway because, while it may allow you to create all sorts of fancy lettering designs, it will also be a lot slower than plain text.

- When you do use graphics, take advantage of the ALT attribute in the <IMG> tag. This attribute lets you supply some text information that will be visible to those who can't see the image. This way, the text-only surfer will at least know what the picture he can't see is a picture of. When you are using the image as a link, the ALT attribute text will also serve as an alternate link to the same location.

- Don't assume that the character formatting will be displayed in a given manner. Most dumb terminals have some way of highlighting text, whether it's showing the text in reverse colors, making it appear brighter, or making it underlined. However, those terminals are less likely to have italics, and almost definitely will not have different sizes of lettering. As such, instead of typing a line in your document that says the books that I have in my collection are in italics, you might want to use a line that says the books that I have in my collection are displayed <EM>like this</EM>. That way, the user will be able to recognize the highlighting in whatever way it appears on his screen.

- Don't use *mapped* graphics. A mapped graphic allows a user to follow different links by clicking on different parts of the graphic. (This function can be achieved either by using a CGI-BIN program or by using the Microsoft extension USEMAP.)

Checking for Proper HTML Codes

It's very easy to make minor mistakes when entering HTML code. After all, it's a combination of typing (where it's easy to make an error) and programming (which requires some logic).

A lot of errors will show up quickly when you test your pages. If the page doesn't look the way you expected, that's a sign that there is something wrong. However, most browsers are forgiving of certain types of mistakes, which is great when you're looking at a flawed Web site—but bad when you're trying to find the flaws in your own. After all, you can't count on other people's browsers ignoring the same errors that yours does.

Missing Half of a Pair of Items

Possibly the most common error is leaving out one of the items of what is supposed to be a pair. One example would be missing one of the quotation marks around URLs in an HREF attribute. Another would be missing one of the angled brackets of a tag. Navigator's source display has built-in features that can help detect both of those errors.

To find a missing angle bracket or quotation mark in your HTML source, follow these steps:

1. Display your page in Netscape Navigator.
2. Pull down the **View** menu and select the **Document Source** command.
3. Look for a lot of words in bold (see Figure 11.7).

   As you saw before, categories of items appear in different colors, and keywords and their attributes appear in bold text. This will instantly help you detect a missing closing bracket because the source code display assumes that everything after the first word between brackets is an attribute. When you suddenly see a whole lot of words in bold that aren't *supposed* to be attributes, you know that the source display found an opening bracket and assumed that everything was supposed to be an attribute up until the *next* closing tag.

4. Look for light blue blinking text.

The source display also has automatic detection for missing quotation marks. When it finds a place where it thinks a quotation mark is missing, it displays all of the text between the quotation mark that it did find and the next quotation mark in blinking light blue text.

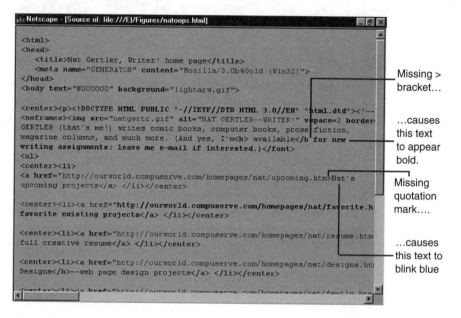

Figure 11.7 Two errors show up on this source display.

Another pairing error would be a missing tag that is needed to make up a paired opening and closing tag set, such as <CENTER> and </CENTER>. Paired tags like these are called *elements*, and you should always make sure that both tags are in place (except with the <P> tag, where </P> is optional). You need the ending tag even if you want the tag to effect the entire page. In that case, you put the closing tag just before the </BODY> tag at the end of the file.

A common cause of this pairing error is forgetting to put the slash in the closing tag, which leaves you with two opening tags and no closing tag! Some

HTML-oriented editors automatically put the closing tag in for you when you insert the second tag, in which case it's okay if you forget about it.

Other Tag Errors

Another common error is using the wrong tag. This is particularly easy when you're using some of the smaller tags such as <DD>, <DT>, <TR>, and <TD> (which you use to build lists and tables).

When building tables and lists, you also have to be careful to get all the tags in the right order. You have to remember that the <TABLE> tag comes before the first piece of information about the table, and the </TABLE> tag comes after the last piece. Similarly, <TR> comes before the first entry for the row, and </TR> comes after the last. <TD> comes before the information for each cell, and </TD> comes afterward. As such, your table specification should end with </TD></TR></TABLE>, which mark the last cell, the last row, and the end of the whole table in that order.

Creating Readable Source Code

Making sure your source file is readable is second in importance to avoiding errors. Not only is this polite to the people who might want to look at your code and figure out how you did your tricks, but it will also help you a lot when you go to change your pages six months later and have to figure just how they work! If you can't figure it out, well, you won't be the first person to look back and think "This stuff works? I must've either been a genius or a madman when I did this!"

You can do three things to make your HTML source code more readable:

- *Comment everything that is unusual or unclear.* If you're using complex constructions, using strange HTML extensions, or calling a CGI-BIN program, you should definitely add a comment.
- *Insert carriage returns into your file.* As you may remember, those carriage returns will be ignored on the displayed page. But they will sure make the file a lot easier to view. You shouldn't have more than about 80 characters on a line, and you should put a blank space between different sections and elements of your document so it's easy to see where one section ends and another begins.

455

- *Indent your tables and complex list structures.* Each list item should be on a new line with a tab before it. If you create a list within a list, indent the inner list by another tab.

  How you indent tables depends on their size and content. If you have a small table, where the contents of each row can fit on a single line, you should probably indent the whole table one level and put each row on one line. However, if you have a complex table with extensive information on each row, you should put each row element (designated by the <TR> and </TR> tags) on its own line indented by a tab, and you should put the contents of each of the cells that make up the row on its own line indented one tab further. That way, it's easy to see where each row starts and ends.

These are all just guidelines. The most important thing is that the file be readable to you. You're the best judge of what it will take to do that.

Figures 11.8 and 11.9 show the difference that using carriage returns, comments, and indents can make. These two files will generate the exact same Web page. But which would you rather try to maintain?

```
Netscape - [Source of: file:///I/DOCS/INTERNET/Test Documents/menuleft.htm]

<!DOCTYPE HTML PUBLIC "-//IETF//DTD HTML//EN//2.0">
<HTML>
<BODY>
<!-- This is an example of types of lists in HTML 2.0. -->

    <UL>
        <LH><B>&ltUL></B> Unnumbered list</LH>
        <LI>bullet 1
        <LI>bullet 2
        <LI>bullet 3
    </UL>
    <MENU>
        <LH><B>&ltMENU></B> Menu list</LH>
        <LI>Selection 1
        <LI>Selection 2
        <LI>Selection 3
    </MENU>
    <DL>
        <LH><B>&ltDL></B> Definition list</LH>
        <DT>Term 1<DD>Definition 1
        <DT>Term 2<DD>Definition 2
    </DL>
</BODY>
</HTML>
```

Figure 11.8   An HTML source that uses carriage returns, comments, and indents.

Figure 11.9 The same page without carriage returns, comments, or indents. Yikes!

Test Your Links

You should check all the links on your Web site at regular intervals. If a user clicks your link to a file and that file no longer exists, they will see an error message like the one shown in Figure 11.10.

Basically, you need to check the internal links only when you make changes to your Web site. That's the only time that any internal link can change. To check links, you simply make sure you have not renamed or eliminated something that one of the links points to.

However, you need to check your external links more regularly. URLs are changed or disconnected more often than phone numbers. People change URLs for all sorts of reasons. For example, sometimes they remove old files that they think are no longer needed. Sometimes they move their site from one server to another looking for either cheaper storage or faster delivery. And sometimes they just get rid of their Web site altogether. Whatever the reason, if you're lucky, the old URL will still have a small file that displays a link to the new site (see Figure 11.11). Test that link. If it works, use the new address in place of the old one.

457

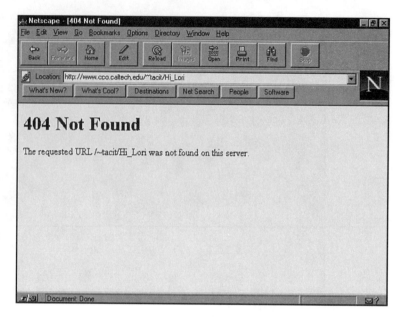

Figure 11.10 When you follow a link to a file that doesn't exist, you usually see this error.

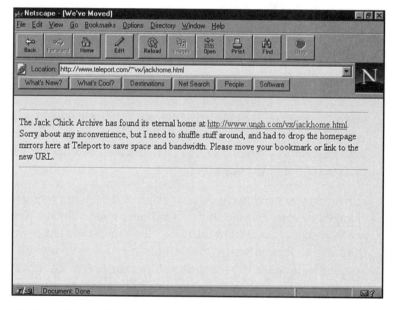

Figure 11.11 A forwarding link.

Even if you don't find a forwarding link, you still have some options. If you were linking to a specific file, try dropping the file name, entering just the directory path as the URL. If you don't see a home page or any files listed, try removing subdirectories from the path until you find something.

If you get all the way back to where you're trying the domain name as the URL and that doesn't bring anything up, or if Navigator tells you that the domain name is not listed, that doesn't mean that the site isn't out there somewhere. Check the search engines or directories to see if it's registered. Even if you can't find it now, try again in a few weeks.

Whatever you do, don't just leave a dead link on your Web site. People will forgive a dead link or two, but the more dead links you have at your site, the more it makes your site seem useless.

Do Unto Others...   The corollary to all this is that if you change URLs, be sure to notify everyone who you know has links to you so that people can find you. Also, put up a forwarding link at your old site if at all possible.

In this lesson, you learned how to make sure your pages work correctly for everyone who wants to view them. In the next lesson, you'll learn how to make your pages load fast and take up less disk space on the server.

Designing for Speed and Space

In this lesson, you learn how to make your Web page load fast and take up less space on the server.

The Importance of Speed and Compactness

Your Web site can run into two limitations: speed and space. If your Web site cannot get information out on the screen fast enough, the user will become disinterested and will go someplace else. In most cases, you will have a limited amount of space to store your site on, whether it's the gigabyte of hard disk space on your company's own Web server or the single megabyte of space that your network service allows you for your personal page. Commercial providers may offer you as much space as you want, but they'll charge you for each megabyte that you use. The more information you can fit into less space, the better.

On one hand, size and speed complement each together: smaller HTML and image files are transferred across the Net more quickly than larger ones. On the other hand, sometimes you have to choose between doing something that will transfer quickly and something that will take up less space, but not both. For example, you can split one big page into three little pages, each of which will load faster, but will take up more space than the single page. You can end up facing a decision between making your site smaller or faster. In any case, efficiency is not something to be ignored.

Making Your Pages Load Fast

Four primary factors contribute to how quickly your Web page appears on a visitor's screen:

- The speed of the visitor's modem
- The speed of the Internet (For all its bandwidth, the Internet can become overcrowded and slow during periods of heavy use.)
- The speed of your server
- The size of the files that make up your page

The last two are the only factors you can control. If you find that it's taking a long time for your page to come up, while similar pages elsewhere are coming up lickity-split, it's time to put your site on a new server. Cheap Web space is no bargain if it's so slow that no one sticks around to see your site.

However, most of the work that you will do to keep your site swift will be focused on the last category. File size is something that you have to keep in mind from the moment you start putting your pages together.

It's very easy to put together a Web site that looks wonderful on your hard disk, where everything comes up instantly. It's not much more difficult to make a page that looks great when viewed from a corporate T1 communications line.

TERM **T1** A type of communication line used for high-speed data communications, which is like a direct tap into the trunk of the phone system. T1 is too pricy for home use, but is commonly used by corporations and universities.

But the truth is, there are millions of people out there getting onto the Internet via ordinary modems—and not even the fastest modems. Plenty of your visitors are likely to be dialing in at 14,400 bits per second, 9,600 bits per second, or even slower. And the slower a person's connection is, the longer it will take his or her browser to load your page.

Suppose your page has 10 images that are 35,000 bytes each, as well as a 10,000 byte background image and a 40,000 byte main HTML file. That adds up to 400,000 bytes. Under *ideal* conditions, a 14,400 modem downloads fewer than 2,000 bytes per second, which means it would take three and a half minutes for that page to appear fully! The less-than-ideal conditions that frequently afflict the Internet can easily double that time.

A Rough Estimate   When the Internet is busy, a 14,400 modem will receive about a thousand bytes (or 1 kilobyte) of data per second. Windows Explorer lists file sizes in kilobytes. If you add up the sizes Windows Explorer lists for the HTML file and all the graphic files on that page, the number you get is approximately the same as the number of seconds it will take to download that page.

This degree of concern is only temporary. Newer technologies are on the way that should significantly increase the speed at which most people are connected. Home ISDN service (which is provided by phone companies) connects people at four times the speed of those 14.4 modems. In addition, cable modems (which hook up through the same wiring as your cable TV) will let users get information at rates as quick as 10 *million* bits per second. Those technologies are available today and should be common within a few years. Of course, you don't want to wait a few years for people to view your site.

When you're designing a Web page, you should be concerned with two speed measurements: how long it will take for the user to see anything, and how long it will take for him to see the complete page. If there is text on the page, the user usually starts seeing that text immediately; the graphics take longer, appearing in stages (see Figure 12.1).

When Text Comes Later   The exception is that if you are using a background graphic, some browsers won't display the text until after the background has loaded. This is a good argument for not using background graphics, particularly on pages with lots of text to load up.

First impressions are important, so it's very important that the first page people go to loads quickly. A good goal is to make sure all of the information on the first page will fit on a typical screen, without any need for scrolling. This screen should include the name of the site, a simple introduction that tells what the site is all about, and some navigational tools the user can use to find his way around the site.

For later pages, you may want to consider just how much you really need on each page. You can have too much on a page, which makes it load slowly, or you can have too little on a page, which makes the user go through a lot of pages to find what he wants.

Suppose, for example, that you have a book online. You probably don't want to include the entire book in a single HTML file. Granted, the Web surfer could start reading it immediately, and it is very unlikely that he would read faster than the document could download. But it would still take a long time to load, and distracting things would happen on his screen (such as the scroll bar shrinking and repositioning itself) while he is trying to read the document. And if the part he wanted to read happened to be at the end, he'd have to wait until the entire thing had downloaded to get there. A better solution is to put small portions, such as individual chapters, into separate HTML files.

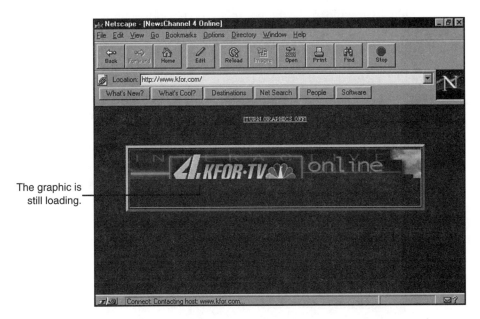

The graphic is still loading.

Figure 12.1 The text appears immediately, but the graphics take more time.

Trying to reduce your file size by removing comments, carriage returns, and tabs that you used to make the source file readable is not worthwhile (unless you have some extremely large comments). Those things generally constitute only a small percentage of your file's size.

Speedy Graphics Tricks

The images on a page will slow down the speed at which the page appears. Not only does it take time for the graphic to download to the machine, but the visitor's computer has to read the HTML file, find all the <IMG> tags, and request each image file separately.

A picture may be worth a thousand words, but on the Internet, many picture files are as big as a file with ten thousand words, or more. Here are some things to think about that can help you keep a lid on the size of your Web pages.

Reduce the Number of Graphics

Many useful Web pages do not have any graphics at all. They might not be visually exciting, but they present the information effectively. If you want a more exciting page, though, you will need graphics. This doesn't mean that you should use as many graphics as possible. Part of the problem with many Web pages is *too many* graphics, which can make the pages hard to read in addition to being slow to download. A site that relies too heavily on graphics ends up looking like one of those gaudy new magazines filled with design elements that make it hard for you to keep your eyes on the words.

Figure 12.2 shows a Web page that uses graphics to provide the second typeface for the table. Most browsers use only two typeface families: one for proportionally spaced characters and one for monospace. However, magazine-style layouts often use two proportional typefaces that blend well together. To make this page look more like published material, the creator used graphics for the second typeface. Except for the numbers, everything on the page is sent as an image instead of as text. Not only does this download much more slowly than it would if it were written entirely in HTML source code as text, but it also forces the reader to read in the font that the designer chose instead of the font he chose when he configured his system. Although these fonts do look good together, that's all for naught if the viewer's system is configured differently from the creator's.

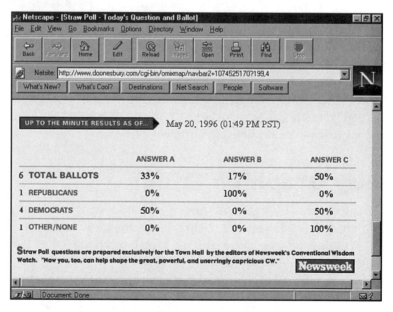

Figure 12.2 This site blends slow graphics with fast text.

Make Your Images Smaller

Many people design their images to be as large and as impressive as possible. Large does not always equal impressive though, particularly when the person who wants to look at the image has to wait for it.

Before you settle on your image size, give it some careful thought. A smaller image downloads faster and is useable in a wider range of browser configurations. By reducing the height and width of your picture by just one third, you can cut your download times in half.

If the image is one that came to you at a certain size, there are plenty of graphics tools that you can use to resize it, such as Photoshop, Graphic Workshop, Conversion Artist, or Collage Image Manager.

 Think Small   If the image you have is 200 pixels wide by 200 pixels high, and you use the HEIGHT and WIDTH attributes with the <IMG> tag to show it as 100 by 100 pixels, you're wasting a lot of time downloading detail you don't show. Resize the image file, shrinking it down to the largest size at which it will actually be displayed.

You can make a large image available to anyone who wants to see it, without forcing the uninterested visitor to wait while the image downloads. For example, let's say you have a 100 kilobyte picture called **BIGPIC.JPG**:

1. Use your graphic program to create a small version of BIGPIC.JPG, perhaps 50 pixels wide and 100 pixels high.

2. On your page, include the following line:

   ```
   <A HREF="bigpic.jpg"><IMG SRC="SMALLPIC.JPG">Click here to see
   BIGPIC.JPG (100K) full size.</A>
   ```

   (Including the size gives the user an idea how long it will take to display the picture.)

3. When you publish your site, be sure to include both BIGPIC.JPG and SMALLPIC.JPG.

If you don't mind having a Netscape-only page, you can forego the process of making a smaller file from the big image. Instead, you can just include the following line in your HTML source:

```
<IMG SRC="bigpic.jpg">Right-click on this image to see BIGPIC.JPG
(100K) full size.
```

Any Navigator user can right-click the file bigpic.jpg and select View Image from the shortcut menu to see the image full-size, in a page all its own.

Choose the Right File Type

An image with only a few colors should always be a GIF file. If you save these sorts of images as JPEG, they are usually larger and don't reproduce well. (You can increase the JPEG compression rate to make the JPEG image smaller, but that distorts it even more.)

The question gets tougher for images with a lot of colors. Generally, a GIF file is smaller than a good JPEG for an image with a lot of sharp, clear angles and curves to it (particularly computer-generated images). JPEG is better for photographs, complex scanned images such as paintings, and ray-traced 3-D graphics.

If you're unsure which to use, try storing the file as both. Then see which is smaller and which looks better on the page. Most good modern art programs (including Photoshop and Graphics Workshop) can read the file as one and save it as the other.

Reduce Your Color Depth

Usually, the fewer colors you use in a GIF, the less space it will take up. This is true even if you store your picture in GIF's 256-color mode.

Color Mode   The GIF file includes a setting for a maximum number of colors that can be used in the image. You have eight modes to choose from: 256 colors (also known as 8 bits), 128 (7 bits), 64 (6 bits), 32 (5 bits), 16 (4 bits), 8 (3 bits), 4 (2 bits), and 2 (1 bit).

However, a big advantage to using fewer colors comes from the fact that you can use one of the lower color modes, sometimes referred to as *bit depths*. Avoid using the 2-color mode, because it doesn't work with some browsers. Ideally, with so many choices, you should use the smallest mode that has at least as many colors as you actually use, because the fewer color modes take less space to describe a color.

Unfortunately, most of the art programs that let you save files as GIFs don't give you that broad range of choices. If you're lucky, they'll give you the choice between two modes: 16 and 256. Even just taking advantage of this can mean major savings. For example, a 2-color drawing stored as a 6 kilobyte file in

256-color mode will probably only take up about 4 kilobytes in 16-color mode. You'll probably also shave a couple of seconds off the amount of time it takes for this image to appear on the screen of a typical Web user. And when you use several images per page, those seconds can really add up!

With larger images, the size difference actually gets proportionately smaller. The 6 kilobyte 256-color file gets one third smaller when reduced to 16-color, but a 60 kilobyte file might only get one-tenth smaller. Still, when you're using large images, you're really using a lot of time and should try to save whatever you can.

Reuse Your Images

Graphical browsers don't automatically start a download every time they see the <IMG> tag. First, the browser checks to see if it has downloaded the image for that URL recently. If it has, it knows that the image is already stored on the hard disk, and it loads the image from there, which is much faster than loading from the Net.

You can use this to your advantage. You can put your logo or your menu buttons on every page, and feel comfortable that they will only actually download once. Just make sure that you're always pointing to the same image file; don't make additional copies of that file for use on different pages.

Figure 12.3 shows an example of the kind of image you can use on several of your pages. As you can see on Netscape's home page, buttons give the user instant access to the "foyers," if you will, of Netscape's various services. Even though this graphic appears on all of Netscape's main pages, it is loaded into the browser only once—when the user links to www.netscape.com. Because the graphic for the button bar on every other Netscape page is the same graphic, the browser doesn't have to request it from the server again; it just recalls the graphic from the local cache, which saves several seconds of download time.

Figure 12.3   Netscape's corporate button bar.

This concept applies even if you want to use smaller versions of the logo on later pages, or even on the same page (see Figure 12.4). Instead of making a smaller version of your logo, you can just use the HEIGHT and WIDTH attributes with the <IMG> tag to manipulate the size at which the image appears on the page. This will not look quite as good as having the image reduced by a really good art program, so you should compare the two and see whether it makes enough of a difference to worry about.

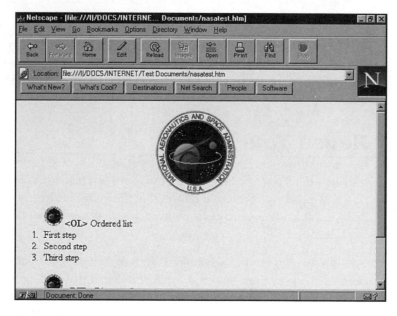

Figure 12.4   You can reuse a big image as a smaller image on the same page.

Make Use of Interlace

Interlacing your GIF images won't actually speed up the transfer rate for your images, but it can decrease how long it takes for a user to recognize what is being seen. Some images look best when seen from the top down, and some won't be recognizable at all until they are in their full resolution. But in most cases, you should lean toward using interlaced graphics.

Combine Images

If you have multiple images with a similar pallet that are supposed to appear next to each other, you should try combining them into a single larger image. Not only can this lead to some compression savings, but it also reduces how many downloading processes the browser has to start.

The series of comic book pages in Figure 12.5 is stored as a single noninterlaced image instead of as separate images for each page. This way, the pages aren't downloading at the same time, with the time being split fairly randomly among the pages. Instead, the first page loads first and is there for the visitor to read while the rest of the pages are downloading.

Anticipating Images If you link from a page that contains a lot of text and no new images to a page that contains an average number of images, you can preload some images for the second page while the reader is reading the first page—but you display the images so small that no one can see them!

At the very bottom of your first page, add the `<IMG SRC="image.gif" HEIGHT=1 WIDTH=1>` tag. This will load the image.gif file (or whatever name you use) and display it as a single pixel. That way, when you go to the next page, this image is already in your buffer! (Avoid the temptation to set `HEIGHT` and `WIDTH` to 0; this may cause some browsers to display the image in an unpredictable format.)

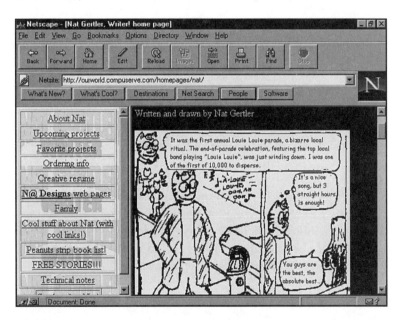

Figure 12.5 You can combine multiple images into a single tiled image.

Working with Limited Disk Space

Images tend to be the biggest culprit when it comes to eating up limited disk space. After all, if you're limited to text, you can fit a good-sized novel in a megabyte. But a megabyte will only hold about ten full-screen, full-color low-compression JPEG photographs.

Most of the techniques you can use to speed up your images will serve you well when you're trying to work with limited disk space. Keeping your images at a minimum, keeping them small, and reusing them will keep you from eating up disk space unnecessarily. You can also try the tricks covered in the next two sections.

Display Images Stored on Other Servers

If there's an image on someone else's page that you'd like to have on yours, it doesn't have to take up any of your limited site space. You can direct your visitor's browser to get the image off of the other site's server and display it in your page.

To do this, follow these steps:

1. Get the permission of the site owner to point to his file. Not only is this polite, but there are legal concerns about using someone's image without his permission.
2. Get the URL of the image you want to use. To do this, right-click the image and select **Copy this Image Location**.
3. Paste that URL into the SRC attribute of your <IMG> tag.

That's all there is to it. And there's another bonus: if you're providing a link to the site you're borrowing the image off of, it will speed things up for the visitor when he follows that link because that image will already be in his buffer. (The reverse is also true: if the visitor gets to your site by following a link from this other site, your page will appear faster.)

CAUTION

The Image's Owner Still Has Control   You don't have any control over an image located on another server. The person who runs the other site can remove it at any time without warning, and you'll be left with a symbol for an unloadable image on your page. (This can, however, serve as your own visual warning that the site has closed down.) You might want to keep a spare copy of that file somewhere (not taking up server space, obviously) just in case you need it.

Another possible problem can occur if you have borrowed the image without asking permission. The owner can change it on purpose simply to cause you problems.

Take Advantage of Other Server Space

Your entire site does not have to be on one server. If you're running out of space on one server or another account, there's no reason that you can't put some of your pages or some of your image files on any other server or account space that you can lay your hands on. With many online services and Internet access providers giving out free Web space to all of their customers, you may have several sites available. Unless the visitor looks at the URLs, he will have no way of knowing that he's switching servers as he moves among pages. (And even if he found out, why would he care?)

If you don't have any additional space (and can't borrow some from a friend), you might want to find out if there is someone else interested in carrying one of your pages for you. If you have useful, informative pages, other people who are interested in that topic would probably be happy to give room to those files. This can be a problem if they are files that need to be updated regularly because that person would have to give you controlling access to his Web space. "Mature" pages that don't need maintenance are the best for passing off to someone else.

In this lesson, you learned various tricks for making your Web pages load faster and take up less server space. In the next lesson, you learn how to design your pages so that they are more readable.

Designing for Readability

In this lesson, you will learn to make your Web pages more readable.

Text Colors

The ability to set the colors of the text in your Web pages can be used or abused. If you choose the right colors, your pages look great and can even evoke a certain mood. If you make poor color choices, however, your pages will be indecipherable.

If your sole objective is readability, your best bet is not to set the text or background colors at all. By letting the visitor's browser configuration control the font and background colors, you can be sure that your page will appear in colors the visitor is comfortable with.

If you do choose to set the text color, you should also set the background color. Otherwise, you might choose a text color that exactly matches the visitor's default background color, and your text will be invisible. Don't assume that everyone uses gray as the background color! The key to ensuring that your colors are visible is *contrast*. Be sure that there is a big difference between your text colors and the background color.

The surprising thing, however, is that it's not really the basic color that makes the difference—it's the brightness. If you think about it, this makes sense. After all, most graphical browsers default to readable black text on a light gray background. And what is gray but a light version of black? It's also clearly true for all of those people (including many laptop users) who browse the Web from black-and-white screens.

Here's a quick rule of thumb for checking contrast:

1. Take the text color code you're using (for example, "#A310F2") and jot down the first, third, and fifth characters after the number sign (in this example, A, 1, and F).

2. If you have a letter A, change it to 10. Then change B to 11, C to 12, D to 13, E to 14, and F to 15. Then, in the example, you have 10, 1, and 15.

3. Add these numbers together (10 plus 1 plus 15 equals 26). The result is a brightness value for this color.

4. Repeat steps 1–3 with your background color (for example, the brightness for the dark gray color #777777 would be 7 plus 7 plus 7, or 21).

5. Subtract the smaller of the two brightness numbers from the larger of the two: 26 minus 21 equals 5. This result is your contrast value.

For readable text, you really want a contrast of at least 15 (although a higher contrast would be better). Knowing that, you can see the colors we considered in the previous example aren't going to look good together.

Note that it doesn't make a difference which color is brighter and which is darker. Even though we're used to reading black text on a white background, having bright text on a dark background can be quite effective (see Figure 13.1). In fact, bright text seems to pop out from a black background and can really grab the reader. You wouldn't want to create huge documents like this because after a while it can tire the eyes. But for something that's going to take only a few minutes to read, it's fine.

Backgrounds

If you're setting a background *color*, the only real concern for readability is its contrast with the text. Yet you should choose your background color for its emotional effect. Blue tends to be calming, red is exciting, and white looks businesslike. Other colors have other subtle effects.

However, if you want to use an *image* as a background, a lot of other concerns surface. Remember that your text has to contrast with all of the background; you wouldn't want to put black text on a mostly-white-but-some-black background because the background parts that are black will make the black text unreadable.

You should make sure that you don't have much contrast within the background image. Otherwise, it will be too busy and distract from the text.

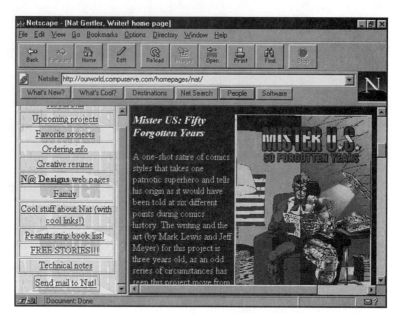

Figure 13.1   White text stands out on a black background.

When you use an image as a background, it is repeated vertically and horizontally. You might want to add some border space around the image so the images don't run together at the edges (see Figure 13.2).

Subtle Beauty   Subtle backgrounds that contain one or two colors with minor variations in darkness can look very nice. However, when viewed by a browser on a system configured for few colors (16 or even 256), two colors with minor variations can be interpreted as the same color.

When used properly, the repetition of images enables you to create some interesting designs. If you create an image whose left edge is designed to connect to its right, and its top to its bottom, you can create what looks like a single endless image. You have to be careful that the images line up cleanly, however. Otherwise, the visitor will be able to detect where the images don't line up, and will see clearly where one copy of the image ends and the next begins. Some people don't have a problem with this, but for others, it's very distracting.

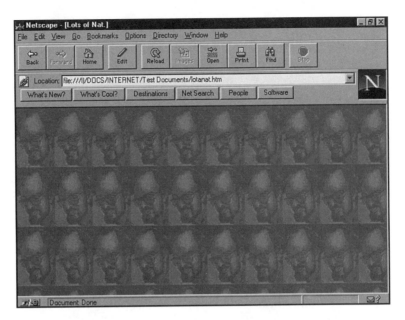

Figure 13.2 Without border space, it's hard to tell where one guy's beard ends and the next guy's hair begins!

Figure 13.3 shows a repeating checkered flag pattern. Notice how the partial squares at the top or left are lined up with the rest of the same square at the bottom or right. This creates a continuous seamless pattern.

Figure 13.3 Some patterns look seamless when repeated in the background of your Web page.

Creating an Overlapping Background Image

Creating your background design so that it overlaps or interlocks can be a little tricky. The best way to design it is often not to try to draw its interlocking form directly. Instead, you can follow these steps:

1. In your art program, draw one copy of the image. For example, take a look at the Escher-inspired image shown in Figure 13.4.

Figure 13.4   Draw the image that you want repeated.

2. Make a copy of the figure, move it directly horizontally, and paste it exactly where you want to see the figure repeated.

3. Make a copy of both of these figures, move it directly downward, and paste it where you want the image to repeat. Now you should have a figure that looks something like Figure 13.5, where you can actually see the pattern repeating.

Figure 13.5   This segment of the image appears in a dotted outline; it is the image that you will save as your background GIF.

4. Using the rectangular area select tool, select an area starting with a point in the middle of the upper-left version of the image and ending one pixel above and one pixel to the left of the same point in the lower-right image.

5. Choose the **Copy** command (it's probably in your program's **Edit** menu).

6. Then start a new file with just the image that you copied (most painting programs let you do this with a command like **New Image from Clipboard**).

This new image probably won't look like much. It has all of the parts of the original image, but they're all over the place. However, when you repeat this image as your background, everything should connect correctly, and you'll see an endless chain of your image.

A Diagonal Look

The standard image repetition tends to suggest strong vertical lines, which can be disconcerting. Some of the best designs feature little images that appear to be repeating diagonally. The background in Figure 13.6 is a good example of this.

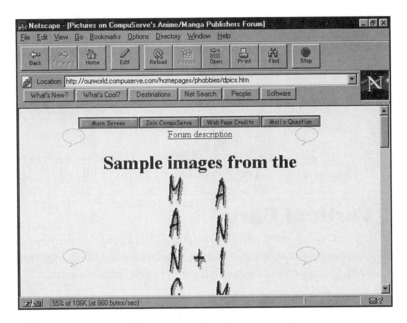

Figure 13.6 A background designed for diagonal repetition.

This effect may seem tricky. What's making the alternating rows of the image indent as they do? It's actually very simple. The image contains not just one copy of the little icon, but two. Figure 13.7 shows the actual image that was used to create the background.

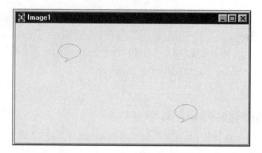

Figure 13.7   Your eyes might fool you into thinking the pattern repeats diagonally.

To get this to work, you need to make sure of two things:

- The width and the height of the image must both be an even number of pixels.
- Any given point on one of the little word balloons must be exactly half the width and half the height away from the same point on the other word balloon.

You can also do images with other sorts of diagonal lines. Just make sure that the lines wrap from one side of the image to the other and from top to bottom.

Vertical Bars

If you create a very wide image for a tiled background, you can be sure that it won't repeat horizontally. Using that image as the background, you can create vertical lines and patterns that don't repeat across the page.

You can achieve one professional-looking effect by building a table element for the entire page and placing a single background image behind the table to add visual effects to the borders. Figure 13.8 shows a GIF that looks like a slightly wrinkled sheet of paper as the background image. This image appears to have a vertical border about one-quarter of the way over from the left of the image (which is actually the left border of the text area of your Web page). The separate column in the left margin of the table creates a clearly separate border for comments or headers.

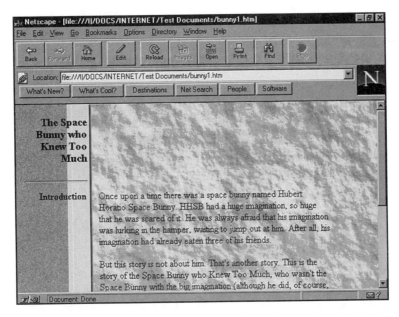

Figure 13.8 The background image is a thin horizontal line, colored at the left end and white across the rest.

Although you could use the <IMG> tag to place an image inside a single table cell, you couldn't display text on top of it. The only way to put text on top of an image is to make the image the background for the page. So when drawing your background image, you have to picture in your mind where your table cell boundaries will appear, or use the rule guides in your drawing program to keep track of the width of columns whose border effects you're currently drawing.

Plan Ahead Make sure that your image (it should be a GIF) is very wide, so that people with large display areas won't see the image start to repeat. An image 1,000 pixels wide should work for most users. Of course, if you think it's possible that someone with one of those huge UNIX workstations might open his browser window to full size, you should make it 1,800 pixels wide.

Although you see two sections here, this is actually a three-column table: the second column serves as a margin between the first and third. To create this effect, within the <TABLE> element of your HTML source, use the WIDTH attribute of the <TH> tag to set the width of the first two columns of the table (measured in pixels, such as <TH WIDTH=170>). The first column should be at least 30 pixels narrower than the colored area in the middle of your GIF background, but just wide enough for any comments you want to include in it. Create a second column with a width of 30 pixels to leave some space between the text in the margin area and the text in the third column (the text for the main body of the document).

Keeping Text Within Two Margins

The next obvious step is to figure out how to do a right margin. Unfortunately, the answer is that you really can't. You always know that the left margin starts at the first pixel. Because you don't know how wide the browser window is, you don't know where the right margin is.

The most common example of what happens when you make assumptions about the width of the browser screen concerns the variability of the user's browser size. Suppose a page designer is working under the assumption that his page will be viewed on a 640 × 480 screen, and he creates a page with a background GIF that's 640 pixels wide. If the user has a higher resolution screen, 640 pixels does not fill the width of the browser window. As a result, the GIF starts repeating horizontally and to the right.

If you really want to keep text between two designed margins, you need to use tables. To do that, follow these steps:

1. Figure out what you consider the narrowest possible browser width anyone will be using. (The minimum resolution for Windows users is 640 pixels wide; for users of old black-and-white Macintoshes, the resolution is 512 pixels wide.)

2. Create a table with three columns, each a fixed pixel width, where the three columns combined are no wider than the narrowest browser.

3. Create a background GIF that puts one color or pattern behind the first column, another color behind the second, and another (or a repeat of the first) behind the third. Then fill out the right and lower portions of it (in whatever manner you want) to at least the thousandth pixel across, so that people with wider browsers won't see the GIF repeat horizontally.

Using Proper, Readable Text

Proofread your text. Bad spelling, incorrect punctuation, and unfinished sentences make your work hard to read—and make you look unintelligent or uncaring.

Some of the HTML editors have spell checkers that are smart enough to skip over the contents of tags. No spell checker can catch every spelling mistake though. After all, if you meant to type *cat* but instead typed *act*, the spell checker would see that you typed an actual existing word and wouldn't correct you.

Do not use text highlights (such as bold and italics) for large amounts of text. Highlights are like spices. Trying to read ten straight paragraphs in bold italic type with the font size cranked up to 5 is like sitting down to a dinner of nothing but spices.

Preformatted text is a good way to quickly put non-HTML formatted text into an HTML document. There are times when you have a good layout reason to use it. However, if you're using it just so you don't have to convert it to HTML, you should reconsider. Preformatted text doesn't take full advantage of the page width in the way that standard HTML text does. In addition, its monospace format makes it harder to read.

You can find many manuals on text presentation designed for the printed page. These cover such topics as how much blank space you should have on the page and how to control the reader's eye. Unfortunately, these theories do not apply in the same way to Web pages. Reading a Web page is very different from reading a paper document because of the unpredictability of both the user's configuration and the way in which the user will scroll the page. These books might give you something to think about, but their guidelines are probably not applicable to your pages.

In this lesson, you learned to select colors and backgrounds to make your pages more readable. You also learned to work with repeating background images.

Designing and Publishing Web Pages with Netscape Gold

Adding and Formatting Text

In this chapter, you'll see how to use Netscape Gold's Web page editor to start a new Web page, how to put text on it, and how to format the text.

Designing and Publishing Web Pages with Netscape Gold

As you know, the protocol used to create and format Web pages is HTML, or HyperText Markup Language. As you learned in Part 5, you can create your own Web pages using a simple word processor and the proper HTML codes. Because HTML is a complex language, the process of creating a Web page this way is often complex. But Netscape has a solution, with a product called Netscape Navigator Gold (or simply Netscape Gold).

The main difference between Netscape Navigator Gold and Netscape Navigator is that the Gold edition has a built-in Web page designer. (There are some additional differences that you can learn about in Part 1, Lesson 1.) Netscape Gold's editor is an easy-to-learn tool that lets you craft how you want your Web page to look just as you might within a word processor, so you don't have to insert difficult-to-understand HTML commands within a Web page. Because the editor's display looks a lot like what the finished page will look like, this is advertised as a *WYSIWYG* tool.

TERM　**WYSIWYG**　Pronounced *wizzy-wig*, this stands for "what-you-see-is-what-you-get." It describes any computer design or editing tool that displays your work in a format that looks the same on-screen as it will when printed out.

When you're actually editing, the display may not show exactly what you will get. However, at any time, you can bring up a Web browser and see exactly what your Web page would look like if you were to view it from the Web. It's important to remember, however, that it may look very different when other people view the page. This is because people use many different Web browsers on different types of computers with different screen sizes and different option settings.

The Netscape Gold editor takes your finished design and generates an HTML file, a file of commands and data that the visitor's Web browser needs to display the Web page properly. The editor also has a feature that makes it easy for you to upload the files to your server, but this works only with certain specific Web space providers.

Ready to Create Web Pages?   Before you use the Netscape Gold editor, you may want to read Part 5, "Using HTML and the Netscape Extensions to Create Web Pages." Part 5 explains HTML commands that will help you understand just what Netscape Gold's HTML editor is doing behind the scenes. Even if you don't read it first, consider going back and reading it afterward because it has many good tips on how to design effective Web pages, particularly those that will look good to users using different Web browsers.

Starting a New Page

The best way to start with Netscape Gold's Web page editor is to jump right in with both feet (or, more importantly, all of your typing fingers). To start a new page, follow these steps:

1. Start Netscape Gold.

2. Open the **File** menu and select **New Document**. In the submenu that appears, select **Blank**. The Netscape editor window opens (see Figure 1.1), with a blinking cursor in the upper-left corner of the open area. (You can also open the editor by clicking the **Edit** button in Netscape Gold.)

3. Type the text below, pressing **Enter** to end each paragraph. If you make mistakes, you can use the cursor keys to move through the text and the Backspace and Delete keys to remove the mistakes.

   ```
   Herbert's Big Art-a-torium!

   Get famous near-masterpieces at going-out-of-business prices! Check
   out our fine selection:
   ```

First up is VonGertler's most influential piece, Portrait of the
Artist as a Blueberry Muffin. This was last sold at Danish auction
for 3.5 million latkes, but it can be yours for a mere $300, plus
$15,000 postage and handling (mostly handling).

Also available is McDragos's abstract ultimasterpiece, Nude Defending
Staircase. Once the crown heads of Europe threatened to go to war
over ownership of the piece; now you can get it just by threatening
to send in $499!

To order, just print out a copy of our order-form and mail it!

4. Save your file so you don't accidentally lose your work. (Open the **File**
   menu and select the **Save** command.) Because this file doesn't have a name
   yet, the Save as dialog box appears.

5. Click the **Create New Folder** icon. A new folder named "New Folder"
   appears.

6. Type **Practice** and press **Enter**, and the folder's name changes to that.

7. Double-click the **Practice** folder, and the folder opens.

8. Click in the **File Name** field and type **catalog**; then press **Enter**. The file is
   saved with that name and the extension .HTM.

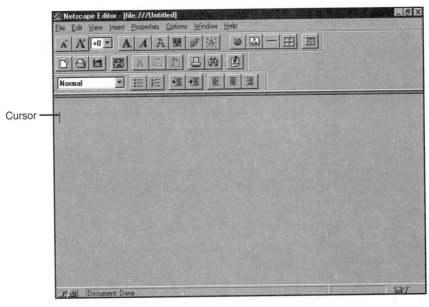

Cursor

Figure 1.1   The Netscape Editor window, where you type the text for your Web page.

Save Typing The editor accepts standard cut and paste commands. To put word processor text into a Web page, just select the text in the word processor, click the word processor's **Copy** button, switch to the Web page document, and then click the Web editor's **Paste** button.

Text Enhancement

Now you have a dull, flat Web page—just flat text on a flat background. It's time to liven up the text a bit. The Netscape Editor has several tools for enhancing your text, as shown in Table 1.1.

Table 1.1 Text Enhancement Tools

Tool	Name	Function
A	Bold	Makes text thick
A	Italic	Makes text slanted
A	Fixed Width	Spaces text evenly
⊞	Font Color	Changes text color
A	Clear All Styles	Makes text plain

To enhance your text, follow these steps:

1. Continue with the document that you created in the previous task. Select the words **Portrait of the Artist as a Blueberry Muffin** (click at the beginning of the first letter and drag to just past the last letter).
2. Click the **Italic** button, and the words appear italicized.
3. Select the words **Nude Defending Staircase**, and then click the **Fixed Width** button. The font changes to a *monospace* font (in which each letter takes up the same width of space).
4. Click the **Font color** button. The dialog box in Figure 1.2 appears.

Figure 1.2 The font Color dialog box.

5. Click on a red box and click **OK**. The selected text does not visibly change color immediately.

6. Select **Portrait of the Artist as a Blueberry Muffin** again. When you do, the other phrase becomes deselected, and you can see its real color: red.

7. Click the **Clear All Styles** button. This turns off the italic on the selected text, so the text returns to normal.

8. Click the **Bold** button, and the text becomes bold.

Undo! If you make any mistakes, pull down the **Edit** menu and select the **Undo** command to unmake the mistake!

Formatting Paragraphs

In addition to formatting individual words, you can also format entire paragraphs. The paragraph formatting tools shown in Table 1.2 let you change how whole paragraphs appear.

Table 1.2   Paragraph Formatting Tools

Tool	Name	Function
Normal ▾	Paragraph Style	Indicates current paragraph's format
	Bullet List	Turns text into a bulleted list
	Numbered List	Turns text into a numbered list
	Decrease Indent	Moves text left
	Increase Indent	Moves text right
	Left Align	Keeps left margin even
	Center	Centers text
	Right Align	Keeps right margin even

The Paragraph Style tool enables you to apply different predefined styles to your paragraphs. The available styles are:

- *Normal*, which gives you standard-sized text, usually displayed with a blank line following each paragraph.
- *Heading 1* through *Heading 6*, which are designed for headlines and section designations. Each gives you a different size or emphasis of text, ranging from 1 (biggest) to 6 (smallest). The program automatically skips a line after the heading.
- *Address*, which usually appears in italics.
- *Formatted*, which displays a monospace font and doesn't automatically wrap at the margins. You have to insert the start of a new line by clicking where the previous line should end and then pressing Enter. This style does not automatically add an extra line between formatted paragraphs.

- *List Item*, which indents the paragraph and puts a bullet in front of it (as in this list). No line is skipped between list items.
- *Description Title* and *Description Text*, which you can use on alternating lines to create a list of items with information on each. The item name (the Title) will stay at the left edge, while the information is indented. No lines are skipped.

To try out some of the tools, follow these steps:

1. Click anywhere on the first line of text.
2. Click on **Paragraph Style** drop-down arrow, and a list of format styles appears. Click **Header 1**. That line now appears in large letters.
3. Select the two paragraphs describing the artwork and click the **Numbered List** button. The two paragraphs become indented, and pound signs (##) appear in front of them. These pound signs will be replaced by actual numbers later.
4. Click the second line of text (the **Get famous** line), and then click the **Increase Indent** button twice to indent it to the second level.
5. Click the **Decrease Indent** button once so that the selected text is indented only one level.
6. The last three buttons in the row control the *alignment*. Click the last line of text, click the **Center** button, and then click the **Left Align** button to see the effects.

The details of how each of these changes will appear on the finished page depends on the viewer's browser and options.

TERM   **Alignment**   The settings that control where the text appears across the page's width. Each alignment button shows a picture of how text will look when you click that button.

Changing Text Size

The Netscape Gold Editor lets you work with seven sizes of text. You already saw the Heading paragraph styles, which let you use different sizes of text, but which apply only to whole paragraphs. Using the buttons shown in Table 1.3, you can change as much or as little text as you want.

Table 1.3   Font Size Tools

Tool	Name	Function
A⁻	Decrease Font Size	Makes text smaller
A⁺	Increase Font Size	Makes text larger
+0 ▾	Font Size	Sets a specific text size

Of the seven different text sizes you can use, normal size is size 0. There are two smaller sizes (–1 and –2) and 4 larger sizes (+1 through +4). To experiment with the font size tools, follow these steps:

1. Select the word **Big** in the first line. The Font Size field should show **+3** because this is a large heading.

2. Click the **Increase font size** button. The word "Big" gets bigger, and the Font Size field shows **+4**.

3. Select **plus $15,000 postage and handling (mostly handling)** from the first art description, which is currently size 0, but really should be small print. Click the **Decrease font size** button to lower it to –1.

4. Select the whole last line.

5. Click the **Font Size** drop-down arrow and select **+2** from the list of font sizes. The line increases in size. Your page should look like the one in Figure 1.3.

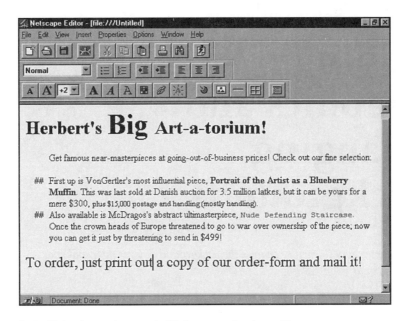

Figure 1.3 This chapter's sample Web page after formatting.

Checking Your Work

When you finish formatting the text on your page—or if you want to check your work periodically before you're done—you can click the **View in Browser** button to see how your page will look to people surfing the Web. To see how your page will look in a browser, follow these steps:

1. Click the **View in Browser** button to see how those numbered lists will actually look when encountered on the Web. A dialog box appears, asking if you want to save the changes to the file.

2. Click **Yes**, and a new browser window displays the page. Notice that there are actual numbers by the list, instead of number signs.

3. To close the browser window, click the **Close** (X) button.

4. Click the **Save** button (the one with a picture of a disk) to save the changes you've made to the file. Then click the **Close** (X) button to close the editor window.

In this lesson, you learned how to start a Web page, add text to it, and format the text. In the next lesson, you'll learn how to use graphics to spice up the page even more.

Adding Graphics and Changing Backgrounds

LESSON **2**

In this chapter, you'll learn to change the background of your page and add graphics to your page.

Changing the Background Color

If you don't specify what color the page background should be, it will default to whatever background the person viewing it has configured for his browser. Usually, this will be a dull gray or a clean white. If you want to add excitement to the page or if you want to make sure that your colored text will be visible, you should specify a background color. To do that, follow these steps:

1. Start Netscape Navigator Gold (if you don't already have it open), pull down the **File** menu, and select the **Open file in editor** command. A dialog box appears.

2. Open the **Practice** folder, click **catalog.htm** (which you created in Lesson 1), and click the **Open** button. The editor window opens and displays the file.

3. Open the **Properties** menu and select the **Document** command. The Document Properties dialog box appears.

4. Click the **Appearance** tab to see the options shown in Figure 2.1. Most of them will be grayed out.

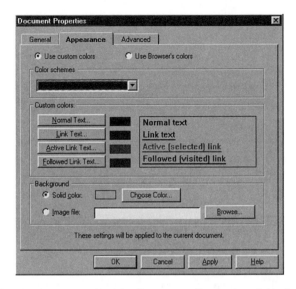

Figure 2.1 The Appearance tab of the Document Properties dialog box.

5. Click the **Use custom colors** option button. A dot appears in the circle, and everything that was grayed out comes to life (which makes the on-screen dialog box look like the one in this figure).

6. Click the **Choose Color** button near the middle of the dialog box, and the Color dialog box appears.

7. In the **Basic colors** chart, click the light blue that's in the fifth column of the first row.

8. Click **OK** to close the Color dialog box.

9. Click **OK** to close the Document Properties dialog box. The background of the page is now the light blue that you selected.

Using a Background Image

If you want a fancier-looking page, you can select a GIF or JPEG image to go behind the text. If the image isn't big enough to fill the user's browser window, the browser will repeat the image horizontally and vertically to fill the space.

Get Some Graphics   In order to perform this task, you need a couple of graphic files (either GIF or JPEG pictures). If you don't have any, they're easy to get. Go to any Web page with graphics (try **http://www.mcp.com/que/new_users/6n1.html**), right-click on any picture, and select **Save Image As**. Smaller images will be a bit easier to work with than large ones. Put these graphics in the Practice folder that you created in the previous lesson.

Most images don't make good backgrounds because it's hard to read text that's in front of them. So it's likely that the images you've got aren't going to look great. Still, this is just a learning exercise, so let's throw something in there.

1. With your Web page open, open the **Properties** menu and select the **Document** command. The Document Properties dialog box appears.

2. Click the **Appearance** tab.

3. Click the **Image file** option button, and a dot appears in it.

4. Click the **Browse** button. The dialog box that appears lists all the GIF and JPEG files in your Practice directory.

5. Click the name of the one of the files and click **Open**. The path to that image appears in the field next to the Browse button.

6. Click **OK**, and the image becomes *tiled* behind your page (see Figure 2.2).

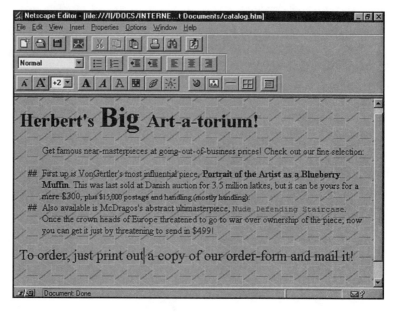

Figure 2.2   A tiled background. Of course, yours will look different, depending on the image you chose.

Tiled The effect produced when an image is repeated both vertically and horizontally to fill the available space.

It doesn't matter what your background looks like for the rest of the lesson, but if the image you chose makes it difficult to read on-screen text, get rid of it. To do so, open the **Properties** menu, select the **Document** command, click the **Solid color** option button, and click **OK**.

Adding a Horizontal Line

The simplest nontext element that you can add to a document is a *horizontal rule*, a horizontal line that separates one section of the document from another. To add a horizontal rule to your Web page, follow these steps:

1. Click at the end of the first line of text to place the cursor there.

2. Click the **Insert Horizontal Line** button. The horizontal line immediately appears below the first line of text, on its own line.

Adding an Image

By default, an image on a Web page appears as part of a line of text. If there is too much text on one line for the image to fit on that line, the browser wraps it down to the beginning of the next line just as it would a word that wouldn't fit on the screen.

To place an image on your page, follow these steps. (Remember that if you don't have any graphics lying around, you can go to **http://www.mcp.com/que/new_users/6n1.html**, right-click on a graphic, select **Save Image As**, and put it in your Practice folder.)

1. Click to the left of the words "Portrait of the Artist as a Blueberry Muffin" to put the cursor there. This indicates where you want the picture inserted.

2. Click the **Insert Image** button, and the Properties dialog box shown in Figure 2.3 appears.

497

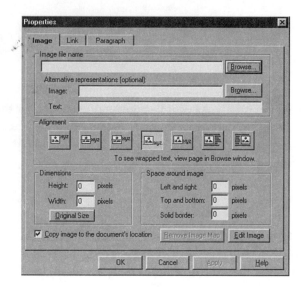

Figure 2.3   The Image tab of the Properties dialog box.

3. Click the **Browse** button next to Image file name. A dialog box appears, listing the image files in your Practice directory.

4. Click one of the files (not the one you used previously as your background), and then click **Open**. You're returned to the Properties dialog box.

5. In the **Text** text box, type **Blueberry Muffin picture**. (These words will be visible to people whose browsers don't support graphics or who are waiting for the image to download.)

6. Click **OK**. The dialog box disappears, and the image is inserted into the line of text (see Figure 2.4).

Give It Some Breathing Room   If you want the image to be on its own line (with no text on either side), add a blank line before you insert the image. To do that, place the cursor where you want the blank line to start and press **Enter**. Then press the up arrow key to move the cursor up to the blank line.

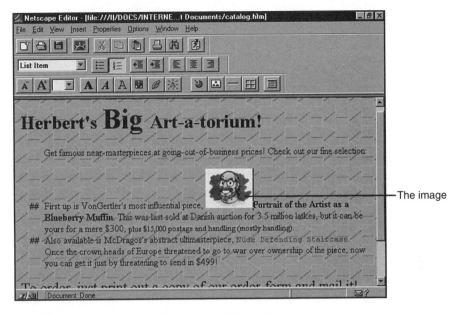

Figure 2.4   The image appears in the middle of the text.

Formatting an Image

Putting an image into a line of text is fine if it's a very small image or if you can put it in on the first line of the paragraph. However, if you insert a big image in the middle of a paragraph, you end up with big gaps between the lines of text because the one line of text has to have enough space to hold the whole image.

As you might guess, there are ways you can format the image to make it fit better and to make the text wrap around it. To learn about the changes you can make, follow these steps to change the image you just inserted.

1. Click the image, and a border appears around it to indicate that it is selected.

2. Click the **Object Properties** button. The Properties dialog box appears (refer to Figure 2.3).

3. The buttons in the Alignment area show five ways the image can line up with the text on the line, as well as two ways you can wrap the text around the image. Click the rightmost button.

499

4. In the Dimensions area, change the **Height** field to **80** and the **Width** to **60**. This forces the image to be squished and stretched to that size.

5. In the Space around the image area, change both the **Left and right** and **Top and bottom** fields to **8**. This keeps the text from running into the edge of the picture, which makes it hard to read.

6. Click **OK**, and the dialog box disappears. You can see that there is more space around the image.

Don't Expect to See It Although there is more space around the image now, it still seems to be on the same line as the text. This is because the text-wrapping isn't displayed on the editor screen.

CAUTION

7. Click the **Save** button to save the changes to the file on disk.

8. Click the **View in Browser** button, and you will see the file as it will be displayed on the Web. As you can see in Figure 2.5, the text does wrap around the image.

9. Click the **Close** (X) button or select **File**, **Close** to close the browser window.

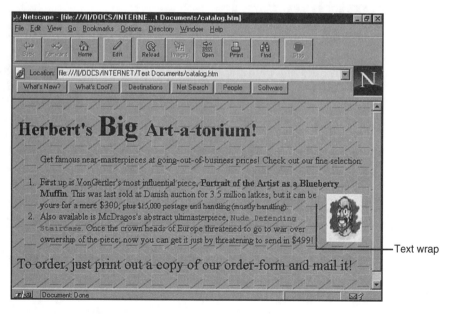

Figure 2.5 Now the text wraps around the image.

You Don't Have to Be an Artist   You don't have to be good at creating your own graphics. Plenty of companies offer computer *clip art*, prepared graphics that you can use.

In this lesson, you learned to use backgrounds and graphics to enhance your page. In the next lesson, you'll learn to create links the visitor can use to go from one page to another.

Creating Links

In this lesson, you'll learn to add links that will take the visitor to other pages, and you'll learn to add targeted links that will take him to a specific part of a page.

Getting Ready to Link

The capability to link pages to one another is a big part of what gives the Web its special feel. Having an immediate link to a related item enables you to follow your curiosity almost instantly. A page that contains links really is part of the Web—not just a stand-alone document.

Before you create any links on your page, however, you really should give the page a name. That way, when people follow a link to your page, they'll know where they are! To name your page, follow these steps:

1. Open the **catalog.htm** file in the Web page editor. (If you just finished working through the previous lesson, you probably still have it open.)

2. Pull down the **Properties** menu and select the **Document** command. The Document Properties dialog box appears.

3. Click the **General** tab, and the Document Properties dialog box shown in Figure 3.1 appears. The fields will be empty except for the Title, which will say **file:///Untitled**. (Because you're starting with a blank file, it is untitled.) The Author field shows the name of the registered user of this program; if it's not your name, change the field's contents.

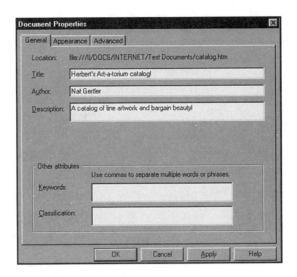

Figure 3.1   The Document Properties dialog box.

4. In the Title field, type **Herbert's Art-a-torium Catalog!**

5. In the **Description** field, type a description of the page's contents.

6. When you finish, click **OK**.

All of this information is embedded into your HTML file. The author and description information will be useful for Web search tools, such as Yahoo and Lycos, that take the information and store it as the description of your page. The title will appear on the visitor's screen—usually in the title bar—when he accesses your page. (Right now, the title appears in the editor's title bar as well.)

If you're going to create a link, you will need a page to link to. To quickly create a page, follow these steps:

1. Click the **New Document** button (see Table 3.1). The Create New Document dialog box appears.

2. Click the **Blank Document** button, and a new editor window opens.

3. In the new window, type **This is a dull but simple document to link to** and click the **Save** button.

4. When the file browser opens, enter the name **linkto** and click **Save**. This saves that file with the name linkto.htm.

5. Click the **Close** (X) button to close the editor window.

Table 3.1 Editing Buttons

Tool	Name	Function
	New Document	Starts a new Web page
	Open file to edit	Gets page from disk to edit
	Save	Saves page as HTML file
	View in Browser	Opens browser and displays page
	Cut	Moves selection to Clipboard
	Copy	Copies selection to Clipboard
	Paste	Pastes Clipboard's contents to page
	Print	Prints current page
	Find	Finds text on page
	Publish	Starts the process of uploading to a server

Creating a Link to a Page Within Your Web Site

Now everything is in place to create a simple link. Follow these steps:

1. In the editor window, select the words **order-form** in the last line of text.
2. Click the **Make Link** button. The Properties dialog box shown in Figure 3.2 appears.

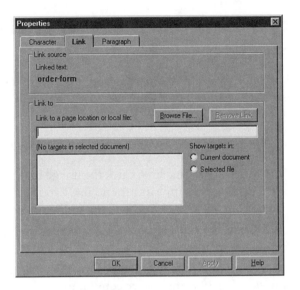

Figure 3.2   The Properties dialog box.

3. Click the **Browse File** button.

4. In the dialog box that appears, click **linkto.htm** and click **Open**. You're returned to the Properties dialog box.

5. Click **OK**. The words **order-form** are now underlined. Deselect the text, and you'll see that they are also a different color to indicate that they are a link.

6. Click the **Save** button to save the file. Then, to test the link, click the **View in Browser** button.

7. When Navigator opens, click the words **order-form**. The linked-to page appears. Click the **Close** (X) button to close the browser.

Because catalog.htm and linkto.htm are in the same directory and will be in the same directory when the Web site is published, you don't have to worry about including the path to the link. However, you do have to make sure that your directory structure on the disk is the same as the structure that will be on the Web server. Having all the files in the same directory is the simplest way to organize things. If you do have subdirectories with files in them, make sure that the same files are in the same directories on the server.

Creating a Link to a Page Outside Your Web Site

You'll probably want to create links to someone else's Web site at some point. Because these files aren't on your hard disk, you won't be able to use the File Open dialog box to locate them.

The following steps walk you through creating an outside link.

1. This will be a graphic link. Click the image that's in the first catalog entry, and a black frame appears around it. (If you were creating a text link, you'd select the text to link, and it would appear in inverse colors.)

2. Click the **Make Link** button. The Properties dialog box opens, with the Link tab displayed.

3. In the **Link to a page location or local file** field, type the URL **http://ourworld.compuserve.com/homepages/nat/**.

Get the URL Right! It's easy to make a typo when entering the URL. The best way to ensure that you get it right is to go the page you're linking to with the browser, right-click the **Location** field, and select **Copy**. Then when you're asked to enter the URL here, right-click the field and select **Paste**.

4. Click **OK**.

Targeted Links

There will be times when you want to provide a link not just to a page, but to a specific place on a page. Many people do this on long pages that are broken into sections, for example. The place on the page that you want to link to is called a *target*, and the link to it is called a *targeted link*.

Often, the place that you are linking to is on the same page as the link. This way, you can have an index at the top of the page that quickly links to any part of the page that someone wants to find.

First, you need to create the target and give it a name:

1. Click on the beginning of the second catalog entry (the one about **Nude Defending Staircase**).

2. Click the **Insert Target** button. The Target Properties dialog box appears (see Figure 3.3).

Figure 3.3 The Target Properties dialog box.

3. Type **staircase** as the target name and click **OK**. A small target symbol appears at the specified location, as shown in Figure 3.4. This is only an editor's symbol; it won't be seen by visitors who view the page.

The target icon —

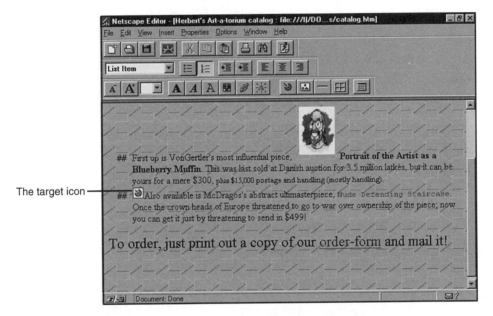

Figure 3.4 The target icon appears so that you will remember where your target is.

To create a link to that target, follow these steps:

1. Add a new line of text to the page by clicking at the start of the second line of text ("Get famous near-masterpieces"). Then type **Check out today's special!!!** and press **Enter**.

2. Select that line of text by clicking in the left margin in front of the line.

3. Click the **Make Link** button. The Properties dialog appears, with the Link tab displayed.

4. The "Select named target in current document" field lists all the targets on the current page—which is only one: staircase. Click the target name you want to link to.

5. #staircase appears in the Link field. Click **OK** to accept this link.

6. Click the **Save** button.

7. Click the **View in Browser** button, and a browser window opens, displaying the current page.

8. As you can see, the whole page fits on one screen. In order to see how clicking the link affects the page, you need to make the Navigator window smaller. Click the **Restore** button to make the window smaller. Only the headline and the link should be showing (see Figure 3.5).

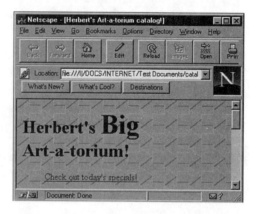

Figure 3.5 The reduced browser window.

9. Click **Check out today's special!!!**, and the entry for "Nude Defending Staircase" appears in the browser window. Click the **Close** (X) button to close the browser.

The procedure for linking to a targeted location on another page of your site is similar. However, when you make the link, you have to click the **Browse file** button to select the page with the target before you can select the target from the list on the page.

Changing the Color of Links

People recognize a link in text in two ways. One is that text links are usually underlined (unless the browser has been configured not to show them that way). The other is that text links show up in a different color. When you create pages, you can configure the colors for each page. Actually, you can configure the color for three distinct items:

- A link to a page or target that the viewer hasn't visited recently
- A link that has been visited recently
- The link the visitor is currently clicking

Why would you want to change those colors? Some folks want to change them just to make their pages prettier. But it can really be important to change them if you create a page that has a background color or background images. You have to make sure that your links will show up well against that color.

To set link colors, follow these steps:

1. With a page open in the editor, click the **Properties** menu and select the **Document** command. The Document Properties dialog box appears.

2. Click the **Appearance** tab to see the options shown in Figure 3.6.

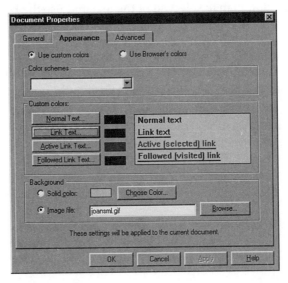

Figure 3.6 You can select link colors in the Document Properties dialog box.

3. Click the **Use custom colors** option button if it is not already selected. In the Custom colors area, you will see the settings for all three link types and for the normal text color against the currently selected background color.

TIP

Match Your Background Color   Even if you have a background *image*, the text in the sample shown in the Document Properties dialog box appears against the selected background *color*. Because of this (and other reasons as well!), you should set your background color value to match the main color of your background image.

4. Click the **Link Text** button, and a color selection dialog box appears.

5. Click a color that will show up well against your background and click **OK**.

6. Repeat steps 4 and 5 for the **Active Link Text** and **Followed Link Text** buttons.

7. Click **OK**, and the dialog box disappears. Your settings immediately take effect in the displayed page.

8. Click the **Save** button to save these changes to your page.

As you probably noticed, there was also a button to change the normal text. If you want to change the color of most of the text on your page, it's better to use that button than to select all of the text and use the Font Color button. Some browsers will be able to show a color you select using the Normal Text button but won't be able to show a color you select with the Font Color button.

In this lesson, you learned to create links. In the next lesson, you will learn to use Netscape's Web page wizard to make simple, good-looking Web pages easily.

Using the Netscape Page Wizard

In this lesson, you will learn to use the Netscape Page Wizard to make simple, good-looking Web pages easily.

What's a Wizard?

Netscape Gold gives you access to the Netscape Page Wizard, an automated program that practically lays out a Web page for you. Because the wizard is designed to create one basic type of page, it's not a very flexible program and isn't well-suited to multipage sites. Still, if you want to put together a good-looking page as quickly as possible, this is a tool for you.

Netscape Page Wizard does not come with your copy of Netscape Navigator or Netscape Navigator Gold; it is located on Netscape's servers. As such, you access it via a Web page. One advantage to having the design program reside on Netscape's servers instead of on your computer is that Netscape can add features to it at any time, and everyone can use those features immediately without having to download new software. Therefore, it's entirely possible that between the time you read this section and the time you use the wizard, other features will have been added!

Running the Wizard

To have the wizard program put your page together, follow these steps:

1. Connect to the Internet and Start Netscape Gold.

2. Open Netscape's **File** menu and select **New Document**. A secondary menu appears to the right. Select the **From Wizard** command.

3. A browser window opens up the three-framed document shown in Figure 4.1. Only the upper-right frame has anything in it. Scroll down to the bottom of this frame and click the **Start** button.

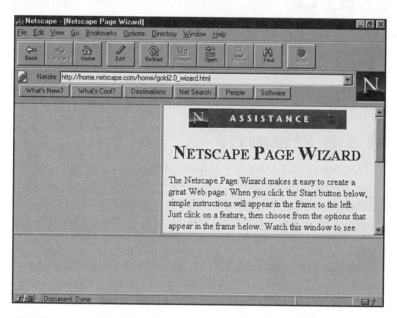

Figure 4.1   The initial screen of the wizard.

4. The upper-left frame contains instructions for using the wizard, and the upper-right frame has a preview of the page you're designing. The under-lined links in the left frame are commands for the wizard. Click the **give your page a title** command.

5. A simple form with just one field appears in the bottom frame (see Figure 4.2). Select the text that is there, and then type **The Well-Meaning Zippy-Doo Page**.

6. Click the **Apply** button, and this unlikely title appears in the preview document.

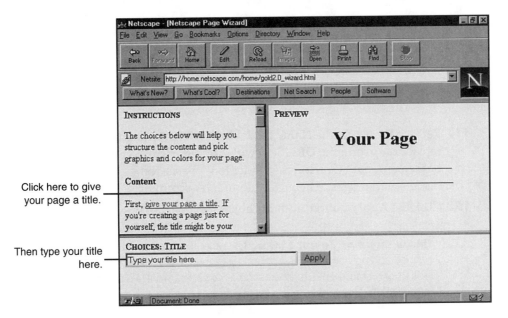

Click here to give
your page a title.

Then type your title
here.

Figure 4.2 Use the wizard to choose a title.

TIP

Fix Your Mistakes If you discover that you messed up your entry for any of the commands, just select that command again. The form will reappear, and you can change what you selected!

7. A little lower in the left frame (you may have to scroll down to find it), click the **type an introduction** command. Another one-field form appears in the bottom frame.

8. Replace the text in this field (which can hold up to 1,000 characters) with **This page will keep you up to date with the latest in Zippy-Dooism, and how you can do the doo with the best of them!**

9. Click the **Apply** button, and this text is added to the preview frame.

10. In the left frame, scroll to and click the **add some hot links to other Web pages** command. A two-field form appears in the bottom frame as shown in Figure 4.3.

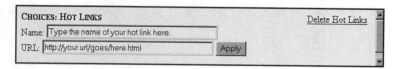

Figure 4.3 Choose your links here.

11. Replace the text in the **Name** field with **Nat Gertler, author supreme!** and replace the text in the **URL** field with **http://ourworld.compuserve.com/ homepages/nat/**. (Forcing the reader to type nice things about you is one of the few advantages of being a computer book author.)

12. Click the **Apply** button, and this link appears in the preview frame.

More Links or Fewer Links Note that if you repeat this command, you will be adding another link, not replacing the existing one. You can string together as many links to interesting sites as you want. To delete your links, click **Delete Hot Links**. In the list that appears, click to remove the check marks next to the links you want to delete.

13. In the left frame, scroll to and click the **type a paragraph of text to serve as a conclusion** command. Another 1,000-character text field appears in the bottom frame.

14. In this field, type **For all those Zippy-Doos and those who love them: be kind to each other, if anyone is watching**.

15. Click the **Apply** button, and the wizard adds that text to the preview frame.

16. Click the **add an e-mail link** command, and another one-field form appears in the bottom frame. Type your e-mail address into this field and click **Apply** to put it on the preview frame.

17. Now that you have all the text on the page, it's time to worry about how it looks. Click the **a preset color combination** command, and the wizard displays color choices in the bottom frame (see Figure 4.4).

Figure 4.4 In color, this looks a lot more, well, *colorful!*

18. Click one of the squares with bright text on a dark background. The preview frame immediately takes on the color combination used in that square. (The background of the preview frame becomes the selected background color, most text becomes the color of the word "text," and the links become the color of the word "links.")

19. Skip over the next few commands, which let you set the background and text colors individually. Click the **choose a bullet style** command, and the bullet style choices shown in Figure 4.5 appear in the bottom frame.

Figure 4.5 The bullet styles from which you can choose.

20. Click the *bullet* (a typography term for a highlighting mark) with the white star on a blue background. The choices disappear, and the selected bullet appears in front of the link (or links, if you added several) in the preview frame.

Not Everyone Can See It Move If you choose an animated (changing) bullet or an animated horizontal rule, other users with the current version of Netscape will see it as animated, but most other browsers don't support animation.

CAUTION

21. Click the **choose a horizontal rule style** command. A column of separation lines appears in the bottom frame (see Figure 4.6).

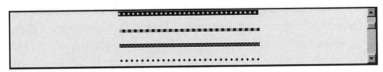

Figure 4.6 Pick a style for your horizontal rules.

22. Click the line made up of alternating black and gray boxes, and it appears in the preview frame, separating the sections of your page.

23. Scroll to the bottom of the left frame, and you will see several buttons. Click the **Build** button, and your finished page appears, taking up the entire window, as shown in Figure 4.7.

515

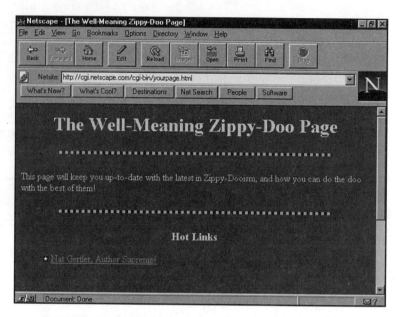

Figure 4.7 Your finished masterpiece!

The good news is that your page is now complete. The bad news is that it is still on Netscape's computer, and you have to move it to your computer before you can publish it. (You might also want to do some editing on it before you publish it, adding things that the wizard didn't take care of, for example, or deleting the built-in advertisement for Netscape that's at the bottom of the page.)

Copying a Page to Your Computer

The method you use to save the page that the wizard generated will also work with *any* page that you find online. It does a lot more than the File, Save as command, which saves only the HTML file to your hard disk. This command saves not only the HTML file, but also all of the page's graphics files (such as the bullets on the Wizard-composed pages or the illustrations on other pages). It also translates all of the links for local items on the page, so that those links will work when the page is on your hard disk.

To copy the page to your computer, follow these steps:

1. Open the **File** menu and select the **Edit Document** command.

2. An editor window opens, displaying the page and the Save Remote Document dialog box shown in Figure 4.8. Check both of the check boxes if they are not already checked. Then click the **Save** button.

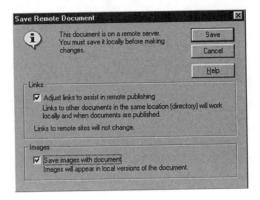

Figure 4.8   You can save your page to your computer.

3. A dialog box appears warning you that **You are about to download a remote document or image. You should get permission to use any copyrighted images or documents.** Heed the advice, and click **OK**.

Copy? Right!   You don't have to worry about the copyright on Netscape-created bullets and horizontal rules that the wizard put on your page. Netscape put them there for you to use!

4. In the dialog box that appears, double-click the **Practice** folder to save the files there.

5. In the **File name** field, replace **yourname.htm** with **zippydoo**. Then click the **Save** button to save the file.

6. A Saving Document dialog box appears, listing each text and graphics file as it downloads, and counting off the number of files it has left to download. When the download is complete, the page appears in your editor window, ready for you to edit (see Figure 4.9).

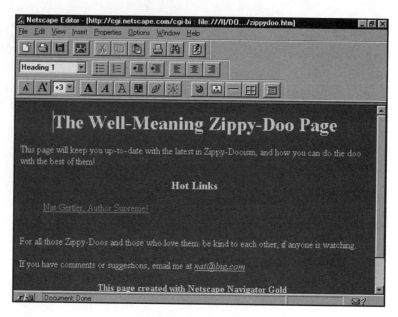

Figure 4.9   Lay the groundwork with the wizard, and then tweak your page in the Netscape Editor.

Because you can save any Web page to your hard drive, if you find a page with a layout you like, you can copy it. Of course, you have to be sure to replace all the text and images with your own (or get permission to use the existing elements), but you can take advantage of a useful structure that already exists.

In this lesson, you used the Netscape Page Wizard to automate the creation of a basic Web page. In the next lesson, you will see how to use Netscape Gold's built-in publishing capabilities to put your Web pages onto your server.

Publishing Your Web Pages

In this lesson, you'll learn how to use Netscape Gold's one-button publisher to put your Web pages onto a Web server where everyone can see them!

Getting Your Page Out on the Web

Unless you've been working directly on a *Web server* (a computer that stores Web sites where people browsing the Web can see them), you will have to take the additional step to *publish* your Web pages.

TERM **Publish** To copy your files to the proper directory on a Web server. This is called "publishing" because it enables people to read your pages, just as publishing a book makes copies of the book available for people to read.

There are two items of good news and one item of bad news about publishing. The first item of good news is that publishing is usually a fairly simple process. The second item of good news is that Netscape Navigator Gold's Web page editor has a built-in publishing feature. The bad news is that, unfortunately, the built-in publishing feature doesn't work with most Web servers. It works only with Web servers that have software designed to work with this feature.

Your Web space provider should be able to tell you if their system works with the publishing feature. If it doesn't, they will probably provide you with their own publishing software and full instructions on how to use it. Table 5.1 lists Internet service providers that currently allow you to use the built-in publishing feature when publishing your Web site on their system (you may have to pay extra to get some Web space with your account—or some may come free).

Table 5.1 Providers That Support Netscape's Publishing Feature

AT&T WorldNet Service

CERFnet, Inc.

Concentric Network Corporation

EarthLink Network

GTE Intelligent Network Services

Internet & Web Services Corporation

NETCOM On-line Communication Services

Portal Information Network

PSINet's PSIWeb

US WEST's !NTERACT Service

Web Communications

You Tools/FASTNET

More providers are supporting this feature all the time. If your Web space provider does not support this feature, you can skip the rest of this chapter. Contact your service provider and ask how their users go about getting Web pages up on the server.

Configuring the Publisher

In order to publish your page, the publisher needs to know your user name, your password, and your Web site address. Your Web space provider should have given you all of this information. If you do not have it, contact them before you do anything else.

Once you have that information, follow these steps to configure the publisher:

1. Pull down Netscape's **Options** menu and select the **Editor Preferences** command. The Editor Preferences dialog box appears.

2. Click the **Publish** tab, and you'll see the form displayed in Figure 5.1. You need to fill out the lower half section.

3. In the **Publish to (FTP or HTTP)** field, type the address of your Web site. This has to be a directory address, not a Web address; if the address you're using ends in **.htm** or **.html**, delete everything after the last slash.

4. Enter your user name in the **User name** field.

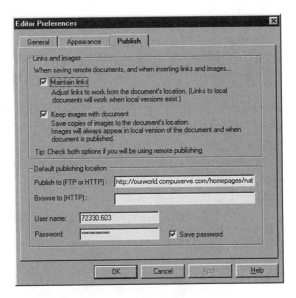

Figure 5.1 Tell the publisher where you want the page located, as well as your user name and password.

5. Type your password in the **Password** field. As you type each character, an asterisk (*) appears in the field instead of the letter you typed. This way, if anyone else looks at this information, he or she won't see your password.

6. (Optional) If you don't want to have to retype the password every time you publish, check the **Save password** check box.

Be Aware of Reduced Security If someone else has access to your computer, and if you have enabled the Save password feature, that person can put pages into your site and change the pages that are there. This opportunity for mischievous hi-jinx might be too much for some people to resist!

CAUTION

7. Click **OK** to enter this information into your configuration.

Publishing Your Pages

You can use the publisher to publish any pages you have, whether they were created with the Web page editor or with any other tool. You can even mix pages from different sources. Just make sure that all of the pages you want to publish are in the same directory on your hard drive before you begin.

Before you publish your pages, check them carefully for content errors. Although you can always correct a page and republish it later, it's better to find and fix the mistake before anyone sees it. To publish your pages, follow these steps:

1. Open the editor with one of the pages that you want to publish on it.

2. Click the **Publish** button, and the Publish Files dialog box appears (see Figure 5.2).

3. If you did not configure the publisher with the Save password option enabled, enter your password now.

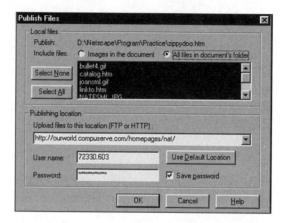

Figure 5.2   The Publish Files dialog box.

4. To publish just this one page, click the **Images in the document** option button, which will upload the HTML file for this page, along with all of the files for graphics on the page. To publish all the pages in the current directory, click the **All files in document's folder** option button.

5. Click **OK** to start the publishing process. The publisher connects to the Internet if you were not already connected. The Publishing Document dialog box appears, listing the name of each file as it is uploaded, and showing the number of files that have been uploaded in relation to the total number to be uploaded. When all the files have been uploaded, this box disappears. Congratulations! Your material is now out on the Web!

In this lesson, you learned to automatically publish your pages on the Web. In the next lesson, you will learn two methods of inserting additional HTML information into your page, so that you can add features that the Web page editor cannot generate itself.

Adding HTML Tags

In this lesson, you'll learn to add HTML tags directly to your document in Netscape Gold's Web page editor, as well as to call up the HTML file in a text editor.

Inserting and Checking the Tags

Netscape's Web page editor is very powerful, but it can't do everything that you can do by actually writing HTML code (which is explained in Part 5—read it!). For example, the editor won't generate the tags to build a table or to include a form on the page. However, you can use the Web editor to insert tags that it's not designed to generate automatically.

To add tags to a Web page file in the editor, follow these steps:

1. Open up the **catalog.htm** page in the Web page editor. (If you haven't been following these lessons in order, you can try any other .htm file with text that you have.)
2. Click to the left of the phrase "going-out-of-business" (in the third line of text) to place the cursor there. (If you're using another .htm page, just pick any text.)
3. Pull down the **Insert** menu and select **HTML tag**. The HTML Tag dialog box shown in Figure 6.1 appears.
4. Type `<BLINK` into the field and click the **Verify** button to tell the program to check the tag's basic syntax.
5. You'll see an error message indicating that the tag is missing a > at the end (HTML tags need brackets on both ends). Click **OK**.
6. Add the > to the end of the tag and click the **Verify** button again. There will be no response, which means that the tag is good.

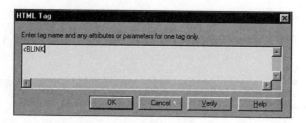

Figure 6.1 Type an HTML tag into the HTML Tag dialog box.

7. Click **OK**. A triangular tag symbol appears in the editor, right where you placed the cursor.2

8. Click at the end of "going-out-of-business" to put the cursor there, and then choose **Insert, HTML tag** again.

9. This time type **</BLINK>** and click the **Verify** button. Then click **OK** to enter it.

TIP

BLINK The <BLINK> and </BLINK> tags cause everything between them to blink. The Web editor can generate this effect, but there's no button for it. Instead, you have to pull down the **Properties** menu, select **Character**, and select **Blink** from the secondary menu. (This menu also contains commands for Superscript, Subscript, and Strikethrough.)

10. While Netscape is showing you the full Web page you are working on, it's actually storing the whole thing as a file of HTML codes (sometimes called the *source*, since it is the basis for what gets displayed), which is what Web browsers understand. To see the HTML source for the page, open the **View** menu and select the **View Document Source** command. A source display window appears (see Figure 6.2).

11. Verify that the tags you've added are really there, and then click the **Close** (X) button on the title bar to close the window.

12. Click the editor's **Save** button to save the changes to your hard disk. Then click the **View in Browser** button to see the effect of these tags in your Web page. The browser window appears. If you wait for a couple of seconds, you'll see the words between the tags blinking on and off (see Figure 6.3).

13. Click the **Close** (X) button on the title bar to close the browser window.

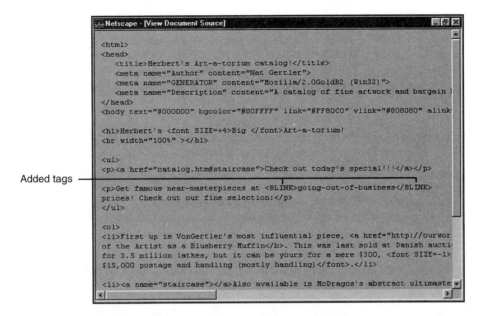

Added tags

Figure 6.2 The underlying HTML source code, with your new tags inserted.

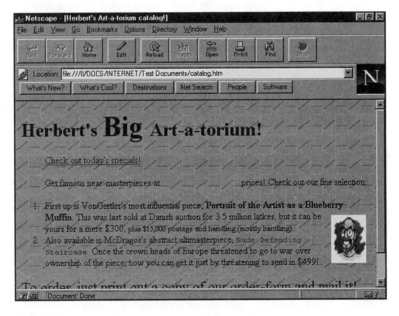

Figure 6.3 The words have momentarily blinked off.

Editing the HTML File

If you have a large chunk of HTML code to add, adding it one tag at a time can be slow and awkward. Instead, you can tell the Web editor where your favorite text editor is, and then you can edit the source code with a single command. Follow these steps:

1. Open the **Options** menu and select the **Editor preferences** command. The Editor Preferences dialog box appears.

2. Click the **General** tab, and the form shown in Figure 6.4 appears.

Figure 6.4   The General tab of the Editor Preferences dialog box.

3. Click the uppermost of the two **Browse** buttons, and a file selector marked **Select HTML Editor Application** appears.

4. Locate and select your text editor. Then click the **Open** button.

 WordPad and Notepad   You can find the WordPad text editor at C:\Program Files\Accessories\Wordpad.exe in Windows 95; you can find the Notepad text editor at C:\windows\notepad.exe in older versions of Windows. (This is assuming that your operating system is installed on Drive C:.)

5. Click **OK** to close the dialog box.

6. Open the **View** menu and select the **Edit Document Source** command. The editor you picked opens and displays the HTML source document. Figure 6.5 shows such a document in WordPad.

7. Move the cursor down to one of the blank lines and add `<P>You gotta love it, it's ART!</P>` to the document.

8. Open the editor's **File** menu and select the **Save** command to save this change.

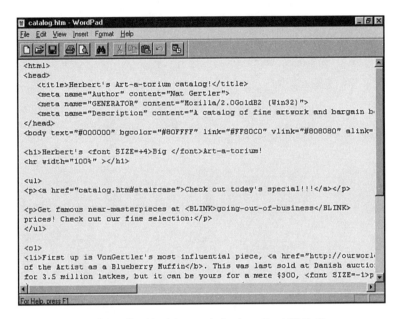

Figure 6.5 An editor (WordPad in this case) displays the HTML file.

9. Click the **Close** (X) button on the editor's title bar to close the editor.

10. The Web page editor displays a dialog box saying **This document has been modified by another editor. Reload document to see changes?** Click the **Yes** button. The editor reloads the page, and the phrase "You gotta love it, it's ART!" appears right where you added it.

Notice that the yellow symbols that indicated where you added the `<BLINK>` tags in the previous procedure are gone now. That's because when you first added these tags, the Netscape Editor didn't check to see if it knew them, but whenever it reloads the page, it checks all the tags. Because it recognizes the `<BLINK>` tags, it treats them as a standard part of the document. If it had found a tag it didn't recognize, it would have shown the yellow symbol, indicating that there was an unknown tag.

In this lesson, you learned how to directly add tags to your document in Netscape Editor. You also learned how to open and edit the file in a text editor such as Notepad or WordPad.

527

Appendixes

HTML Reference Section

Table A.1 lists all of the HTML tags and attributes supported by the Netscape Navigator browser. Listed under each tag are the attributes that can be used within the brackets of the tag. For attributes that take variables (such as SIZE=3 or HREF="www.me.com"), you'll see the following standard variables:

- *alignment* is used to relate an image to the surrounding text or to relate text to the surrounding area. Possible values are ABSBOTTOM, ABSMIDDLE, BASELINE, BOTTOM, LEFT, MIDDLE, RIGHT, TEXTTOP, and TOP. (Not all tags or all browsers support all settings.)

- *color* represents a number sign followed by a six-digit hexadecimal value, where the first two digits indicate the amount of red, the second two the amount of green, and the third two the amount of blue (example: #80F700). In Netscape, *color* can also be set to one of 140 different color names, but that feature is not fully supported by any other browser.

- *framesize* indicates the size of a frame and can stand for any number of formats. If it's a number, it represents a pixel measurement. If it's a percentage, it represents a percentage of the whole page width. If it ends with an asterisk, it represents a share of the space remaining after the pixel- and percentage-measured frames have been accounted for. For example, if you have one width listed as 2* and one listed as just *, the space left over will be divided so that the first column (the one with 2*) gets twice as much width as the other column (the one with just *).

- *URL* is a uniform resource locator. This can indicate the location of a directory (http://www.fish.com/recipes/), a file (http://www.fish.com/recipes/sandwich.htm), or a targeted position in the file (http://www.fish.com/recipes/sandwich.htm#ingredients). A URL can also be relative to the current position (recipes/sandwich.htm) instead of being a full path.
- *pixels* is a measurement of screen size in pixels. This is just a standard decimal number (such as 20).

Any other variables are described in their individual entries. A variable followed by ,... can have more than one of the same variable separated by commas. A tag can generally have any number of attributes as long as they don't conflict with one another. The attributes can be in any order.

The "Other Browsers?" column of this table indicates whether this tag is supported by current revisions of popular non-Netscape graphical browsers. The possible values in this column are **none** (Netscape-only tags), **all** (generally supported tags), and **some** (tags supported in certain non-Netscape browsers, but not all). Take this information into account when considering whether to include these tags in your pages.

Note that, while this list is accurate as of the time of this writing, new revisions are in the works for most of the popular browsers, and some tags that few of them currently support will soon be supported by more. (Of course, nongraphical browsers will be unable to handle any tag requiring a graphic display and will interpret font-altering tags differently.)

Table A.1   Netscape HTML Tags and Attributes

Tag Attributes	Description	Other Browsers?
`<!—text—>`	Comment (text is ignored)	all
`<!DOCTYPE>`	Header information about file format	all
`HTML`	Indicates an HTML file	all
`PUBLIC`	Indicates a readable document	all
`"standard"`	Indicates the HTML standard in use	all
`</tag>`	Ends the effect of the indicated tag	all
`<A HREF="URL">`	Marks the start of a link to a document	all
`METHODS="method,..."`	(Advanced) Lists functions document supports	some

Tag Attributes	Description	Other Browsers?
REL="*value,...*"	(Advanced) Lists relationship of link	some
REV="*value,...*"	(Advanced) Reverses relationship of link	some
TARGET="*frame*"	Puts the document in the listed frame	none
TITLE="*text*"	Gives a name for the page linked to	some
URN="*URN*"	(Advanced) Resource Name of document	some
<A NAME=*name*>	Names a location, for use as a target	all
<ADDRESS>	Text format for mailing addresses	all
<APPLET>	Loads a Java applet	none
ALIGN=*alignment*	Locates applet display within text	none
ALT="*text*"	Text for display by non-Java browsers	none
CODE="*URL*"	(Required) Indicates the program file	none
CODEBASE="*URL*"	Directory the program files are in	none
HEIGHT=*pixels*	(Required) Applet display area	none
HSPACE=*pixels*	Horizontal space from applet to text	none
NAME="*name*"	Names applet for intertask messages	none
VSPACE=*pixels*	Vertical space from applet to text	none
WIDTH=*pixels*	(Required) Applet display area	none
<AREA>	Describes one link on a mapped image	some
COORDS="*pixels,...*"	Left, top, right, bottom of link area	some
HREF="*URL*"	Location to link to	som
NOHREF	This area isn't a link	some
SHAPE="RECT"	Rectangular map area	some
TARGET="*frame*"	Links to indicated frame	none
<B>	Makes text bold	all
<BASE>	Changes defaults for URLs in document	all
HREF="*URL*"	The new base for relative URLs	all
TARGET="*frame*"	Specifies default frame for links	none
<BASEFONT>	Changes default for fonts in document	some
SIZE=*number*	Sets default font size (1–7)	some
<BIG>	Increases text size	some
<BLINK>	Causes text to blink	none
<BODY>	Starts the page content	all
ALINK="*color*"	Sets active link color	all
BACKGROUND="*url*"	Sets an image as page backdrop	all
BGCOLOR="*color*"	Sets background color for page	some
LINK="*color*"	Sets unvisited link color	all
TEXT="*color*"	Sets default text color	all
VLINK="*color*"	Sets visited link color	all

continues

533

Table A.1 Continued

Tag Attributes	Description	Other Browsers?
` `	Starts a new text line	all
CLEAR=ALL	Starts next line below any images	some
CLEAR=LEFT	Starts new line below image on left	some
CLEAR=RIGHT	Starts new line below image on right	some
`<CAPTION>`	Sets a caption for a table	some
ALIGN=BOTTOM	Puts caption below table	some
ALIGN=TOP	Puts caption above table (default)	some
`<CENTER>`	Centers text and images across page	all
`<CITE>`	Text format for citations	all
`<CODE>`	Text format for program code	all
`<DIR>`	A directory list	all
TYPE=CIRCLE	Uses open circle bullets on list	none
TYPE=DISC	Uses dot bullets on list	none
TYPE=SQUARE	Uses square bullets on list	none
`<DIV>`	Creates a division of text	none
ALIGN=*alignment*	(Required) Positions text across page	none
`<DD>`	Descriptor in definition list	all
`<DL>`	A definition list	all
COMPACT	Reduces list size	none
`<DT>`	Defined term of a definition list	all
`<EM>`	Emphasizes text (italic)	all
`<EMBED>`	Puts area for a plug-in onto page	none
ALIGN=*align*	Positions area relative to text	none
BORDER=*pixels*	Sets border color	none
HEIGHT=*pixels*	Area size	none
SRC="*url*"	(Required) Indicated document file	none
WIDTH=*pixels*	Area size	none
`<FONT>`	Changes font attributes	some
COLOR=*color*	Changes font color	some
SIZE=*number*	Changes font to size *number* (1–7)	some
SIZE=+*number*	Increases font size (up to 6)	some
SIZE=-*number*	Decreases font size (down to −6)	some
`<FORM>`	Structures a data input form	all
ACTION="*URL*"	Location to send data to	all
METHOD=*protocol*	Selects transfer protocol (GET or PUT)	all
ENCTYPE=*MIMEtype*	Format for data	all

Tag Attributes	Description	Other Browsers?
<FRAME>	Sets the attributes for a frame	some
MARGINHEIGHT=*pixels*	Space at top and bottom of frame	some
MARGINWIDTH=*pixels*	Space at side edges of frame	some
NAME=*frame*	Gives the frame a name	some
NORESIZE	Prevents frame borders from being moved	some
SCROLLING=YES	Frame has scroll bars	some
SCROLLING=NO	Frame doesn't have scroll bars	some
SCROLLING=AUTO	Frame has scroll bars if needed	some
SRC="*URL*"	Page to put in frame	some
<FRAMESET>	Breaks screen into frames	some
COLS="*framesize,…*"	Sets the width of frame columns	some
ROWS="*framesize,…*"	Sets height of frame rows	some
<H*number*>	Headline text format level *number* (1–6)	all
ALIGN=CENTER	Centers the headline	some
<HEAD>	Indicates the page's header	all
<HR>	Horizontal rule line	all
ALIGN=*alignment*	Positions line across page	all
NOSHADE	Flat line rather than shaded line	all
SIZE=*pixels*	Thickness of line	all
WIDTH=*number*%	Line width, as percentage of space	all
WIDTH=*pixels*	Line width	all
<HTML>	Identifies document as being HTML	all
<I>	Italic font	all
<IMG>	Inserts an image (graphic)	all
ALIGN=*alignment*	Positions image relative to text	all
ALT="*text*"	Text is displayed if graphic can't be	all
BORDER=*pixels*	Thickness of border around graphic	some
HEIGHT=*pixels*	Vertical size of image on page	all
HSPACE=*pixels*	Horizontal space between image and text	some
ISMAP	This image maps to multiple links	some
LOWSRC="*URL*"	Displays this image before SRC image	none
SRC="*URL*"	(Required) Image to be displayed	all
VSPACE=*pixels*	Vertical space between image and text	some
WIDTH=*pixels*	Horizontal size of image	all
USEMAP="*URL*"	File describes links for this image	some
<INPUT>	A form field	all
ACCEPT="*type,…*"	File types OK in file submission field	none

continues

Table A.1 Continued

Tag Attributes	Description	Other Browsers?
ALIGN=*alignment*	Positions image field relative to text	all
CHECKED	Check box or option button is selected	all
MAXLENGTH=*number*	Maximum characters user can enter	all
NAME="*name*"	Gives field a name	all
SIZE=*number*	Size of field in characters	all
SRC="*URL*"	Image file for button on form	all
TYPE=CHECKBOX	Check box (yes/no) field	all
TYPE=FILE	Field for submission of file	none
TYPE=HIDDEN	Field not seen by user	all
TYPE=IMAGE	Form submission button with graphic	all
TYPE=PASSWORD	Text entry field; text isn't displayed	all
TYPE=RADIO	An option select field (option button)	all
TYPE=RESET	Button that clears all fields	all
TYPE=SUBMIT	Form submission button	all
TYPE=TEXT	Single-line text field	all
TYPE=TEXTAREA	Multiple-line text field	all
VALUE="*text*"	Default value for field	all
<ISINDEX>	Indicates page is a searchable index	all
ACTION="*URL*"	Program to send search request to	none
PROMPT="*text*"	Text appears on search form	some
<KBD>	Text in keyboard format (monospace)	all
<LI>	Start of new item on list	all
TYPE=1	(Default) Arabic numbers (1, 2, 3, etc.)	some
TYPE=a	Lowercase letters (a, b, c, etc.)	some
TYPE=A	Uppercase letters (A, B, C, etc.)	some
TYPE=CIRCLE	Use circle as bullet (unordered list)	none
TYPE=DISC	Use dots as bullet (unordered list)	none
TYPE=i	Lowercase Roman numerals (i, xiv, etc.)	some
TYPE=I	Uppercase Roman numerals (I, XIV, etc.)	some
TYPE=SQUARE	Use square as bullet (unordered list)	none
VALUE=*number*	Sets entry counter for an ordered list	some
<LINK>	Shows relationship to another document	all
METHODS="*method,...*"	(Advanced) Lists functions document supports	some
REL="*value,...*"	(Advanced) Lists relationship of link	some
REV="*value,...*"	(Advanced) Reverses relationship of link	some
TITLE="*text*"	Gives a name for the page linked to	some
URN="*URN*"	(Advanced) Resource Name of document	some

Tag Attributes	Description	Other Browsers?
`<LISTING>`	Text format with a fixed spacing	some
`<MAP>`	Describes what areas of image are links	some
`NAME="name"`	(Required) Names the map	some
`<MENU>`	A menu list	all
`TYPE=CIRCLE`	Use open circle bullets on list	none
`TYPE=DISC`	Use dot bullets on list	none
`TYPE=SQUARE`	Use square bullets on list	none
`<META>`	Holds information to identify page	all
`CONTENT="text"`	(Required) The information being held	all
`HTTP-EQUIV="text"`	Relates info with HTTP response field	all
`NAME="text"`	Name for the information	all
`<NEXTID>`	Machine-picked identifier for document	all
`N="text"`	Identifier for document	all
`<NOBR>`	Insert no line breaks into text	some
`<NOFRAMES>`	Browsers with frames skip this section	all
`<OL>`	Ordered (numbered or lettered) list	all
`START=number`	First value on list	some
`TYPE=a`	Lowercase letters (a, b, c, etc.)	some
`TYPE=A`	Uppercase letters (A, B, C, etc.)	some
`TYPE=i`	Lowercase Roman numerals (i, xiv, etc.)	some
`TYPE=I`	Uppercase Roman numerals (I, XIV, etc.)	some
`TYPE=1`	(Default) Arabic numbers (1, 2, 3, etc.)	some
`<OPTION>`	A choice on a form menu	all
`DISABLED`	This choice cannot be picked	some
`SELECTED`	This choice appears as the default	all
`VALUE="text"`	Text sent to host if option is chosen	all
`<P>`	A text paragraph	all
`ALIGN=alignment`	Positions text across page	some
`<PARAM>`	Passes parameters to an applet	none
`NAME=name`	(Required) Name of attribute being set	none
`VALUE=value`	(Required) Value attribute is set to	none
`<PLAINTEXT>`	Treat rest of document as text	some
`<PRE>`	Preformatted text	all
`<SAMP>`	Text format for text samples	all

continues

Table A.1 Continued

Tag / Attributes	Description	Other Browsers?
`<SCRIPT>`	A Java script	none
`LANGUAGE="JAVASCRIPT"`	Indicates script language	none
`SRC="URL"`	Script program file	none
`<SELECT>`	A menu field on a form	all
`MULTIPLE`	Allows more than one selection	some
`NAME="text"`	Name for the field	all
`SIZE=number`	Number of items visible at a time	all
`<SMALL>`	Use a smaller font	some
`<STRIKE>`	Display text with a line through it	some
`<STRONG>`	Highlighted text (usually bold)	all
`<SUB>`	Subscript text	some
`<SUP>`	Superscript text	some
`<TABLE>`	Create a grid	some
`ALIGN=alignment`	Position text within the cell	some
`BORDER`	Display a border on the table	some
`BORDER=pixels`	Display a border of a certain thickness	some
`CELLPADDING=pixels`	Distance between cell frame and contents	some
`CELLSPACING=pixels`	Distance between cells	some
`HEIGHT=number%`	Table height as percentage of space	some
`HEIGHT=pixels`	Table height	some
`WIDTH=number%`	Table width as percentage of space	some
`WIDTH=pixels`	Table width	some
`<TD>`	Table cell contents	some
`ALIGN=alignment`	Horizontal position of text in cell	some
`COLSPAN=number`	Number of columns this cell covers	some
`HEIGHT=number%`	Cell height as percentage of table	some
`HEIGHT=pixels`	Cell height	some
`NOWRAP`	No line breaks in cell	some
`ROWSPAN=number`	Number of table rows this cell covers	some
`VALIGN=alignment`	Vertical position of text in cell	some
`WIDTH=number%`	Cell width as percentage of table	some
`WIDTH=pixels`	Cell width	some
`<TEXTAREA>`	A multiline text field in a form	all
`COLS=number`	(Required) Field width, in characters	all
`NAME="name"`	(Required) Names the field	all
`ROWS=number`	(Required) Field height, in characters	all
`WRAP=OFF`	(Default) No word wrap	none
`WRAP=PHYSICAL`	Word wrap affects display and data	none
`WRAP=VIRTUAL`	Affects display but not sent data	none

Tag Attributes	Description	Other Browsers?
<TH>	Table header cell (cell with bold text)	some
ALIGN=*alignment*	Horizontal position of text in cell	some
COLSPAN=*number*	Number of columns this cell covers	some
HEIGHT=*number*%	Cell height as percentage of table	some
HEIGHT=*pixels*	Cell height	some
NOWRAP	No line breaks in cell	some
ROWSPAN=*number*	Number of table rows this cell covers	some
VALIGN=*alignment*	Vertical position of text in cell	some
WIDTH=*number*%	Cell width as percentage of table	some
WIDTH=*pixels*	Cell width	some
<TITLE>	Sets page title, displayed in title bar	all
<TR>	Table row	some
ALIGN=*alignment*	Horizontal position of text in cells	some
VALIGN=*alignment*	Vertical position of text in cells	some
<TT>	Teletype format (fixed width font)	all
<UL>	Unnumbered list	all
TYPE=CIRCLE	Use open circle bullets on list	none
TYPE=DISC	Use dot bullets on list	none
TYPE=SQUARE	Use square bullets on list	none
<VAR>	Text format for program variables	all
<WBR>	Allows a break even in <NOBR> area	some
<XMP>	Example text format	all

Glossary

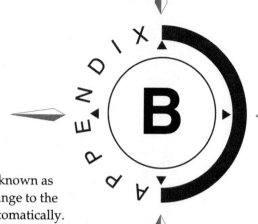

alias   A copy of an e-mail address is known as an alias because when you make a change to the original entry, the copy is changed automatically.

anchor   The part of a link that causes the mouse pointer to turn into a pointing finger. See also *links*.

anonymous login   The process of connecting to a system incognito. Many FTP sites (places where you can get files) allow users to connect anonymously and access public areas. Anonymous login privileges usually do not allow you to place files on the server or change anything.

applet   A small, single-purpose application, such as a loan calculator or a tic-tac-toe game. Java applets, which are found on Web pages, cannot run by themselves; they run in conjunction with a compatible Web browser (such as Netscape).

Archie   An Internet search tool that helps you find files on FTP sites. In most cases, you need to know the exact name of the file or a partial file name. See also *Jughead* and *Veronica*.

associate   To establish a connection between a given file type and the helper application needed to view or play that file type. In Navigator, you must create file associations so Navigator will know which application to run when you choose to view, watch, or listen to a file. For example, you might associate movie files that end in .mpg with an MPEG movie helper application.

attribute   A parameter that further defines an HTML command, giving such specific information as the size or color, for example.

BBS   Short for *bulletin board system*, a BBS is a computer to which multiple users can send messages for the purpose of conversing or exchanging files and information. Special interest groups, professional organizations, and software companies often set up BBSs.

bookmark   A Navigator tool that lets you mark your favorite Web pages so you can quickly return to them later.

Boolean operators   Conjunctions including "and" and "or" that are used to separate search terms. For example, if you search for "Clinton and Whitewater," you get a list of all resources that relate to both "Clinton" and "Whitewater." If you use "or," the search is much broader, finding anything that relates to either "Clinton" or "Whitewater."

bps   Short for *bits per second*, this is a unit used to measure the speed of data being transferred between two computers. Most transfers on the Web take place at 14,400bps or higher.

browser   See *Web browser*.

bullet   A small graphic used to highlight each item within a list.

cache   A temporary storage area that Navigator creates both in RAM and on your hard disk. Navigator stores Web pages in the cache so that it can quickly load these pages if you decide to return to them. In other words, because Netscape saves the Web pages you've visited recently in this cache, the pages don't have to be transferred over the phone lines again.

channel   The equivalent of a conference room. When you chat on the Internet, you first connect to a chat server, and then you tune in to a channel. Each channel is supposed to deal with a different topic, but some are open for general conversation about the weather and where people are from. See also *chat room*.

chat   To "talk" to another person by typing at your computer. What you type appears on the other person's screen, and what the other person types appears on your screen. You can't chat with Navigator; you need another program such as Netscape Chat if you want to get chatty.

chat room   You enter into a conversation on a chat server by opening a channel, called a chat room. Conversations carried on within a room are copied to everyone else on that channel (in the same room).

client   Of two computers, the computer that's being served. Whenever you connect to a Web site, the computer at that site is the *server*, and your computer is the client or customer.

compressed file   A file that has been condensed so that it takes up less disk space and travels faster through network and modem connections. Before you can use a compressed file, you must decompress (or expand) it using a special program.

cyberspace   The universe created by the connection of thousands of computers. Computer users can use modems to enter cyberspace and converse with other users. This term was first used by William Gibson in his novel *Neuromancer*. In the novel, people plugged their brains into cyberspace. If you've ever seen the glazed look people get when they're wired to the Web, you know that Gibson's notion is not too far from the truth.

decompress   To expand a compressed file and make it usable. Popular decompression programs include PKZIP (for DOS) and WinZip (for Windows).

Dial-Up Networking   A program that comes with Windows 95 that establishes the Internet connection you need in order to run Navigator and access the World Wide Web.

document   On the Web, this could be anything: an index of topics, several screens full of text, or even a page full of pictures. See also *Web page*.

document source   The coded document that controls the way Web pages look. See also *HTML*.

domain name   A unique identification for an Internet site; also known as *host name*. Each computer on the Internet has a domain name that distinguishes it from other computers on the Internet. Domain names usually provide some vague indication of the establishment that runs the server. For example, the domain name of the White House server is www.whitehouse.gov.

domain name server (DNS)   A computer that matches a site's name to a number that identifies that site. All servers on the Internet have a domain name, such as ncsa.uiuc.edu. Each server also has a unique IP (Internet Protocol) number, such as 128.252.135.4. Your Internet service provider has an electronic database, called a DNS (Domain Name Server) that matches the domain to the IP number to find the server that has the data you've requested. As you innocently click links, the DNS is matching domain names and IP numbers to make sure you get where you're supposed to be.

download   To copy a file from another computer (usually an FTP server) to your computer. See also *upload*.

EDI   Short for *electronic data interchange*, EDI is a protocol through which information sent between two designated parties is encrypted so that it can be sent over the Internet in a secure manner.

e-mail   A system by which people can send and receive messages through their computers, either on a network or by using modems. Each person has a designated mailbox that stores messages sent by other users. He can then retrieve and read messages from the mailbox.

FAQ   (Pronounced "fak") Short for *frequently asked questions*, this is a list of answers to the most often-asked questions at a particular Internet site. Good Internet etiquette demands that you read the FAQ at a site before you post any questions.

finger   A special UNIX command that pokes around through a directory of users and finds information about that person, including the person's e-mail address, and whether or not that person has read her mail recently or even logged in.

flame   To verbally abuse another user during an online discussion, via e-mail or in a newsgroup. Common flaming techniques include name-calling, abusive innuendos about one's parents, and other puerile gems of wit.

form   A fill-in-the-blank Web document. Sites commonly use forms to take credit card orders, ask for your password, register downloaded software, or request search instructions.

frame   A new Navigator feature that allows two parts of the same Web document to appear in the same window. For example, one frame might contain an outline of the document, and if you click on a heading in that outline, the other frame shows the contents under that heading.

FTP   Short for *File Transfer Protocol*, a set of rules that governs the transfer of files between computers. You can download files off the Internet with an FTP program or with Netscape.

GIF file   Pronounced "giff file" or "jiff file," this is a picture file that's often a photograph or painting. GIF is short for *Graphic Interchange Format*, a format developed by CompuServe for transferring graphic files. This format is good for storing a lot of graphic information in very little space.

Gopher An indexing system that allows you to access various Internet services by selecting menu options. Whenever you connect to a Gopher site, it presents you with an opening menu. When you select a menu item, the server presents you with another submenu containing additional options and/or files. These options may kick you out to another Gopher server, an FTP server, a newsgroup, or other Internet servers. You proceed through the menus until you find the information you want... or until you reach a dead end.

handle A user's computerized nickname or ID number. When you look for a person using Whois, you might find the person's handle. You can often find out more about a person by performing the search again using the person's handle.

helper application A program that performs a specialized job that Navigator is unable to manage. Whenever you click a link to a file that Navigator can't play, Navigator loads the file to disk and then starts the helper application associated with that file. The helper application loads the file and plays it in a separate window. See also *in-line plug-in*.

hexadecimal The notation for a base-16 numeral, which uses the letters A–F as replacements for the numbers 10, 11, 12, and so on. Hexadecimal notation is used in the designation of color values in HTML.

history list A directory of all the Web sites you have visited since you connected. You can view the history list in Navigator by opening the Window menu and clicking History.

hits In a WAIS search, the number of times a search word was found in an article. The higher the number, the more likely it is that the article contains the information you're looking for. See also *score*.

home page The page that greets you when you first start Navigator or first connect to a Web site.

host The host is the computer that has the information. Your computer is the client, requesting information from the host.

host name See *domain name*.

HTML Short for *HyperText Markup Language*, the code used to create Web documents. These codes tell the Navigator how to display the text (titles, headings, lists, and so on), insert anchors that link this document to other documents, and control character formatting (by making it bold or italic).

HTTP   Short for *HyperText Transfer Protocol*, a set of rules that govern the exchange of data between a Web host and a client (your computer). The address for every Web server starts with **http**. If you see an address that starts with different letters (such as "ftp" or "gopher"), the address is for a different type of server. Gopher addresses start with "gopher," FTP with "ftp," WAIS with "wais," Usenet with "news," and Telnet with "telnet."

hyperdocument   A Web page that contains links connecting it to other pages. On the Web, a hyperdocument might contain links to other text, graphics, sounds, or movies.

hyperlinks   Icons, pictures, or highlighted chunks of text that connect two documents. For example, a document about pork might contain a link for sausage. If you click the link, Navigator displays a document about how to make sausage.

hypermedia   A dynamic computerized "soup" that contains movie clips, graphics, sound files, text, and anything else that can be stored in a digitized form. That's the "media" part, anyway. The "hyper" part deals with the fact that these ingredients are interlinked, so you can jump quickly from one to another.

hypertext   Specially formatted text that provides a link to another document, or another part of the same document. You'll find hypertext in most Help systems. When you click a hypertext word such as "save," you're taken to the part of Help that tells you how to save your work. On the Internet, hypertext (more correctly called *hyperlinks*) provides a link to a particular Web document (Web page).

in-line image   A graphic that appears inside a Web document. You can tell Navigator not to display these images if you can't stand waiting for them to load.

in-line plug-in   A program that links itself to Netscape Navigator in order to provide Navigator with some capability it would otherwise not have, such as the capability to play MPEG video files. Unlike helper applications, in-line plug-ins display their work within the Netscape window. See also *helper application*.

interactive   A user-controlled program, document, or game. Interactive programs commonly display on-screen *prompts*, asking the user for input so he can decide how to carry out a particular task. These programs are popular in education, allowing children to follow their natural curiosity to solve problems and gather information.

Internet The world's largest system of interconnected networks. The Internet was originally named ARPAnet after the Advanced Research Projects Agency in the Defense department. The agency developed the ARPAnet in the mid-1970s as an experimental project that would allow various university and military sources to continue to communicate in a state of national emergency. Now, the Internet is used mostly by private citizens for connecting to databases, exchanging electronic mail, and finding information.

IP address A unique number assigned to each computer on the Internet. Most of the time, you work with domain names, such as nasa.uiuc.edu. Behind the scenes, whenever you enter a domain name, your service provider matches that name to the site's IP number (for example 128.252.135.4) and calls that site. The idea here is that it's easier for you to remember names and easier for computers to remember numbers. The domain name/IP number link makes everyone happy.

IRC Short for *Internet Relay Chat*, this is a technology that allows users to type messages back and forth using their keyboards. It's sort of like talking on the phone, but it's less expensive and much slower.

Java A relatively new technology that enables its users to create animations and other moving video clips and embed them in Web pages. All you need to know about Java is that if you click a link for a Java applet (application), Navigator will play it.

JavaScript Developed by Netscape, JavaScript is a variation of pure Java, in which Java code is embedded directly within an HTML document. By contrast, a programmer using only Java creates and saves his program as a separate file. That program is then launched from the HTML page by a single command.

JPEG Short for *Joint Photographic Experts Group*, a file-compression format used for storing graphic files. If you come across a file that ends in .JPG, you can view it in Netscape Navigator, or you can have one of your helper applications display it.

Jughead An Internet search tool used to find resources at a Gopher site. Archie, Veronica, and Jughead (all Internet search tools) are related. Archie searches for FTP servers that contain the files you want to download. Veronica searches all Gopher sites to find the ones that store the various resources you specify. Jughead searches only the current Gopher site to find the specified resources.

links   Also known as *hyperlinks*, these are icons, pictures, or highlighted chunks of text that connect the current page to other pages, Internet sites, graphics, movies, or sounds.

logical codes   In a Web document, codes that provide general directions on how to display text. For example, <em> stands for emphasis, which might mean bold or italic. Physical codes give more precise instructions. For example, <b> means bold. See also *physical codes* and *tags*.

login   To connect to another computer on a network or on the Internet so you can use that computer's resources. The login procedure usually requires you to enter your user name (or user ID) and a password.

logout   To disconnect from another computer on a network or on the Internet.

lurk   To read newsgroup messages posted by other people but not respond to them or post any messages of your own. That way, you can see what's going on before you decide to participate in a particular discussion.

map   A graphical navigational tool used on many Web pages. Think of it as one of those mall maps with the **YOU ARE HERE** arrow on it, but with a Web map, you can actually go places by clicking on different areas of the map.

MIDI   Short for *Musical Instrument Digital Interface*. Some Web pages contain links to files that can play music on MIDI instruments or on MIDI-compatible sound cards within your PC.

MIME   Short for *Multipurpose Internet Mail Extensions*, a protocol that controls all file transfers on the Web. Navigator uses MIME to recognize different file types. If an HTML document arrives, Navigator "knows" to play that file. If an MPG file arrives, Navigator calls the associated helper application. MIME was originally developed to attach different types of files (usually multimedia files) to e-mail messages.

mirror site   A server that contains the same files as the original site. Mirror sites are very useful because some sites are so busy that users might have trouble connecting during peak hours. The mirror sites offer an alternative location that helps users avoid Internet traffic jams.

modem   Short for *modulator-demodulator*, a modem is a device that translates computer information into sound and transmits those sounds over conventional telephone lines or that receives such sounds and translates them into computer data.

monospace   In typesetting, a typeface in which all characters have the same width.

MPEG   Short for *Moving Pictures Expert Group*, a video-compression and movie presentation standard used for most video clips stored on the Web. The only thing that matters is that if you encounter a file that ends in MPG, you need an MPG or MPEG player to watch it.

Netscape Navigator   Popular Web browser. Netscape Navigator transforms Web documents (which consist of boring codes) into exciting multimedia documents complete with sounds, pictures, and movies.

Netscape Navigator Gold   The enhanced version of the popular Netscape Navigator, which includes additional features such as a Web page creator/editor.

newbie   Derogatory term for a new user on the Internet.

newsgroup   An Internet bulletin board for users who share common interests. There are thousands of newsgroups ranging from body art to pets. Newsgroups let you post messages and read messages from other users.

pane   A portion of a window. Netscape Mail uses panes to divide its window into logical areas. See also *frame*.

physical codes   In a Web document, codes that provide specific directions on how to display text. For example, <bold> stands for bold. Logical codes give less precise instructions. For example, <em> means emphasis, which might mean bold or italic.

plan   A text file that a user might attach to his finger file to include more information. A plan might include the person's address, phone number, job interests, or anything else that person wants to make publicly accessible.

port   1) The hardware connection through which a computer sends and/or receives data.   2) An application that's set up on a server. When you specify the server's port, you're actually telling it to run one of its applications.

post   To send a message to a bulletin board or newsgroup for all to see.

postmaster   The person at a given site who is in charge of assigning users their e-mail addresses. You can usually send a message to the postmaster by addressing it to **postmaster@***sitename*.

PPP   Short for *Point-to-Point Protocol*, PPP is a type of Internet connection. What's important is that when you choose an Internet service provider, you get the right connection: SLIP or PPP; otherwise, you won't be able to use Navigator.

protocol   A set of rules that govern the transfer of data between two computers.

proxy   A special connection that allows two incompatible networks to communicate. For example, say you're on the Web with Navigator and you decide to use WAIS to search for a list of articles. You can't use WAIS directly from Navigator, so you have to work through a Web/WAIS proxy. The proxy acts as a middleman, ensuring that the data transfer goes smoothly.

relative reference   In a Web document, a link that refers to the location of another page or file in relation to the address of the current page. For example, if the page is in the /PUB directory, and a linked page is in /PUB/HOME, a relative reference might specify /HOME. An absolute reference would have to give the complete path (/PUB/HOME).

score   In WAIS searches, a number that indicates the relative likelihood that an article will contain the information you need. The topmost article gets a score of 1000. Subsequent scores are relative to 1000, so 500 would mean that the article had half as many occurrences of the search term as did the top article.

search tool   A searchable index of Web pages. Popular Web search tools include Yahoo, InfoSeek, and Lycos.

server   In the politically incorrect world of the Internet, the computer that serves up all the data. The other computer, the client, acts as a customer, demanding specific information.

service provider   The company that you pay for permission to connect to its computer and get on the Internet.

shareware   Computer programs you can use for free and then pay for if you decide to continue using them. Many programmers use the Internet to distribute their programs, relying on the honesty and goodwill of Internet users for their income.

signature file   A text file that usually includes your name and some kind of logo or picture, created by using spaces and other characters such as x, |, and - to form a particular pattern (such as a bird).

SLIP   Short for *Serial Line Internet Protocol*, a type of Internet connection that allows you to connect directly to the Internet without having to run programs off your Internet service provider's computer.

SSL   Short for *Secure Sockets Layer*, this is Netscape's new security technology. Web pages protected with SSL prevent misanthropic hackers from nabbing personal information that you might enter on the page (including your credit card number).

status bar   The area at the bottom of the Navigator window that shows you what's going on as you work. The little key in the status bar indicates whether a document is secure; if the key looks broken, the document is not secure.

stop word   In a search, any word that is excluded from the search. For example, if you are searching a computer database, the database may refuse to look for such common words as "and" and "computer."

subscribe   The process by which you gain access to the messages in a news-group. After subscribing to a newsgroup, its messages are downloaded to your PC so that you can access them.

tags   HTML codes that work behind the scenes to tell Navigator how to display a document and how to open other linked documents. Tags can control the look of text (as in titles and headings), insert anchors that link this document to other documents, and control character formatting (by making it bold or italic).

TCP/IP   Acronym for *Transmission Control Protocol/Internet Protocol*, the pre-ferred method of data transfer over the Internet. With TCP/IP, the sending computer stuffs data into packets and sends it. The receiving computer unstuffs the packets and assembles them into some meaningful and useful form. The most popular TCP/IP program is Winsock.

telnet   To connect to a server and use it to run programs as if you were sitting at its keyboard (or sitting at the keyboard of a terminal that's connected to the server). Think of it as using the computerized card catalog at the local library.

terminal connection   The type of connection you don't want to have if you're using Navigator. A terminal connection makes your computer act like one of your service provider's workstations. You run programs on the service provider's computer and connect to the Internet indirectly through that com-puter. With a SLIP or PPP connection, you connect through the service pro-vider's computer, but you use software on your computer to do all your work.

terminal emulation   A technique used to make one computer act like another so the two computers can carry on a conversation. Some mainframe computers will interact with only a specific type of terminal. If you want to connect to that mainframe computer using your personal computer, you must make your computer act like the required terminal.

texture mapping   A technique in which a three-dimensional object is rendered by computer with a surface taken from a two-dimensional picture, giving that object an apparent "texture" or "feel."

thread   In newsgroups and e-mail, a way of grouping messages so you can quickly tell that they belong to the same topic of conversation.

tiled   Repeating a graphic on a Web page both horizontally and vertically.

UNIX shell   The equivalent of a DOS prompt for computers that are running the UNIX operating system. You type commands at the prompt as if you were using a PC.

upload   To copy a file from your computer to another computer. You usually upload files to share them with other users. See also *download*.

URL   Short for *Uniform Resource Locator*, an address for an Internet site. The Web uses URLs to specify the addresses of the various servers on the Internet and the documents on each server. For example, the URL for the White House server is http://www.whitehouse.gov. The "http" stands for HyperText Transfer Protocol, which means this is a Web document. "www" stands for World Wide Web; "whitehouse" stands for White House; "gov" stands for Government.

Usenet   Short for *user's network*, Usenet sets the standards by which the various newsgroups swap information. See also *newsgroup*.

Veronica   One of many Internet search tools, this one finds Gopher sites that have what you're looking for. For a comparison of popular search tools, see also *Jughead*.

viewer   A program that Navigator uses to play movie clips, sound clips, PostScript files, graphics, and any other file Navigator cannot handle. See also *helper application* and *in-line plug-in*.

virus A computer virus is a program that hides itself inside another file. If you use the file, the virus attaches itself to your system, often destroying data and rendering your system inoperable. Although some viruses are simple pranks, many are extremely dangerous to your data. A virus can only enter your system from within an outside file; typically you copy the diseased file from a floppy disk, or leave an infected floppy disk in its drive during startup. But you can also infect your system by downloading an infected file from the Internet, an online service, or a BBS.

VRML Short for *Virtual Reality Modeling Language*. VRML is a method that enables Netscape to bring a seemingly three-dimensional world to life on your PC's two-dimensional screen.

W3 Another name for the World Wide Web.

WAIS (Pronounced "ways") Short for *Wide Area Information Server*, this is a system that allows you to search various databases on the Internet for specific articles and other resources.

wave table In a sound card, a wave table contains a set of prerecorded sound patches that allows a MIDI device to simulate a musical instrument.

Web browser Any of several programs you can use to navigate the World Wide Web. The Web browser controls the look of the Web documents and provides additional tools for jumping from one Web document to another. Netscape Navigator is a Web browser.

Web page A document on a server that is viewed with a Web browser.

Web server A specialized computer on the Internet that's devoted to storing and serving up Web documents.

Webmaster The person who created and maintains a Web document. If you find an error in a Web document, you should notify the Webmaster (in a nice way).

Whois A UNIX command that you can use to find out a person's e-mail address, mailing address, phone number, or other information, if you know the person's last name and the location of the server that person logs in to.

World Wide Web   A collection of interconnected documents stored on computers all over the world. These documents can contain text, pictures, movie clips, sounds, and links to other documents. You move from one document to another by clicking links.

WWW   See *World Wide Web*.

WYSIWYG   Short for *What-You-See-Is-What-You-Get*. When a document is displayed on-screen in WYSIWYG mode, it looks just like it will when printed.

zip   To compress a file so that it takes up less space and transfers more quickly. If you have a zipped file, you must unzip it before you can use it.

Index

X

Y

Z

Check out Que® Books on the World Wide Web
http://www.mcp.com/que

As the biggest software release in computer history, Windows 95 continues to redefine the computer industry. Click here for the latest info on our Windows 95 books

Make computing quick and easy with these products designed exclusively for new and casual users

Examine the latest releases in word processing, spreadsheets, operating systems, and suites

The Internet, The World Wide Web, CompuServe®, America Online®, Prodigy®—it's a world of ever-changing information. Don't get left behind!

Find out about new additions to our site, new bestsellers and hot topics

In-depth information on high-end topics: find the best reference books for databases, programming, networking, and client/server technologies

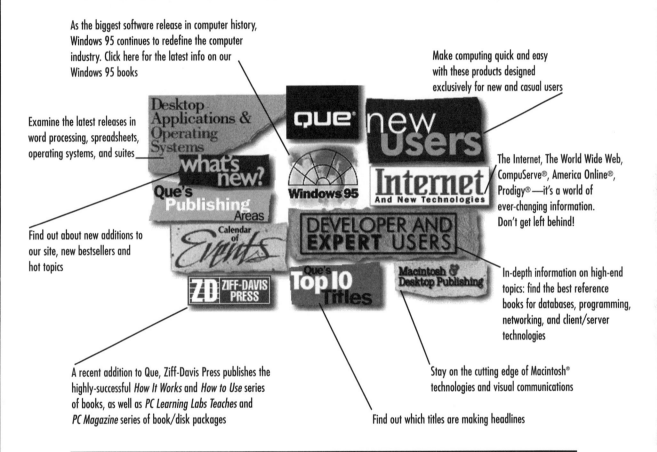

A recent addition to Que, Ziff-Davis Press publishes the highly-successful *How It Works* and *How to Use* series of books, as well as *PC Learning Labs Teaches* and *PC Magazine* series of book/disk packages

Stay on the cutting edge of Macintosh® technologies and visual communications

Find out which titles are making headlines

With 6 separate publishing groups, Que develops products for many specific market segments and areas of computer technology. Explore our Web Site and you'll find information on best-selling titles, newly published titles, upcoming products, authors, and much more.

- Stay informed on the latest industry trends and products available
- Visit our online bookstore for the latest information and editions
- Download software from Que's library of the best shareware and freeware

Complete and Return this Card
for a *FREE* Computer Book Catalog

Thank you for purchasing this book! You have purchased a superior computer book written expressly for your needs. To continue to provide the kind of up-to-date, pertinent coverage you've come to expect from us, we need to hear from you. Please take a minute to complete and return this self-addressed, postage-paid form. In return, we'll send you a free catalog of all our computer books on topics ranging from word processing to programming and the internet.

Mr. ☐   Mrs. ☐   Ms. ☐   Dr. ☐

Name (first) ☐☐☐☐☐☐☐☐☐☐☐   (M.I.) ☐   (last) ☐☐☐☐☐☐☐☐☐☐☐☐☐☐☐☐

Address ☐☐☐☐☐☐☐☐☐☐☐☐☐☐☐☐☐☐☐☐☐☐☐☐☐☐☐☐☐☐☐☐☐☐

☐☐☐☐☐☐☐☐☐☐☐☐☐☐☐☐☐☐☐☐☐☐☐☐☐☐☐☐☐☐☐☐☐☐

City ☐☐☐☐☐☐☐☐☐☐☐☐☐☐☐☐☐   State ☐☐   Zip ☐☐☐☐☐ ☐☐☐☐

Phone ☐☐☐ ☐☐☐ ☐☐☐☐   Fax ☐☐☐ ☐☐☐ ☐☐☐☐

Company Name ☐☐☐☐☐☐☐☐☐☐☐☐☐☐☐☐☐☐☐☐☐☐☐☐☐☐☐☐☐☐☐☐

E-mail address ☐☐☐☐☐☐☐☐☐☐☐☐☐☐☐☐☐☐☐☐☐☐☐☐☐☐☐☐☐☐☐☐

1. Please check at least (3) influencing factors for purchasing this book.

Front or back cover information on book .... ☐
Special approach to the content .... ☐
Completeness of content .... ☐
Author's reputation .... ☐
Publisher's reputation .... ☐
Book cover design or layout .... ☐
Index or table of contents of book .... ☐
Price of book .... ☐
Special effects, graphics, illustrations .... ☐
Other (Please specify): _____ ☐

2. How did you first learn about this book?

Saw in Macmillan Computer Publishing catalog .... ☐
Recommended by store personnel .... ☐
Saw the book on bookshelf at store .... ☐
Recommended by a friend .... ☐
Received advertisement in the mail .... ☐
Saw an advertisement in: _____ ☐
Read book review in: _____ ☐
Other (Please specify): _____ ☐

3. How many computer books have you purchased in the last six months?

This book only .... ☐   3 to 5 books .... ☐
2 books .... ☐   More than 5 .... ☐

4. Where did you purchase this book?

Bookstore .... ☐
Computer Store .... ☐
Consumer Electronics Store .... ☐
Department Store .... ☐
Office Club .... ☐
Warehouse Club .... ☐
Mail Order .... ☐
Direct from Publisher .... ☐
Internet site .... ☐
Other (Please specify): _____ ☐

5. How long have you been using a computer?

☐ Less than 6 months   ☐ 6 months to a year
☐ 1 to 3 years   ☐ More than 3 years

6. What is your level of experience with personal computers and with the subject of this book?

	With PCs	With subject of book
New	☐	☐
Casual	☐	☐
Accomplished	☐	☐
Expert	☐	☐

Source Code ISBN: 0-7897-0807-8

7. Which of the following best describes your job title?

Administrative Assistant .... ☐
Coordinator .... ☐
Manager/Supervisor .... ☐
Director .... ☐
Vice President .... ☐
President/CEO/COO .... ☐
Lawyer/Doctor/Medical Professional .... ☐
Teacher/Educator/Trainer .... ☐
Engineer/Technician .... ☐
Consultant .... ☐
Not employed/Student/Retired .... ☐
Other (Please specify): _____ ☐

8. Which of the following best describes the area of the company your job title falls under?

Accounting .... ☐
Engineering .... ☐
Manufacturing .... ☐
Operations .... ☐
Marketing .... ☐
Sales .... ☐
Other (Please specify): _____ ☐

9. What is your age?

Under 20 .... ☐
21-29 .... ☐
30-39 .... ☐
40-49 .... ☐
50-59 .... ☐
60-over .... ☐

10. Are you:

Male .... ☐
Female .... ☐

11. Which computer publications do you read regularly? (Please list)

_____
_____
_____
_____
_____
_____
_____
_____
_____
_____

Comments: _____
_____
_____

Fold here and scotch-tape to mail.